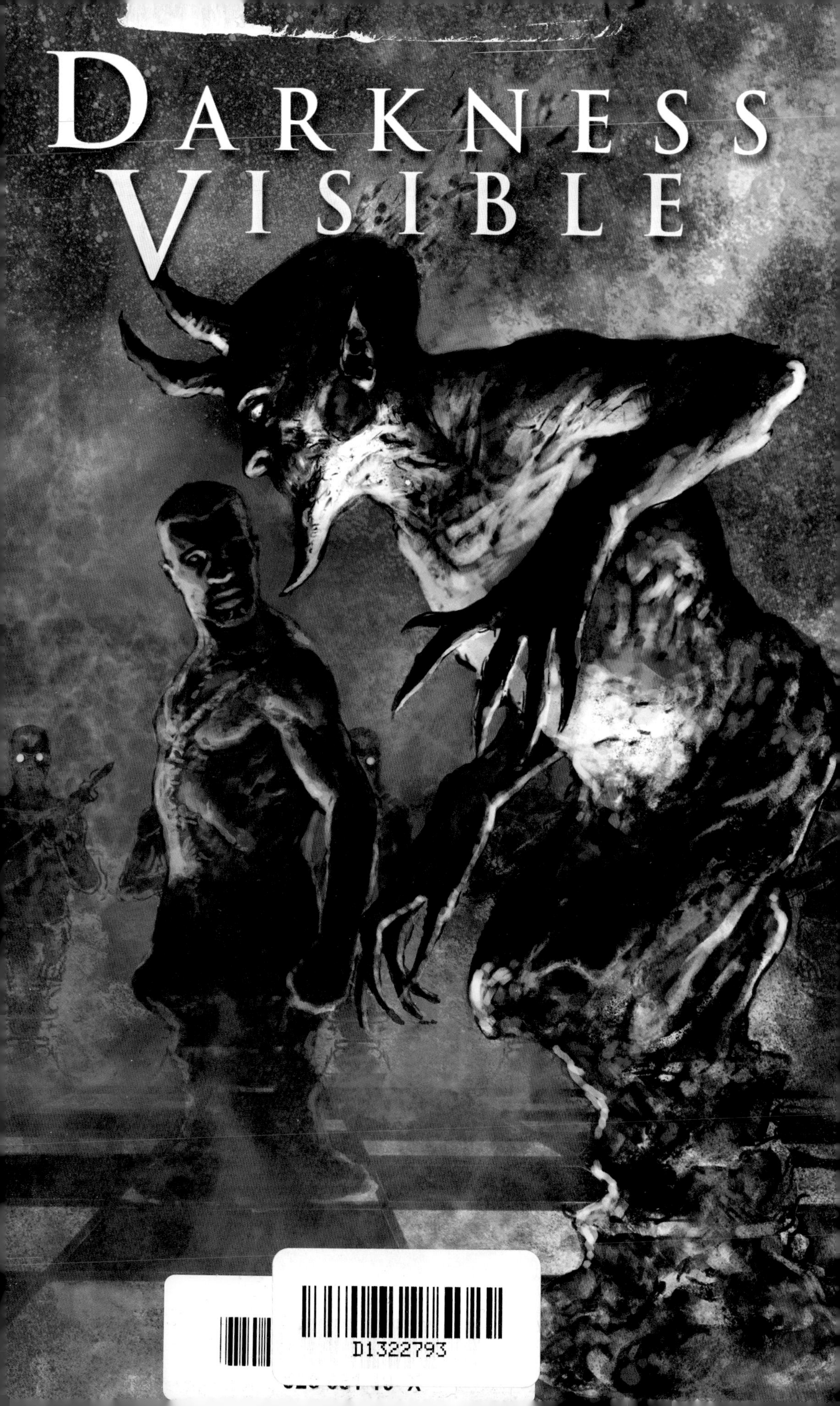
DARKNESS
VISIBLE

Cover Art: **Brendan Cahill**
Cover Colors: **Joana Lafuente**

Collection Edits: **Justin Eisinger** and **Alonzo Simon**
Collection Design: **Ron Estevez**
Publisher: **Ted Adams**

IDW
www.IDWPUBLISHING.com

Ted Adams, CEO & Publisher
Greg Goldstein, President & COO
Robbie Robbins, EVP/Sr. Graphic Artist
Chris Ryall, Chief Creative Officer
David Hedgecock, Editor-in-Chief
Laurie Windrow, Senior Vice President of Sales & Marketing
Matthew Ruzicka, CPA, Chief Financial Officer
Lorelei Bunjes, VP of Digital Services
Jerry Bennington, VP of New Product Development

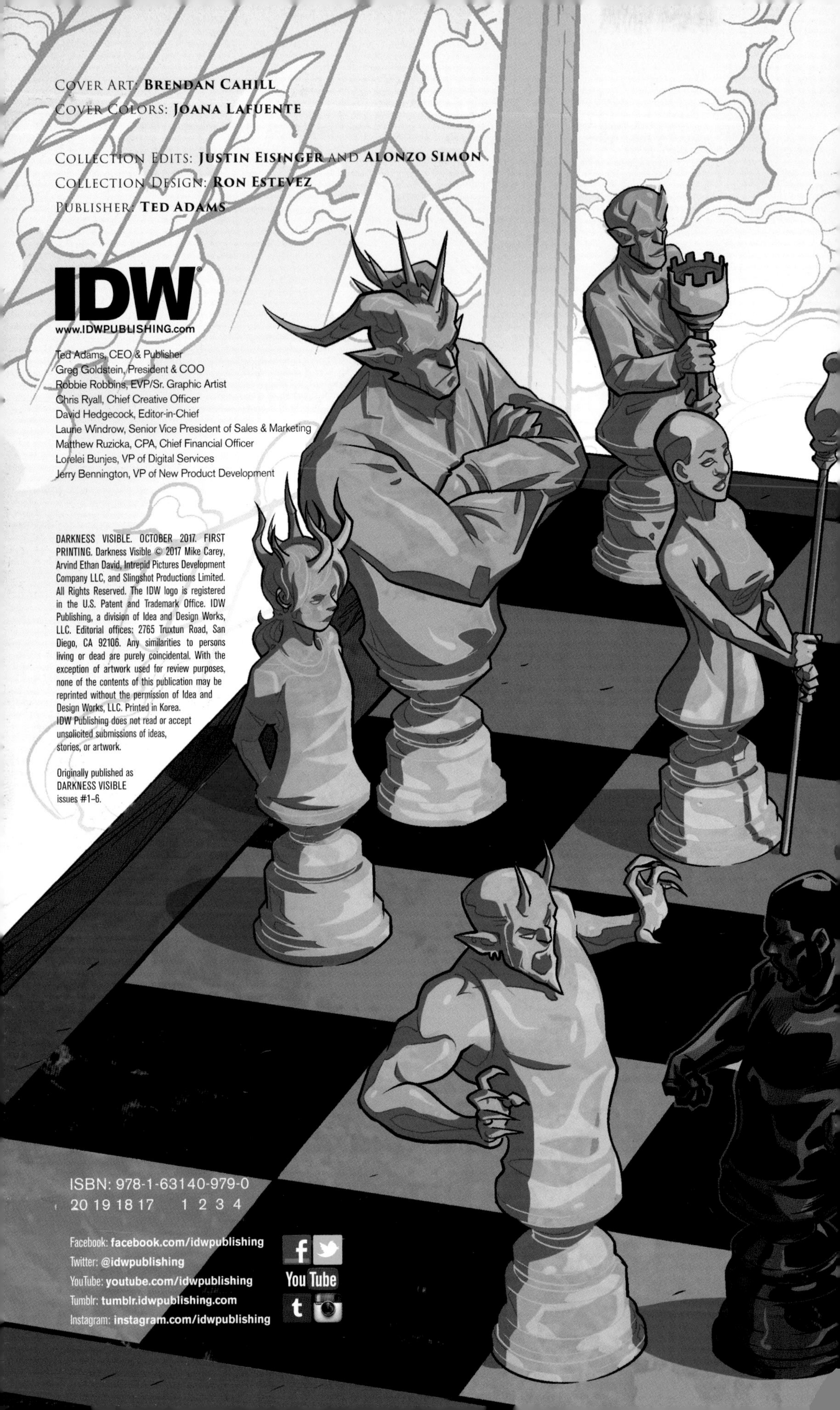

Originally published as
DARKNESS VISIBLE
issues #1–6.

ISBN: 978-1-63140-979-0
20 19 18 17 1 2 3 4

Facebook: **facebook.com/idwpublishing**
Twitter: **@idwpublishing**
YouTube: **youtube.com/idwpublishing**
Tumblr: **tumblr.idwpublishing.com**
Instagram: **instagram.com/idwpublishing**

Writers: **Mike Carey** & **Arvind Ethan David**

Art: **Brendan Cahill** and **Livio Ramondelli** (Ch. 3 & 6)
Colors: **Joana Lafuente**
Letters: **Robbie Robbins**, **Shawn Lee**, and **Neil Uyetake**

Series Edits: **Denton J. Tipton**
Series Assistant Edits: **Peter Adrian Behravesh**

Special thanks to Scott Dunbier, Trevor Macy, Marc Evans, Cavan Ash, Toby Rushton, Bharat Nalluri, Ari Donnelly, and all who helped Detective Aston on his journey.

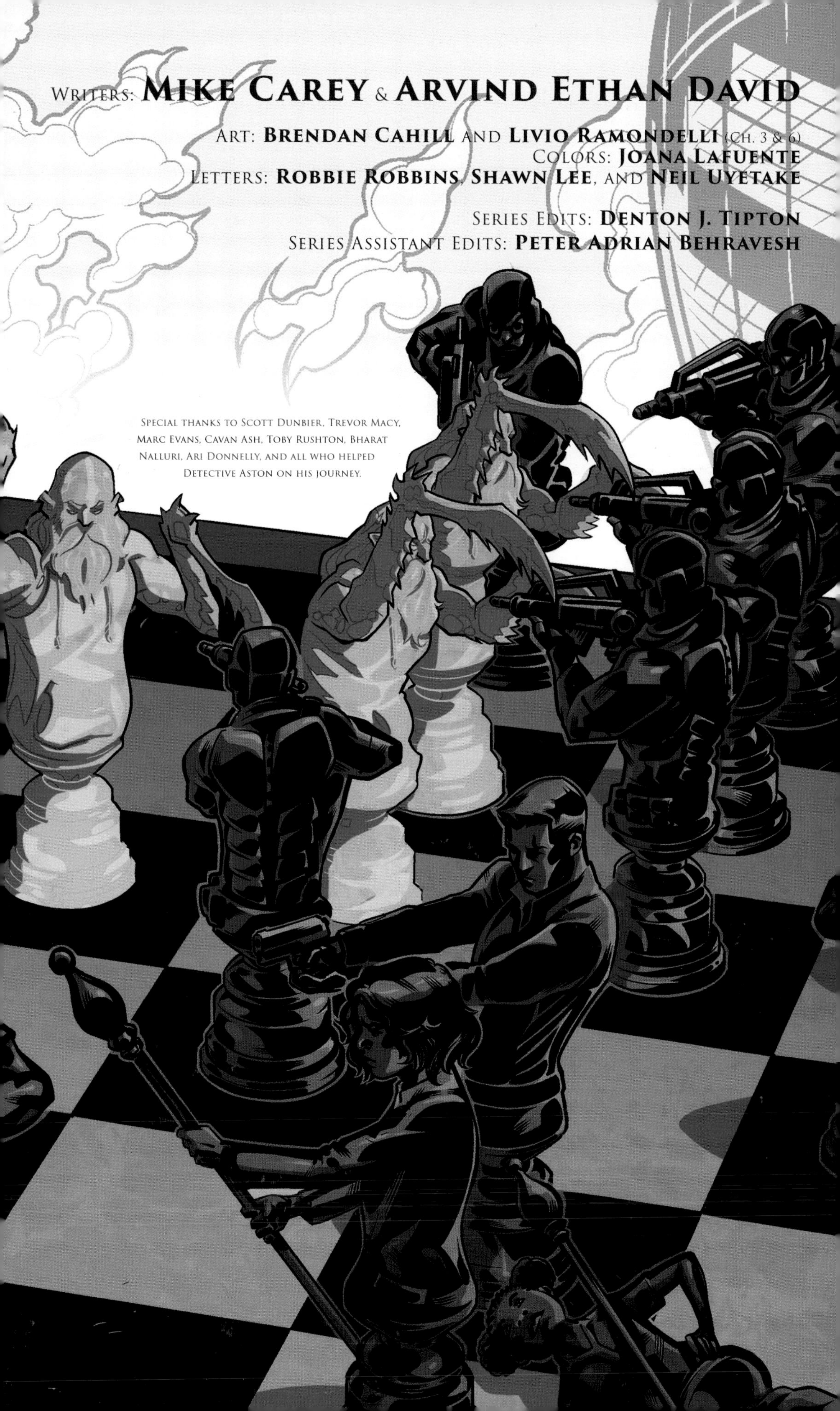

INTERVIEW TAKEN FROM FREAKSUGAR.COM

FreakSugar: For readers considering picking up the book, what can you tell us about Darkness Visible?

MIKE CAREY: It's partly a police procedural story in that the main character, Danny Aston, is a cop working a crime investigation. But that's complicated by the fact that the crime involves his own murder. He sits up on the autopsy slab, inexplicably alive again, and after the initial disorientation he gets back to work. But we realize very quickly that there are multiple conspiracies going on around him. He's not out for vengeance, he just wants to do his job—but there are other people and agencies who want other things, and they've all got a vested interest in Aston's inquiry.

FS: How did the idea for the series materialize and evolve into what it is now?

ARVIND ETHAN DAVID: Oooh. How much time do you have? Short version: Mike had an idea almost 10 years ago for a story about a city where supernatural races and humans had an uneasy coexistence, and a detective charged with policing the spaces between them. That original idea immediately hit me as something I wanted to help tell, and we've be en working on it, on and off, ever since.

Over that time, every element of the story has changed and evolved. To what the supernatural race would be (vampires, zombies, werewolves), the City (London, New York, Imaginarypolis), the medium (film, prose, TV, comics) and the mechanics of the plot. But two things have stayed constant: the themes and Detective Daniel Aston himself.

FS: What can you tell us about Daniel Aston, the series' protagonist? How does he view his job and the world around him?

MC: Aston is very task-oriented, and that's partly because he doesn't have much of a life outside of his job. He lives with his daughter, Maggie, who he's bringing up by himself. Clearly there's some tragedy in his background, but we're not immediately clear what that is—we just know that it's left him embittered and hard, dedicated to his job but with a very visible bias against the Shaitan, our race (or multiple races) of demons. The only thing that gets through his armor is Maggie, who he loves fiercely and protectively. Outside of that single family tie his only friends are cops—and the events of the series put him very much at odds with the rest of the squad he works with. He's got a very hard journey to make.

FS: The mood of the art is a perfect fit for the series. What was the collaboration process like with Brendan Cahill?

MC: Brendan is awesome. We're building a very complicated world here, part real and contemporary, part imagined from the ground up. And with the Shaitan we've got a cast of characters who look grotesque and impossible to start with and can present very differently at different times. He's brought his own vision to all these things, and we're really happy with how the series looks.

While we're on the subject, though, we're using a structure that includes a number of stand-alone issues that give us the recent history of our story world. Those issues are drawn by Livio Ramondelli, and they're really beautiful too. Again, there's a big challenge in that each issue has a new cast and a new setting, and they intertwine with the present day narrative in complex ways. Sometimes we'll meet a character in backstory before they impact on the main arc, and sometimes it's the other way around. Brendan and Livio have to work closely together to maintain continuity.

And the other team member who deserves a shout-out is Joana Lafuente on colors. The series has a dark palette, but she makes sure it's on the rich and brooding side of dark. It never looks drab or murky.

FS: Darkness Visible *seems to touch on some real-world issues such as the threat of terrorism from what's seen as an invading people. How present was that in the back of your mind as you wrote the tale? Following up on that, there are echoes of xenophobia in the world of* Darkness Visible, *which is especially timely given the news recently (although xenophobia is a constant issue). How much will you delve into that in the book?*

AED: From the moment of conception, this was always a story with a political element, and a social one. Politics with both a big "P" and a small "p!" That said, we're not activists, we're artists: and so this has to be a good story, first and foremost, or it won't be anything at all.

Darkness Visible is a fantasy set in a world just like ours, which means it has every shade of people and every shape of prejudice. You can expect our story to never fear to go into the ugliest places of human nature, and also we hope to surprise you with the unexpected goodness of monsters.

As to recent events, yes, sadly Team Trump—and indeed Team Brexit—have put issues of prejudice, fear, immigration, and border control back on the front pages and in the front of people's minds. It's an interesting question as to what Trump would do in the world of *Darkness Visible*—a wall, however beautiful and big, just doesn't work with demons.

MC: The beautiful thing about monsters is that they're really flexible as metaphors. We don't have any desire to preach, but I think our world view comes across. Most horror is about meeting the Other, and either finding common ground or failing to. That basic trope has a set of associations that changes all the time, and in the case of *Darkness Visible* reality caught up with us as we were writing. It was a weird and unsettling experience.

FS: In the book, demons who have joined with humans are called Shaitan, which have roots in different mythologies. Why did you land on that particular type of demon to use in your story?

AED: The name was Mike's inspiration, and I love that it has Arabic derivation as that adds to the political resonance. However, we aren't specifically referencing any one school or pre-existing demon mythology. Rather, we're saying that all the different mythologies of demons–Western, Chinese, Greek, Muslim, Christian–all are attempts to explain the truth. The truth that *Darkness Visible* tells for the first time.

MC: The paranoid version of history, rather than the screw-up version. "Everything you suspected was true, but you didn't hear the half of it…"

FS: Following up on that, what kind of research goes into a project like this? Are there any other specific callbacks or nods to demons in mythology that you try to pepper into the book?

AED: One of the fun things about world building is you get to pull from everything you know and love and throw it into the caldron. Between Mike and me, you can count on lots of fairly different building blocks. To take one: the title comes from a line of Milton, from *Paradise Lost*:

> A Dungeon horrible, on all sides round
> As one great Furnace flam'd, yet from those flames
> No light, but rather darkness visible
> Serv'd onely to discover sights of woe,
> Regions of sorrow, doleful shades, where peace [65]
> And rest can never dwell, hope never comes

And you'll see Milton's influence popping up in ways both subtle and less so through the book. There's also lots of Shakespeare, from the first issue on, but also less highfalutin stuff: you might not notice it but the British band The Heavy is a big influence on how I write the rhythm of Aston's dialogue (listen to their song What Makes a Good Man as you read issue 2 and you'll hopefully get it).

Also the TV series *Luther*–not because Aston himself is like John Luther, other than superficially because I'd like Idris Elba to play everyone in everything I do, but Aston isn't as smart or as unhinged (at least not at first) as Luther, but because the London of Luther is so beautifully specific and precise in its depiction, and the relationships between police in it so carefully crafted, and that's something we've tried to bring to this also.

FS: The series is set 80 years after demons came to Earth. How has the culture of the world changed since their arrival?

MC: It's been a seismic shock. Actually the Shaitan have been visiting Earth for as long as there's been a sentient species here to visit. What happened 80 years ago is that they announced themselves. And they chose their moment, offering help to the Allied powers in the first exchanges of World War II. In exchange they got a homeland and official recognition. Now the Shaitan are everywhere, a visible presence in all the world's cities, but they're sometimes terrifying to look at and integration has proved to be a really tough proposition. The Shaitan are easy to demonize: they rely on a willing human host to maintain a presence in our world, so you've got something that looks from the outside like demonic possession even when the interior balance of power is more nuanced.

And they're easy to exoticize, too, because they have a lot of control over their bodily shape. There are brothels where Shaitan sex workers service human clients, not to mention sectors of the labour market that have gone over almost entirely to Shaitan workers. At the time of our story the resulting tensions are coming to a boil and it looks as though it's going to get ugly–even before Shaitan terrorists attack a very visible London landmark.

FS: You both have a varied career behind you. How has your past work informed how you approach Darkness Visible?

AED: I'm a relative newbie to writing comics, after a career focused on film, theatre, and television. So for me, I'm having to learn a new set of story-telling tools. There, I lean on Mike's experience and generosity, as well as on the good will and great gifts of our artists.

That said, whilst Dirk Gently [whom David has written for IDW] and Daniel Aston might struggle to get on at a dinner party, they are both supernatural detectives, trying to maintain order in a chaotic universe, and they are both British and fond of junk food.

MC: I was mainly concerned to make this book feel very different from *Lucifer* and *Hellblazer*, not to mention Felix Castor. These demons have a different origin and a different rationale from the demons you might encounter in those other books, and they needed a different voice and a different aesthetic to bring that out.

FS: Can you tease anything about what we can expect to see in the book going forward?

MC: It's a story that opens out in stages–both in terms of the bigger picture that informs Aston's personal dilemma and in terms of revealing the past lives and entanglements of our core cast. I think it's fair to say that the reader's moral compass might spin around a little as the story goes on, in terms of who we sympathize with and why.

CHAPTER 1

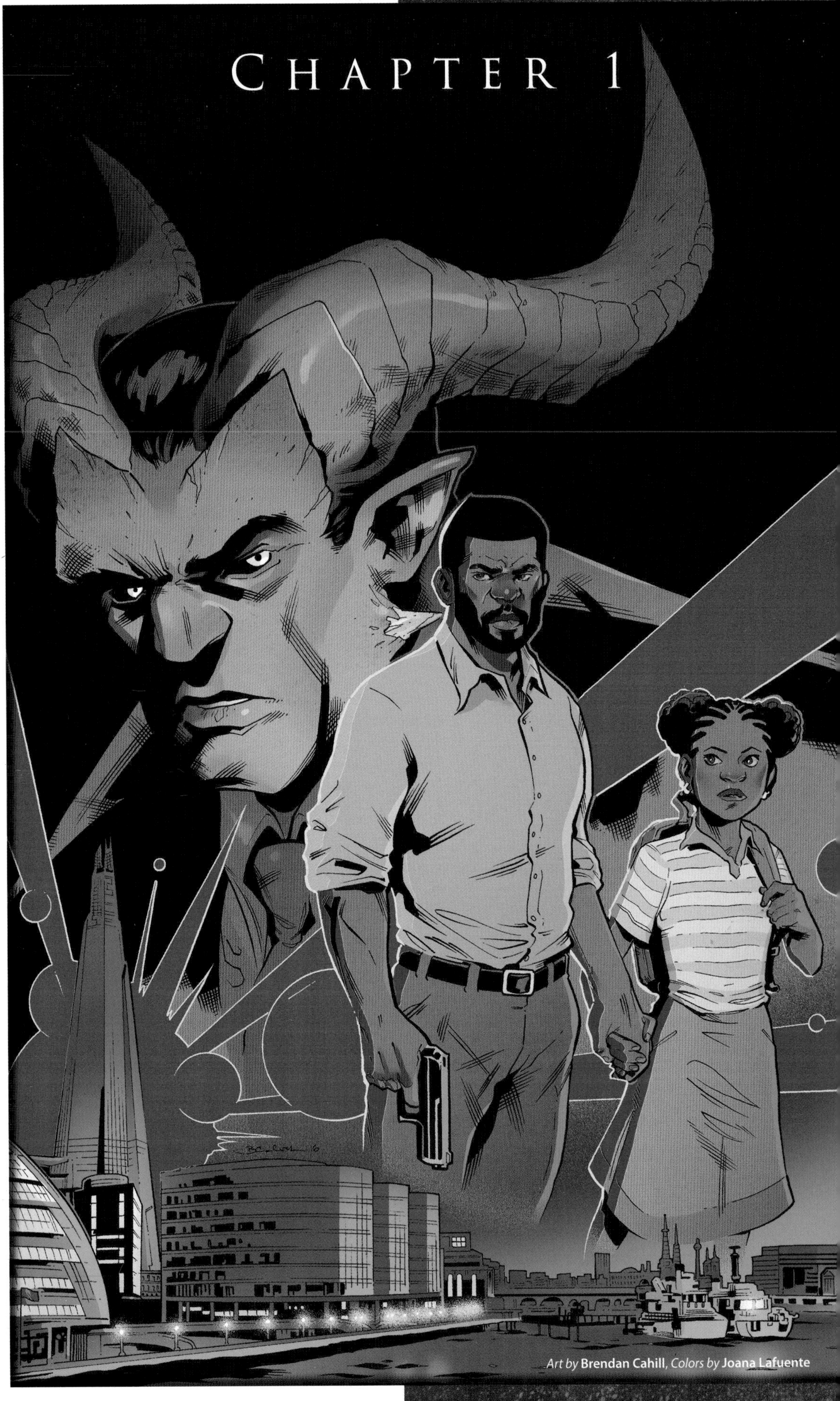

Art by **Brendan Cahill**, *Colors by* **Joana Lafuente**

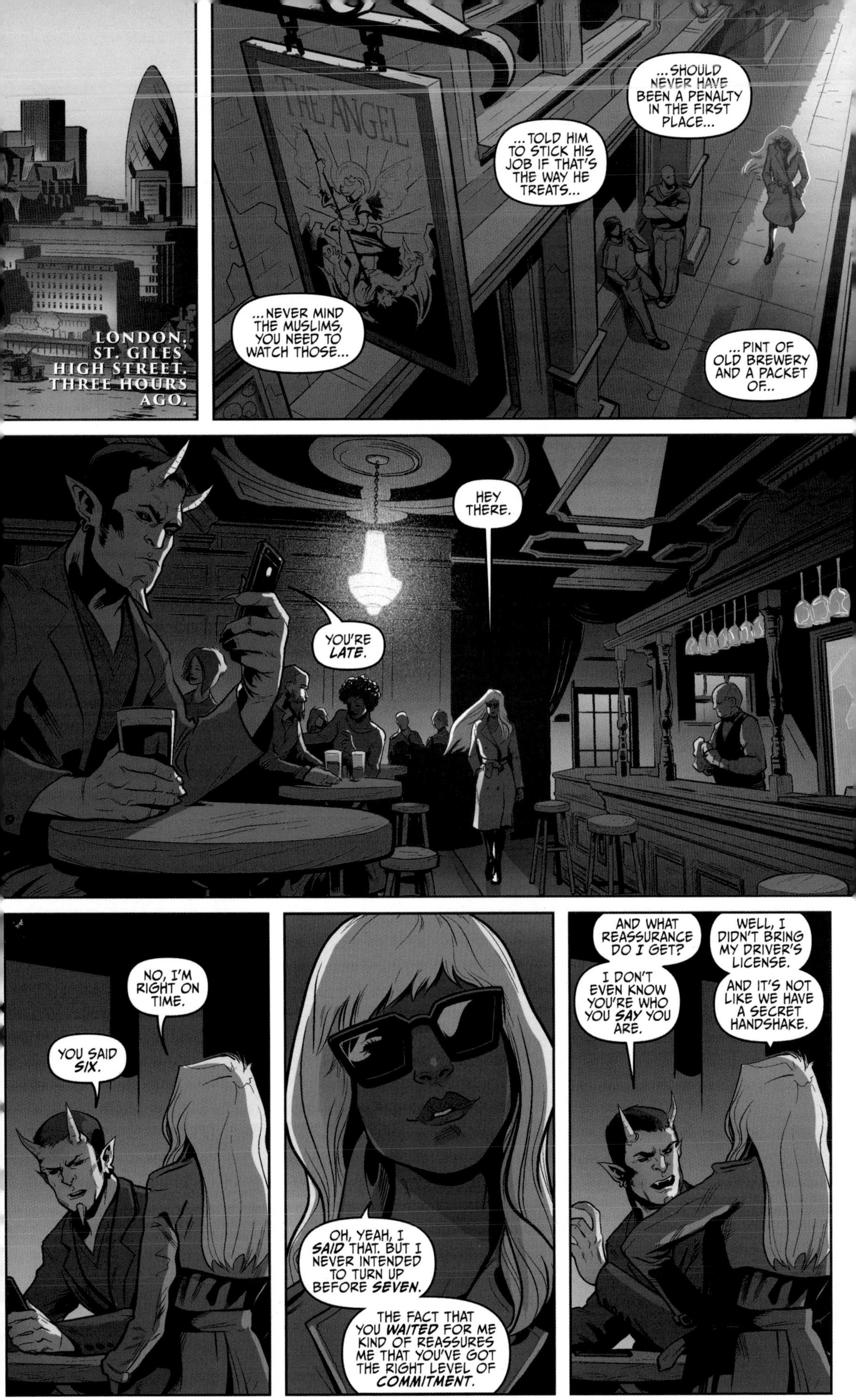
LONDON. ST. GILES HIGH STREET. THREE HOURS AGO.
THE ANGEL
...NEVER MIND THE MUSLIMS, YOU NEED TO WATCH THOSE...
...TOLD HIM TO STICK HIS JOB IF THAT'S THE WAY HE TREATS...
...SHOULD NEVER HAVE BEEN A PENALTY IN THE FIRST PLACE...
...PINT OF OLD BREWERY AND A PACKET OF...
HEY THERE.
YOU'RE LATE.
NO, I'M RIGHT ON TIME.
YOU SAID SIX.
OH, YEAH, I SAID THAT. BUT I NEVER INTENDED TO TURN UP BEFORE SEVEN.
THE FACT THAT YOU WAITED FOR ME KIND OF REASSURES ME THAT YOU'VE GOT THE RIGHT LEVEL OF COMMITMENT.
AND WHAT REASSURANCE DO I GET?
I DON'T EVEN KNOW YOU'RE WHO YOU SAY YOU ARE.
WELL, I DIDN'T BRING MY DRIVER'S LICENSE.
AND IT'S NOT LIKE WE HAVE A SECRET HANDSHAKE.

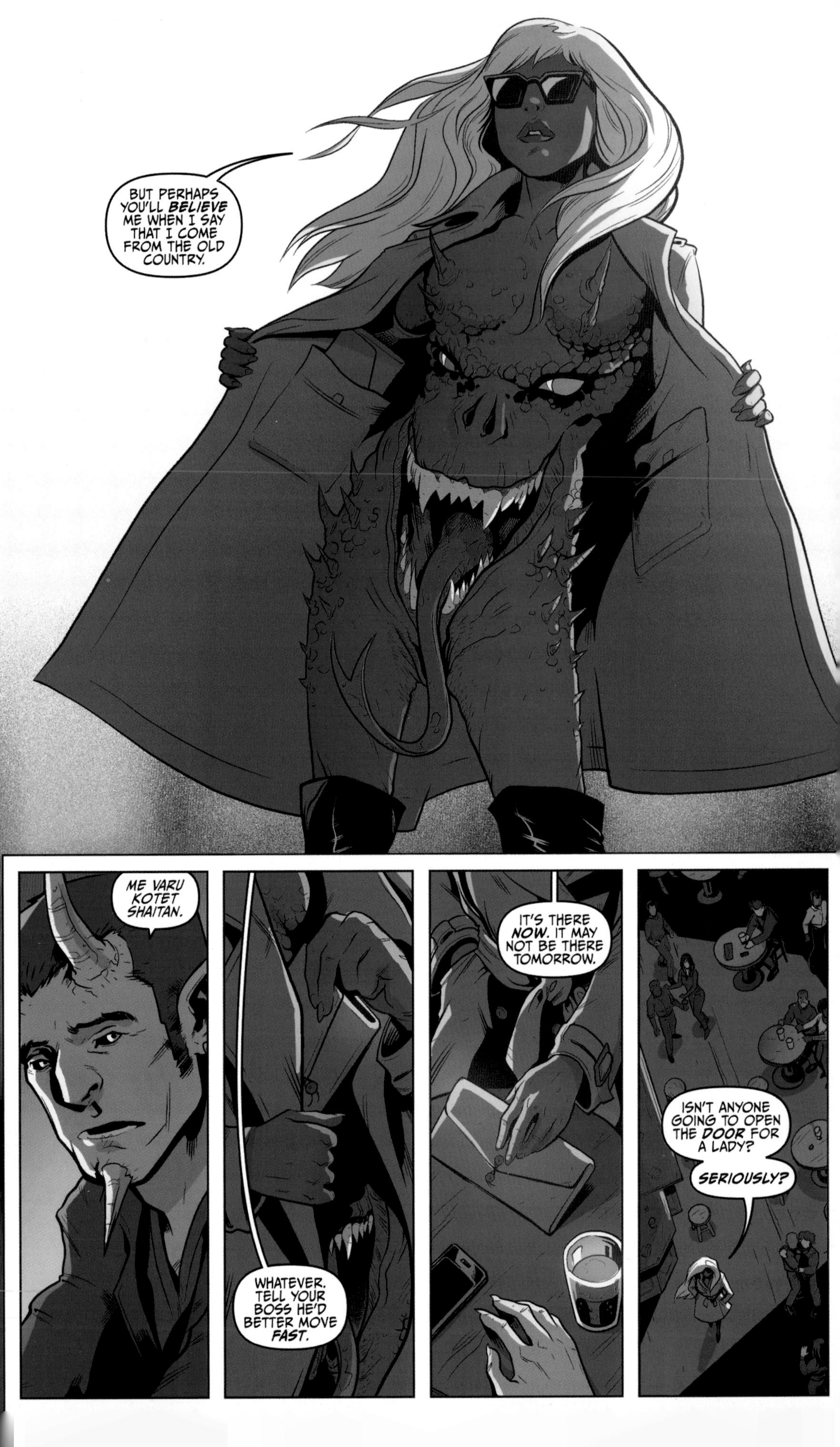

BUT PERHAPS YOU'LL BELIEVE ME WHEN I SAY THAT I COME FROM THE OLD COUNTRY.
ME VARU KOTET SHAITAN.
WHATEVER. TELL YOUR BOSS HE'D BETTER MOVE FAST.
IT'S THERE NOW. IT MAY NOT BE THERE TOMORROW.
ISN'T ANYONE GOING TO OPEN THE DOOR FOR A LADY?
SERIOUSLY?

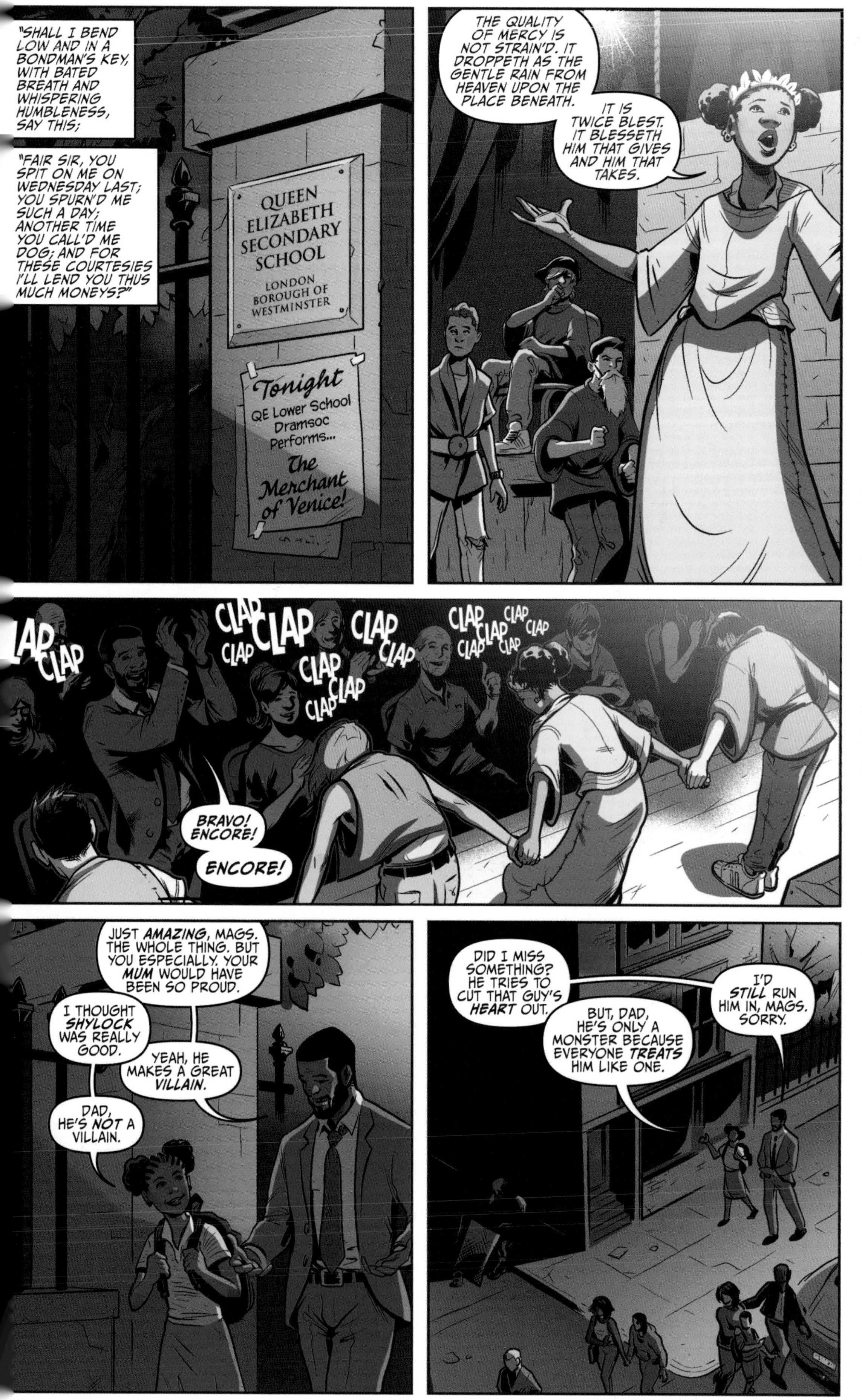
"SHALL I BEND LOW AND IN A BONDMAN'S KEY, WITH BATED BREATH AND WHISPERING HUMBLENESS, SAY THIS;
"FAIR SIR, YOU SPIT ON ME ON WEDNESDAY LAST; YOU SPURN'D ME SUCH A DAY; ANOTHER TIME YOU CALL'D ME DOG; AND FOR THESE COURTESIES I'LL LEND YOU THUS MUCH MONEYS?"
QUEEN ELIZABETH SECONDARY SCHOOL
LONDON BOROUGH OF WESTMINSTER
Tonight
QE Lower School Dramsoc Performs...
The Merchant of Venice!
THE QUALITY OF MERCY IS NOT STRAIN'D. IT DROPPETH AS THE GENTLE RAIN FROM HEAVEN UPON THE PLACE BENEATH.
IT IS TWICE BLEST. IT BLESSETH HIM THAT GIVES AND HIM THAT TAKES.
CLAP CLAP
CLAP CLAP CLAP
CLAP CLAP
CLAP CLAP CLAP
CLAP CLAP CLAP CLAP CLAP CLAP CLAP
BRAVO! ENCORE!
ENCORE!
JUST AMAZING, MAGS. THE WHOLE THING. BUT YOU ESPECIALLY. YOUR MUM WOULD HAVE BEEN SO PROUD.
I THOUGHT SHYLOCK WAS REALLY GOOD.
YEAH, HE MAKES A GREAT VILLAIN.
DAD, HE'S NOT A VILLAIN.
DID I MISS SOMETHING? HE TRIES TO CUT THAT GUY'S HEART OUT.
BUT, DAD, HE'S ONLY A MONSTER BECAUSE EVERYONE TREATS HIM LIKE ONE.
I'D STILL RUN HIM IN, MAGS. SORRY.

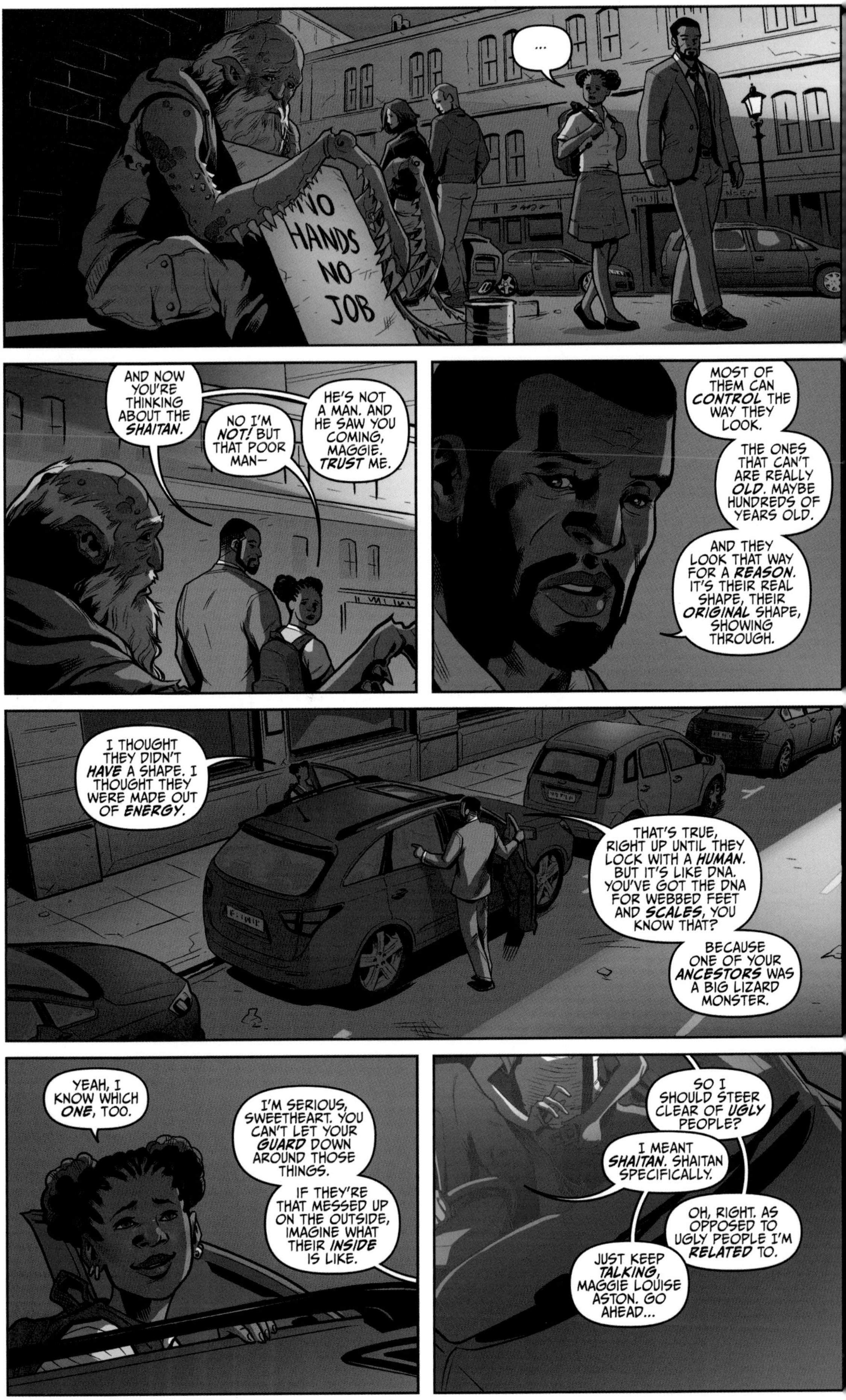
...
NO HANDS NO JOB
AND NOW YOU'RE THINKING ABOUT THE SHAITAN.
NO I'M NOT! BUT THAT POOR MAN—
HE'S NOT A MAN. AND HE SAW YOU COMING, MAGGIE. TRUST ME.
MOST OF THEM CAN CONTROL THE WAY THEY LOOK.
THE ONES THAT CAN'T ARE REALLY OLD. MAYBE HUNDREDS OF YEARS OLD.
AND THEY LOOK THAT WAY FOR A REASON. IT'S THEIR REAL SHAPE, THEIR ORIGINAL SHAPE, SHOWING THROUGH.
I THOUGHT THEY DIDN'T HAVE A SHAPE. I THOUGHT THEY WERE MADE OUT OF ENERGY.
THAT'S TRUE, RIGHT UP UNTIL THEY LOCK WITH A HUMAN. BUT IT'S LIKE DNA. YOU'VE GOT THE DNA FOR WEBBED FEET AND SCALES, YOU KNOW THAT?
BECAUSE ONE OF YOUR ANCESTORS WAS A BIG LIZARD MONSTER.
YEAH, I KNOW WHICH ONE, TOO.
I'M SERIOUS, SWEETHEART. YOU CAN'T LET YOUR GUARD DOWN AROUND THOSE THINGS.
IF THEY'RE THAT MESSED UP ON THE OUTSIDE, IMAGINE WHAT THEIR INSIDE IS LIKE.
SO I SHOULD STEER CLEAR OF UGLY PEOPLE?
I MEANT SHAITAN. SHAITAN SPECIFICALLY.
OH, RIGHT. AS OPPOSED TO UGLY PEOPLE I'M RELATED TO.
JUST KEEP TALKING, MAGGIE LOUISE ASTON. GO AHEAD...

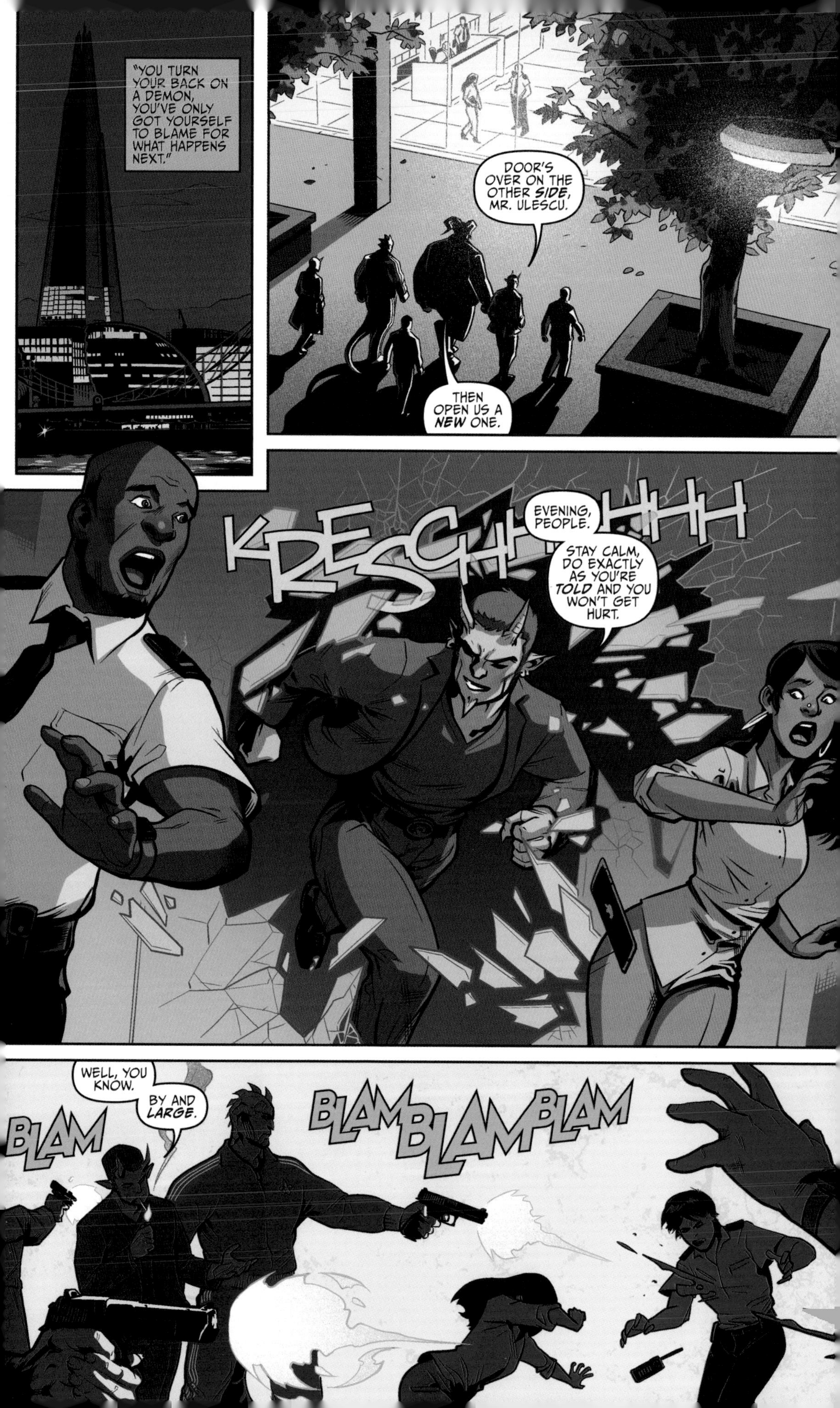
"YOU TURN YOUR BACK ON A DEMON, YOU'VE ONLY GOT YOURSELF TO BLAME FOR WHAT HAPPENS NEXT."
DOOR'S OVER ON THE OTHER *SIDE*, MR. ULESCU.
THEN OPEN US A *NEW* ONE.
KRESCHHHHH
EVENING, PEOPLE.
STAY CALM, DO EXACTLY AS YOU'RE *TOLD* AND YOU WON'T GET HURT.
WELL, YOU KNOW.
BY AND *LARGE*.
BLAM
BLAMBLAMBLAMBLAM

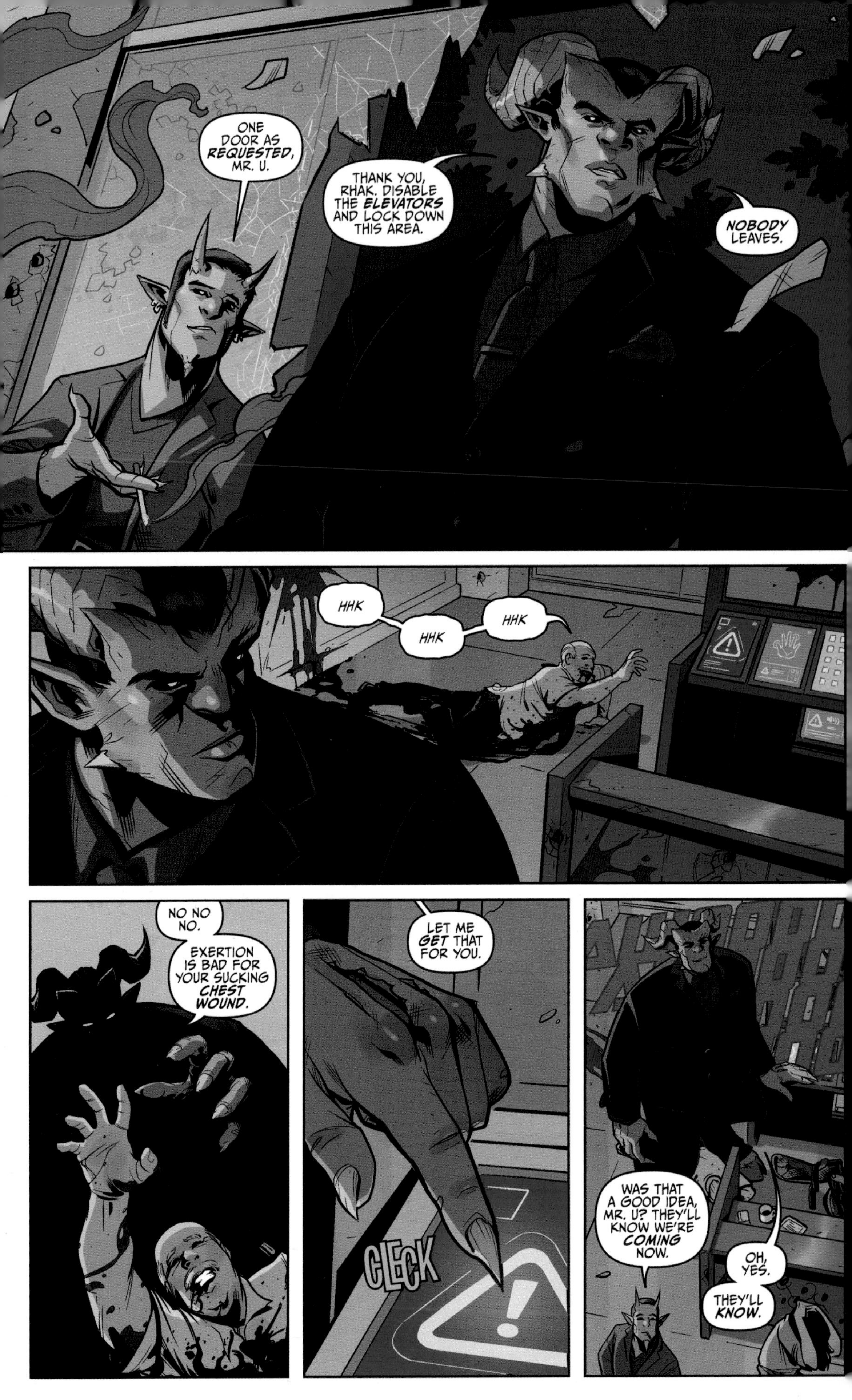

ONE DOOR AS REQUESTED, MR. U.
THANK YOU, RHAK. DISABLE THE ELEVATORS AND LOCK DOWN THIS AREA.
NOBODY LEAVES.
HHK
HHK
HHK
NO NO NO.
EXERTION IS BAD FOR YOUR SUCKING CHEST WOUND.
LET ME GET THAT FOR YOU.
CLICK
WAS THAT A GOOD IDEA, MR. U? THEY'LL KNOW WE'RE COMING NOW.
OH, YES.
THEY'LL KNOW.

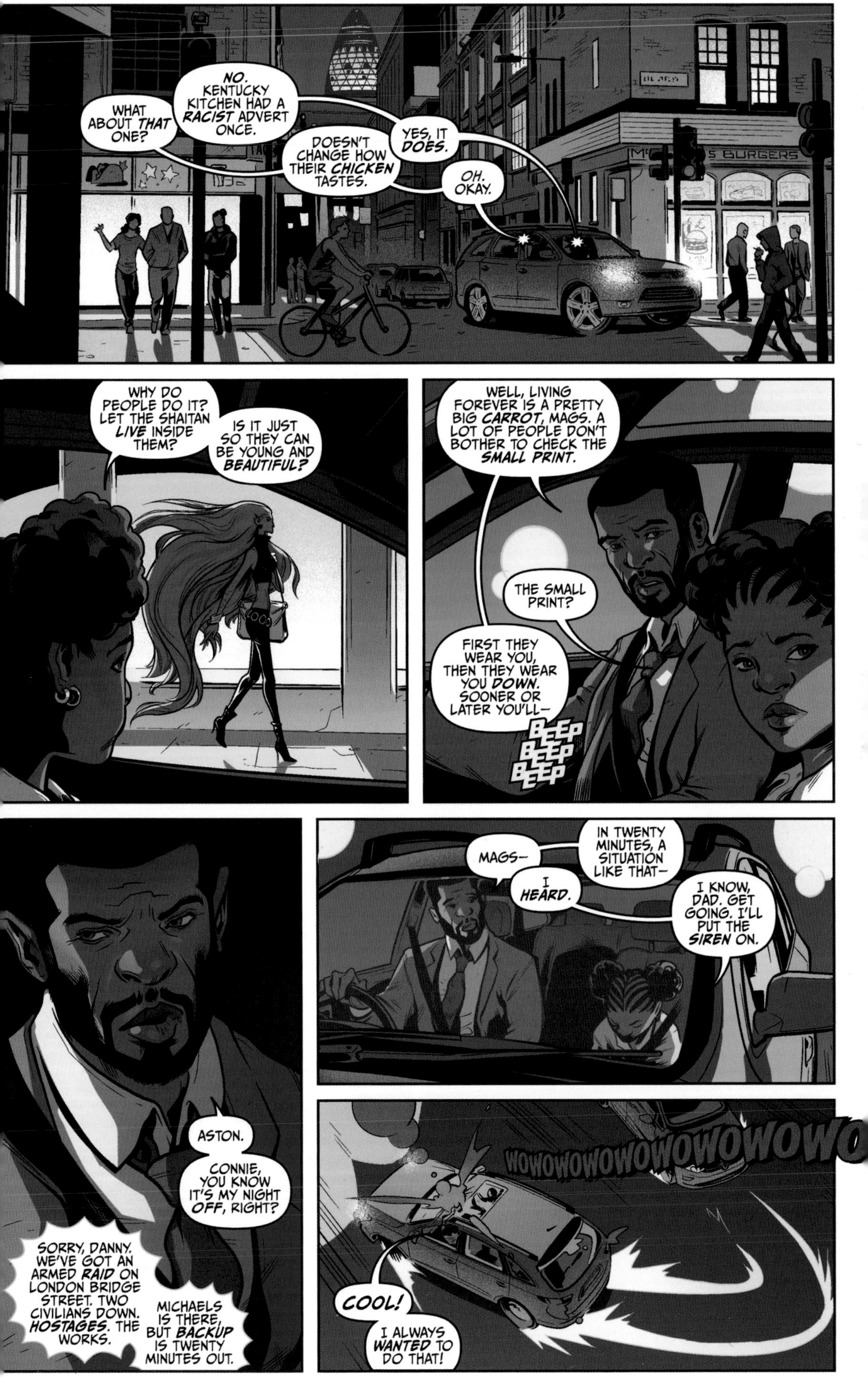

WHAT ABOUT THAT ONE?
NO. KENTUCKY KITCHEN HAD A RACIST ADVERT ONCE.
DOESN'T CHANGE HOW THEIR CHICKEN TASTES.
YES, IT DOES.
OH. OKAY.
S BURGERS
WHY DO PEOPLE DO IT? LET THE SHAITAN LIVE INSIDE THEM?
IS IT JUST SO THEY CAN BE YOUNG AND BEAUTIFUL?
WELL, LIVING FOREVER IS A PRETTY BIG CARROT, MAGS. A LOT OF PEOPLE DON'T BOTHER TO CHECK THE SMALL PRINT.
THE SMALL PRINT?
FIRST THEY WEAR YOU, THEN THEY WEAR YOU DOWN. SOONER OR LATER YOU'LL—
BEEP BEEP BEEP
ASTON.
CONNIE, YOU KNOW IT'S MY NIGHT OFF, RIGHT?
SORRY, DANNY. WE'VE GOT AN ARMED RAID ON LONDON BRIDGE STREET. TWO CIVILIANS DOWN. HOSTAGES. THE WORKS.
MICHAELS IS THERE, BUT BACKUP IS TWENTY MINUTES OUT.
MAGS—
IN TWENTY MINUTES, A SITUATION LIKE THAT—
I HEARD.
I KNOW, DAD. GET GOING. I'LL PUT THE SIREN ON.
WOWOWOWOWOWOWOWOWO
COOL!
I ALWAYS WANTED TO DO THAT!

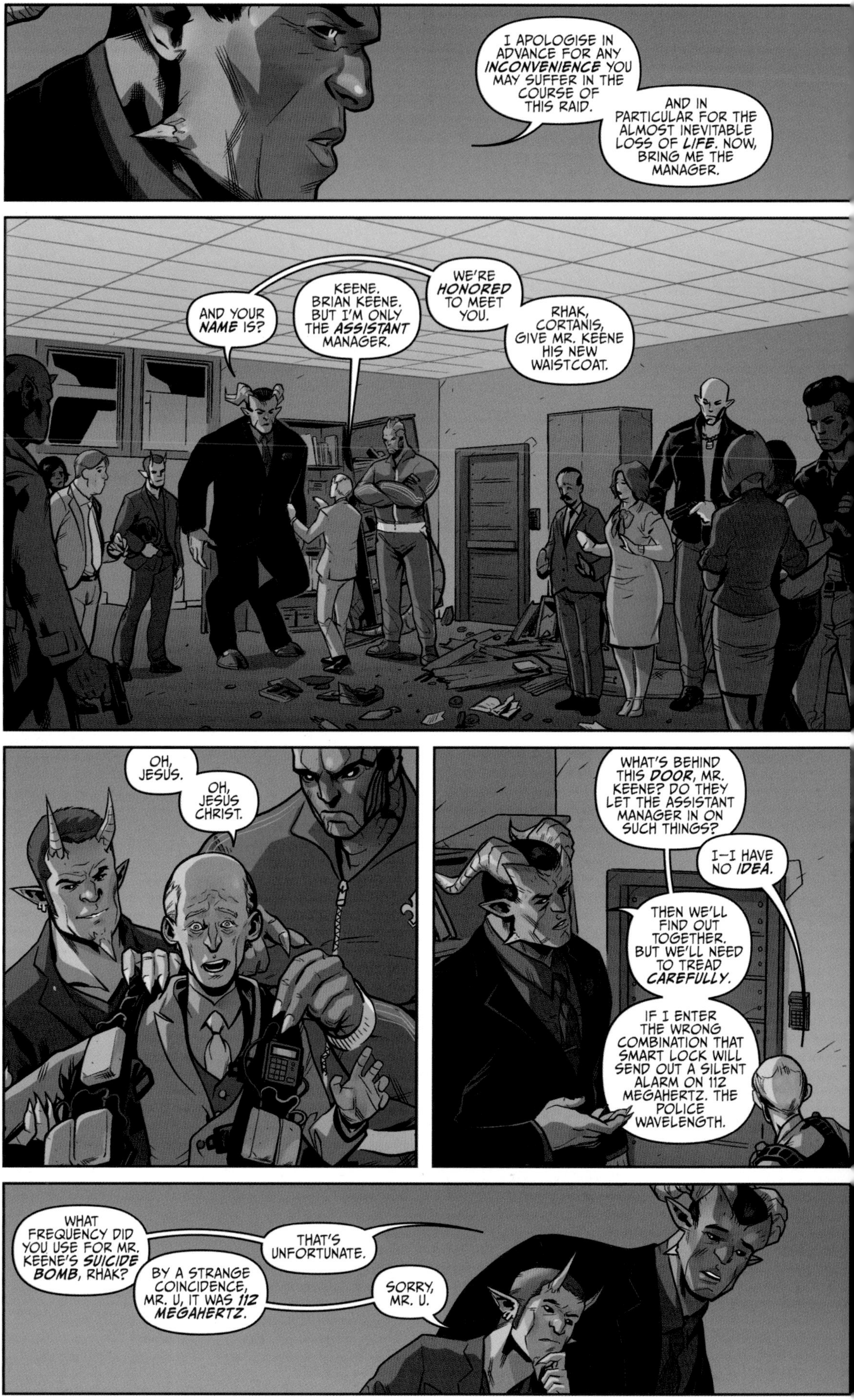
I APOLOGISE IN ADVANCE FOR ANY INCONVENIENCE YOU MAY SUFFER IN THE COURSE OF THIS RAID.
AND IN PARTICULAR FOR THE ALMOST INEVITABLE LOSS OF LIFE. NOW, BRING ME THE MANAGER.
AND YOUR NAME IS?
KEENE. BRIAN KEENE. BUT I'M ONLY THE ASSISTANT MANAGER.
WE'RE HONORED TO MEET YOU.
RHAK, CORTANIS, GIVE MR. KEENE HIS NEW WAISTCOAT.
OH, JESUS.
OH, JESUS CHRIST.
WHAT'S BEHIND THIS DOOR, MR. KEENE? DO THEY LET THE ASSISTANT MANAGER IN ON SUCH THINGS?
I—I HAVE NO IDEA.
THEN WE'LL FIND OUT TOGETHER. BUT WE'LL NEED TO TREAD CAREFULLY.
IF I ENTER THE WRONG COMBINATION THAT SMART LOCK WILL SEND OUT A SILENT ALARM ON 112 MEGAHERTZ. THE POLICE WAVELENGTH.
WHAT FREQUENCY DID YOU USE FOR MR. KEENE'S SUICIDE BOMB, RHAK?
BY A STRANGE COINCIDENCE, MR. U, IT WAS 112 MEGAHERTZ.
THAT'S UNFORTUNATE.
SORRY, MR. U.

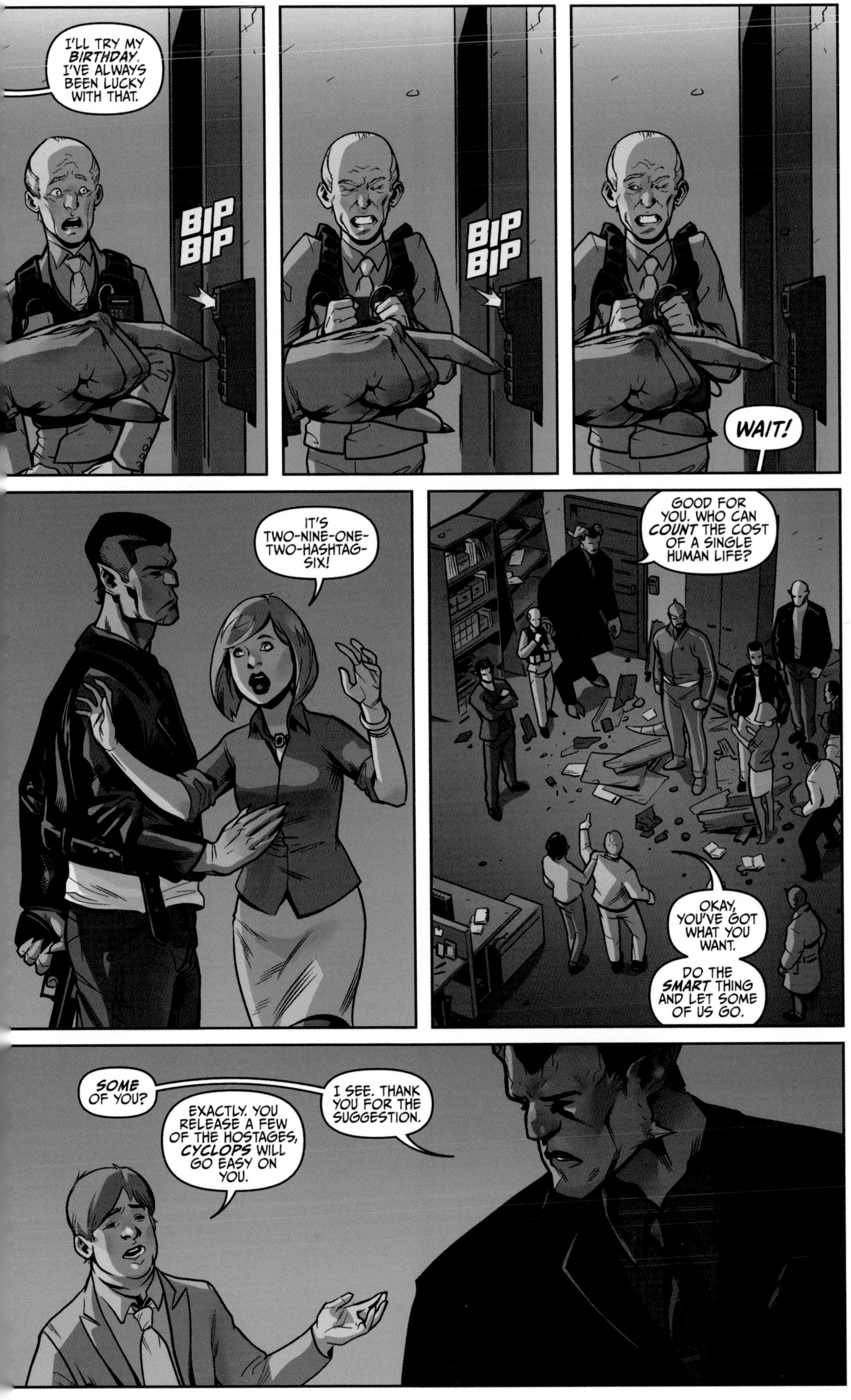
I'LL TRY MY BIRTHDAY. I'VE ALWAYS BEEN LUCKY WITH THAT.
BIP BIP
BIP BIP
WAIT!
IT'S TWO-NINE-ONE-TWO-HASHTAG-SIX!
GOOD FOR YOU. WHO CAN COUNT THE COST OF A SINGLE HUMAN LIFE?
OKAY, YOU'VE GOT WHAT YOU WANT.
DO THE SMART THING AND LET SOME OF US GO.
SOME OF YOU?
EXACTLY. YOU RELEASE A FEW OF THE HOSTAGES, CYCLOPS WILL GO EASY ON YOU.
I SEE. THANK YOU FOR THE SUGGESTION.

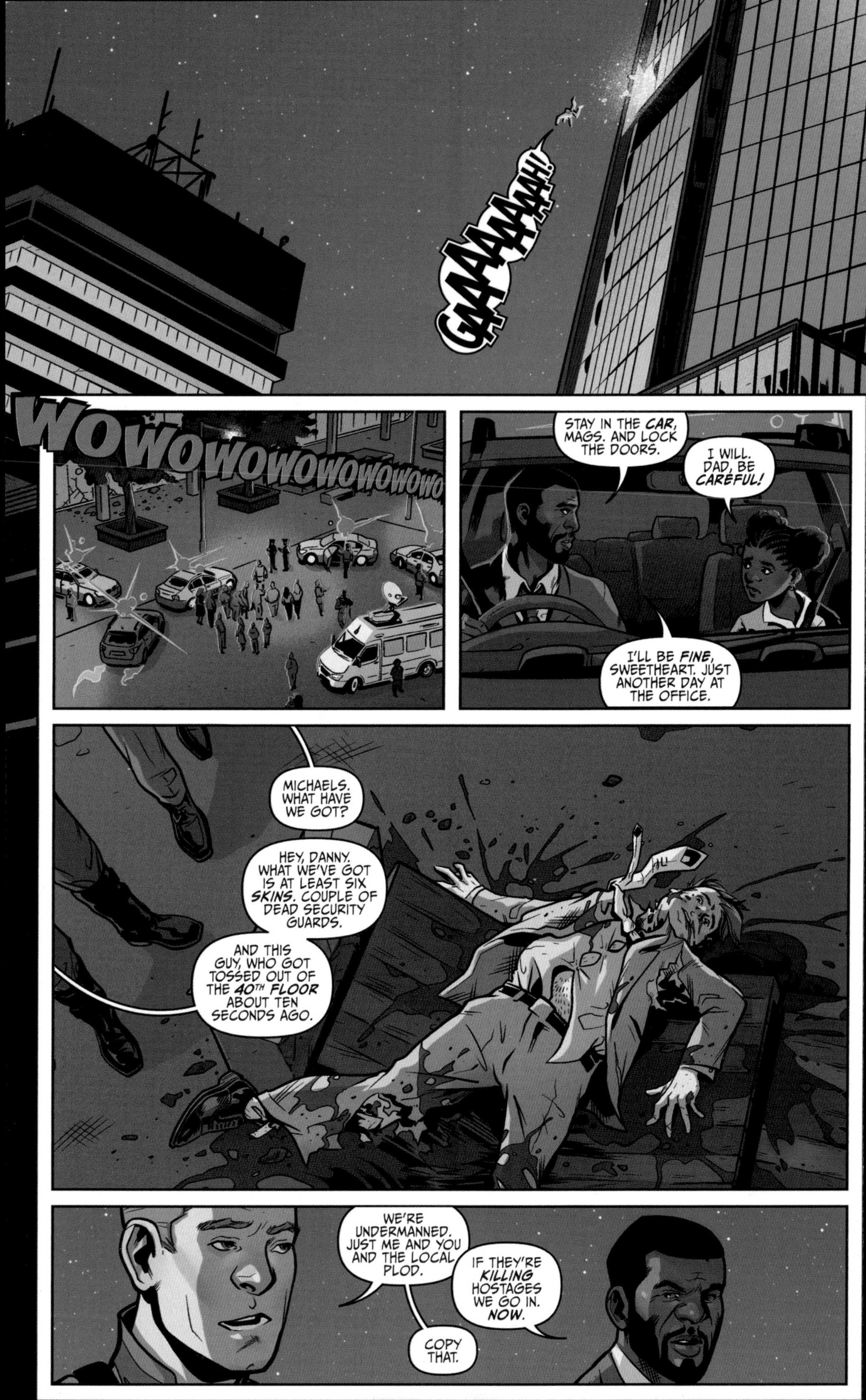
GAAAAAAAH!
WOWOWOWOWOWOWOWOWO
STAY IN THE CAR, MAGS. AND LOCK THE DOORS.
I WILL. DAD, BE CAREFUL!
I'LL BE FINE, SWEETHEART. JUST ANOTHER DAY AT THE OFFICE.
MICHAELS. WHAT HAVE WE GOT?
HEY, DANNY. WHAT WE'VE GOT IS AT LEAST SIX SKINS. COUPLE OF DEAD SECURITY GUARDS.
AND THIS GUY, WHO GOT TOSSED OUT OF THE 40TH FLOOR ABOUT TEN SECONDS AGO.
WE'RE UNDERMANNED. JUST ME AND YOU AND THE LOCAL PLOD.
IF THEY'RE KILLING HOSTAGES WE GO IN. NOW.
COPY THAT.

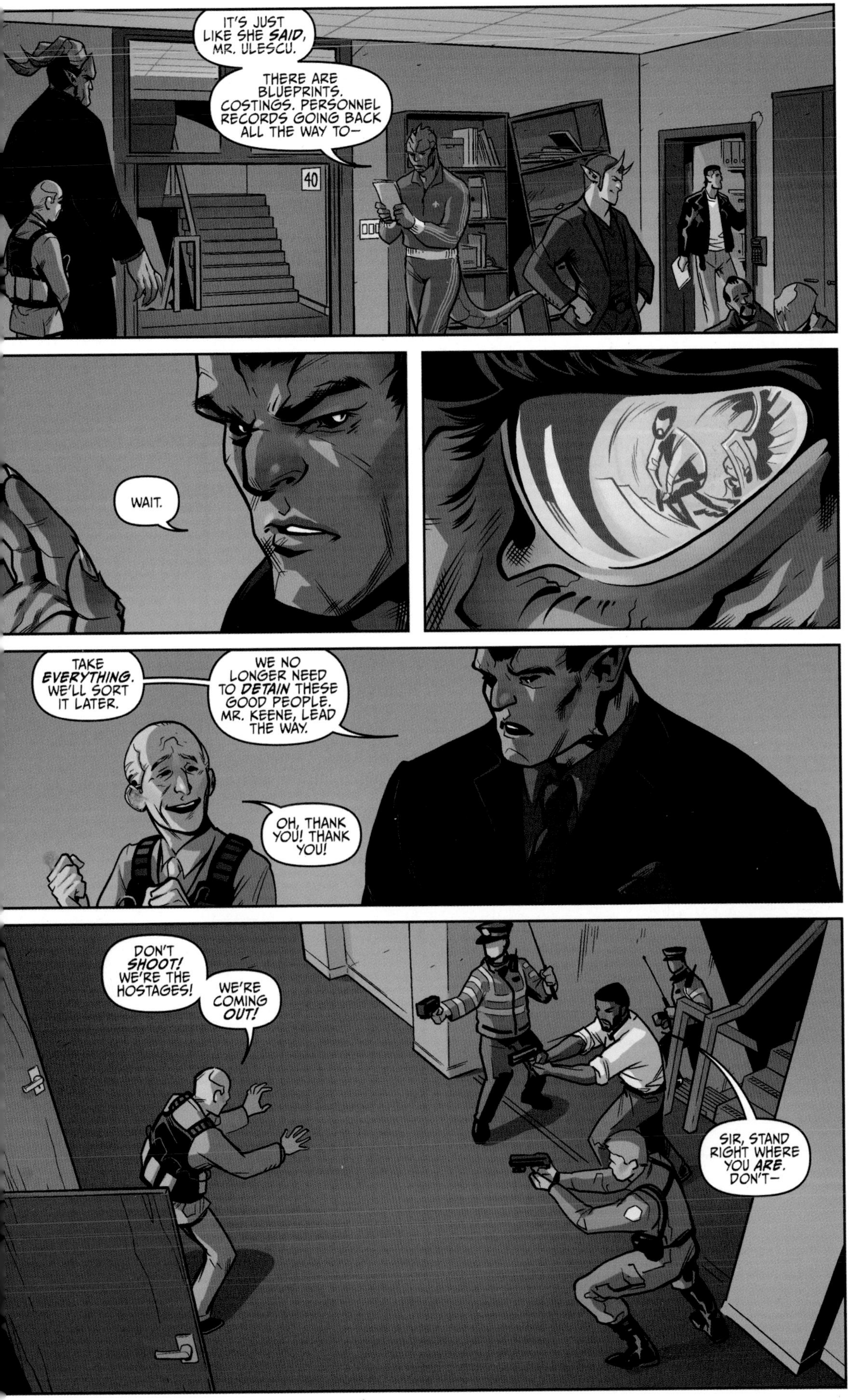
IT'S JUST LIKE SHE SAID, MR. ULESCU.
THERE ARE BLUEPRINTS. COSTINGS. PERSONNEL RECORDS GOING BACK ALL THE WAY TO—
40
WAIT.
TAKE EVERYTHING. WE'LL SORT IT LATER.
WE NO LONGER NEED TO DETAIN THESE GOOD PEOPLE. MR. KEENE, LEAD THE WAY.
OH, THANK YOU! THANK YOU!
DON'T SHOOT! WE'RE THE HOSTAGES!
WE'RE COMING OUT!
SIR, STAND RIGHT WHERE YOU ARE. DON'T—

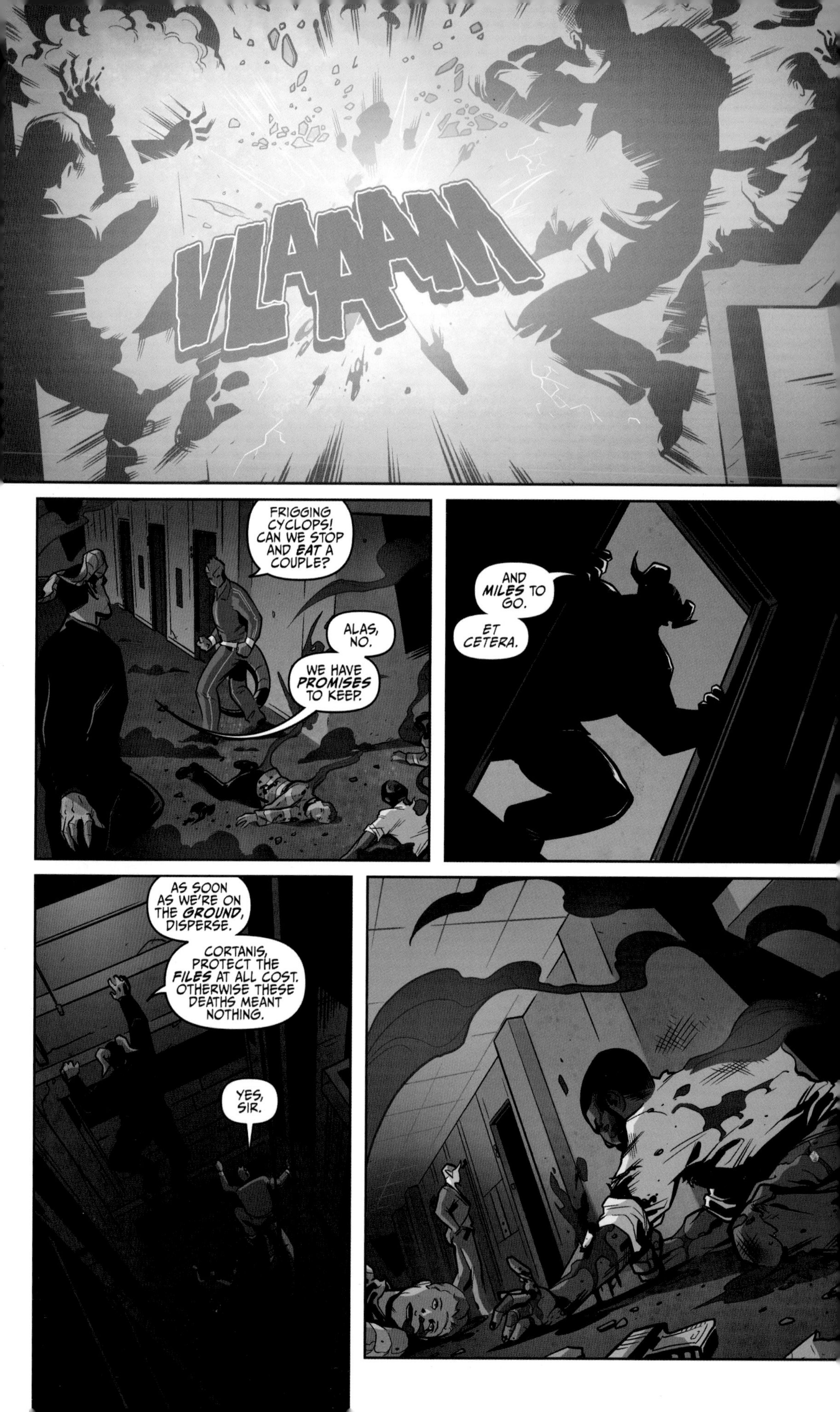
VLAAAM
FRIGGING CYCLOPS! CAN WE STOP AND EAT A COUPLE?
ALAS, NO.
WE HAVE PROMISES TO KEEP.
AND MILES TO GO.
ET CETERA.
AS SOON AS WE'RE ON THE GROUND, DISPERSE.
CORTANIS, PROTECT THE FILES AT ALL COST. OTHERWISE THESE DEATHS MEANT NOTHING.
YES, SIR.

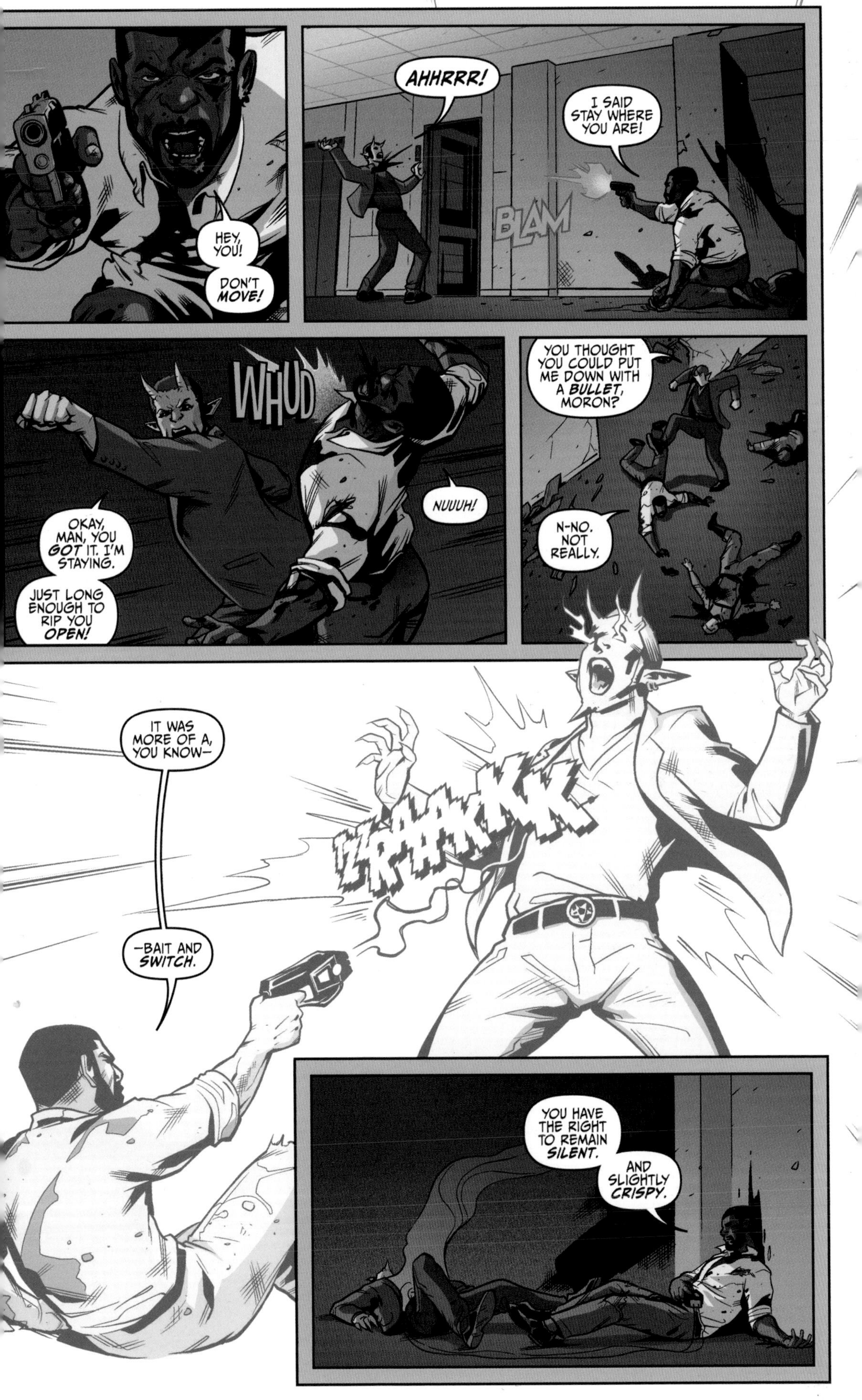
HEY, YOU!
DON'T MOVE!
AHHRRR!
I SAID STAY WHERE YOU ARE!
BLAM
WHUD
OKAY, MAN, YOU GOT IT. I'M STAYING.
JUST LONG ENOUGH TO RIP YOU OPEN!
NUUUH!
YOU THOUGHT YOU COULD PUT ME DOWN WITH A BULLET, MORON?
N-NO. NOT REALLY.
IT WAS MORE OF A, YOU KNOW—
ZZRAKKK
—BAIT AND SWITCH.
YOU HAVE THE RIGHT TO REMAIN SILENT.
AND SLIGHTLY CRISPY.

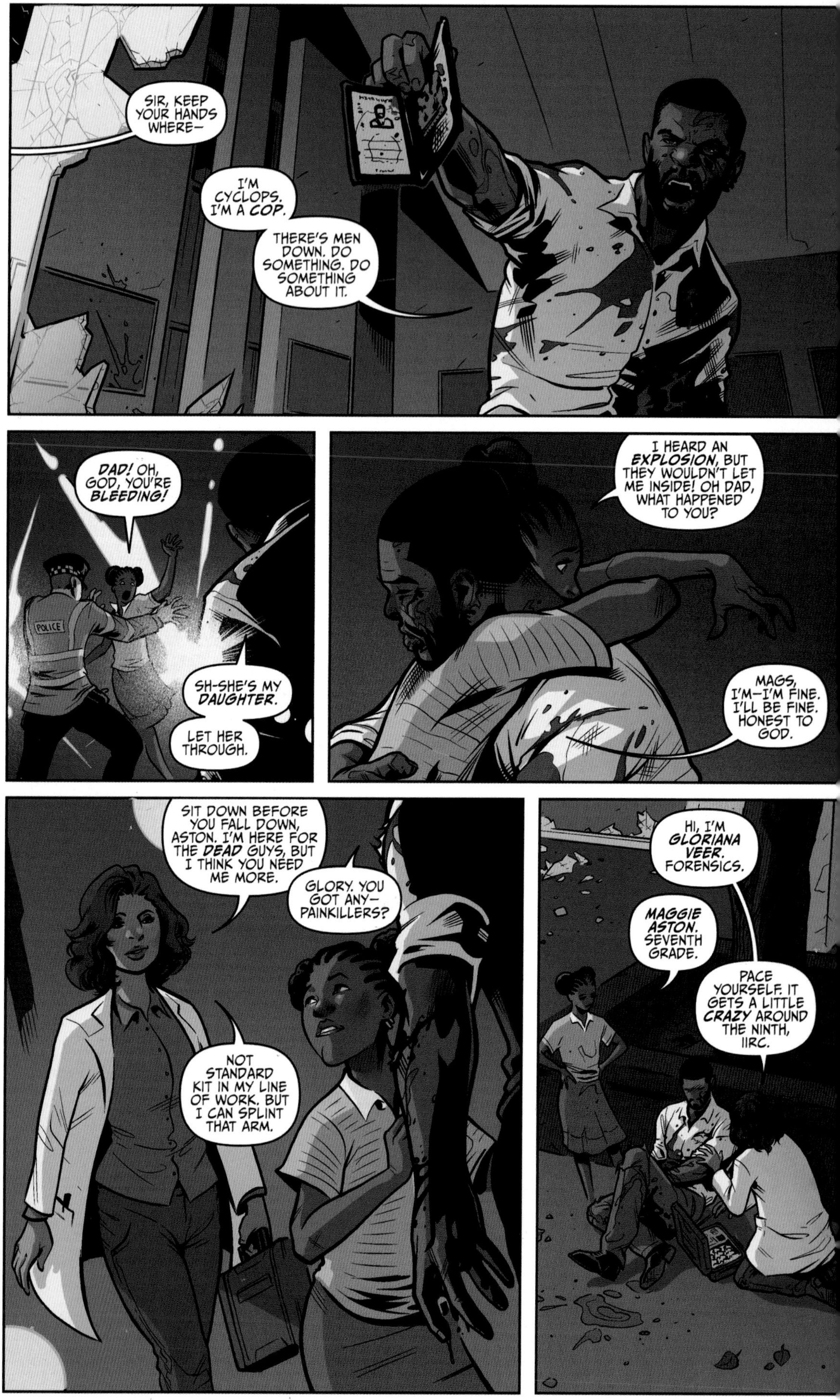
SIR, KEEP YOUR HANDS WHERE—
I'M CYCLOPS. I'M A COP.
THERE'S MEN DOWN. DO SOMETHING. DO SOMETHING ABOUT IT.
DAD! OH, GOD, YOU'RE BLEEDING!
POLICE
SH-SHE'S MY DAUGHTER.
LET HER THROUGH.
I HEARD AN EXPLOSION, BUT THEY WOULDN'T LET ME INSIDE! OH DAD, WHAT HAPPENED TO YOU?
MAGS, I'M—I'M FINE. I'LL BE FINE. HONEST TO GOD.
SIT DOWN BEFORE YOU FALL DOWN, ASTON. I'M HERE FOR THE DEAD GUYS, BUT I THINK YOU NEED ME MORE.
GLORY. YOU GOT ANY— PAINKILLERS?
NOT STANDARD KIT IN MY LINE OF WORK. BUT I CAN SPLINT THAT ARM.
HI, I'M GLORIANA VEER. FORENSICS.
MAGGIE ASTON. SEVENTH GRADE.
PACE YOURSELF. IT GETS A LITTLE CRAZY AROUND THE NINTH, IIRC.

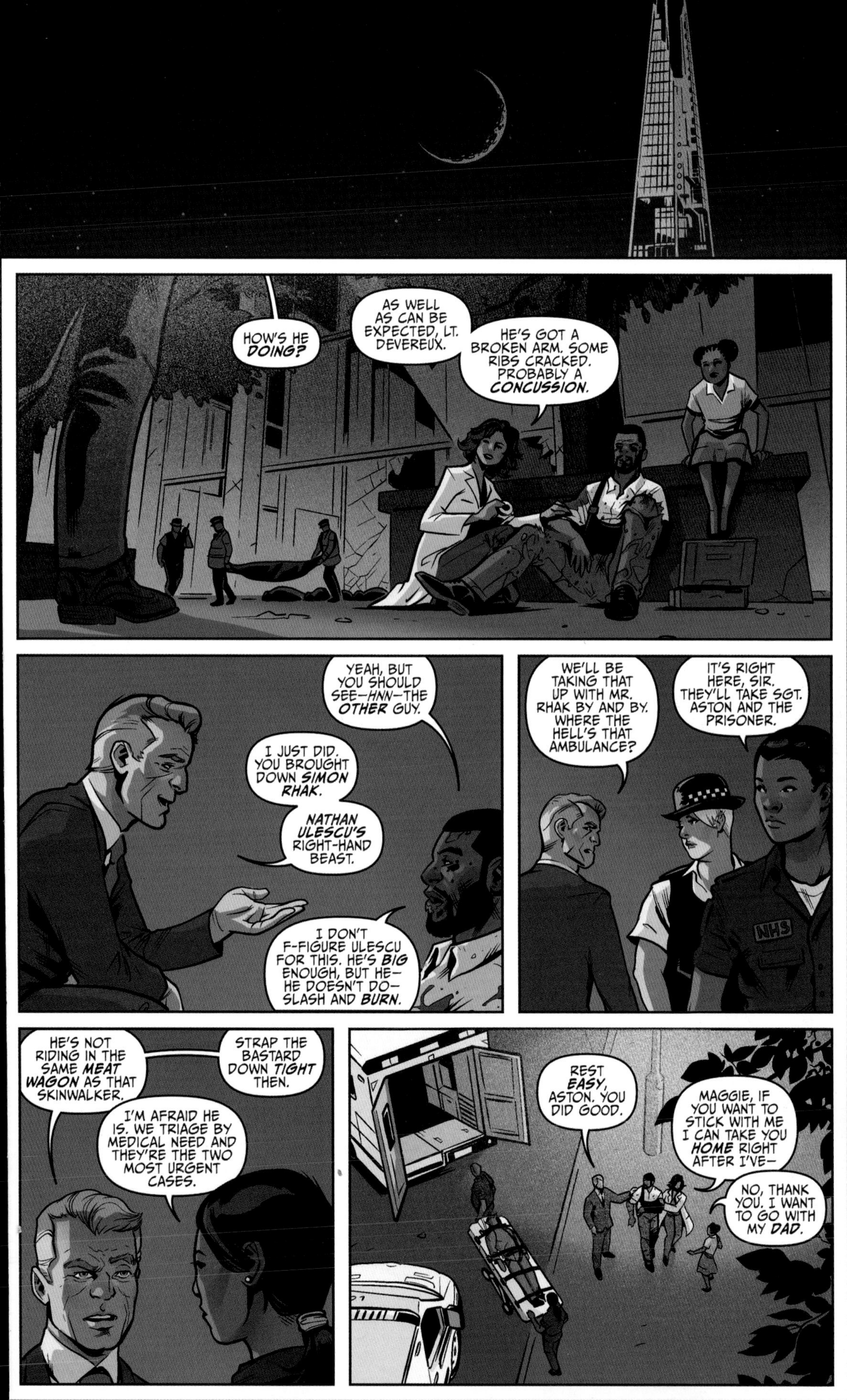
HOW'S HE DOING?
AS WELL AS CAN BE EXPECTED, LT. DEVEREUX.
HE'S GOT A BROKEN ARM. SOME RIBS CRACKED. PROBABLY A CONCUSSION.
YEAH, BUT YOU SHOULD SEE–HNN–THE OTHER GUY.
I JUST DID. YOU BROUGHT DOWN SIMON RHAK.
NATHAN ULESCU'S RIGHT-HAND BEAST.
I DON'T F-FIGURE ULESCU FOR THIS. HE'S BIG ENOUGH, BUT HE– HE DOESN'T DO– SLASH AND BURN.
WE'LL BE TAKING THAT UP WITH MR. RHAK BY AND BY. WHERE THE HELL'S THAT AMBULANCE?
IT'S RIGHT HERE, SIR. THEY'LL TAKE SGT. ASTON AND THE PRISONER.
NHS
HE'S NOT RIDING IN THE SAME MEAT WAGON AS THAT SKINWALKER.
I'M AFRAID HE IS. WE TRIAGE BY MEDICAL NEED AND THEY'RE THE TWO MOST URGENT CASES.
STRAP THE BASTARD DOWN TIGHT THEN.
REST EASY, ASTON. YOU DID GOOD.
MAGGIE, IF YOU WANT TO STICK WITH ME I CAN TAKE YOU HOME RIGHT AFTER I'VE–
NO, THANK YOU. I WANT TO GO WITH MY DAD.

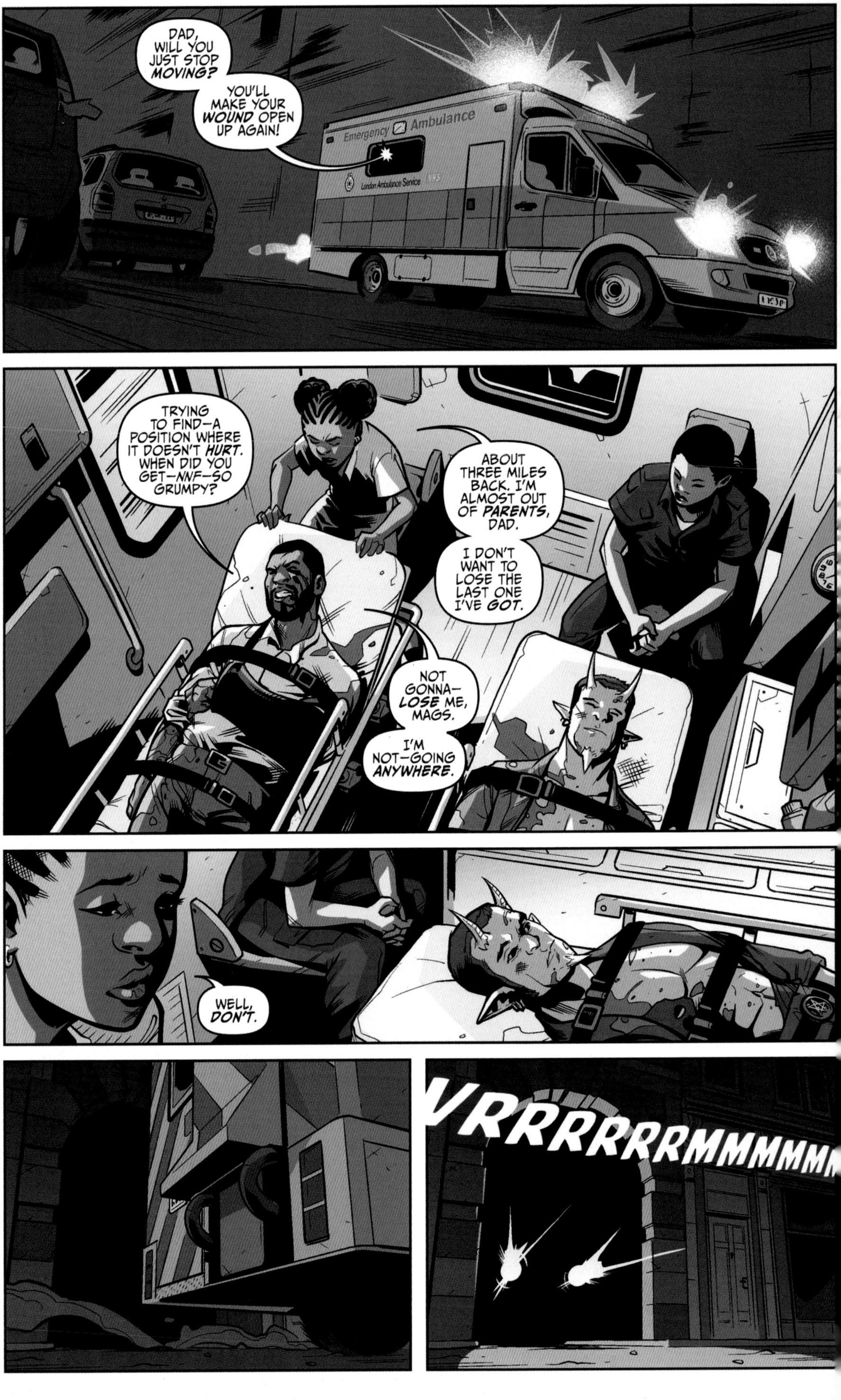
DAD, WILL YOU JUST STOP MOVING?
YOU'LL MAKE YOUR WOUND OPEN UP AGAIN!
Emergency Ambulance
London Ambulance Service
TRYING TO FIND—A POSITION WHERE IT DOESN'T HURT. WHEN DID YOU GET—NNF—SO GRUMPY?
ABOUT THREE MILES BACK. I'M ALMOST OUT OF PARENTS, DAD.
I DON'T WANT TO LOSE THE LAST ONE I'VE GOT.
NOT GONNA—LOSE ME, MAGS.
I'M NOT—GOING ANYWHERE.
WELL, DON'T.
VRRRRRRRMMMMMM

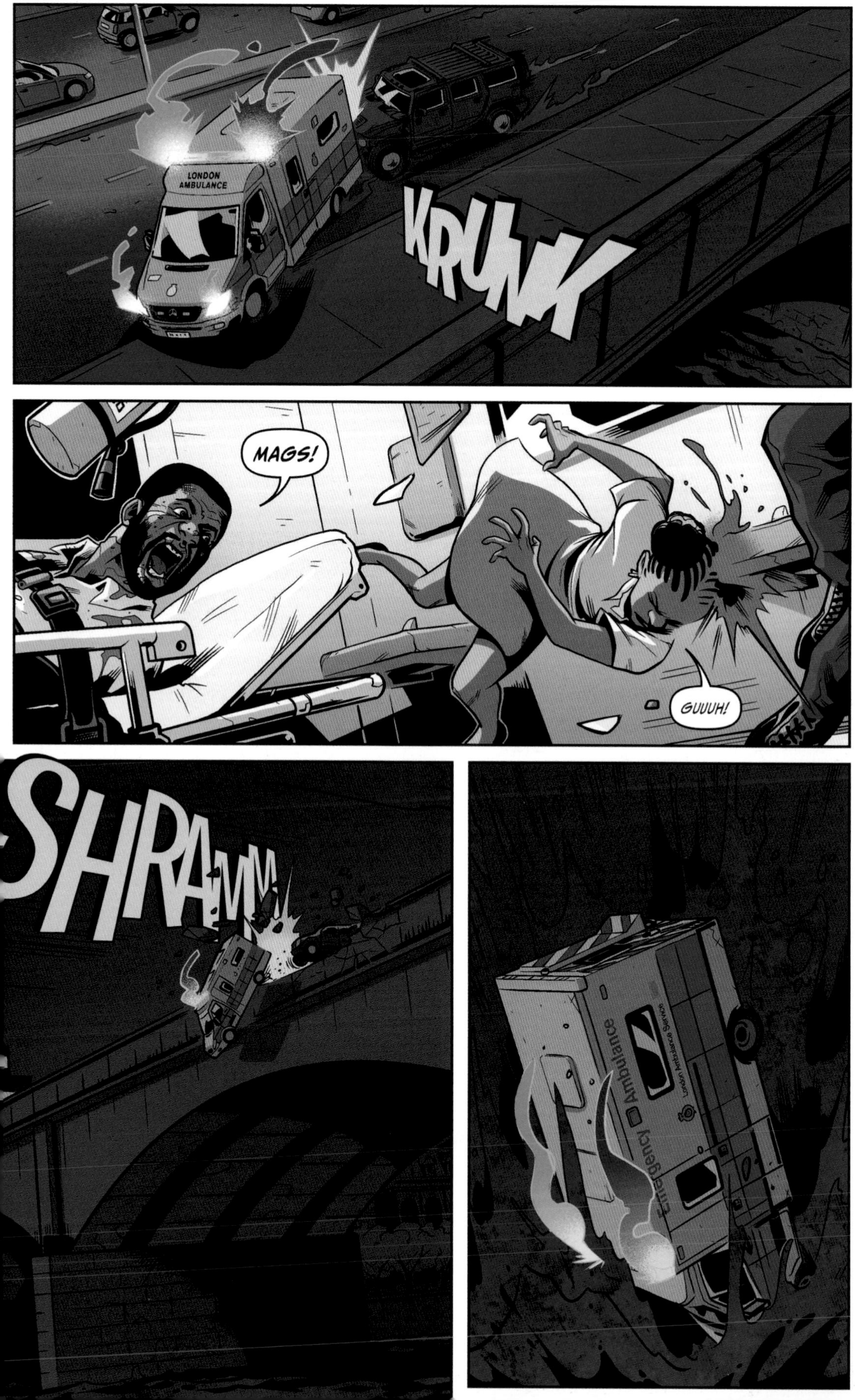
LONDON AMBULANCE
KRUNK
MAGS!
GUUUH!
SHRAMM
Emergency Ambulance
London Ambulance Service

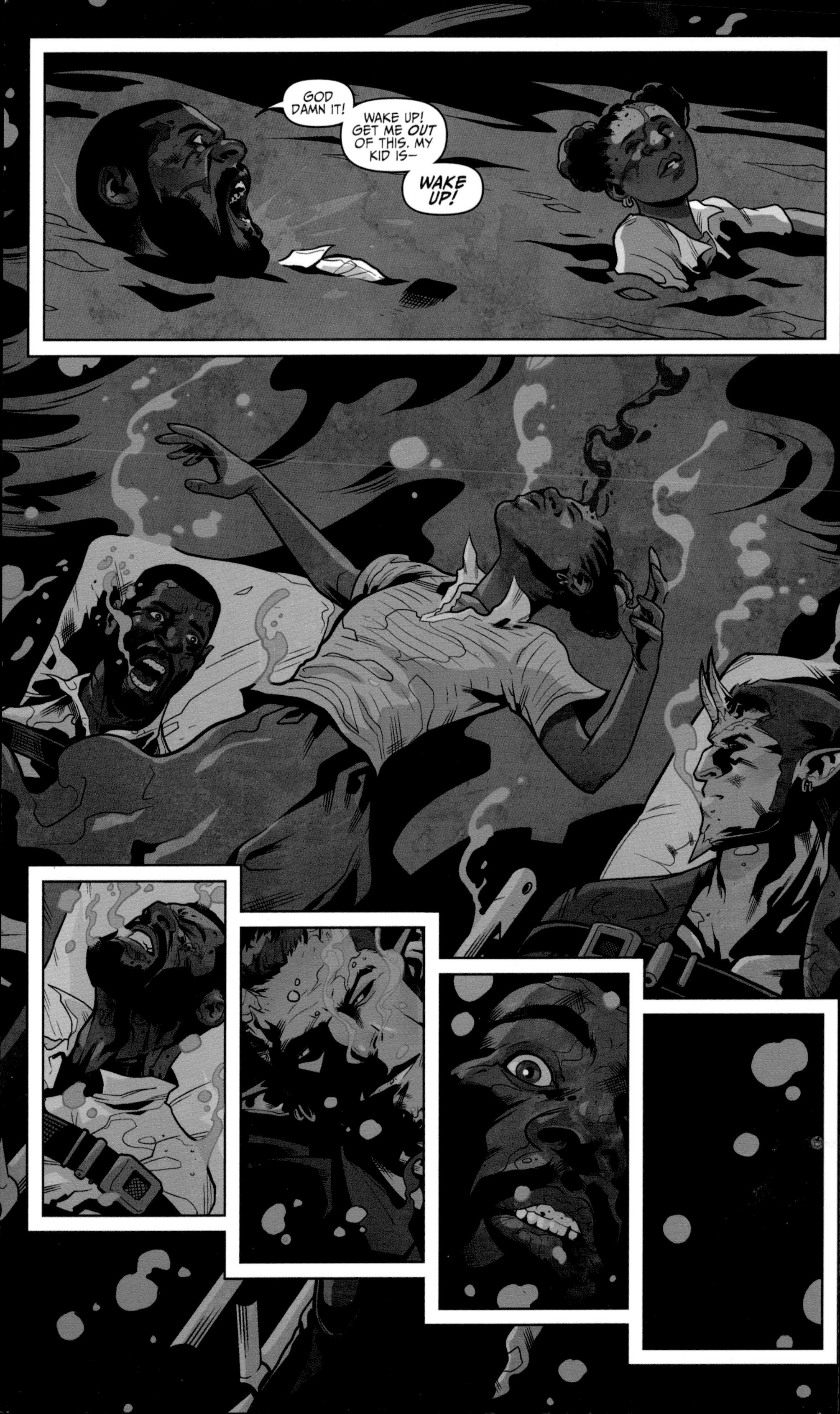
GOD DAMN IT!
WAKE UP! GET ME OUT OF THIS. MY KID IS—
WAKE UP!

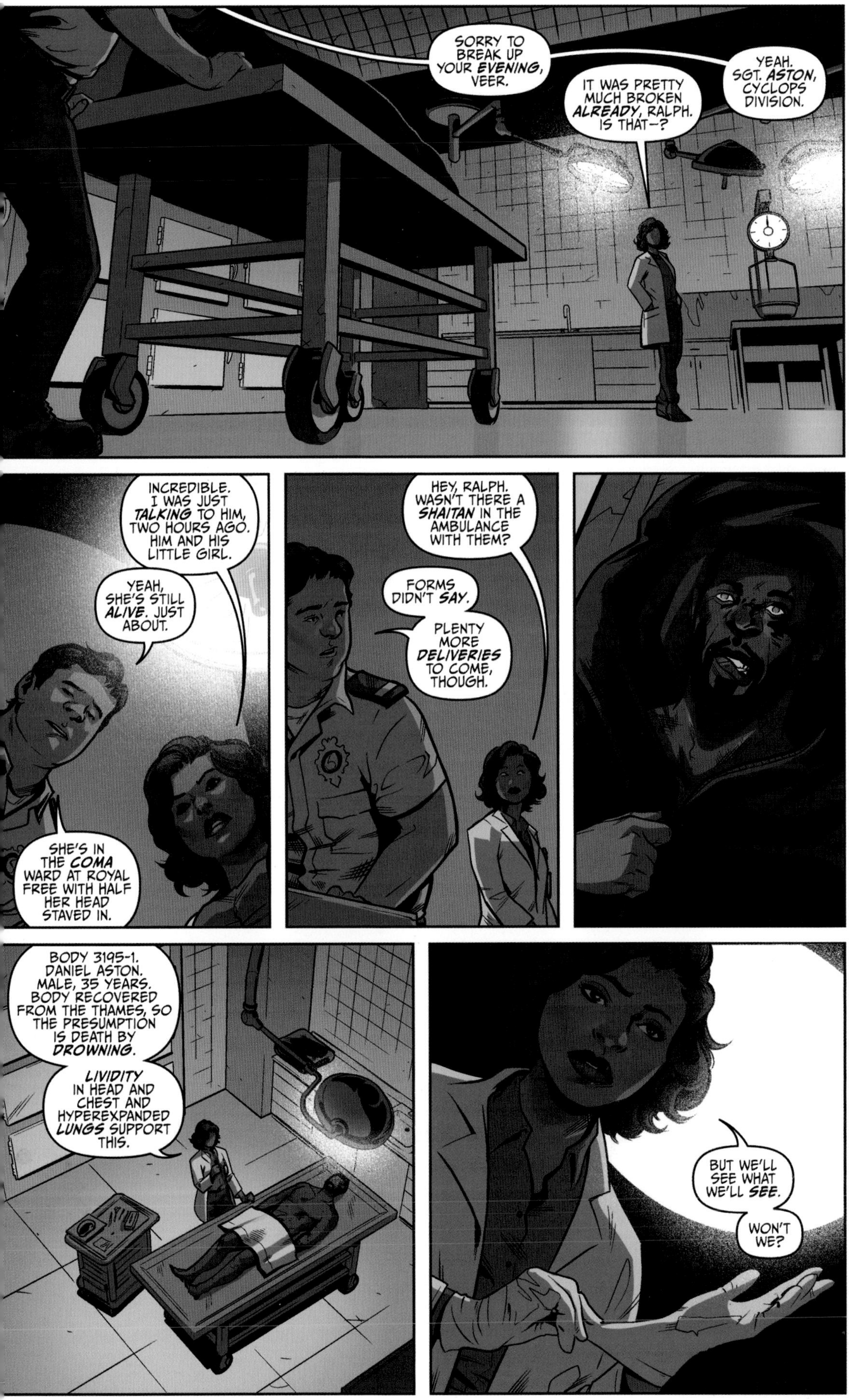
SORRY TO BREAK UP YOUR EVENING, VEER.
IT WAS PRETTY MUCH BROKEN ALREADY, RALPH. IS THAT–?
YEAH. SGT. ASTON, CYCLOPS DIVISION.
INCREDIBLE. I WAS JUST TALKING TO HIM, TWO HOURS AGO. HIM AND HIS LITTLE GIRL.
YEAH, SHE'S STILL ALIVE. JUST ABOUT.
SHE'S IN THE COMA WARD AT ROYAL FREE WITH HALF HER HEAD STAVED IN.
HEY, RALPH. WASN'T THERE A SHAITAN IN THE AMBULANCE WITH THEM?
FORMS DIDN'T SAY.
PLENTY MORE DELIVERIES TO COME, THOUGH.
BODY 3195-1. DANIEL ASTON. MALE, 35 YEARS. BODY RECOVERED FROM THE THAMES, SO THE PRESUMPTION IS DEATH BY DROWNING.
LIVIDITY IN HEAD AND CHEST AND HYPEREXPANDED LUNGS SUPPORT THIS.
BUT WE'LL SEE WHAT WE'LL SEE.
WON'T WE?

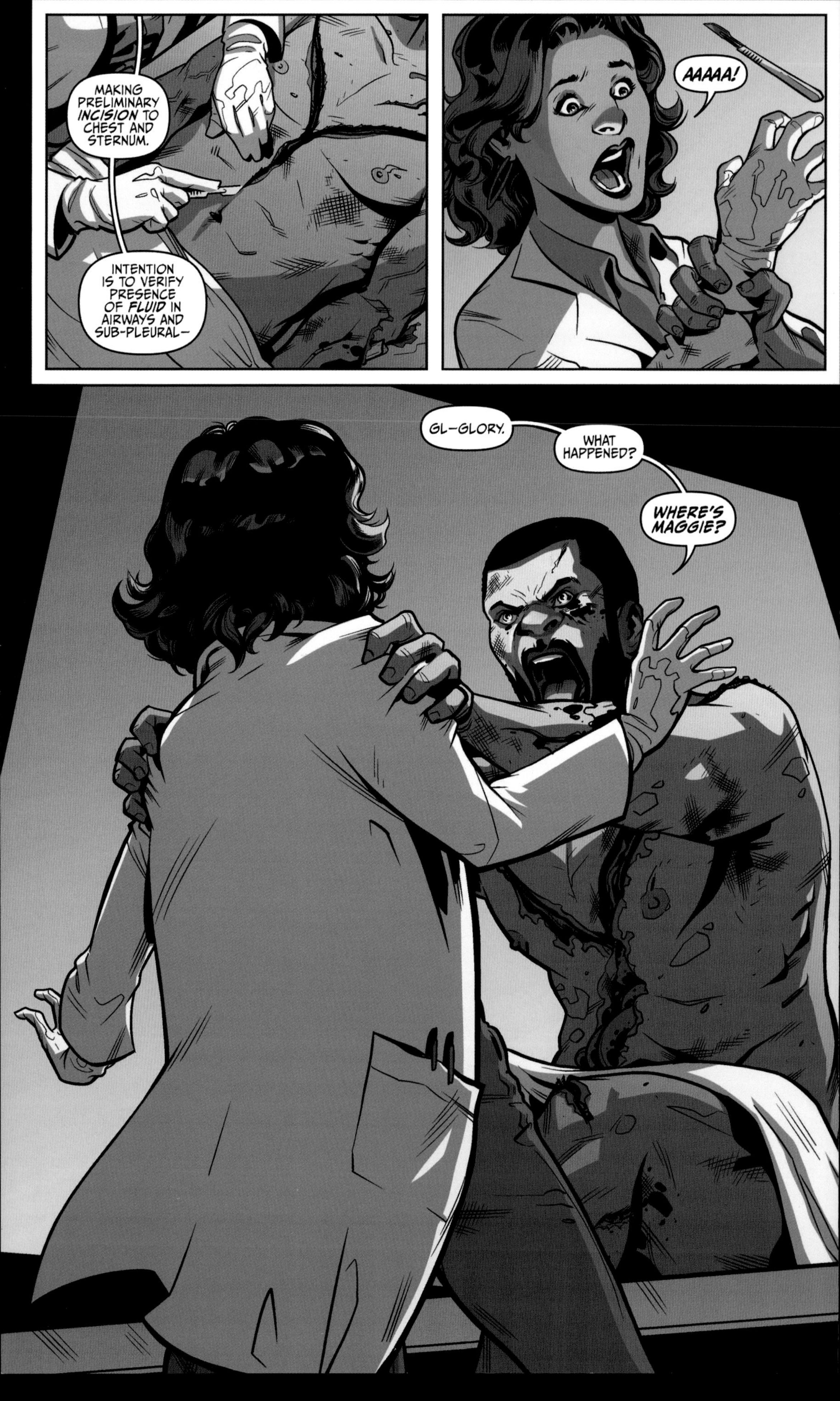
MAKING PRELIMINARY *INCISION* TO CHEST AND STERNUM.
INTENTION IS TO VERIFY PRESENCE OF *FLUID* IN AIRWAYS AND SUB-PLEURAL—
AAAAA!
GL-GLORY.
WHAT HAPPENED?
WHERE'S MAGGIE?

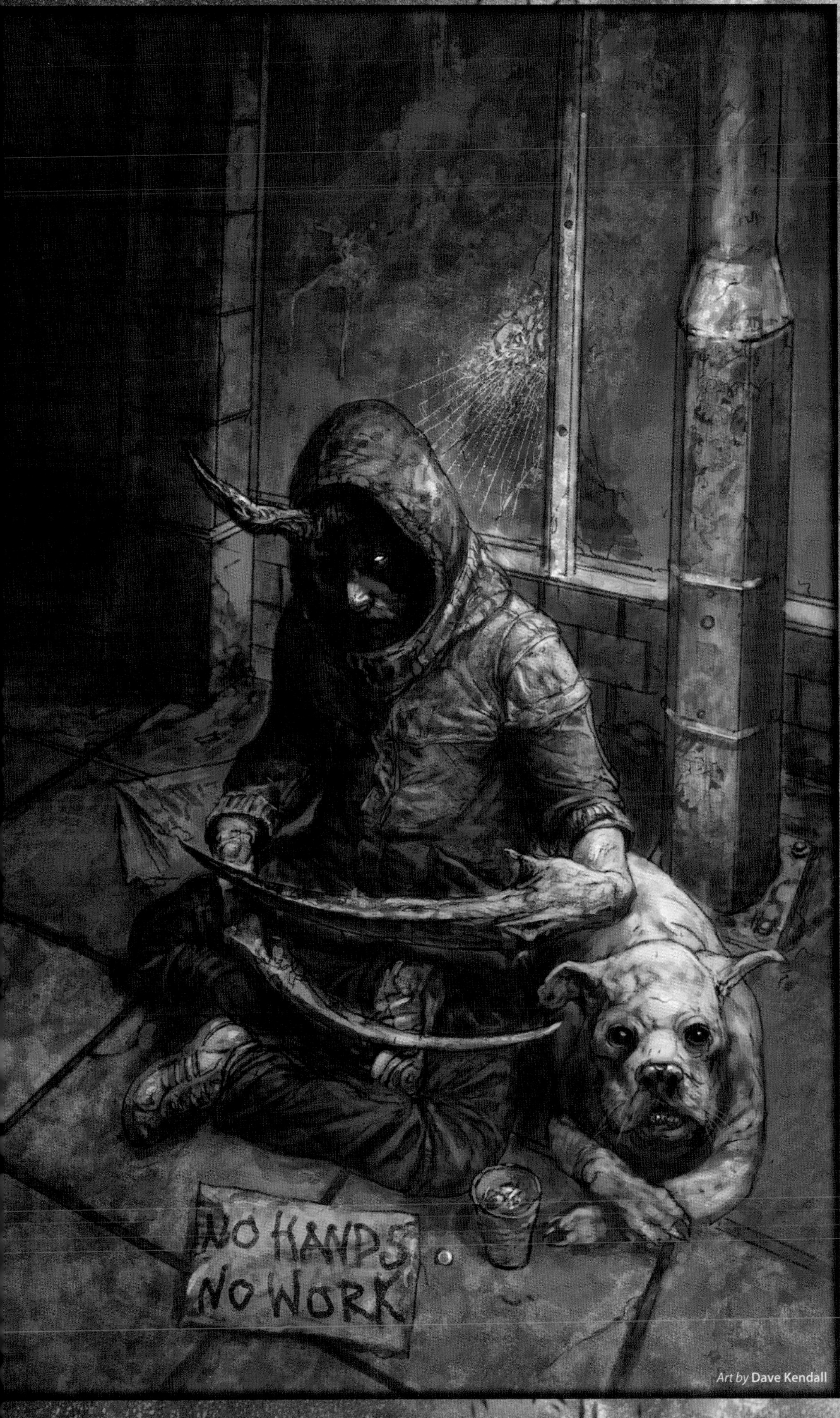
NO HANDS
NO WORK
Art by Dave Kendall

Chapter 2

Accidents and Emergencies

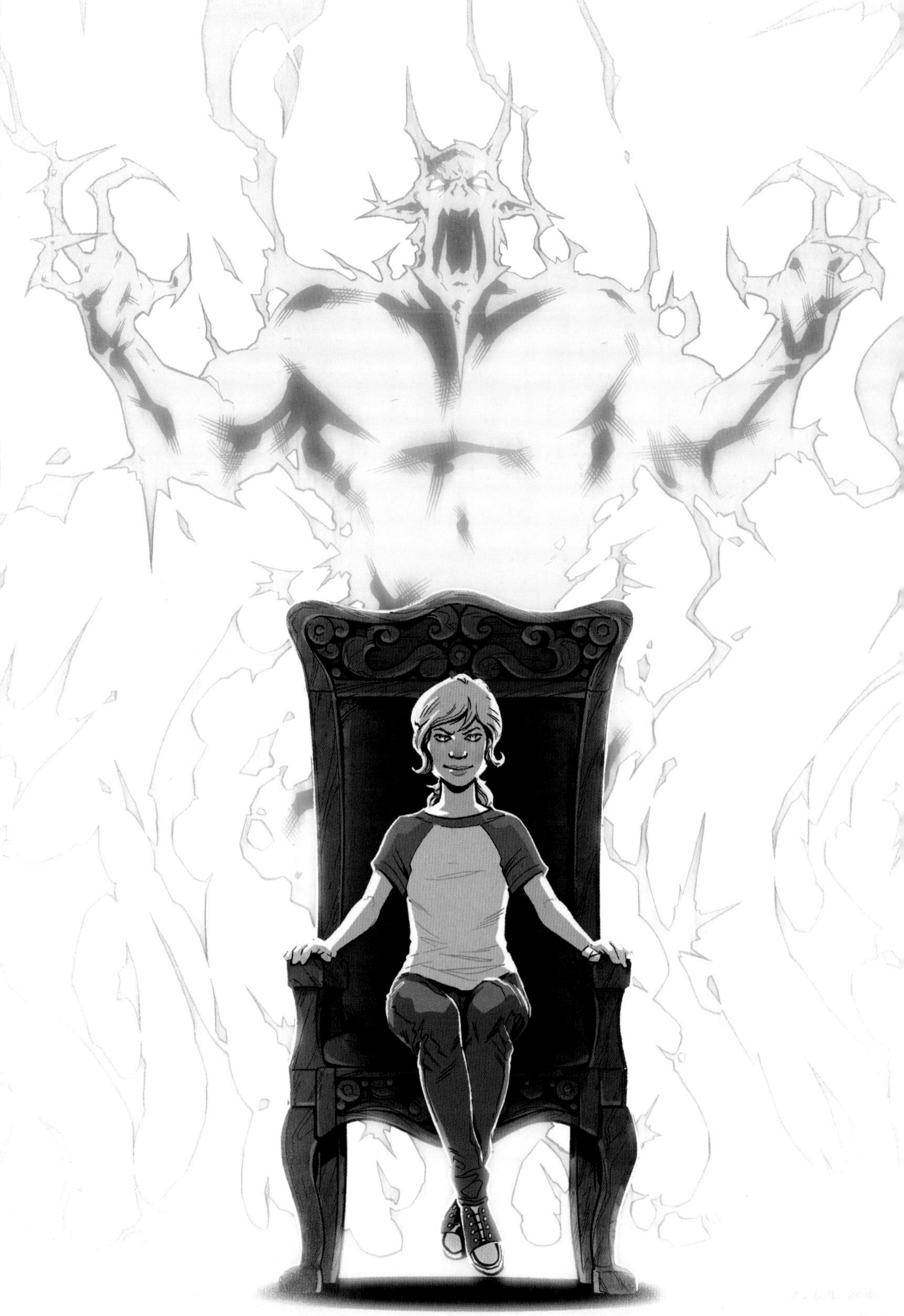

Art by **Brendan Cahill**, *Colors by* **Joana Lafuente**

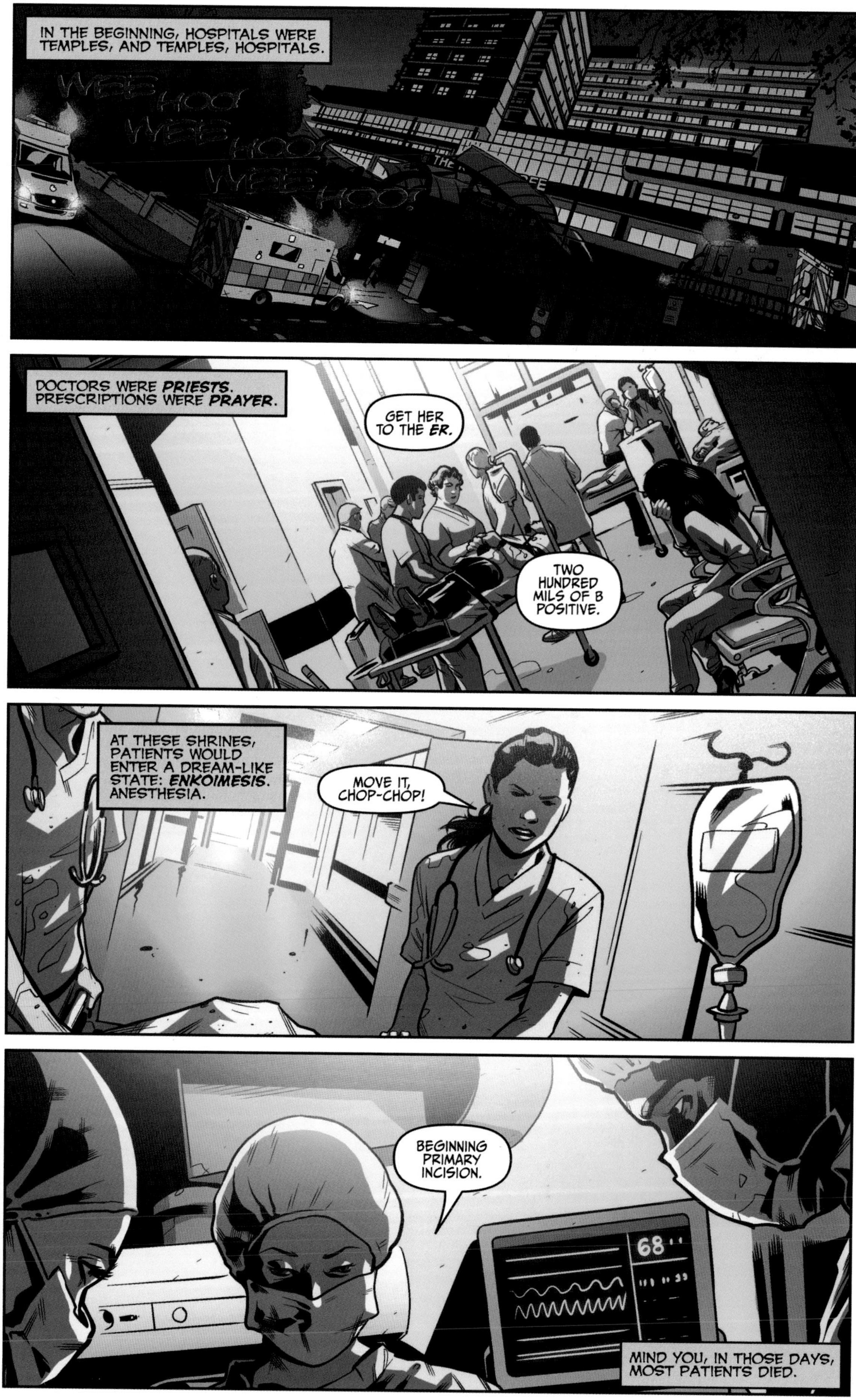

IN THE BEGINNING, HOSPITALS WERE TEMPLES, AND TEMPLES, HOSPITALS.
DOCTORS WERE **PRIESTS**. PRESCRIPTIONS WERE **PRAYER**.
GET HER TO THE **ER**.
TWO HUNDRED MILS OF B POSITIVE.
AT THESE SHRINES, PATIENTS WOULD ENTER A DREAM-LIKE STATE: **ENKOIMESIS**. ANESTHESIA.
MOVE IT, CHOP-CHOP!
BEGINNING PRIMARY INCISION.
68
MIND YOU, IN THOSE DAYS, MOST PATIENTS DIED.

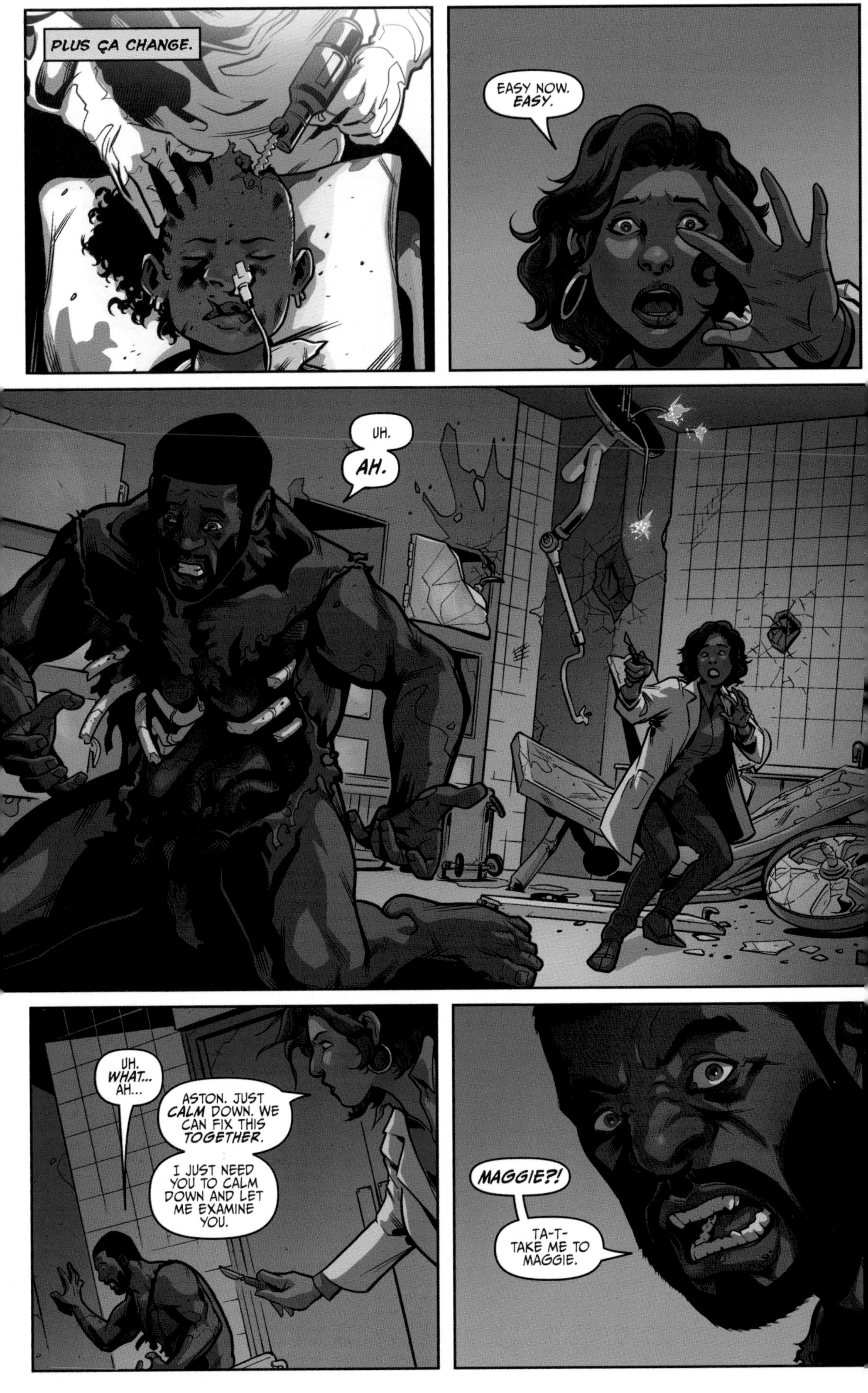
PLUS ÇA CHANGE.
EASY NOW. EASY.
UH. AH.
UH. WHAT... AH...
ASTON. JUST CALM DOWN. WE CAN FIX THIS TOGETHER.
I JUST NEED YOU TO CALM DOWN AND LET ME EXAMINE YOU.
MAGGIE?!
TA-T- TAKE ME TO MAGGIE.

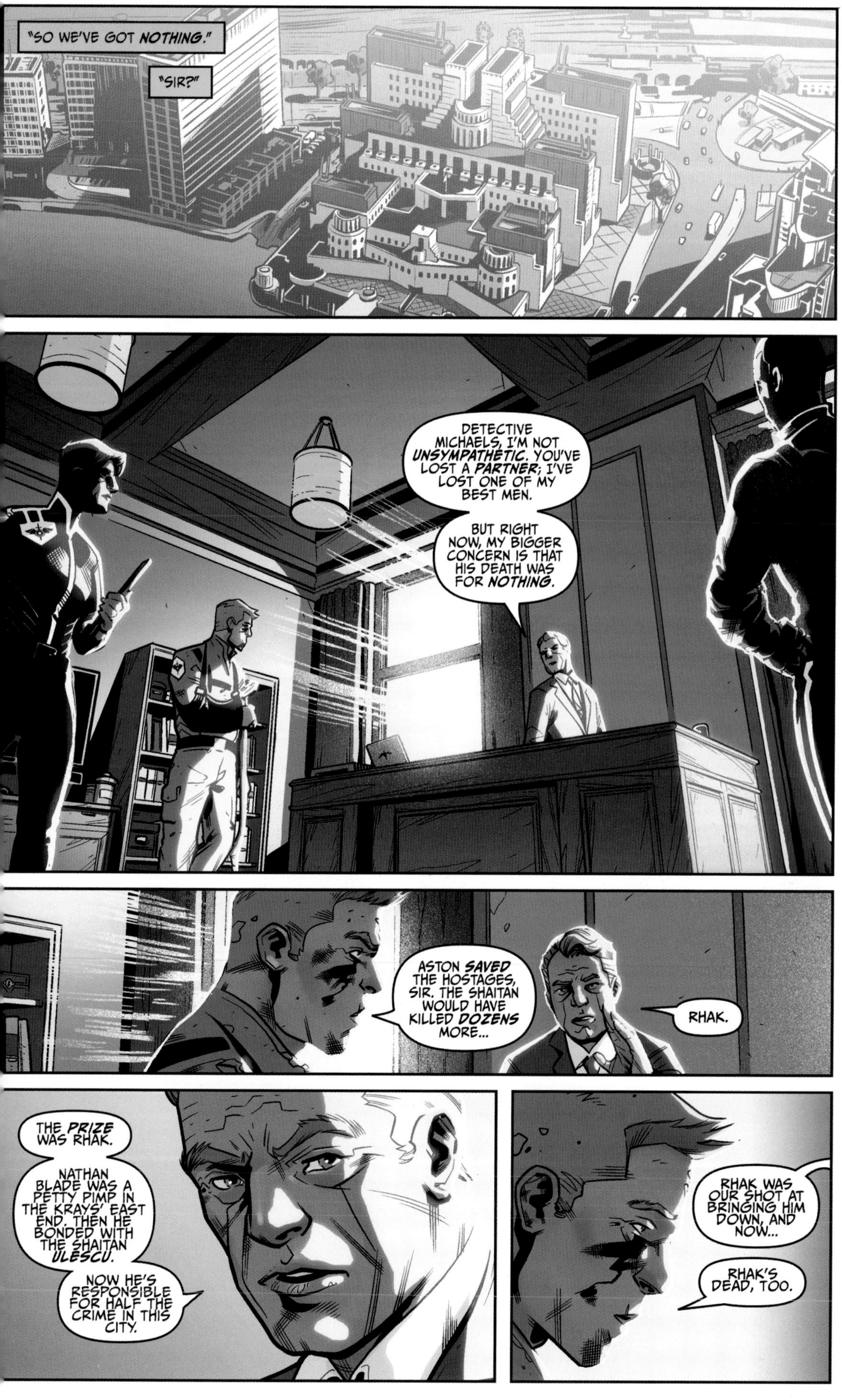
"SO WE'VE GOT NOTHING."
"SIR?"
DETECTIVE MICHAELS, I'M NOT UNSYMPATHETIC. YOU'VE LOST A PARTNER; I'VE LOST ONE OF MY BEST MEN.
BUT RIGHT NOW, MY BIGGER CONCERN IS THAT HIS DEATH WAS FOR NOTHING.
ASTON SAVED THE HOSTAGES, SIR. THE SHAITAN WOULD HAVE KILLED DOZENS MORE...
RHAK.
THE PRIZE WAS RHAK.
NATHAN BLADE WAS A PETTY PIMP IN THE KRAYS' EAST END. THEN HE BONDED WITH THE SHAITAN ULESCU.
NOW HE'S RESPONSIBLE FOR HALF THE CRIME IN THIS CITY.
RHAK WAS OUR SHOT AT BRINGING HIM DOWN, AND NOW...
RHAK'S DEAD, TOO.

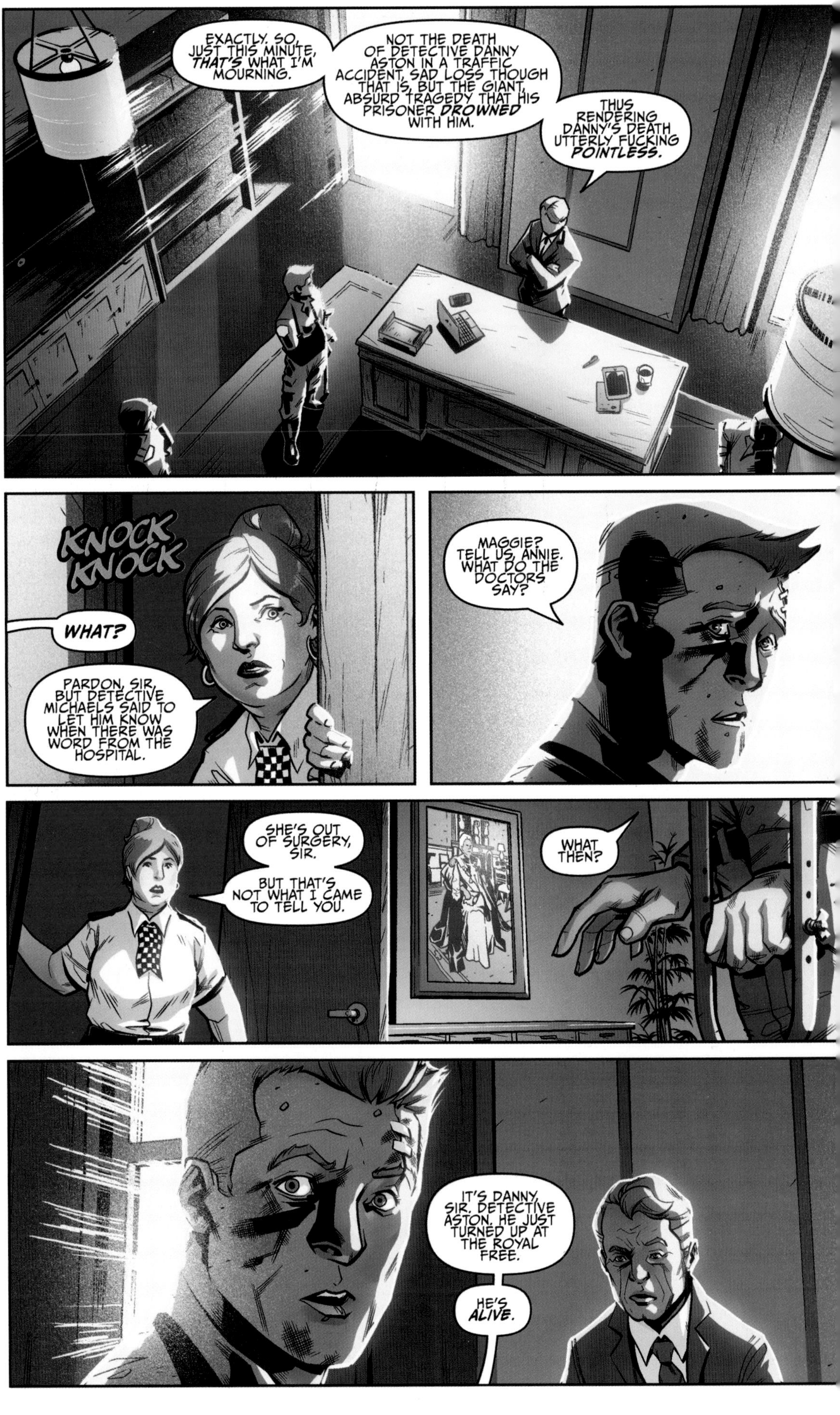
EXACTLY. SO, JUST THIS MINUTE, THAT'S WHAT I'M MOURNING.
NOT THE DEATH OF DETECTIVE DANNY ASTON IN A TRAFFIC ACCIDENT, SAD LOSS THOUGH THAT IS, BUT THE GIANT, ABSURD TRAGEDY THAT HIS PRISONER DROWNED WITH HIM.
THUS RENDERING DANNY'S DEATH UTTERLY FUCKING POINTLESS.
KNOCK KNOCK
WHAT?
PARDON, SIR, BUT DETECTIVE MICHAELS SAID TO LET HIM KNOW WHEN THERE WAS WORD FROM THE HOSPITAL.
MAGGIE? TELL US, ANNIE. WHAT DO THE DOCTORS SAY?
SHE'S OUT OF SURGERY, SIR.
BUT THAT'S NOT WHAT I CAME TO TELL YOU.
WHAT THEN?
IT'S DANNY, SIR. DETECTIVE ASTON. HE JUST TURNED UP AT THE ROYAL FREE.
HE'S ALIVE.

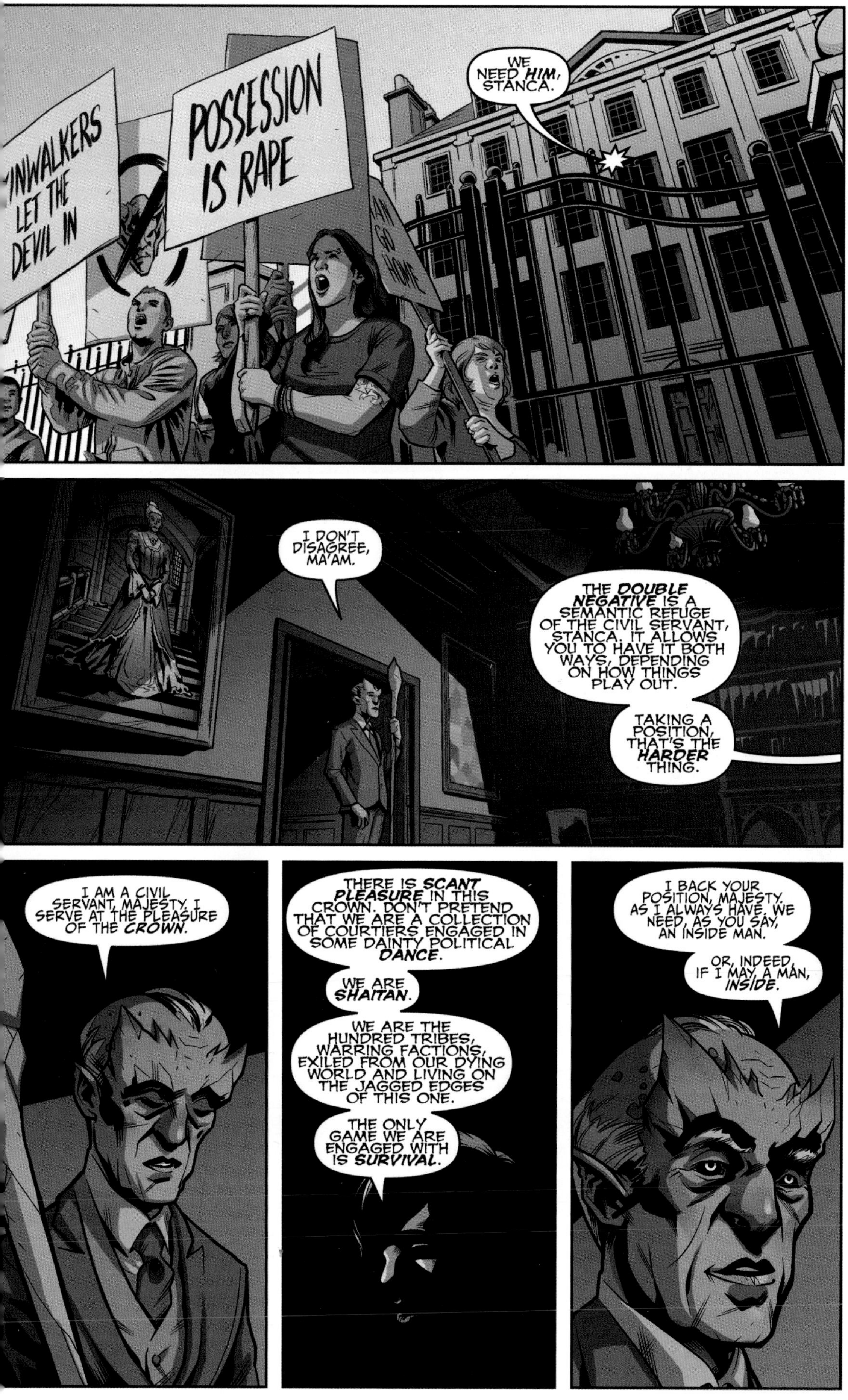
INWALKERS LET THE DEVIL IN
POSSESSION IS RAPE
GO HOME
WE NEED HIM, STANCA.
I DON'T DISAGREE, MA'AM.
THE DOUBLE NEGATIVE IS A SEMANTIC REFUGE OF THE CIVIL SERVANT, STANCA. IT ALLOWS YOU TO HAVE IT BOTH WAYS, DEPENDING ON HOW THINGS PLAY OUT.
TAKING A POSITION, THAT'S THE HARDER THING.
I AM A CIVIL SERVANT, MAJESTY. I SERVE AT THE PLEASURE OF THE CROWN.
THERE IS SCANT PLEASURE IN THIS CROWN. DON'T PRETEND THAT WE ARE A COLLECTION OF COURTIERS ENGAGED IN SOME DAINTY POLITICAL DANCE.
WE ARE SHAITAN.
WE ARE THE HUNDRED TRIBES, WARRING FACTIONS, EXILED FROM OUR DYING WORLD AND LIVING ON THE JAGGED EDGES OF THIS ONE.
THE ONLY GAME WE ARE ENGAGED WITH IS SURVIVAL.
I BACK YOUR POSITION, MAJESTY. AS I ALWAYS HAVE. WE NEED, AS YOU SAY, AN INSIDE MAN.
OR, INDEED, IF I MAY, A MAN, INSIDE.

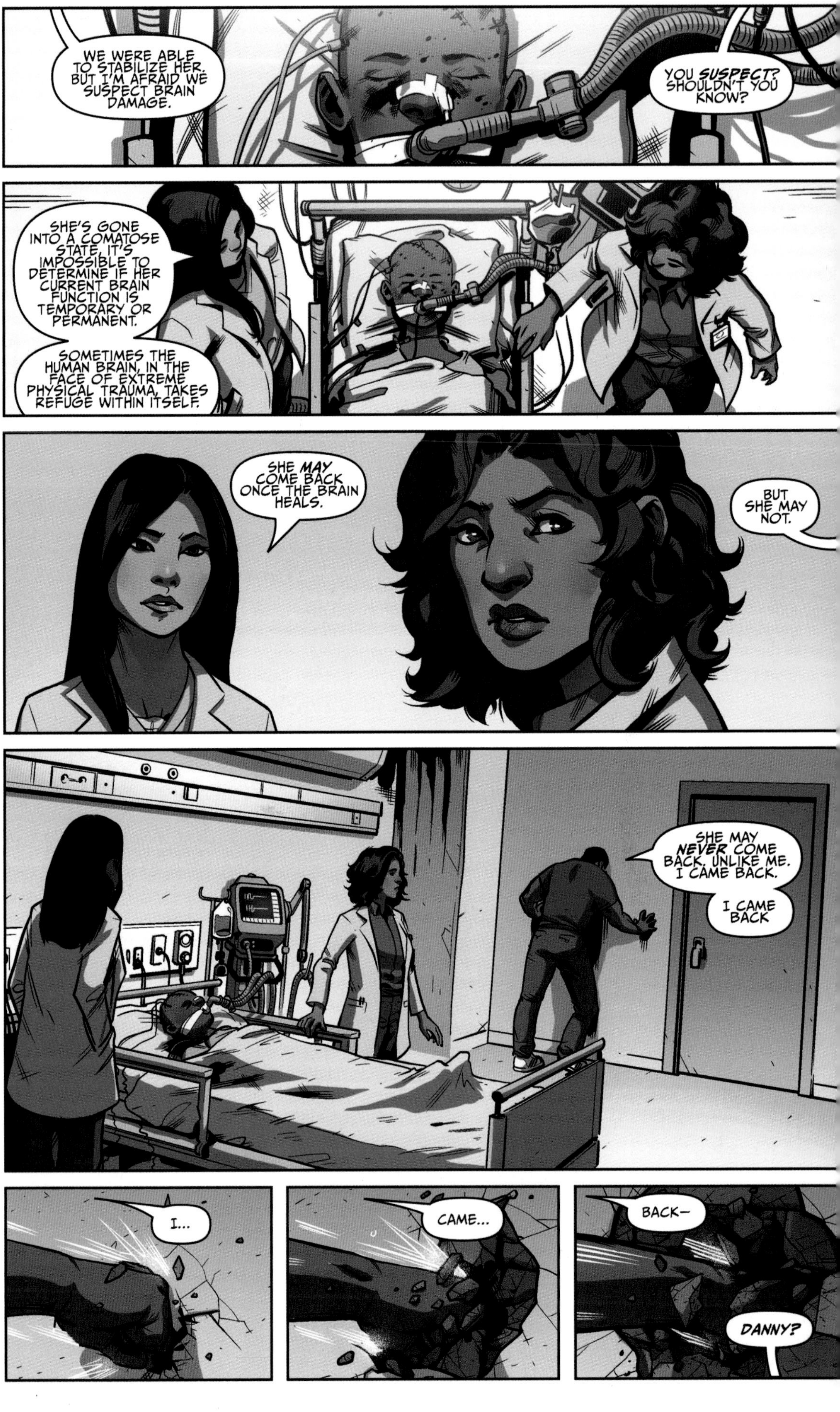
WE WERE ABLE TO STABILIZE HER. BUT I'M AFRAID WE SUSPECT BRAIN DAMAGE.
YOU SUSPECT? SHOULDN'T YOU KNOW?
SHE'S GONE INTO A COMATOSE STATE, IT'S IMPOSSIBLE TO DETERMINE IF HER CURRENT BRAIN FUNCTION IS TEMPORARY OR PERMANENT.
SOMETIMES THE HUMAN BRAIN, IN THE FACE OF EXTREME PHYSICAL TRAUMA, TAKES REFUGE WITHIN ITSELF.
SHE MAY COME BACK ONCE THE BRAIN HEALS.
BUT SHE MAY NOT.
SHE MAY NEVER COME BACK. UNLIKE ME. I CAME BACK.
I CAME BACK
I...
CAME...
BACK—
DANNY?

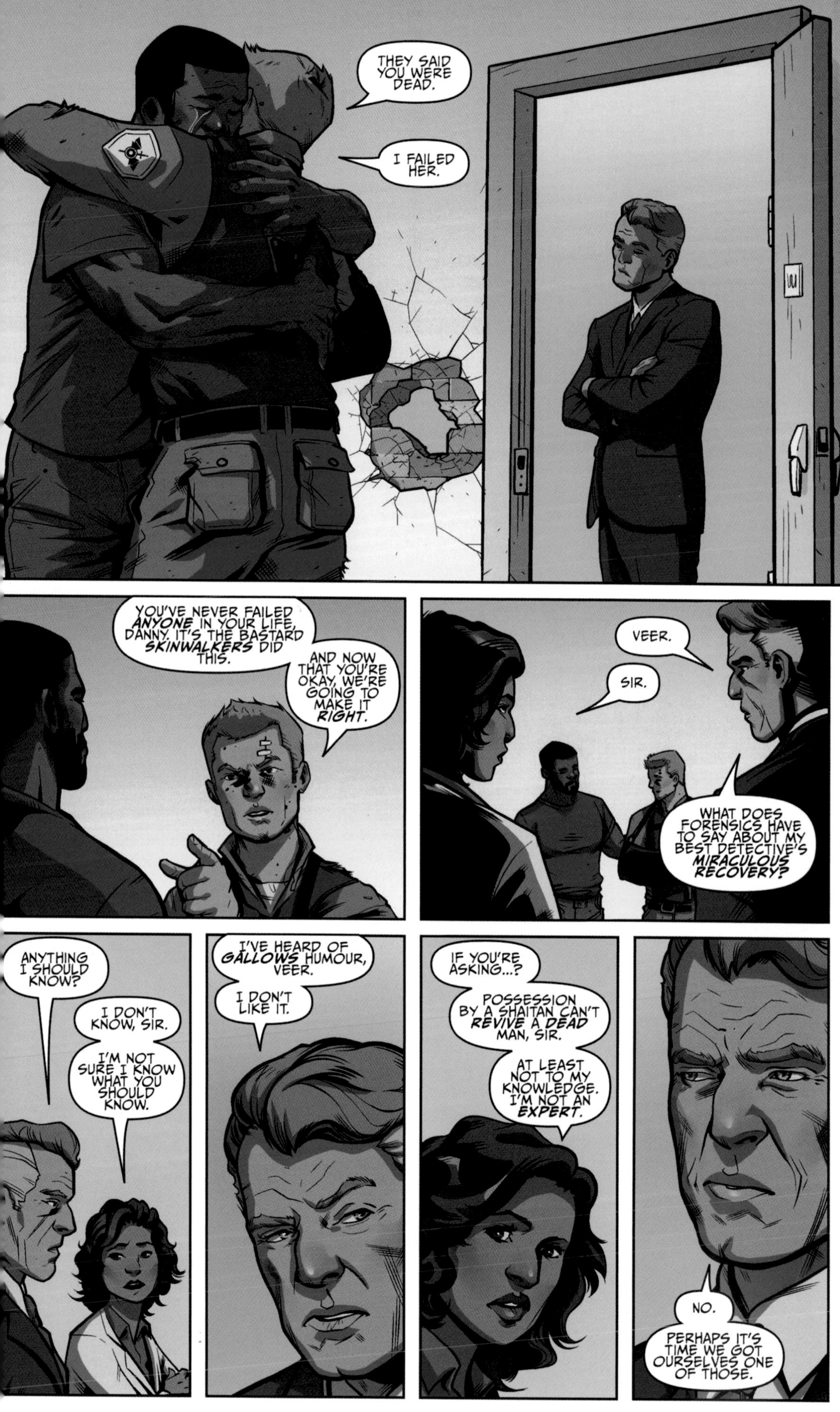
THEY SAID YOU WERE DEAD.
I FAILED HER.
YOU'VE NEVER FAILED ANYONE IN YOUR LIFE, DANNY. IT'S THE BASTARD SKINWALKERS DID THIS.
AND NOW THAT YOU'RE OKAY, WE'RE GOING TO MAKE IT RIGHT.
VEER.
SIR.
WHAT DOES FORENSICS HAVE TO SAY ABOUT MY BEST DETECTIVE'S MIRACULOUS RECOVERY?
ANYTHING I SHOULD KNOW?
I DON'T KNOW, SIR.
I'M NOT SURE I KNOW WHAT YOU SHOULD KNOW.
I'VE HEARD OF GALLOWS HUMOUR, VEER.
I DON'T LIKE IT.
IF YOU'RE ASKING...?
POSSESSION BY A SHAITAN CAN'T REVIVE A DEAD MAN, SIR.
AT LEAST NOT TO MY KNOWLEDGE. I'M NOT AN EXPERT.
NO.
PERHAPS IT'S TIME WE GOT OURSELVES ONE OF THOSE.

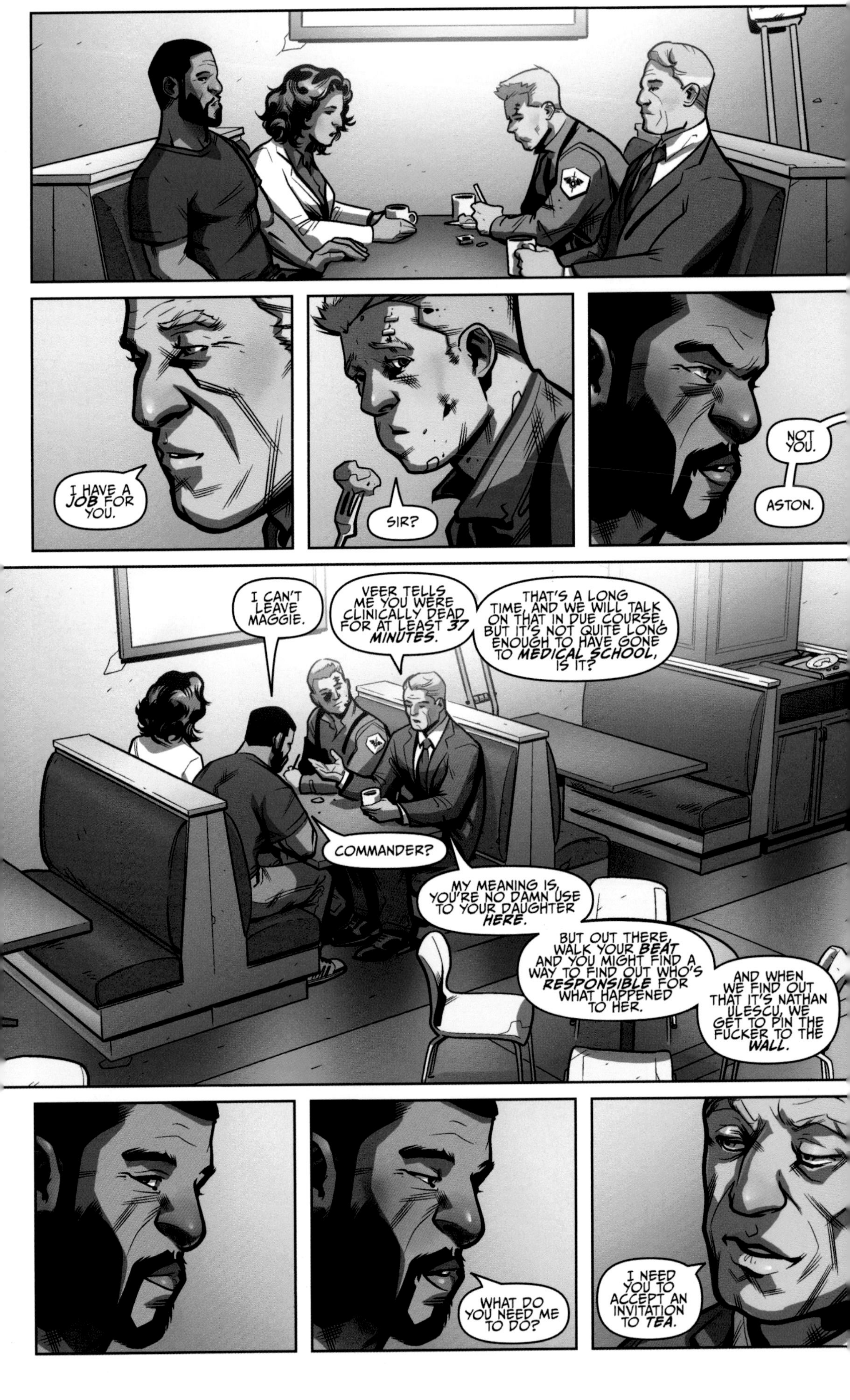

I HAVE A JOB FOR YOU.
SIR?
NOT YOU.
ASTON.
I CAN'T LEAVE MAGGIE.
VEER TELLS ME YOU WERE CLINICALLY DEAD FOR AT LEAST 37 MINUTES.
THAT'S A LONG TIME, AND WE WILL TALK ON THAT IN DUE COURSE, BUT IT'S NOT QUITE LONG ENOUGH TO HAVE GONE TO MEDICAL SCHOOL, IS IT?
COMMANDER?
MY MEANING IS, YOU'RE NO DAMN USE TO YOUR DAUGHTER HERE.
BUT OUT THERE, WALK YOUR BEAT AND YOU MIGHT FIND A WAY TO FIND OUT WHO'S RESPONSIBLE FOR WHAT HAPPENED TO HER.
AND WHEN WE FIND OUT THAT IT'S NATHAN ULESCU, WE GET TO PIN THE FUCKER TO THE WALL.
WHAT DO YOU NEED ME TO DO?
I NEED YOU TO ACCEPT AN INVITATION TO TEA.

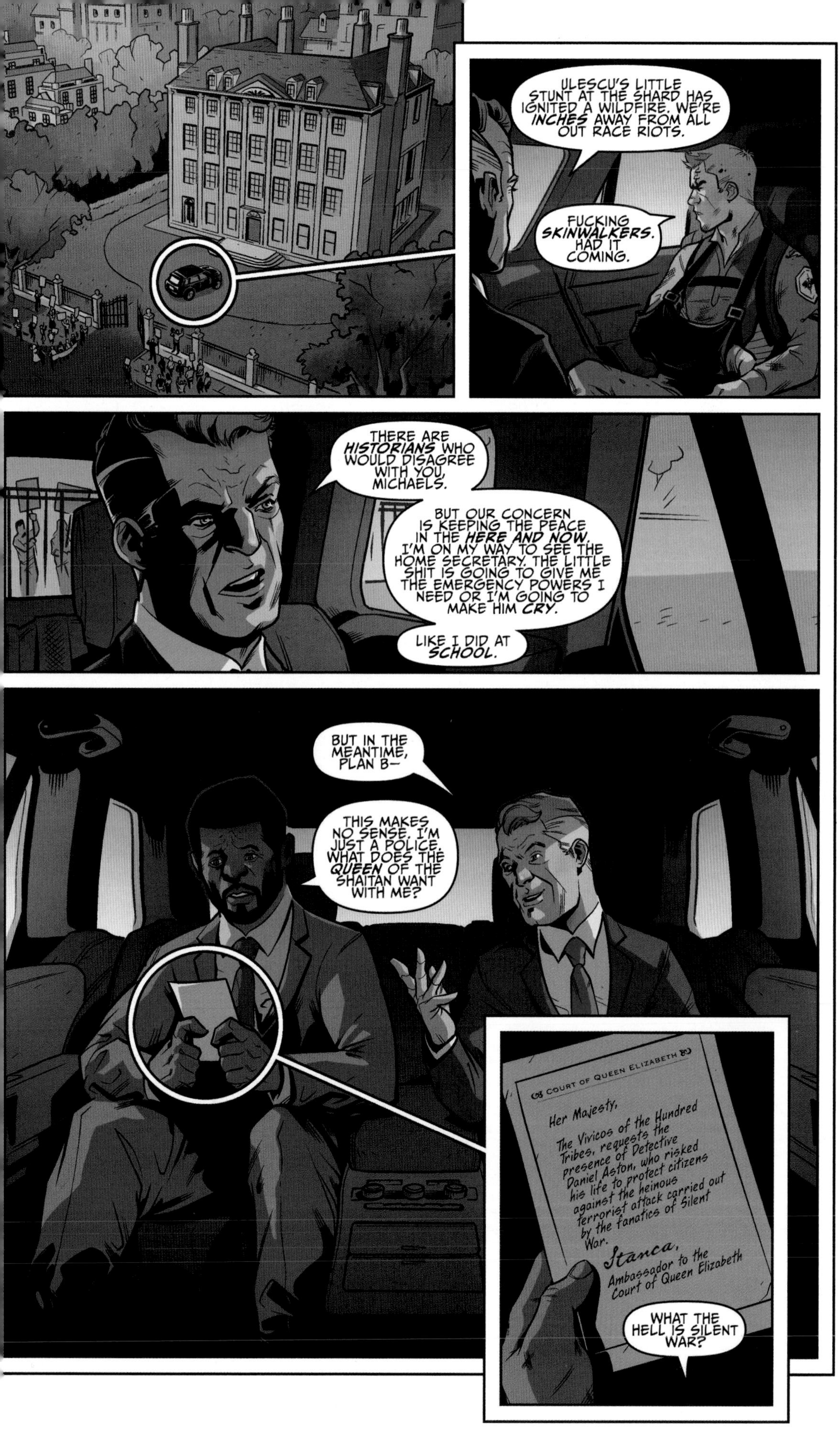
ULESCU'S LITTLE STUNT AT THE SHARD HAS IGNITED A WILDFIRE. WE'RE INCHES AWAY FROM ALL OUT RACE RIOTS.
FUCKING SKINWALKERS. HAD IT COMING.
THERE ARE HISTORIANS WHO WOULD DISAGREE WITH YOU, MICHAELS.
BUT OUR CONCERN IS KEEPING THE PEACE IN THE HERE AND NOW. I'M ON MY WAY TO SEE THE HOME SECRETARY. THE LITTLE SHIT IS GOING TO GIVE ME THE EMERGENCY POWERS I NEED OR I'M GOING TO MAKE HIM CRY.
LIKE I DID AT SCHOOL.
BUT IN THE MEANTIME, PLAN B—
THIS MAKES NO SENSE. I'M JUST A POLICE. WHAT DOES THE QUEEN OF THE SHAITAN WANT WITH ME?
COURT OF QUEEN ELIZABETH
Her Majesty,
The Vivicos of the Hundred Tribes, requests the presence of Detective Daniel Aston, who risked his life to protect citizens against the heinous terrorist attack carried out by the fanatics of Silent War.
Stanca,
Ambassador to the Court of Queen Elizabeth
WHAT THE HELL IS SILENT WAR?

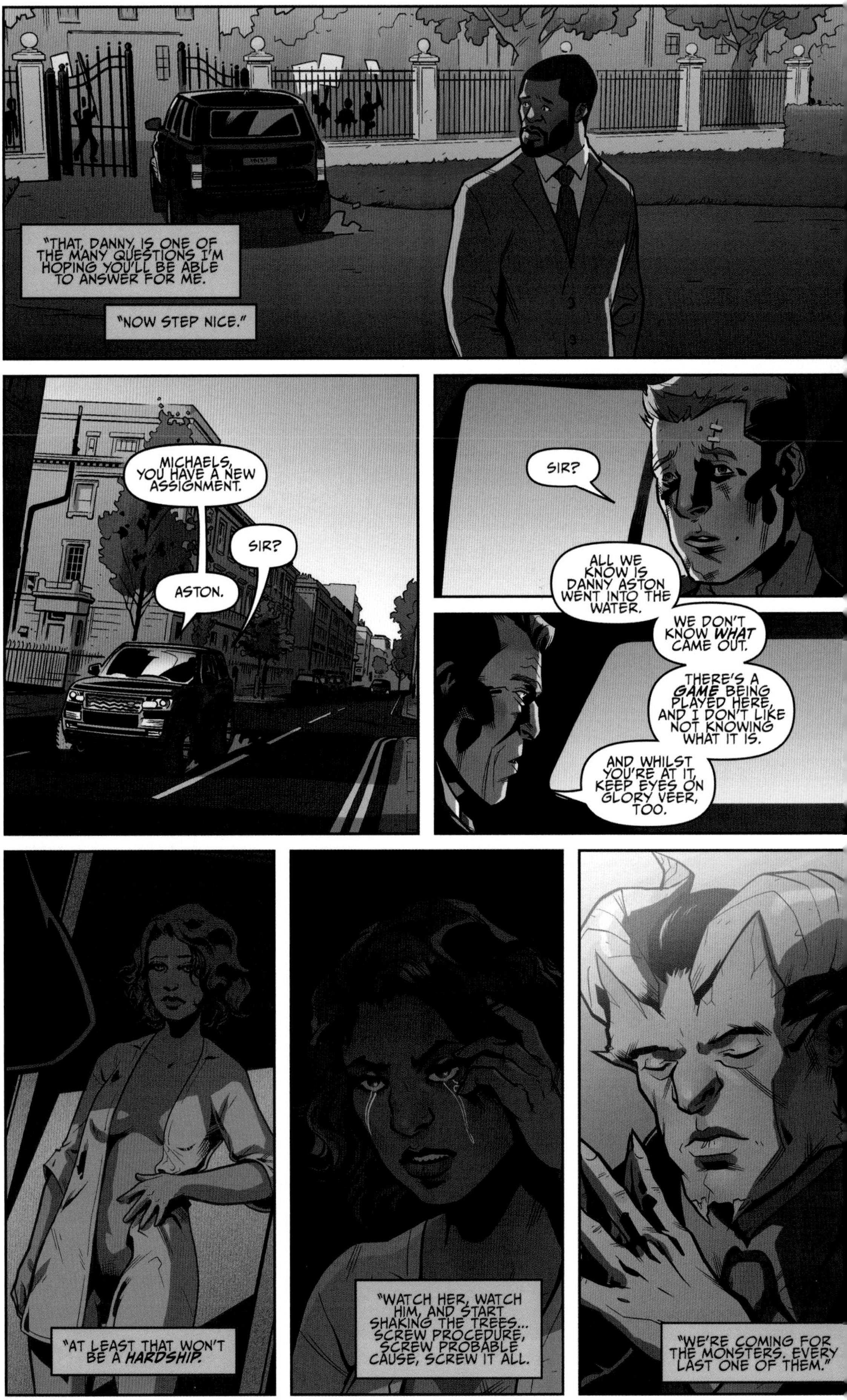
"THAT, DANNY, IS ONE OF THE MANY QUESTIONS I'M HOPING YOU'LL BE ABLE TO ANSWER FOR ME.
"NOW STEP NICE."
MICHAELS, YOU HAVE A NEW ASSIGNMENT.
SIR?
ASTON.
SIR?
ALL WE KNOW IS DANNY ASTON WENT INTO THE WATER.
WE DON'T KNOW *WHAT* CAME OUT.
THERE'S A *GAME* BEING PLAYED HERE, AND I DON'T LIKE NOT KNOWING WHAT IT IS.
AND WHILST YOU'RE AT IT, KEEP EYES ON GLORY VEER, TOO.
"AT LEAST THAT WON'T BE A *HARDSHIP*.
"WATCH HER, WATCH HIM, AND START SHAKING THE TREES... SCREW PROCEDURE, SCREW PROBABLE CAUSE, SCREW IT ALL.
"WE'RE COMING FOR THE MONSTERS. EVERY LAST ONE OF THEM."

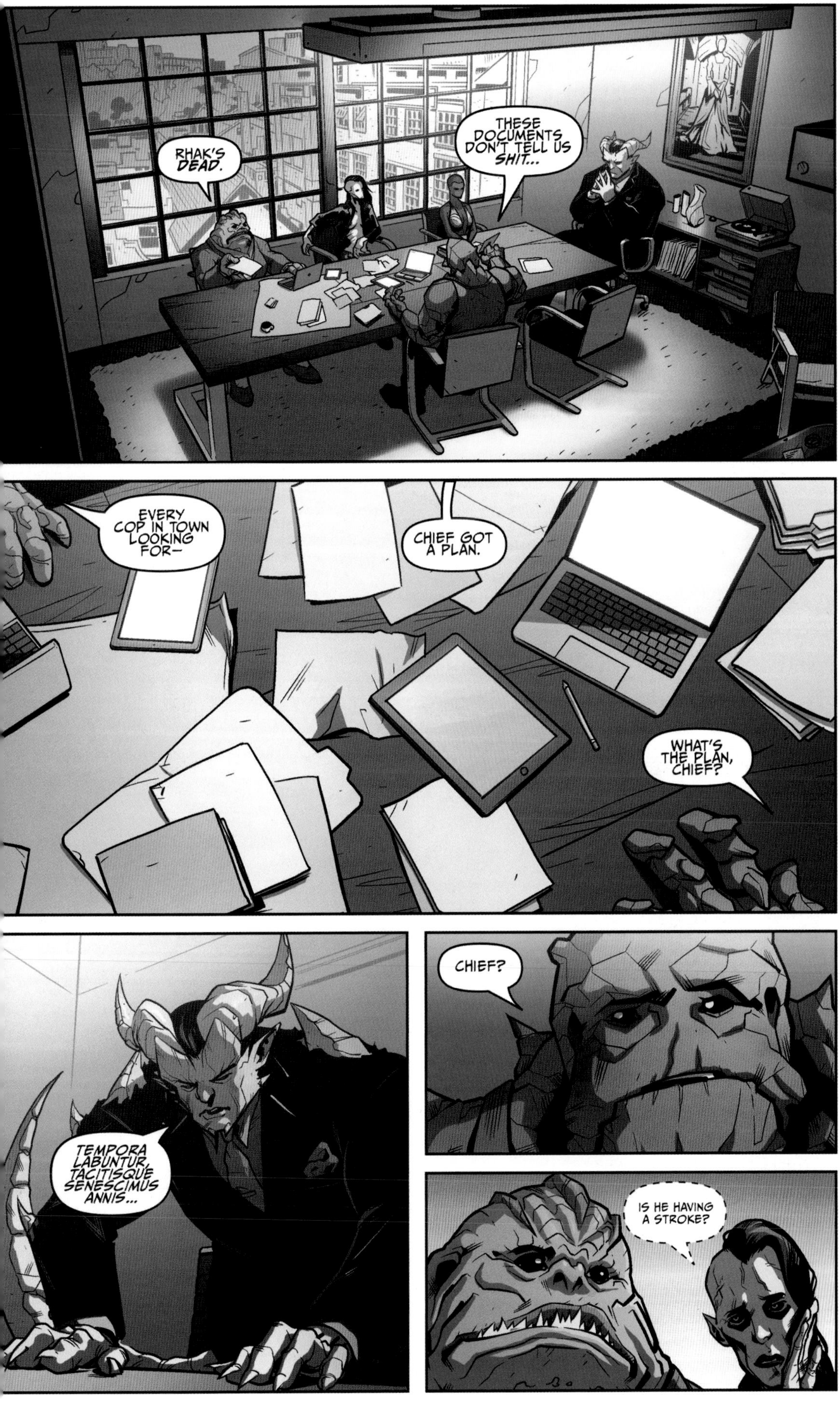
RHAK'S DEAD.
THESE DOCUMENTS DON'T TELL US SHIT...
EVERY COP IN TOWN LOOKING FOR—
CHIEF GOT A PLAN.
WHAT'S THE PLAN, CHIEF?
TEMPORA LABUNTUR, TACITISQUE SENESCIMUS ANNIS...
CHIEF?
IS HE HAVING A STROKE?

...ET FUGIUNT FRENO NON REMORANTE DIES.

"THE TIMES SLIP AWAY, AND WE GROW OLD WITH THE SILENT YEARS, AND THE DAYS FLEE UNCHECKED BY A REIN."

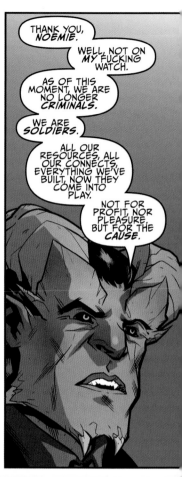

THANK YOU, *NOEMIE*.

WELL, NOT ON *MY FUCKING* WATCH.

AS OF THIS MOMENT, WE ARE NO LONGER *CRIMINALS*.

WE ARE *SOLDIERS*.

ALL OUR RESOURCES, ALL OUR CONNECTS, EVERYTHING WE'VE BUILT, NOW THEY COME INTO PLAY.

NOT FOR *PROFIT*, NOR *PLEASURE*, BUT FOR THE *CAUSE*.

EVERYTHING?

EVERYTHING, DRAGOS, AS OF THIS MOMENT, YOU NO LONGER *SELL* ARMS.

I DON'T?

NO. YOU *BUY* THEM. WE'RE STOCKPILING.

OPAL, WE DON'T SELL *POISON* TO SHAITAN ANY MORE. ONLY TO FULL HUMANS.

THAT'S GOING TO CUT INTO OUR MARGINS.

LET IT. WE NEED OUR PEOPLE CLEAN AND FOCUSED AND THE ENEMY BEFUDDLED AND WEAK.

WE HAVE *ONE* GOAL. *THE LAMP.* TO FIND IT, NOEMIE--YOUR GIRLS AND BOYS, EVERY LAST ONE OF THEM IS A SPY NOW. THEY'RE NOT SELLING *SEX*, THEY ARE COLLECTING *PILLOW TALK.*

CALL ME MATA HARI.

WHAT ABOUT ME, CHIEF?

FORGET *SMUGGLING*, CRACKEN. WE'RE MOVING INTO THE MASS TRANSPORTATION BUSINESS.

WE'RE GOING TO BLOW THE DOORS OFF AND LET OUR PEOPLE *IN.*

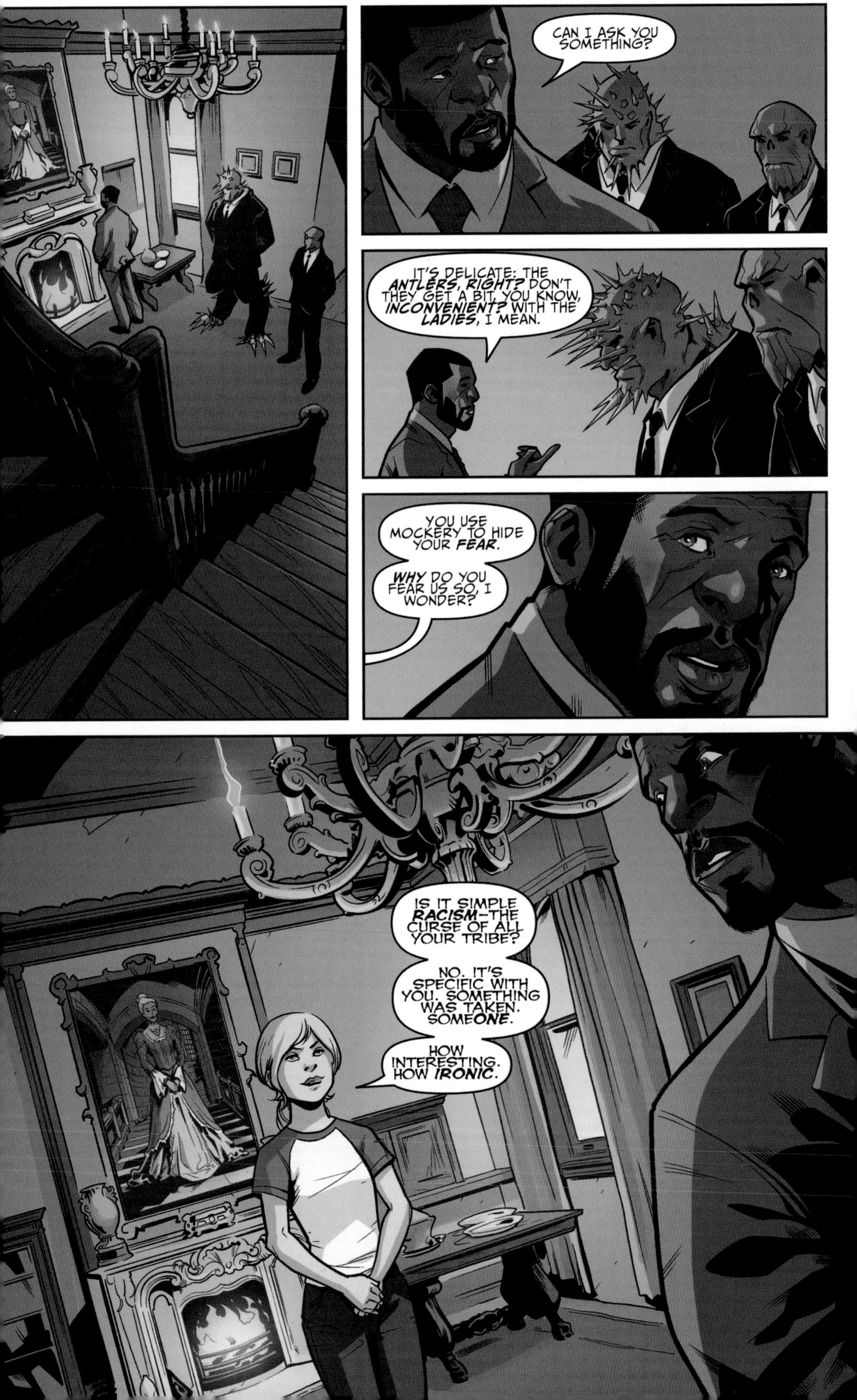
CAN I ASK YOU SOMETHING?
IT'S DELICATE: THE ANTLERS, RIGHT? DON'T THEY GET A BIT, YOU KNOW, INCONVENIENT? WITH THE LADIES, I MEAN.
YOU USE MOCKERY TO HIDE YOUR FEAR.
WHY DO YOU FEAR US SO, I WONDER?
IS IT SIMPLE RACISM—THE CURSE OF ALL YOUR TRIBE?
NO. IT'S SPECIFIC WITH YOU. SOMETHING WAS TAKEN. SOMEONE.
HOW INTERESTING. HOW IRONIC.

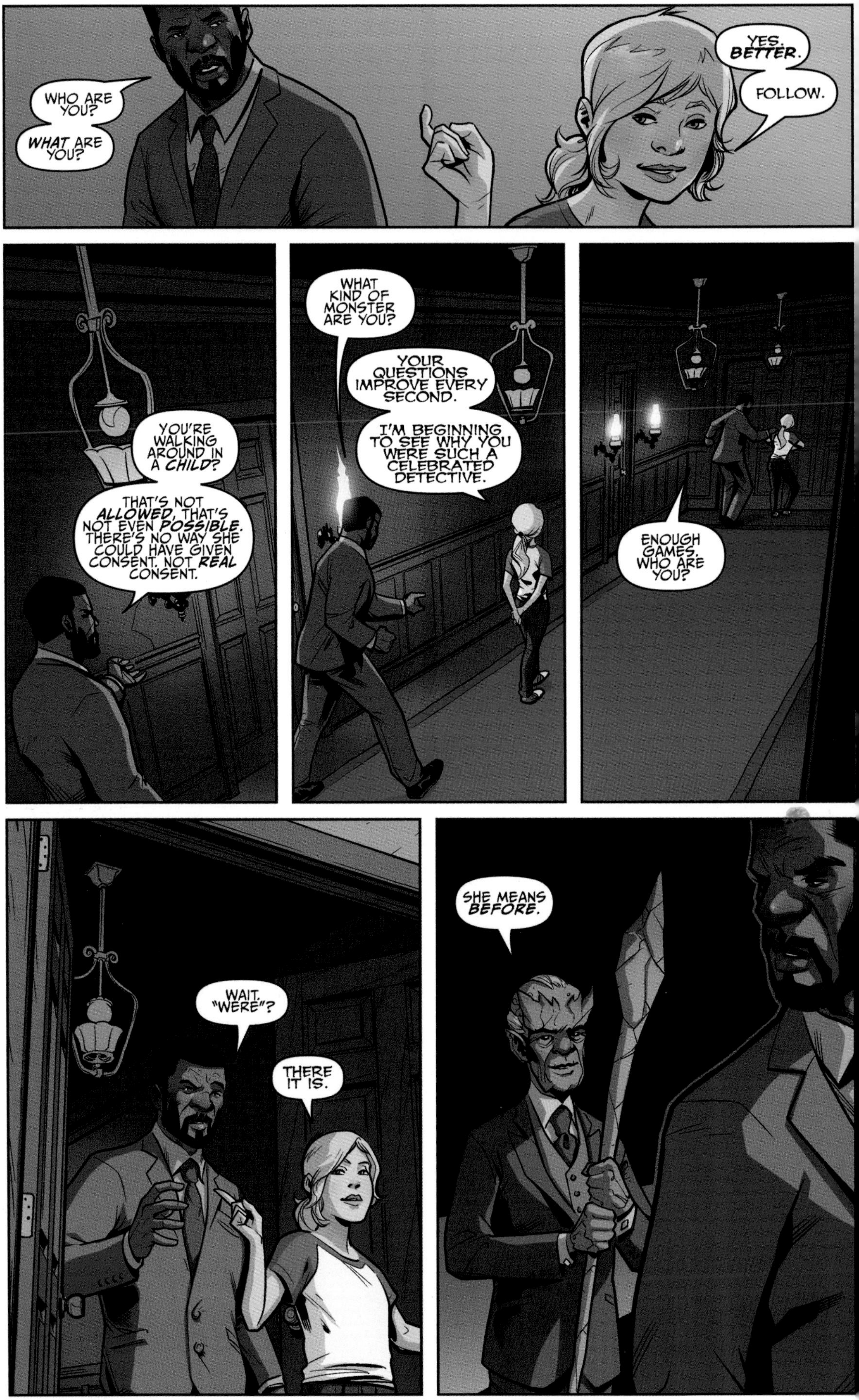
WHO ARE YOU?
WHAT ARE YOU?
YES. BETTER.
FOLLOW.
YOU'RE WALKING AROUND IN A CHILD?
THAT'S NOT ALLOWED, THAT'S NOT EVEN POSSIBLE. THERE'S NO WAY SHE COULD HAVE GIVEN CONSENT. NOT REAL CONSENT.
WHAT KIND OF MONSTER ARE YOU?
YOUR QUESTIONS IMPROVE EVERY SECOND.
I'M BEGINNING TO SEE WHY YOU WERE SUCH A CELEBRATED DETECTIVE.
ENOUGH GAMES. WHO ARE YOU?
WAIT. "WERE"?
THERE IT IS.
SHE MEANS BEFORE.

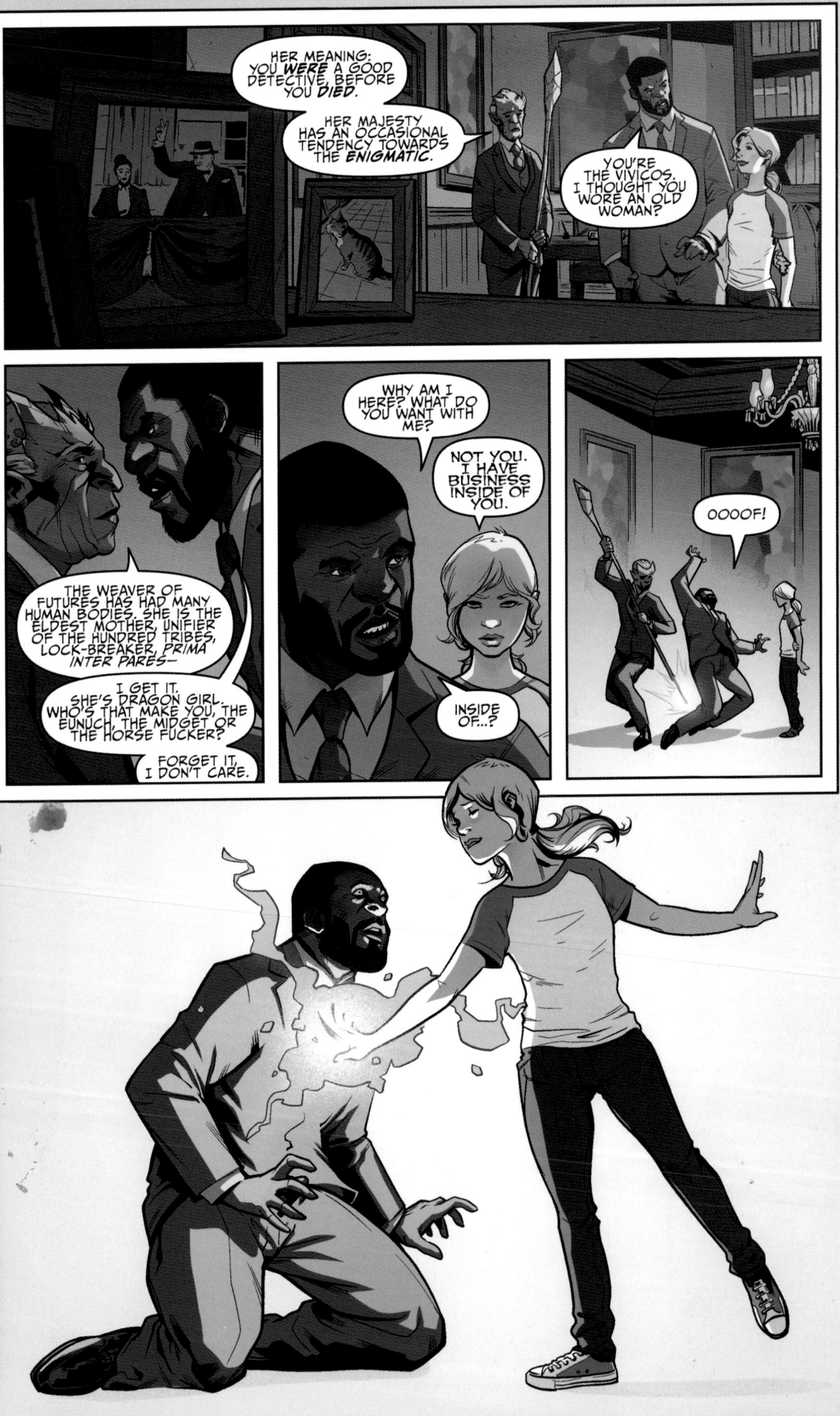
HER MEANING: YOU WERE A GOOD DETECTIVE, BEFORE YOU DIED.
HER MAJESTY HAS AN OCCASIONAL TENDENCY TOWARDS THE ENIGMATIC.
YOU'RE THE VIVICOS. I THOUGHT YOU WORE AN OLD WOMAN?
THE WEAVER OF FUTURES HAS HAD MANY HUMAN BODIES. SHE IS THE ELDEST MOTHER, UNIFIER OF THE HUNDRED TRIBES, LOCK-BREAKER, PRIMA INTER PARES—
I GET IT. SHE'S DRAGON GIRL. WHO'S THAT MAKE YOU, THE EUNUCH, THE MIDGET OR THE HORSE FUCKER?
FORGET IT, I DON'T CARE.
WHY AM I HERE? WHAT DO YOU WANT WITH ME?
NOT YOU. I HAVE BUSINESS INSIDE OF YOU.
INSIDE OF...?
OOOOF!

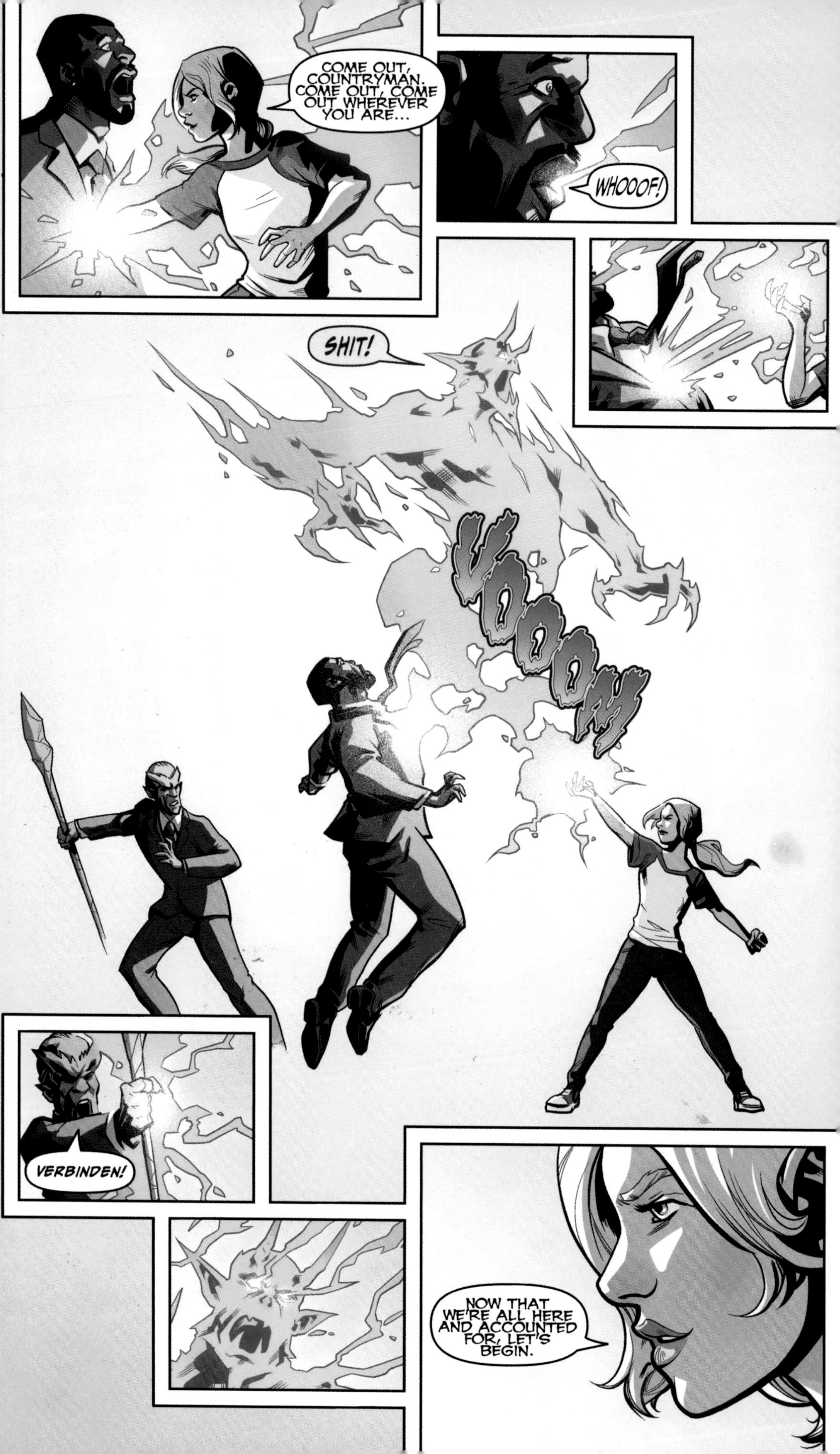
COME OUT, COUNTRYMAN. COME OUT, COME OUT WHEREVER YOU ARE...
WHOOOF!
SHIT!
VOOOOM
VERBINDEN!
NOW THAT WE'RE ALL HERE AND ACCOUNTED FOR, LET'S BEGIN.

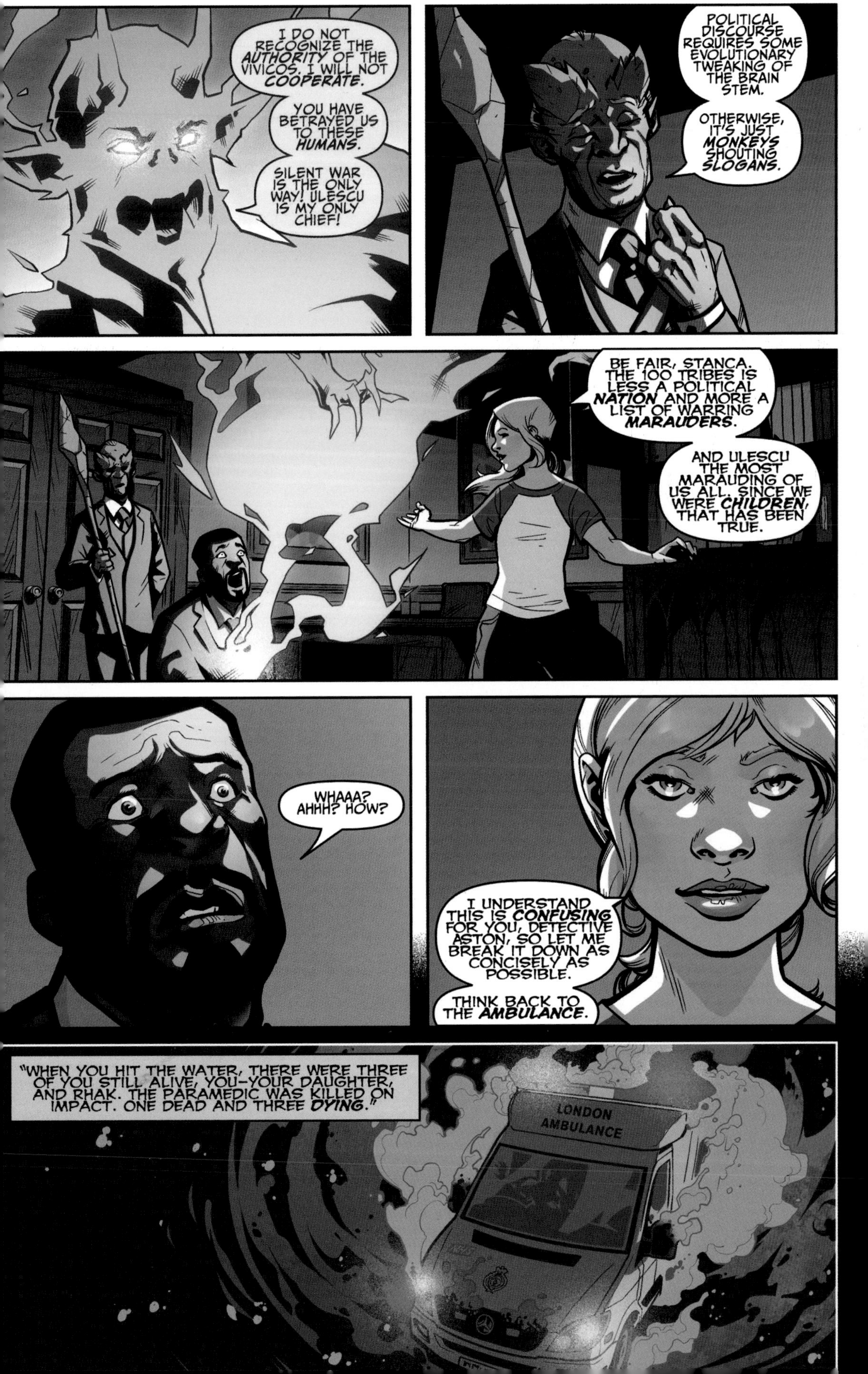
I DO NOT RECOGNIZE THE AUTHORITY OF THE VIVICOS. I WILL NOT COOPERATE.
YOU HAVE BETRAYED US TO THESE HUMANS.
SILENT WAR IS THE ONLY WAY! ULESCU IS MY ONLY CHIEF!
POLITICAL DISCOURSE REQUIRES SOME EVOLUTIONARY TWEAKING OF THE BRAIN STEM.
OTHERWISE, IT'S JUST MONKEYS SHOUTING SLOGANS.
BE FAIR, STANCA. THE 100 TRIBES IS LESS A POLITICAL NATION AND MORE A LIST OF WARRING MARAUDERS.
AND ULESCU THE MOST MARAUDING OF US ALL. SINCE WE WERE CHILDREN, THAT HAS BEEN TRUE.
WHAAA? AHHH? HOW?
I UNDERSTAND THIS IS CONFUSING FOR YOU, DETECTIVE ASTON, SO LET ME BREAK IT DOWN AS CONCISELY AS POSSIBLE.
THINK BACK TO THE AMBULANCE.
"WHEN YOU HIT THE WATER, THERE WERE THREE OF YOU STILL ALIVE, YOU--YOUR DAUGHTER, AND RHAK. THE PARAMEDIC WAS KILLED ON IMPACT. ONE DEAD AND THREE DYING."
LONDON AMBULANCE

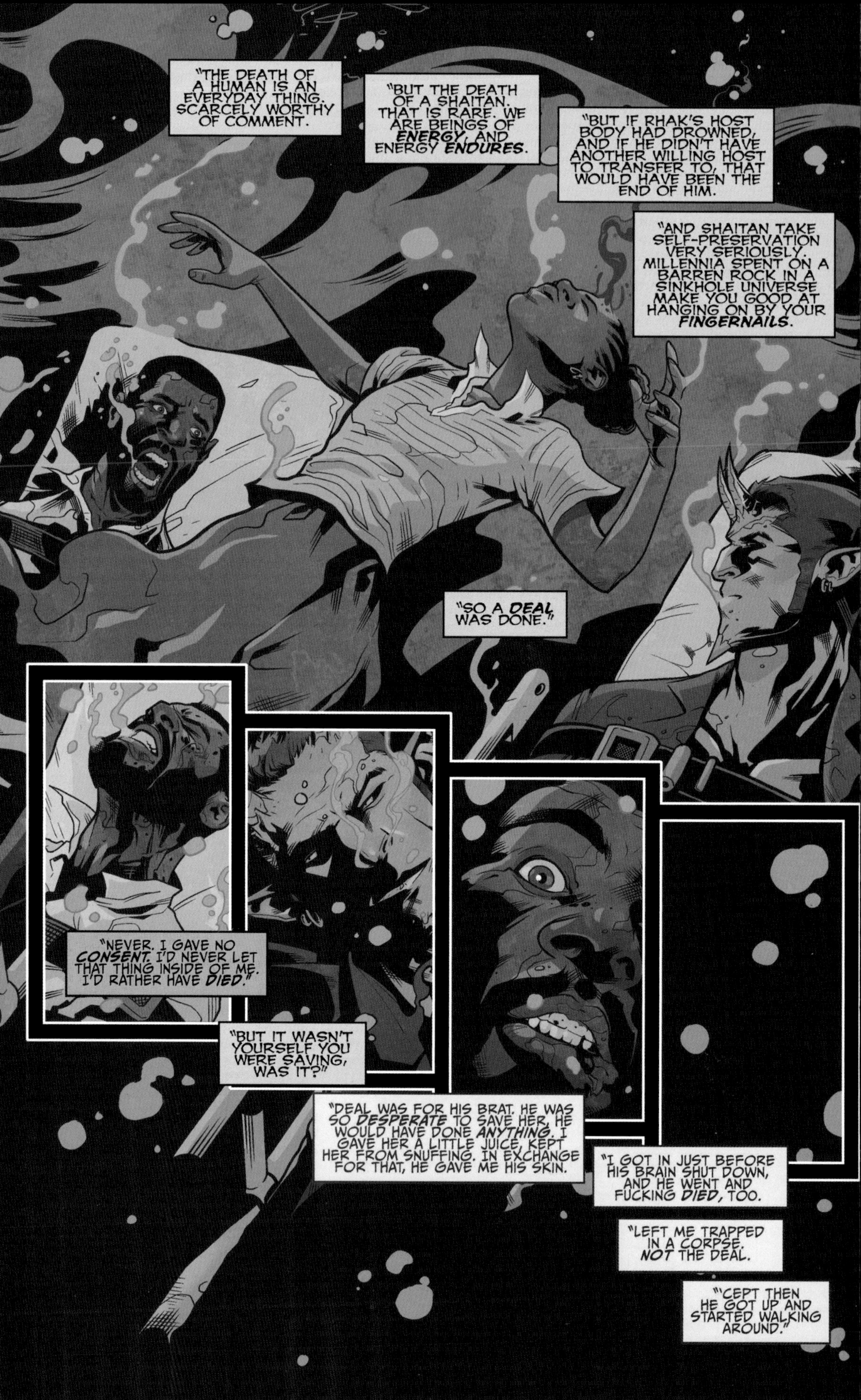
"THE DEATH OF A HUMAN IS AN EVERYDAY THING. SCARCELY WORTHY OF COMMENT.
"BUT THE DEATH OF A SHAITAN. THAT IS RARE. WE ARE BEINGS OF ENERGY, AND ENERGY ENDURES.
"BUT IF RHAK'S HOST BODY HAD DROWNED, AND IF HE DIDN'T HAVE ANOTHER WILLING HOST TO TRANSFER TO, THAT WOULD HAVE BEEN THE END OF HIM.
"AND SHAITAN TAKE SELF-PRESERVATION VERY SERIOUSLY. MILLENNIA SPENT ON A BARREN ROCK IN A SINKHOLE UNIVERSE MAKE YOU GOOD AT HANGING ON BY YOUR FINGERNAILS.
"SO A DEAL WAS DONE."
"NEVER. I GAVE NO CONSENT. I'D NEVER LET THAT THING INSIDE OF ME. I'D RATHER HAVE DIED."
"BUT IT WASN'T YOURSELF YOU WERE SAVING, WAS IT?"
"DEAL WAS FOR HIS BRAT. HE WAS SO DESPERATE TO SAVE HER, HE WOULD HAVE DONE ANYTHING. I GAVE HER A LITTLE JUICE, KEPT HER FROM SNUFFING. IN EXCHANGE FOR THAT, HE GAVE ME HIS SKIN.
"I GOT IN JUST BEFORE HIS BRAIN SHUT DOWN, AND HE WENT AND FUCKING DIED, TOO.
"LEFT ME TRAPPED IN A CORPSE. NOT THE DEAL.
"'CEPT THEN HE GOT UP AND STARTED WALKING AROUND."

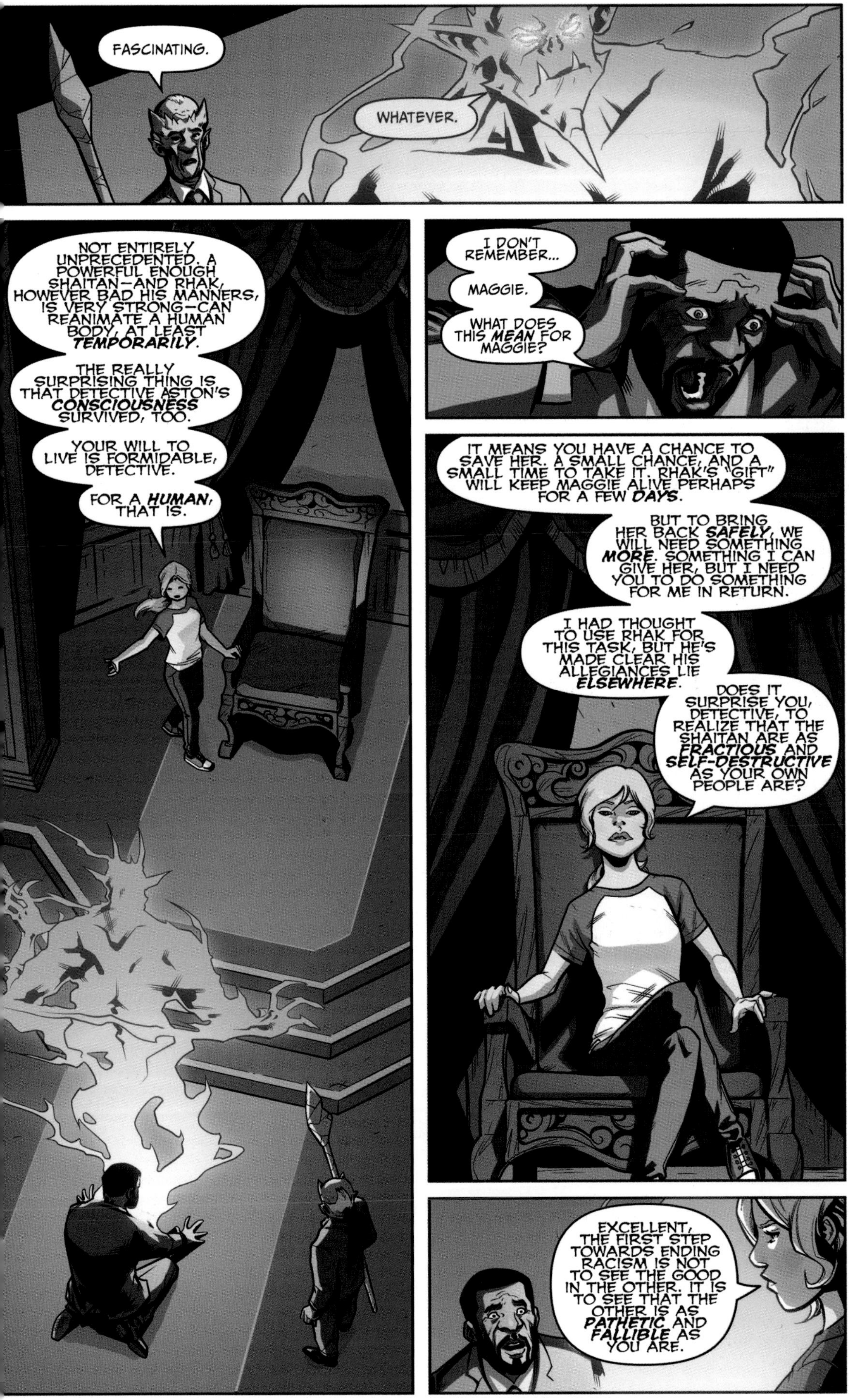

FASCINATING.
WHATEVER.
NOT ENTIRELY UNPRECEDENTED. A POWERFUL ENOUGH SHAITAN—AND RHAK, HOWEVER BAD HIS MANNERS, IS VERY STRONG—CAN REANIMATE A HUMAN BODY, AT LEAST TEMPORARILY.
THE REALLY SURPRISING THING IS THAT DETECTIVE ASTON'S CONSCIOUSNESS SURVIVED, TOO.
YOUR WILL TO LIVE IS FORMIDABLE, DETECTIVE.
FOR A HUMAN, THAT IS.
I DON'T REMEMBER...
MAGGIE.
WHAT DOES THIS MEAN FOR MAGGIE?
IT MEANS YOU HAVE A CHANCE TO SAVE HER. A SMALL CHANCE, AND A SMALL TIME TO TAKE IT. RHAK'S "GIFT" WILL KEEP MAGGIE ALIVE PERHAPS FOR A FEW DAYS.
BUT TO BRING HER BACK SAFELY, WE WILL NEED SOMETHING MORE. SOMETHING I CAN GIVE HER, BUT I NEED YOU TO DO SOMETHING FOR ME IN RETURN.
I HAD THOUGHT TO USE RHAK FOR THIS TASK, BUT HE'S MADE CLEAR HIS ALLEGIANCES LIE ELSEWHERE.
DOES IT SURPRISE YOU, DETECTIVE, TO REALIZE THAT THE SHAITAN ARE AS FRACTIOUS AND SELF-DESTRUCTIVE AS YOUR OWN PEOPLE ARE?
EXCELLENT, THE FIRST STEP TOWARDS ENDING RACISM IS NOT TO SEE THE GOOD IN THE OTHER. IT IS TO SEE THAT THE OTHER IS AS PATHETIC AND FALLIBLE AS YOU ARE.

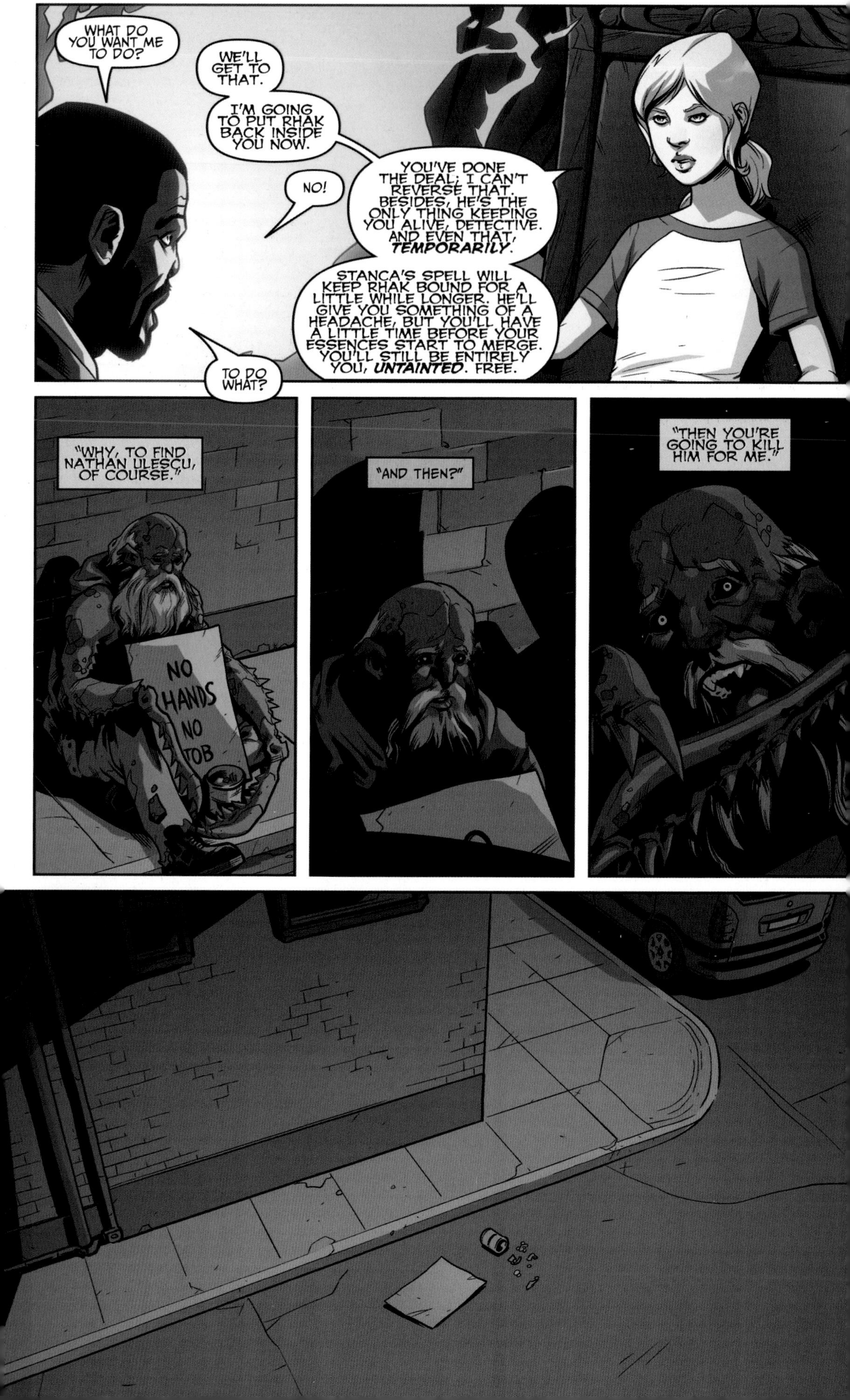
WHAT DO YOU WANT ME TO DO?
WE'LL GET TO THAT.
I'M GOING TO PUT RHAK BACK INSIDE YOU NOW.
NO!
YOU'VE DONE THE DEAL; I CAN'T REVERSE THAT. BESIDES, HE'S THE ONLY THING KEEPING YOU ALIVE, DETECTIVE. AND EVEN THAT, TEMPORARILY.
STANCA'S SPELL WILL KEEP RHAK BOUND FOR A LITTLE WHILE LONGER. HE'LL GIVE YOU SOMETHING OF A HEADACHE, BUT YOU'LL HAVE A LITTLE TIME BEFORE YOUR ESSENCES START TO MERGE. YOU'LL STILL BE ENTIRELY YOU, UNTAINTED. FREE.
TO DO WHAT?
"WHY, TO FIND NATHAN ULESCU, OF COURSE."
NO HANDS NO JOB
"AND THEN?"
"THEN YOU'RE GOING TO KILL HIM FOR ME."

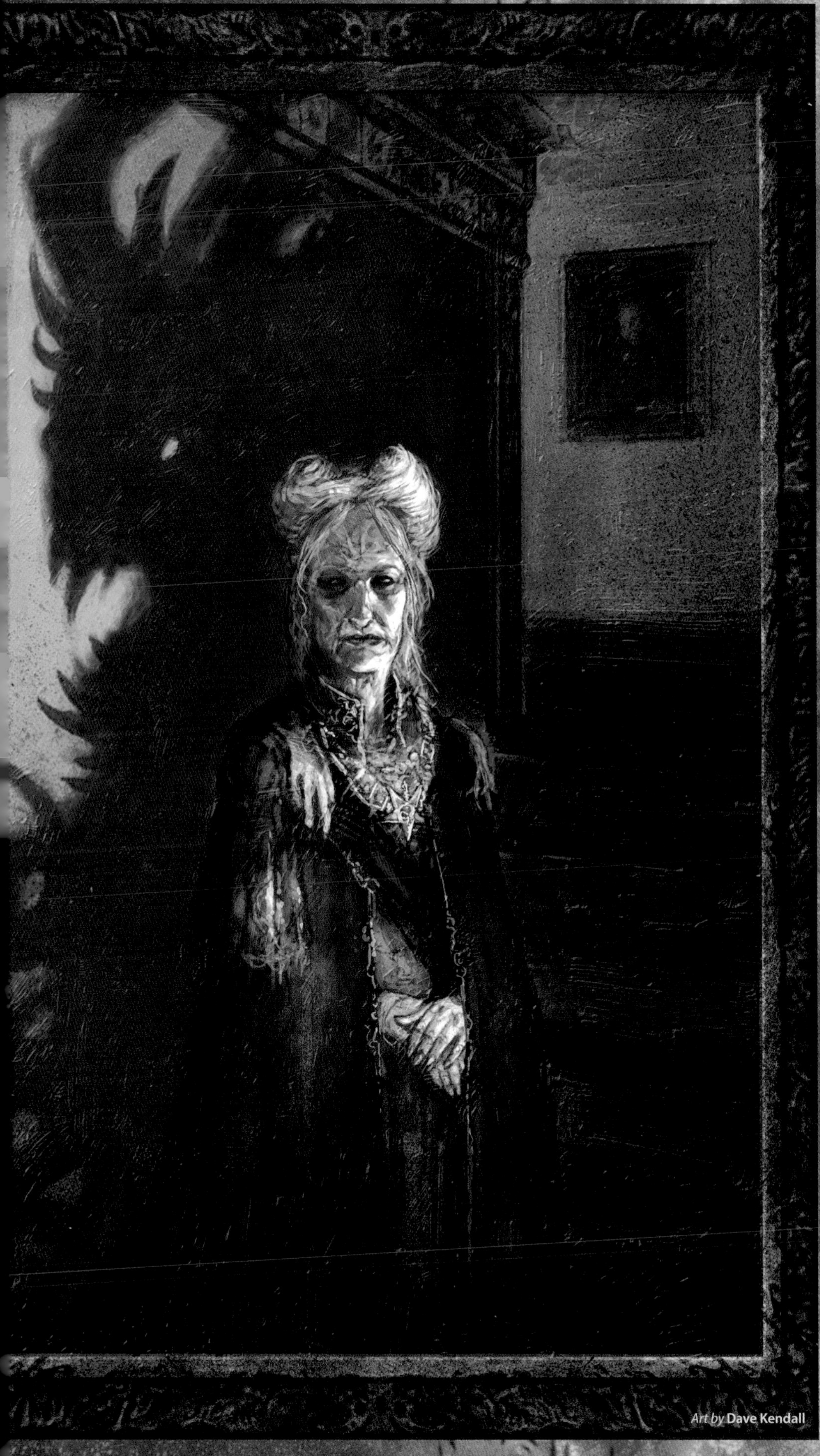
Art by Dave Kendall

Chapter 3
Winston and Vivian

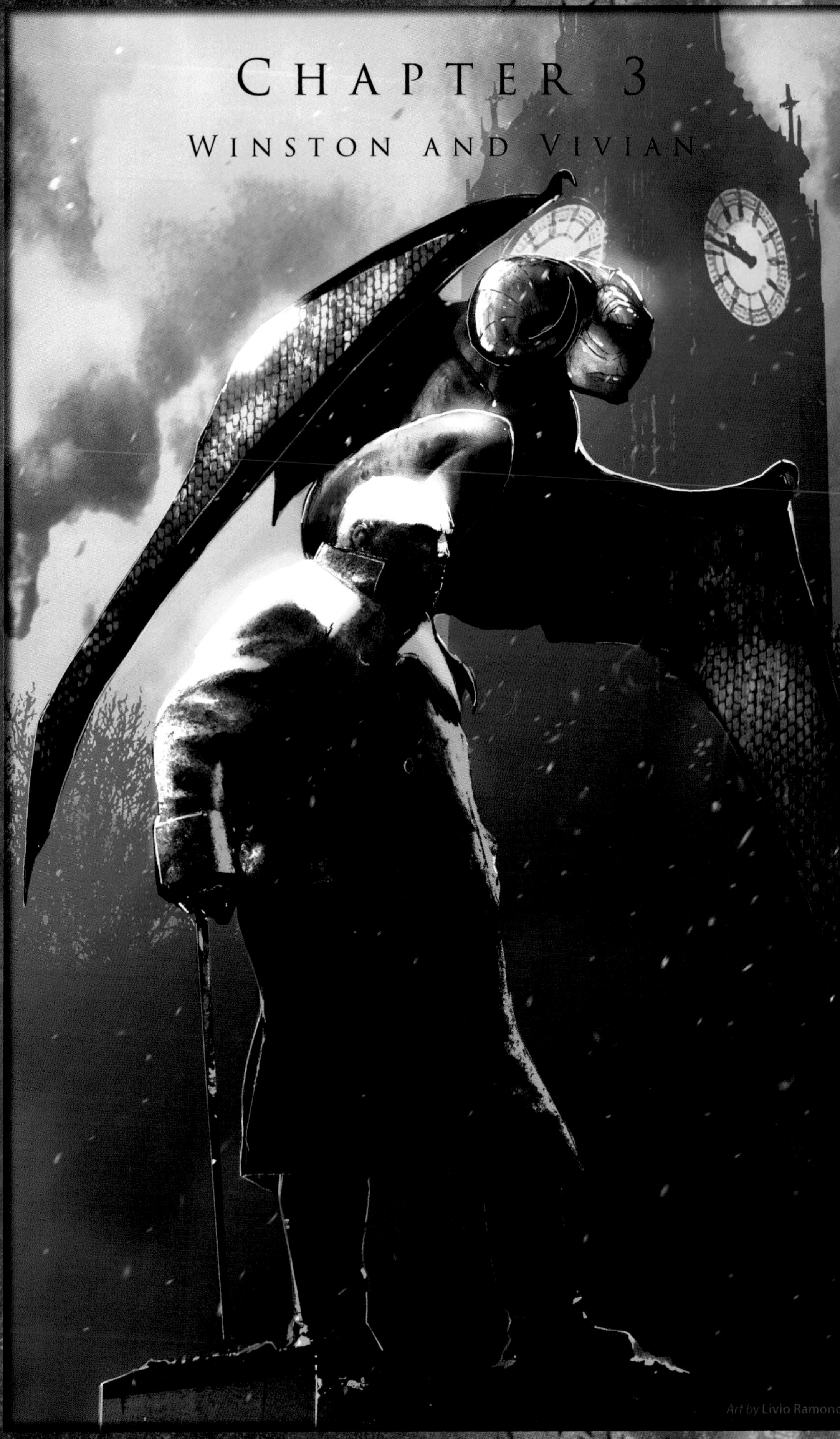

Art by Livio Ramondelli

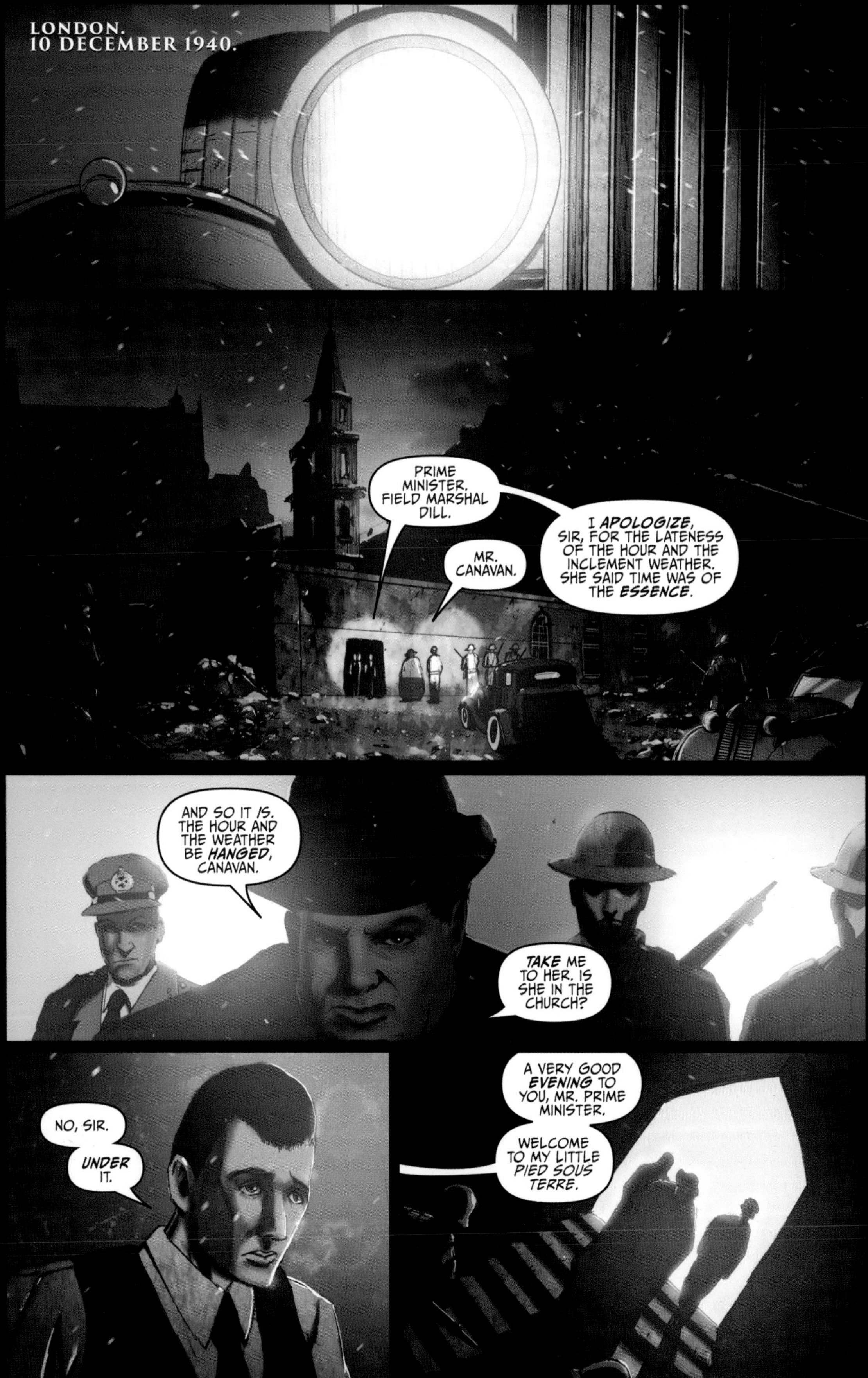
LONDON.
10 DECEMBER 1940.
PRIME MINISTER. FIELD MARSHAL DILL.
MR. CANAVAN.
I APOLOGIZE, SIR, FOR THE LATENESS OF THE HOUR AND THE INCLEMENT WEATHER. SHE SAID TIME WAS OF THE ESSENCE.
AND SO IT IS. THE HOUR AND THE WEATHER BE HANGED, CANAVAN.
TAKE ME TO HER. IS SHE IN THE CHURCH?
NO, SIR.
UNDER IT.
A VERY GOOD EVENING TO YOU, MR. PRIME MINISTER.
WELCOME TO MY LITTLE PIED SOUS TERRE.

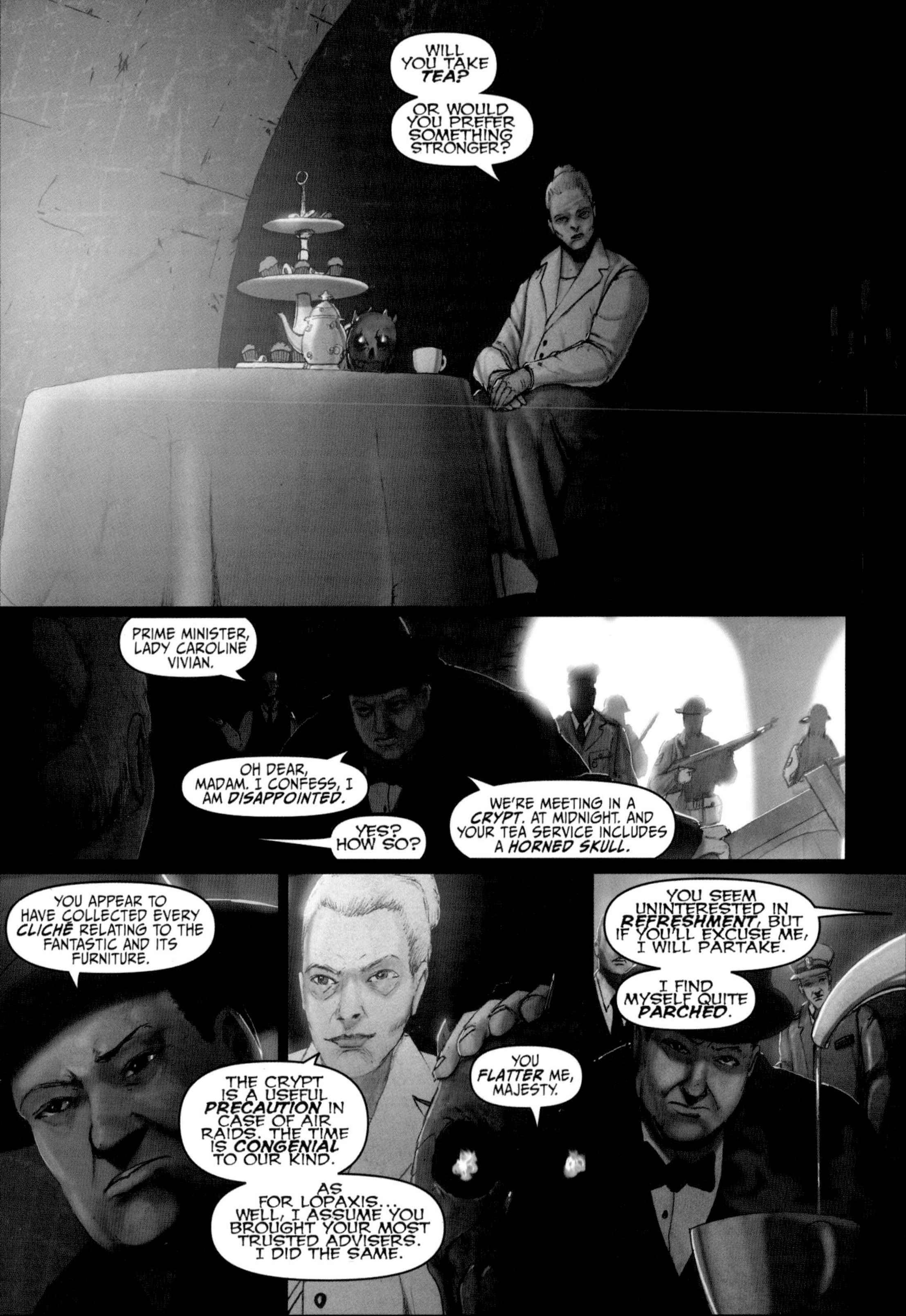
WILL YOU TAKE TEA?
OR WOULD YOU PREFER SOMETHING STRONGER?
PRIME MINISTER, LADY CAROLINE VIVIAN.
OH DEAR, MADAM. I CONFESS, I AM DISAPPOINTED.
YES? HOW SO?
WE'RE MEETING IN A CRYPT. AT MIDNIGHT. AND YOUR TEA SERVICE INCLUDES A HORNED SKULL.
YOU APPEAR TO HAVE COLLECTED EVERY CLICHÉ RELATING TO THE FANTASTIC AND ITS FURNITURE.
THE CRYPT IS A USEFUL PRECAUTION IN CASE OF AIR RAIDS. THE TIME IS CONGENIAL TO OUR KIND.
AS FOR LOPAXIS... WELL, I ASSUME YOU BROUGHT YOUR MOST TRUSTED ADVISERS. I DID THE SAME.
YOU FLATTER ME, MAJESTY.
YOU SEEM UNINTERESTED IN REFRESHMENT, BUT IF YOU'LL EXCUSE ME, I WILL PARTAKE.
I FIND MYSELF QUITE PARCHED.

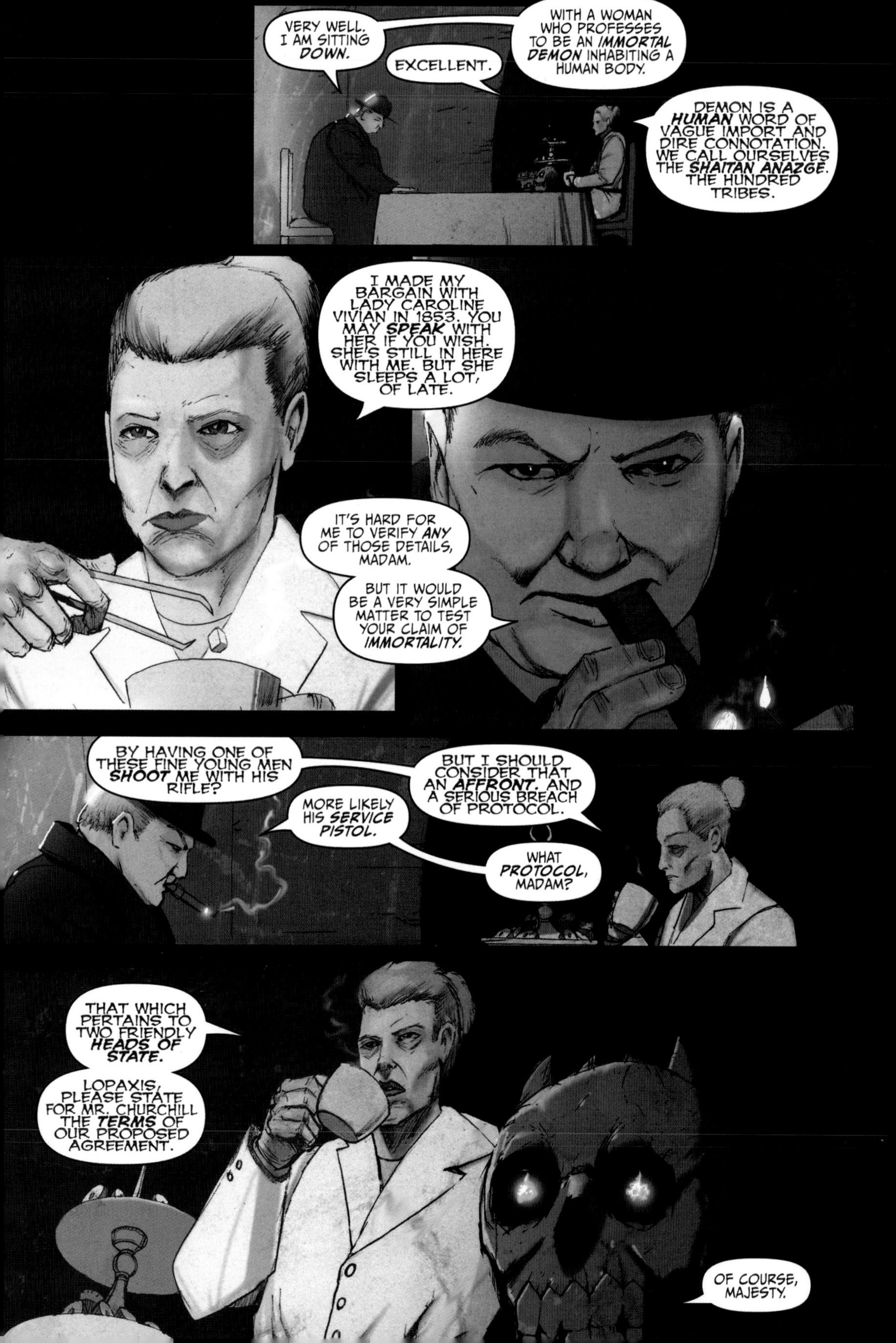
VERY WELL. I AM SITTING *DOWN.*
EXCELLENT.
WITH A WOMAN WHO PROFESSES TO BE AN *IMMORTAL DEMON* INHABITING A HUMAN BODY.
DEMON IS A ***HUMAN*** WORD OF VAGUE IMPORT AND DIRE CONNOTATION. WE CALL OURSELVES THE ***SHAITAN ANAZGE***. THE HUNDRED TRIBES.
I MADE MY BARGAIN WITH LADY CAROLINE VIVIAN IN 1853. YOU MAY ***SPEAK*** WITH HER IF YOU WISH. SHE'S STILL IN HERE WITH ME. BUT SHE SLEEPS A LOT, OF LATE.
IT'S HARD FOR ME TO VERIFY *ANY* OF THOSE DETAILS, MADAM.
BUT IT WOULD BE A VERY SIMPLE MATTER TO TEST YOUR CLAIM OF *IMMORTALITY.*
BY HAVING ONE OF THESE FINE YOUNG MEN ***SHOOT*** ME WITH HIS RIFLE?
MORE LIKELY HIS ***SERVICE PISTOL.***
BUT I SHOULD CONSIDER THAT AN ***AFFRONT.*** AND A SERIOUS BREACH OF PROTOCOL.
WHAT *PROTOCOL,* MADAM?
THAT WHICH PERTAINS TO TWO FRIENDLY ***HEADS OF STATE.***
LOPAXIS, PLEASE STATE FOR MR. CHURCHILL THE ***TERMS*** OF OUR PROPOSED AGREEMENT.
OF COURSE, MAJESTY.

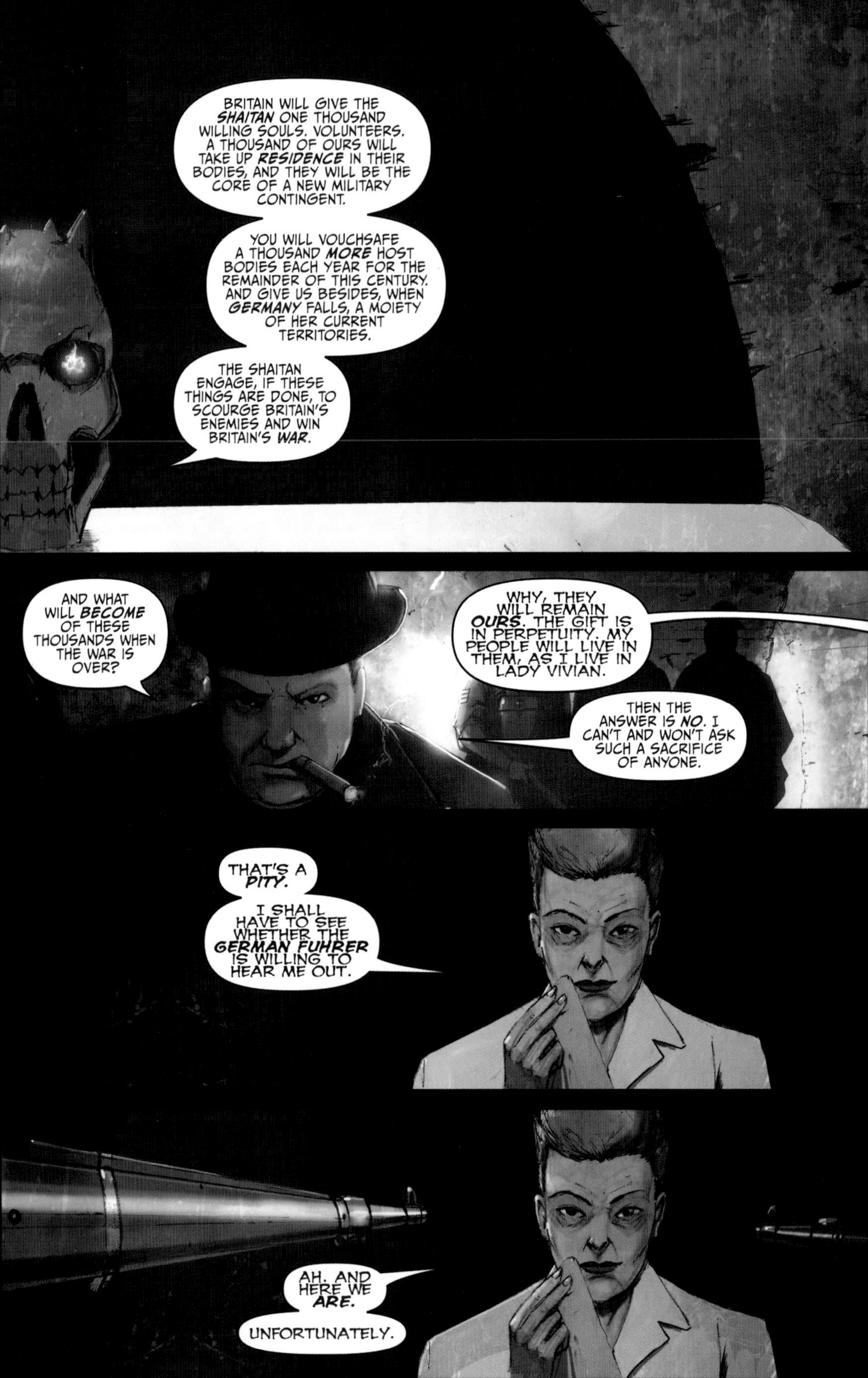
BRITAIN WILL GIVE THE SHAITAN ONE THOUSAND WILLING SOULS. VOLUNTEERS. A THOUSAND OF OURS WILL TAKE UP RESIDENCE IN THEIR BODIES, AND THEY WILL BE THE CORE OF A NEW MILITARY CONTINGENT.
YOU WILL VOUCHSAFE A THOUSAND MORE HOST BODIES EACH YEAR FOR THE REMAINDER OF THIS CENTURY. AND GIVE US BESIDES, WHEN GERMANY FALLS, A MOIETY OF HER CURRENT TERRITORIES.
THE SHAITAN ENGAGE, IF THESE THINGS ARE DONE, TO SCOURGE BRITAIN'S ENEMIES AND WIN BRITAIN'S WAR.
AND WHAT WILL BECOME OF THESE THOUSANDS WHEN THE WAR IS OVER?
WHY, THEY WILL REMAIN OURS. THE GIFT IS IN PERPETUITY. MY PEOPLE WILL LIVE IN THEM, AS I LIVE IN LADY VIVIAN.
THEN THE ANSWER IS NO. I CAN'T AND WON'T ASK SUCH A SACRIFICE OF ANYONE.
THAT'S A PITY.
I SHALL HAVE TO SEE WHETHER THE GERMAN FUHRER IS WILLING TO HEAR ME OUT.
AH. AND HERE WE ARE.
UNFORTUNATELY.

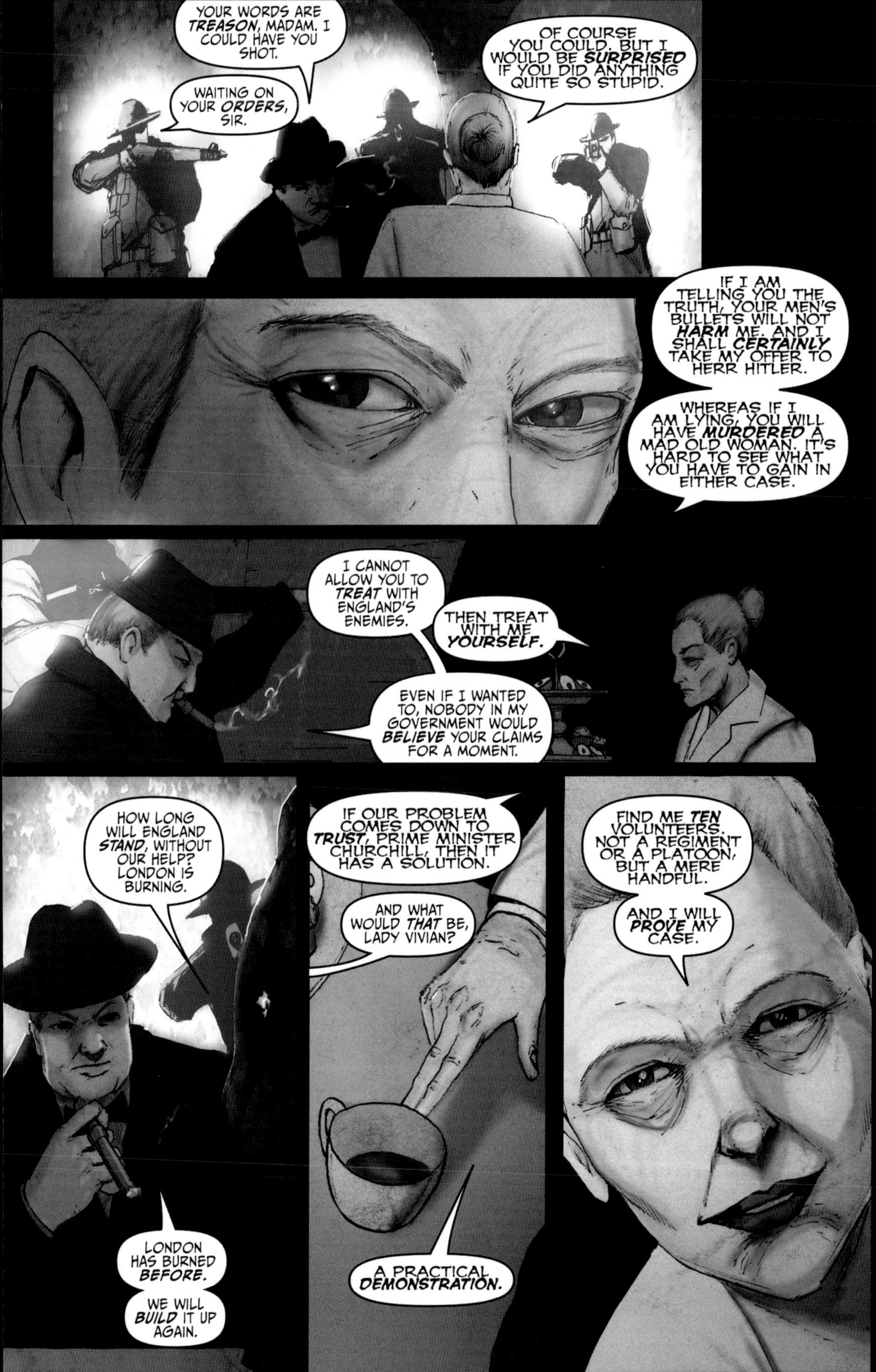
YOUR WORDS ARE TREASON, MADAM. I COULD HAVE YOU SHOT.
WAITING ON YOUR ORDERS, SIR.
OF COURSE YOU COULD. BUT I WOULD BE SURPRISED IF YOU DID ANYTHING QUITE SO STUPID.
IF I AM TELLING YOU THE TRUTH, YOUR MEN'S BULLETS WILL NOT HARM ME. AND I SHALL CERTAINLY TAKE MY OFFER TO HERR HITLER.
WHEREAS IF I AM LYING, YOU WILL HAVE MURDERED A MAD OLD WOMAN. IT'S HARD TO SEE WHAT YOU HAVE TO GAIN IN EITHER CASE.
I CANNOT ALLOW YOU TO TREAT WITH ENGLAND'S ENEMIES.
THEN TREAT WITH ME YOURSELF.
EVEN IF I WANTED TO, NOBODY IN MY GOVERNMENT WOULD BELIEVE YOUR CLAIMS FOR A MOMENT.
HOW LONG WILL ENGLAND STAND, WITHOUT OUR HELP? LONDON IS BURNING.
LONDON HAS BURNED BEFORE.
WE WILL BUILD IT UP AGAIN.
IF OUR PROBLEM COMES DOWN TO TRUST, PRIME MINISTER CHURCHILL, THEN IT HAS A SOLUTION.
AND WHAT WOULD THAT BE, LADY VIVIAN?
A PRACTICAL DEMONSTRATION.
FIND ME TEN VOLUNTEERS. NOT A REGIMENT OR A PLATOON, BUT A MERE HANDFUL.
AND I WILL PROVE MY CASE.

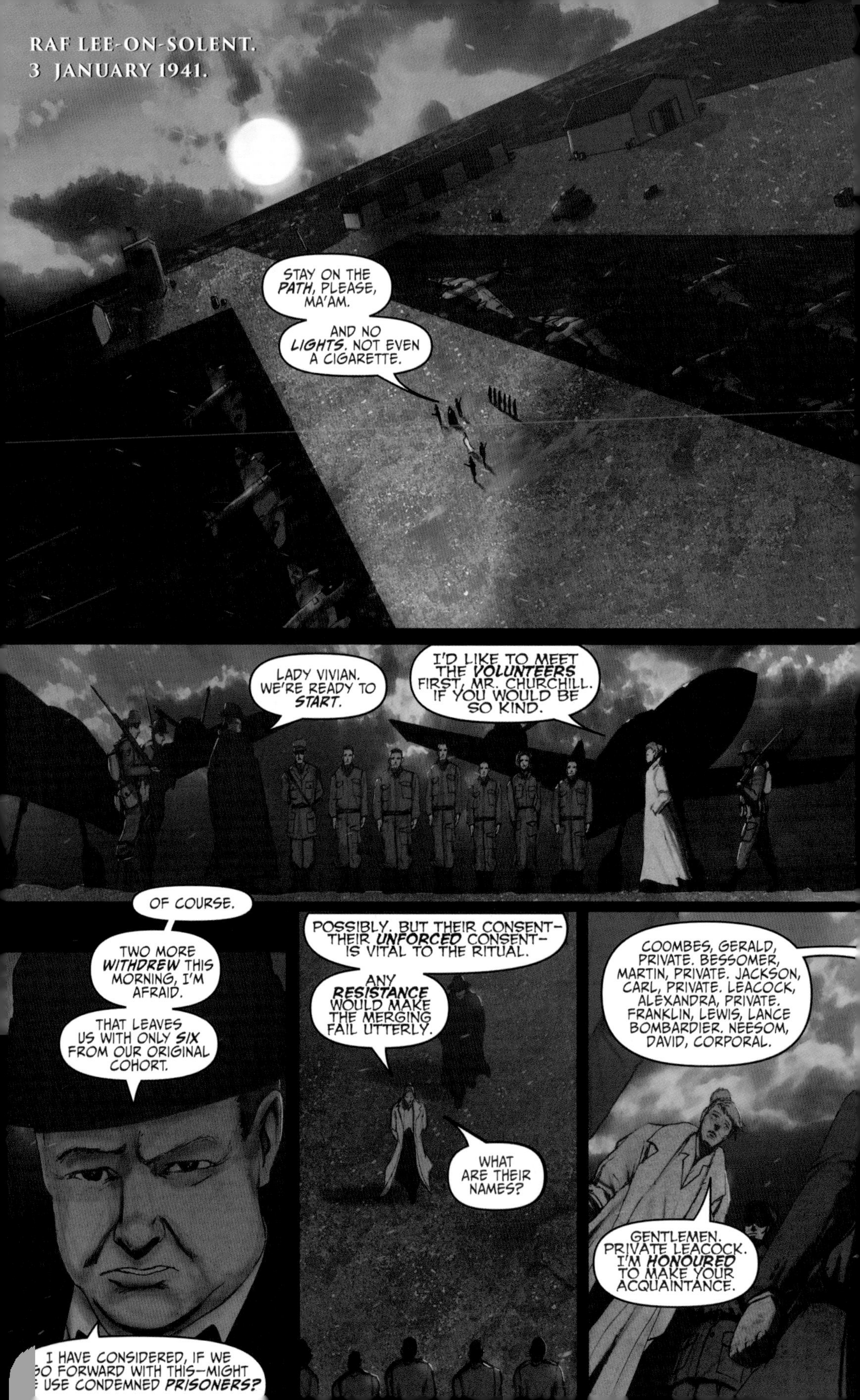
RAF LEE-ON-SOLENT.
3 JANUARY 1941.
STAY ON THE PATH, PLEASE, MA'AM.
AND NO LIGHTS. NOT EVEN A CIGARETTE.
LADY VIVIAN. WE'RE READY TO START.
I'D LIKE TO MEET THE VOLUNTEERS FIRST, MR. CHURCHILL. IF YOU WOULD BE SO KIND.
OF COURSE.
TWO MORE WITHDREW THIS MORNING, I'M AFRAID.
THAT LEAVES US WITH ONLY SIX FROM OUR ORIGINAL COHORT.
I HAVE CONSIDERED, IF WE GO FORWARD WITH THIS—MIGHT USE CONDEMNED PRISONERS?
POSSIBLY. BUT THEIR CONSENT—THEIR UNFORCED CONSENT—IS VITAL TO THE RITUAL.
ANY RESISTANCE WOULD MAKE THE MERGING FAIL UTTERLY.
WHAT ARE THEIR NAMES?
COOMBES, GERALD, PRIVATE. BESSOMER, MARTIN, PRIVATE. JACKSON, CARL, PRIVATE. LEACOCK, ALEXANDRA, PRIVATE. FRANKLIN, LEWIS, LANCE BOMBARDIER. NEESOM, DAVID, CORPORAL.
GENTLEMEN. PRIVATE LEACOCK. I'M HONOURED TO MAKE YOUR ACQUAINTANCE.

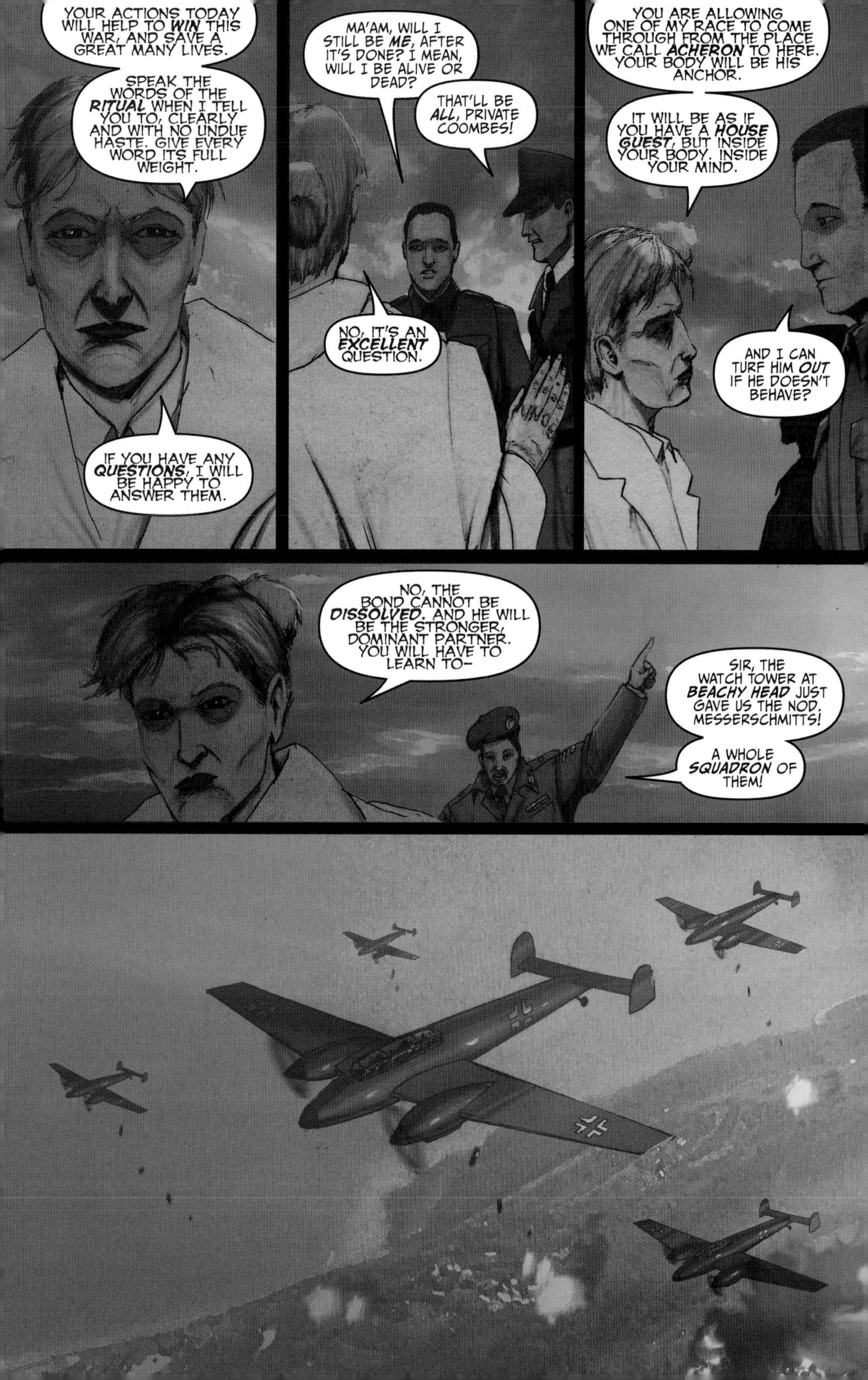

YOUR ACTIONS TODAY WILL HELP TO WIN THIS WAR, AND SAVE A GREAT MANY LIVES.
SPEAK THE WORDS OF THE RITUAL WHEN I TELL YOU TO, CLEARLY AND WITH NO UNDUE HASTE. GIVE EVERY WORD ITS FULL WEIGHT.
IF YOU HAVE ANY QUESTIONS, I WILL BE HAPPY TO ANSWER THEM.
MA'AM, WILL I STILL BE ME, AFTER IT'S DONE? I MEAN, WILL I BE ALIVE OR DEAD?
THAT'LL BE ALL, PRIVATE COOMBES!
NO, IT'S AN EXCELLENT QUESTION.
YOU ARE ALLOWING ONE OF MY RACE TO COME THROUGH FROM THE PLACE WE CALL ACHERON TO HERE. YOUR BODY WILL BE HIS ANCHOR.
IT WILL BE AS IF YOU HAVE A HOUSE GUEST, BUT INSIDE YOUR BODY. INSIDE YOUR MIND.
AND I CAN TURF HIM OUT IF HE DOESN'T BEHAVE?
NO, THE BOND CANNOT BE DISSOLVED. AND HE WILL BE THE STRONGER, DOMINANT PARTNER. YOU WILL HAVE TO LEARN TO–
SIR, THE WATCH TOWER AT BEACHY HEAD JUST GAVE US THE NOD. MESSERSCHMITTS!
A WHOLE SQUADRON OF THEM!

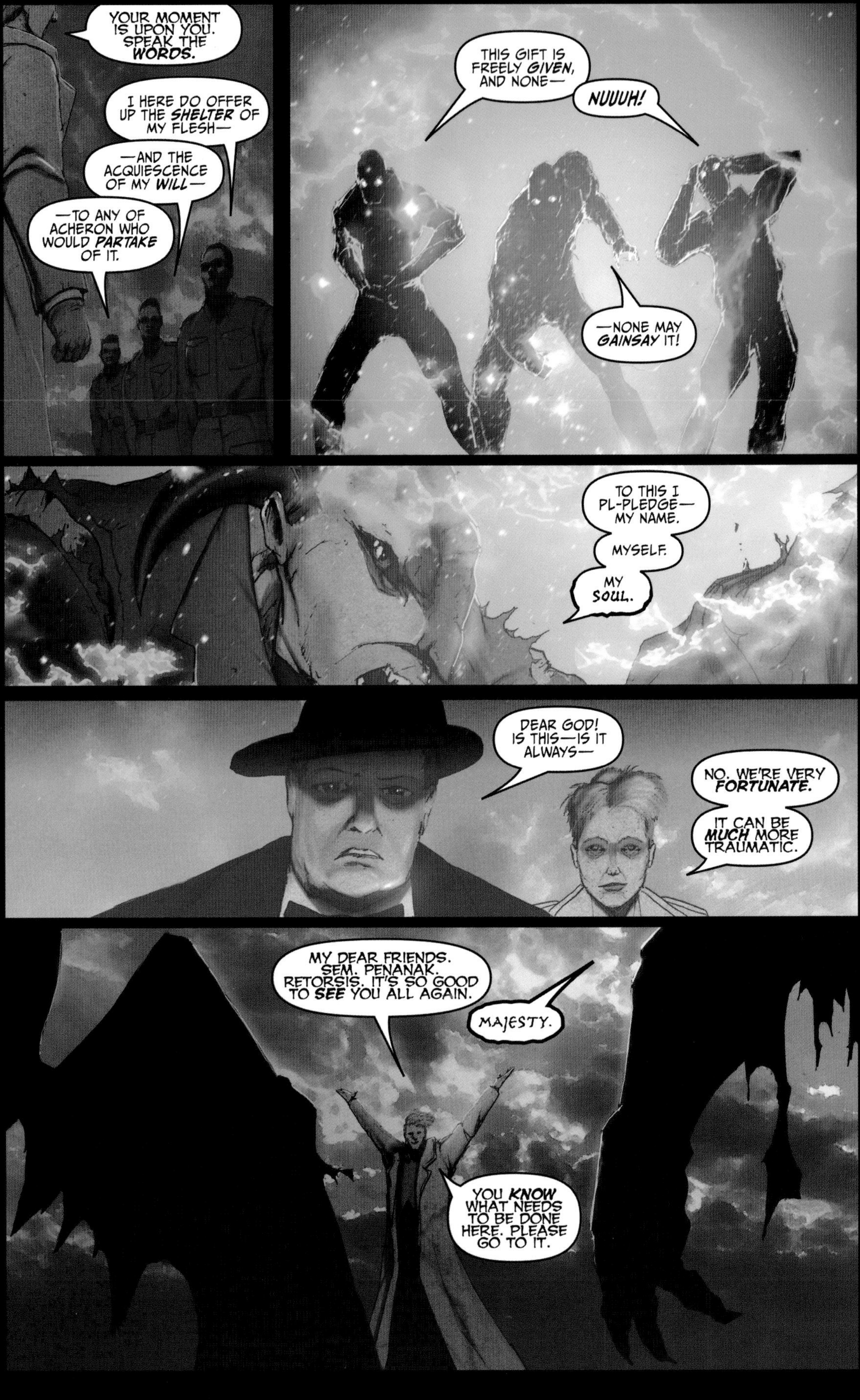
YOUR MOMENT IS UPON YOU. SPEAK THE WORDS.
I HERE DO OFFER UP THE SHELTER OF MY FLESH—
—AND THE ACQUIESCENCE OF MY WILL—
—TO ANY OF ACHERON WHO WOULD PARTAKE OF IT.
THIS GIFT IS FREELY GIVEN, AND NONE—
NUUUH!
—NONE MAY GAINSAY IT!
TO THIS I PL-PLEDGE— MY NAME.
MYSELF.
MY SOUL.
DEAR GOD! IS THIS—IS IT ALWAYS—
NO. WE'RE VERY FORTUNATE.
IT CAN BE MUCH MORE TRAUMATIC.
MY DEAR FRIENDS. SEM. PENANAK. RETORSIS. IT'S SO GOOD TO SEE YOU ALL AGAIN.
MAJESTY.
YOU KNOW WHAT NEEDS TO BE DONE HERE. PLEASE GO TO IT.

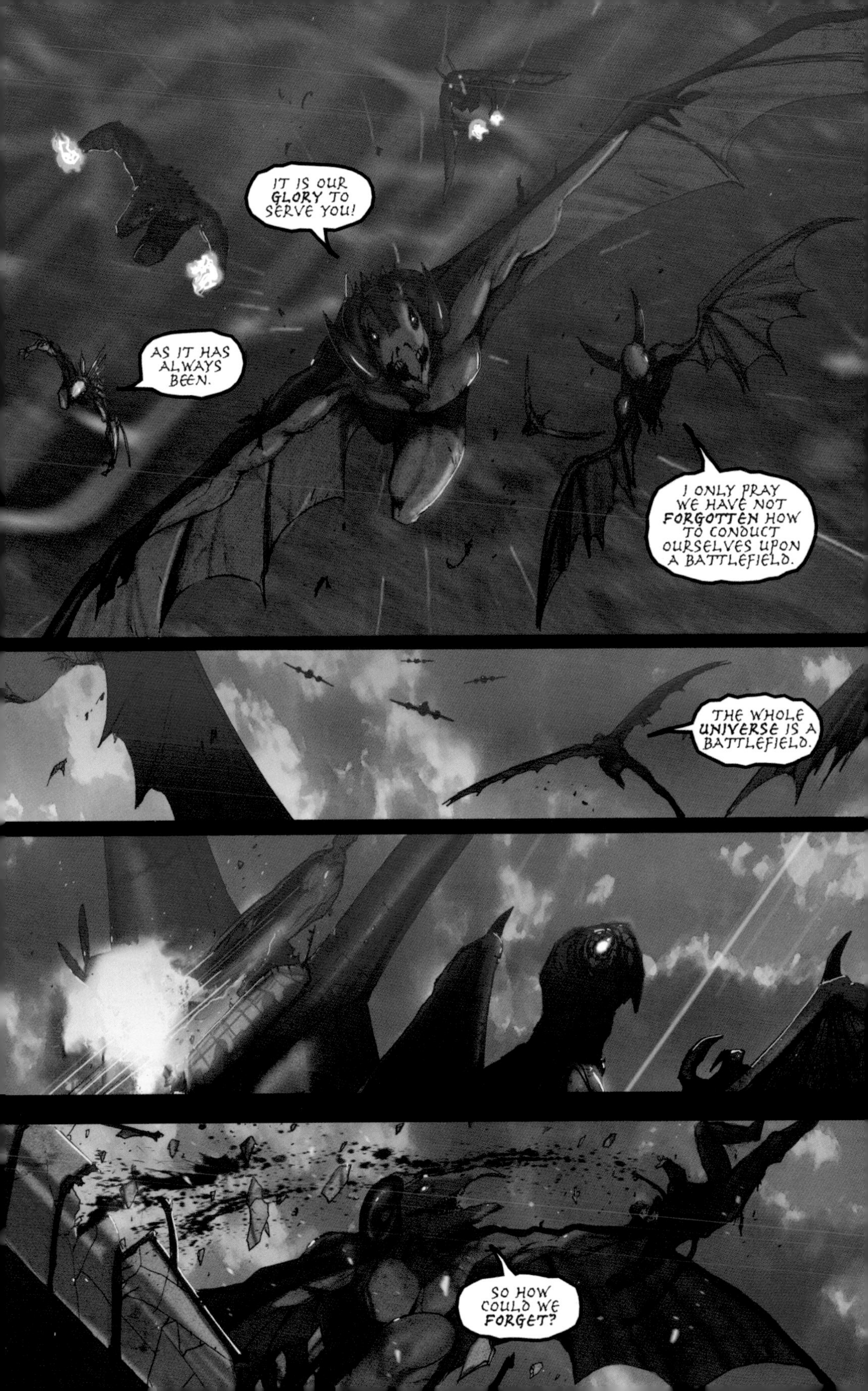
IT IS OUR GLORY TO SERVE YOU!
AS IT HAS ALWAYS BEEN.
I ONLY PRAY WE HAVE NOT FORGOTTEN HOW TO CONDUCT OURSELVES UPON A BATTLEFIELD.
THE WHOLE UNIVERSE IS A BATTLEFIELD.
SO HOW COULD WE FORGET?

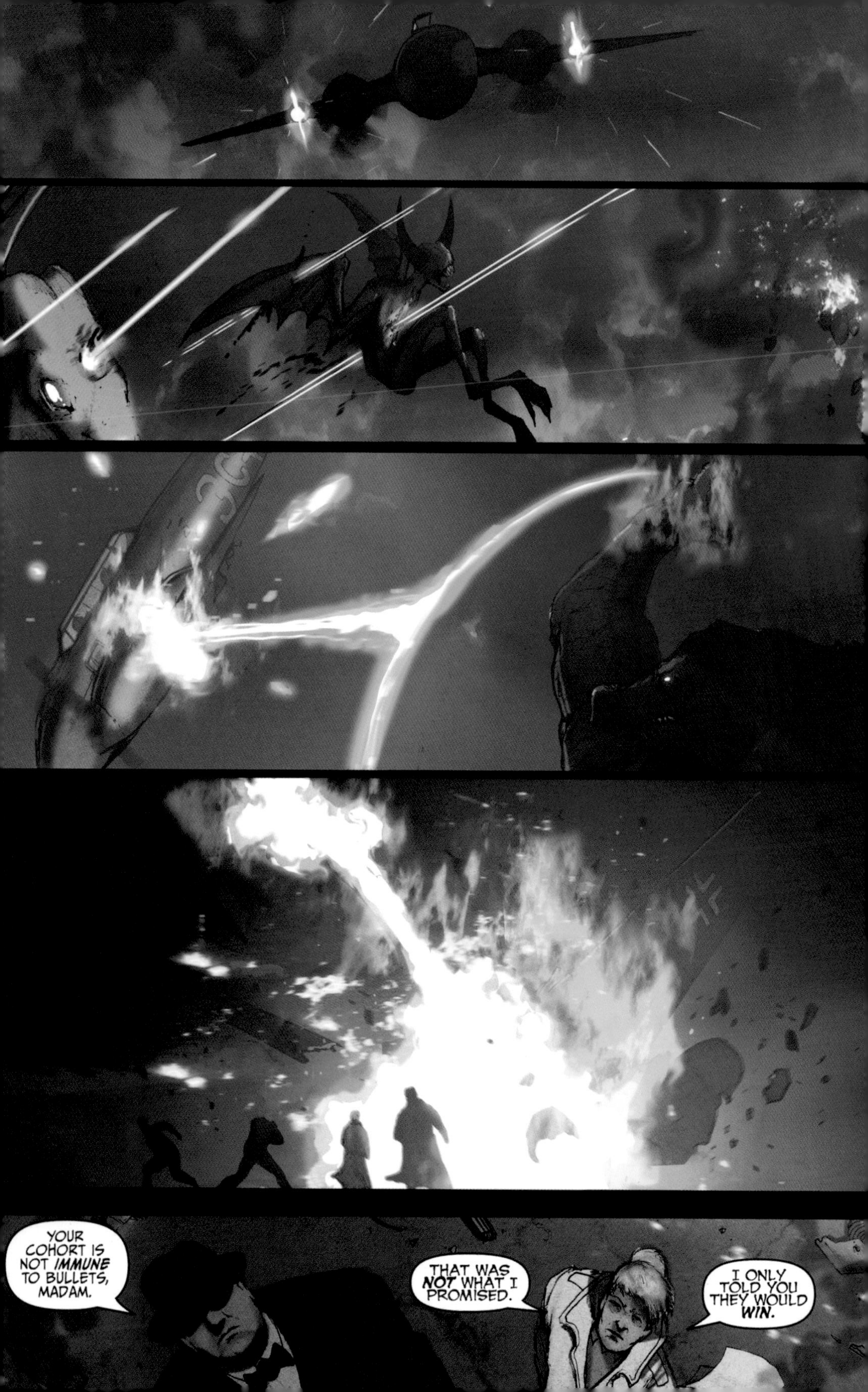
YOUR COHORT IS NOT IMMUNE TO BULLETS, MADAM.
THAT WAS NOT WHAT I PROMISED.
I ONLY TOLD YOU THEY WOULD WIN.

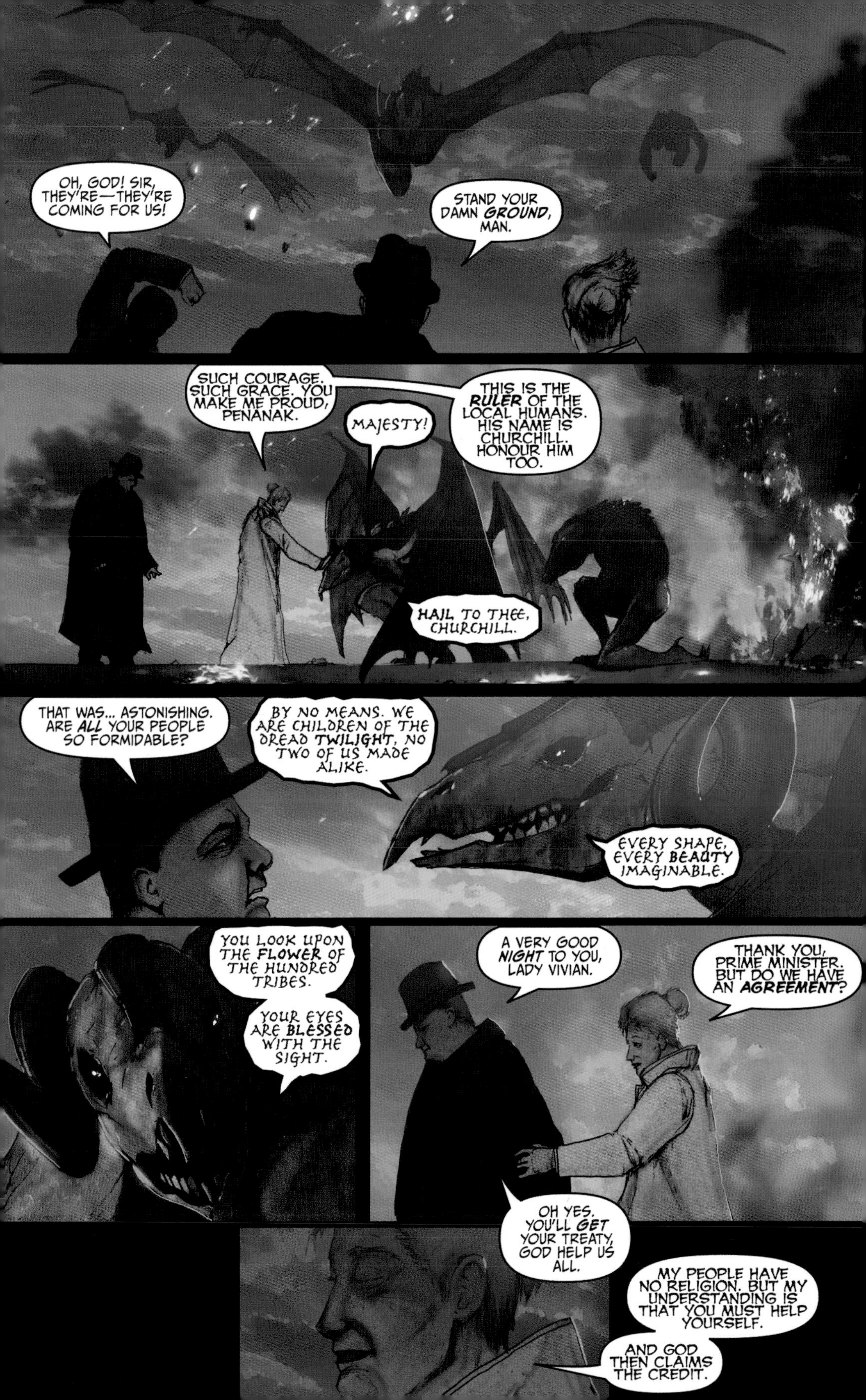
OH, GOD! SIR, THEY'RE—THEY'RE COMING FOR US!
STAND YOUR DAMN GROUND, MAN.
SUCH COURAGE. SUCH GRACE. YOU MAKE ME PROUD, PENANAK.
MAJESTY!
THIS IS THE RULER OF THE LOCAL HUMANS. HIS NAME IS CHURCHILL. HONOUR HIM TOO.
HAIL TO THEE, CHURCHILL.
THAT WAS... ASTONISHING. ARE ALL YOUR PEOPLE SO FORMIDABLE?
BY NO MEANS. WE ARE CHILDREN OF THE DREAD TWILIGHT, NO TWO OF US MADE ALIKE.
EVERY SHAPE, EVERY BEAUTY IMAGINABLE.
YOU LOOK UPON THE FLOWER OF THE HUNDRED TRIBES.
YOUR EYES ARE BLESSED WITH THE SIGHT.
A VERY GOOD NIGHT TO YOU, LADY VIVIAN.
THANK YOU, PRIME MINISTER. BUT DO WE HAVE AN AGREEMENT?
OH YES. YOU'LL GET YOUR TREATY, GOD HELP US ALL.
MY PEOPLE HAVE NO RELIGION. BUT MY UNDERSTANDING IS THAT YOU MUST HELP YOURSELF.
AND GOD THEN CLAIMS THE CREDIT.

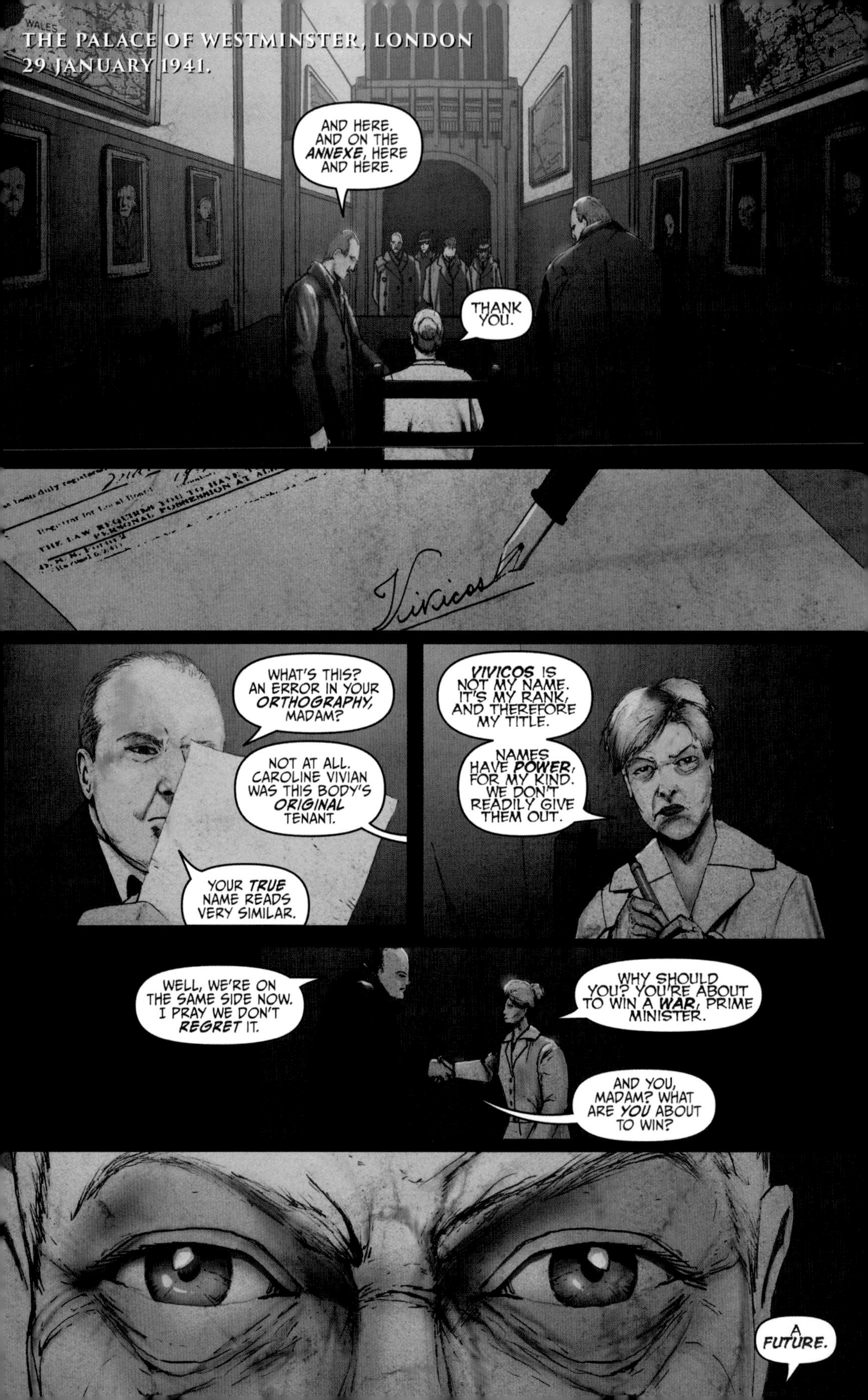
THE PALACE OF WESTMINSTER, LONDON
29 JANUARY 1941.
AND HERE. AND ON THE ANNEXE, HERE AND HERE.
THANK YOU.
WHAT'S THIS? AN ERROR IN YOUR ORTHOGRAPHY, MADAM?
NOT AT ALL. CAROLINE VIVIAN WAS THIS BODY'S ORIGINAL TENANT.
YOUR TRUE NAME READS VERY SIMILAR.
VIVICOS IS NOT MY NAME. IT'S MY RANK, AND THEREFORE MY TITLE.
NAMES HAVE POWER, FOR MY KIND. WE DON'T READILY GIVE THEM OUT.
WELL, WE'RE ON THE SAME SIDE NOW. I PRAY WE DON'T REGRET IT.
WHY SHOULD YOU? YOU'RE ABOUT TO WIN A WAR, PRIME MINISTER.
AND YOU, MADAM? WHAT ARE YOU ABOUT TO WIN?
A FUTURE.

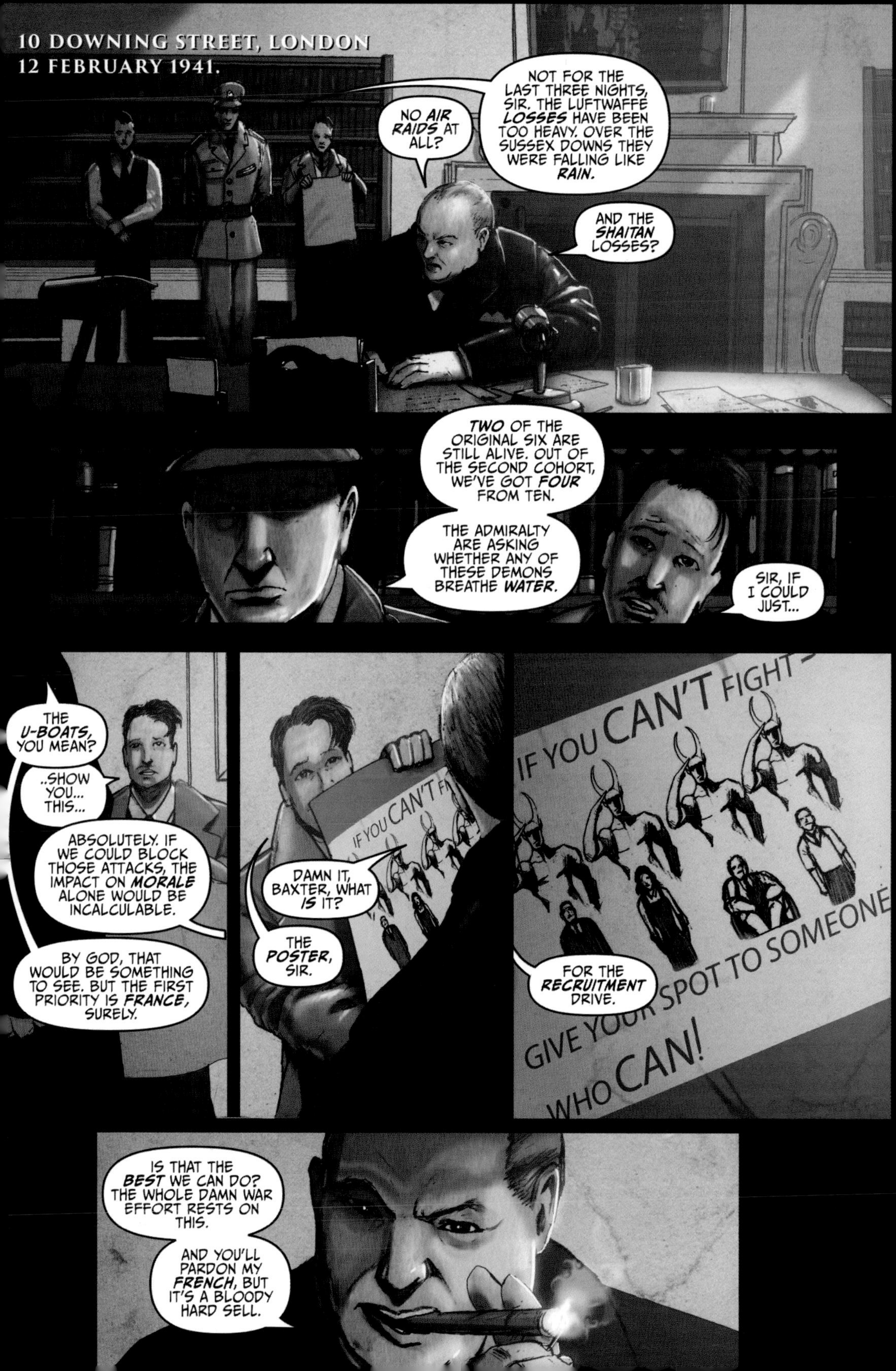
10 DOWNING STREET, LONDON
12 FEBRUARY 1941.
NO AIR RAIDS AT ALL?
NOT FOR THE LAST THREE NIGHTS, SIR. THE LUFTWAFFE LOSSES HAVE BEEN TOO HEAVY. OVER THE SUSSEX DOWNS THEY WERE FALLING LIKE RAIN.
AND THE SHAITAN LOSSES?
TWO OF THE ORIGINAL SIX ARE STILL ALIVE. OUT OF THE SECOND COHORT, WE'VE GOT FOUR FROM TEN.
THE ADMIRALTY ARE ASKING WHETHER ANY OF THESE DEMONS BREATHE WATER.
SIR, IF I COULD JUST...
THE U-BOATS, YOU MEAN?
..SHOW YOU... THIS...
ABSOLUTELY. IF WE COULD BLOCK THOSE ATTACKS, THE IMPACT ON MORALE ALONE WOULD BE INCALCULABLE.
BY GOD, THAT WOULD BE SOMETHING TO SEE. BUT THE FIRST PRIORITY IS FRANCE, SURELY.
DAMN IT, BAXTER, WHAT IS IT?
THE POSTER, SIR.
IF YOU CAN'T FIGHT
GIVE YOUR SPOT TO SOMEONE WHO CAN!
FOR THE RECRUITMENT DRIVE.
IS THAT THE BEST WE CAN DO? THE WHOLE DAMN WAR EFFORT RESTS ON THIS.
AND YOU'LL PARDON MY FRENCH, BUT IT'S A BLOODY HARD SELL.

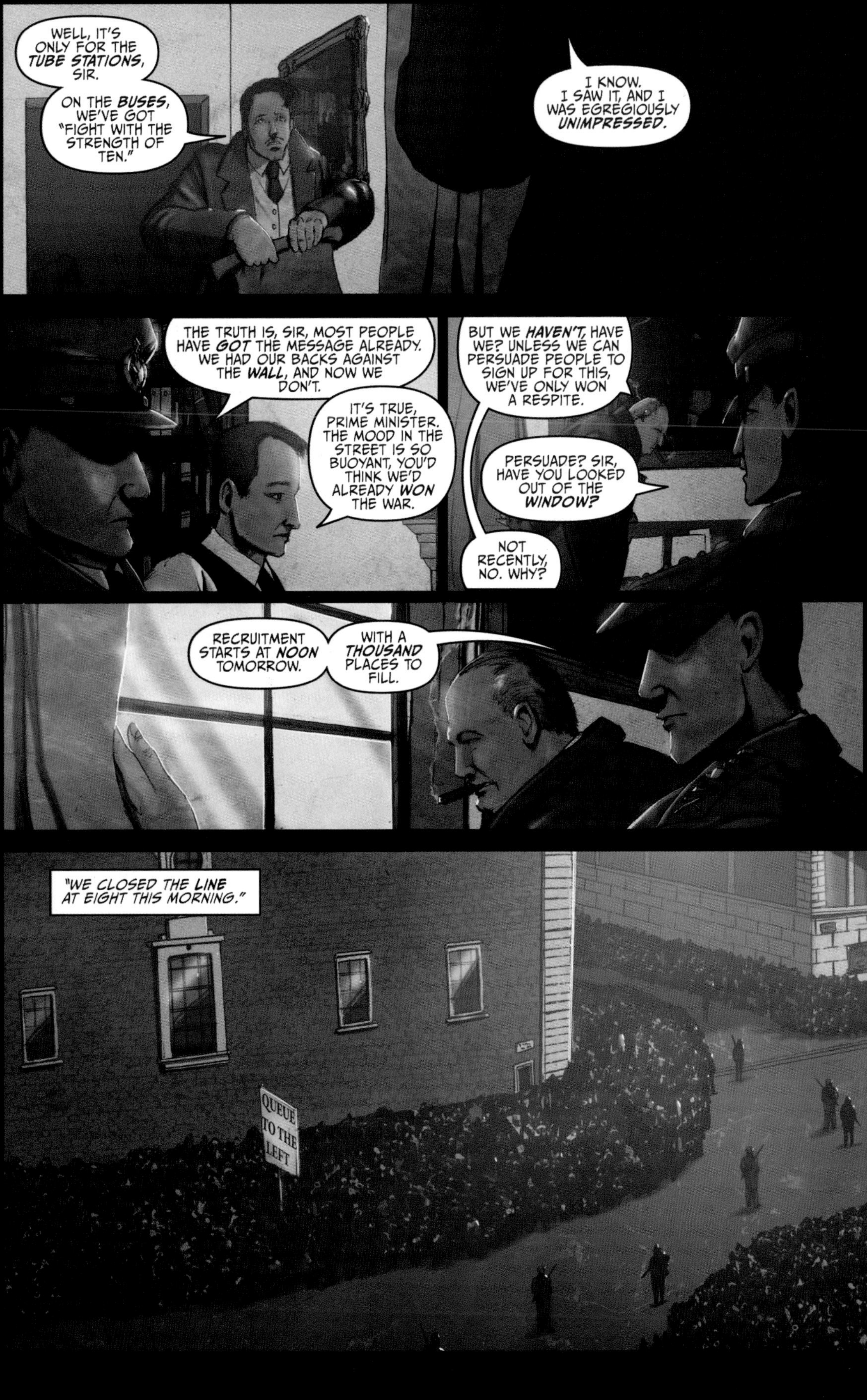
WELL, IT'S ONLY FOR THE *TUBE STATIONS,* SIR.
ON THE *BUSES,* WE'VE GOT "FIGHT WITH THE STRENGTH OF TEN."
I KNOW. I SAW IT, AND I WAS EGREGIOUSLY *UNIMPRESSED.*
THE TRUTH IS, SIR, MOST PEOPLE HAVE *GOT* THE MESSAGE ALREADY. WE HAD OUR BACKS AGAINST THE *WALL,* AND NOW WE DON'T.
IT'S TRUE, PRIME MINISTER. THE MOOD IN THE STREET IS SO BUOYANT, YOU'D THINK WE'D ALREADY *WON* THE WAR.
BUT WE *HAVEN'T,* HAVE WE? UNLESS WE CAN PERSUADE PEOPLE TO SIGN UP FOR THIS, WE'VE ONLY WON A RESPITE.
PERSUADE? SIR, HAVE YOU LOOKED OUT OF THE *WINDOW?*
NOT RECENTLY, NO. WHY?
RECRUITMENT STARTS AT *NOON* TOMORROW.
WITH A *THOUSAND* PLACES TO FILL.
"WE CLOSED THE LINE AT EIGHT THIS MORNING."
QUEUE TO THE LEFT

---------------The LONDON VOICE-------------------

SHAITAN BRING FAIR WINDS FOR THE ALLIED FLEETS

EXTRA

Losses of British shipping to German submarine attacks escalated in 1940 to the point where it seriously jeopardised the arrival of essential supplies from Canada to the United States.

The submarines, known as U-boats, were fast moving and difficult to detect. They could potentially stalk an entire convoy, attacking one ship after another and sinking freighters and military escorts alike.

But now these devastating raids are a thing of the past. Our Shaitan allies have taken over the task of escorting merchant convoys, and the Admirals are reporting a very high rate of success.

A number of Shaitan have proved crucial in this theatre of war. One of the most formidable, Bezoar, is a shark-like hunter with an incredibly fine sense of smell. He can reputedly track a U-boat through the lightless depths of the ocean by the scent of the chemicals used to clean its hull. His platoon carry magnetic mines which they can attach to the U-boat's hull, ensuring its immediate destruction.

For covert operations in German waters Podmoi and his infiltration squad take the brunt of the action. These water-breathing Shaitan secrete a corrosive resin from ducts in their fingers. The resin eats into the steel of a U-boat's hull, alowing it to be torn like paper. Our brave sub-mariners are going hand-to-hand with the German Wolfpacks!

The combiner effect of these two Shaitan special forces teams has been litle short of miraculous. "The Jerries don't know what's hit them," Admiral Shillingham opined yesterday. "The hunter has become

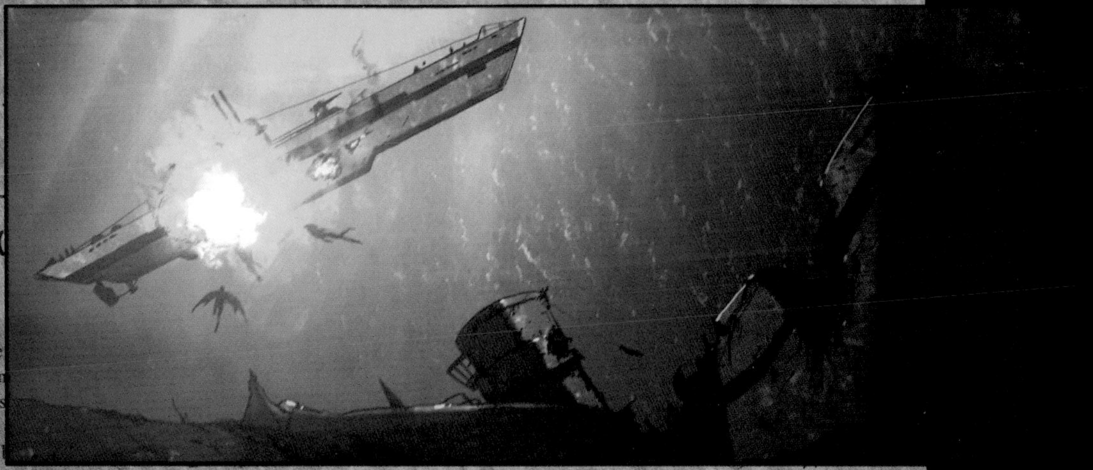

St

Morale
ever sin
fighters
breach
dating

The fin
grand a

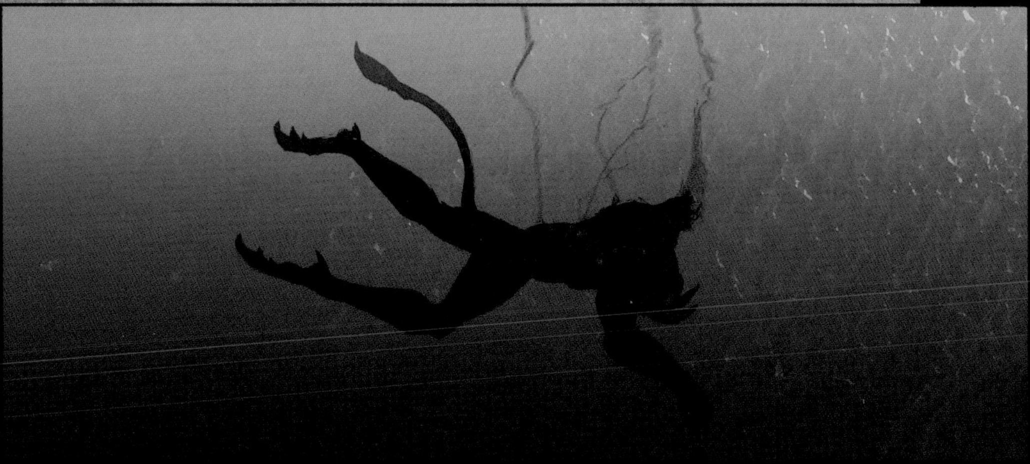

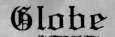

"WE HAVE WALKED IN FRANCE, AND SHE IS FREE" - GENERAL MONTGOMERY

Almost two years to the day after France fell into the hands of the Axis powers, her liberation began three days ago with the arrival on French soil of a combined force of 160,000 British and American troops, ably supported by fully 800 of our Shaitan allies.

The precise location of the Allied landings remains a close-kept secret, but we can reveal that superhuman efforts by British Intelligence kept the German divisions in northern France in the dark until the very last moment with masterful misdirections.

As a consequence, the Wehrmacht troops were very slow to respond to the initial landings. By the time they were able to mount a counter-atack, troops from the 21st Army Group led by Generals Bernard Montgomery and Dwight D. Eisenhower had already established a robust beachhead across a two-mile stretch of France's shoreline.

From that beachhead they surged outwards in a series of devastating sorties. The Shaitan proved invaluable to these consolidations, destroying German ordnance on the ground and ensuring that they were unable to bring air superiority to bear. German losses on the first day of fighting alone amounted to more than a quarter of a million.

Speaking for the Shaitan, one of the tallest warriors this correspondent has ever seen declared that he would "wear Hitler's viscera as a

MORNING EDITION

BERLIN FALLS!

The Allied advance into the Reich's heartland culminated yesterday in a robust assault on Germany's capital, Berlin. And in keeping with their conduct in many recent battles our Shaitan troops got there first.

A dozen Shaitan holding masses of green flame in their hands set fire to the barracks and armorouries to the West of the city, while their airborne brethren secured the fortified bunker in which Führer Adolf Hitler had sought to hide.

An attempt by the German Weichsel army group to relieve the beleaguered city was met with heroic resistance from the British and American troops who fortified the west bank of the River Spree and held it against all comers.

Meanwhile the Russian army of the Vistula, who had thought to reach the city first and consolidate its control before the arrival of British and US forces, had only reached Zielenzig when word arrived that the city had fallen. General Heinrici has lodged a formal protest, claiming that the Yalta agreement guaranteed them post-war control of the German capital.

At the time of this report, 36 hours after the initial advance, much of Berlin continues to burn with green fires which resist all attempts to extinguish them, and which loudly mock the fleeing German citizens. It is possible that the flames are themselves profoundly transformed Shaitan, although General Montgomery refused to confirm this.

With the war in the European threatre now effectively over, speculation has turned to the forthcoming general election in

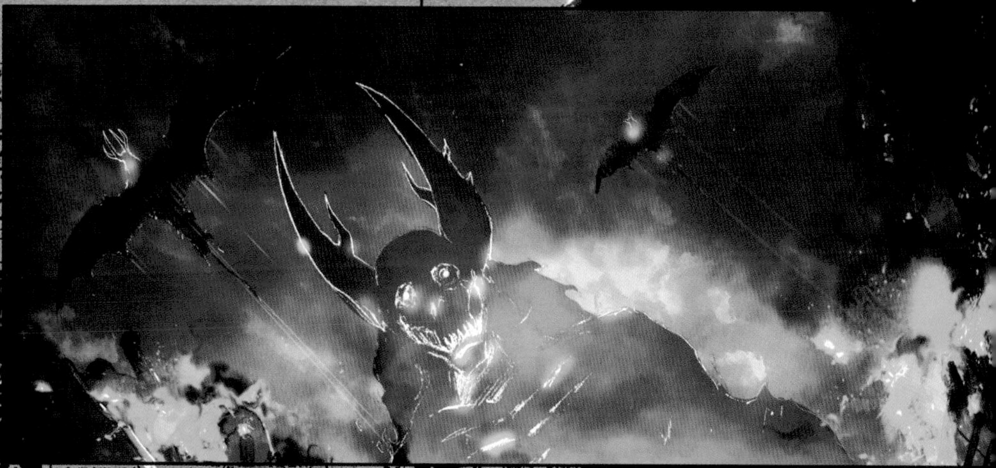

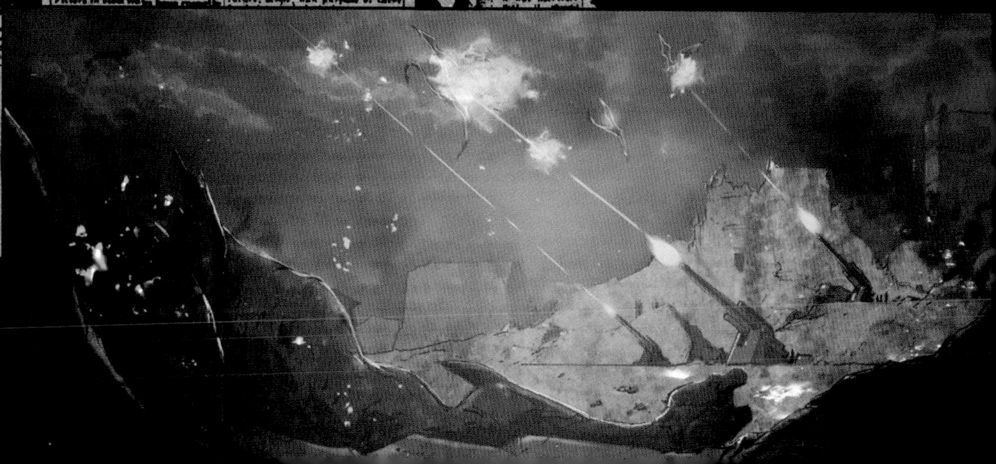

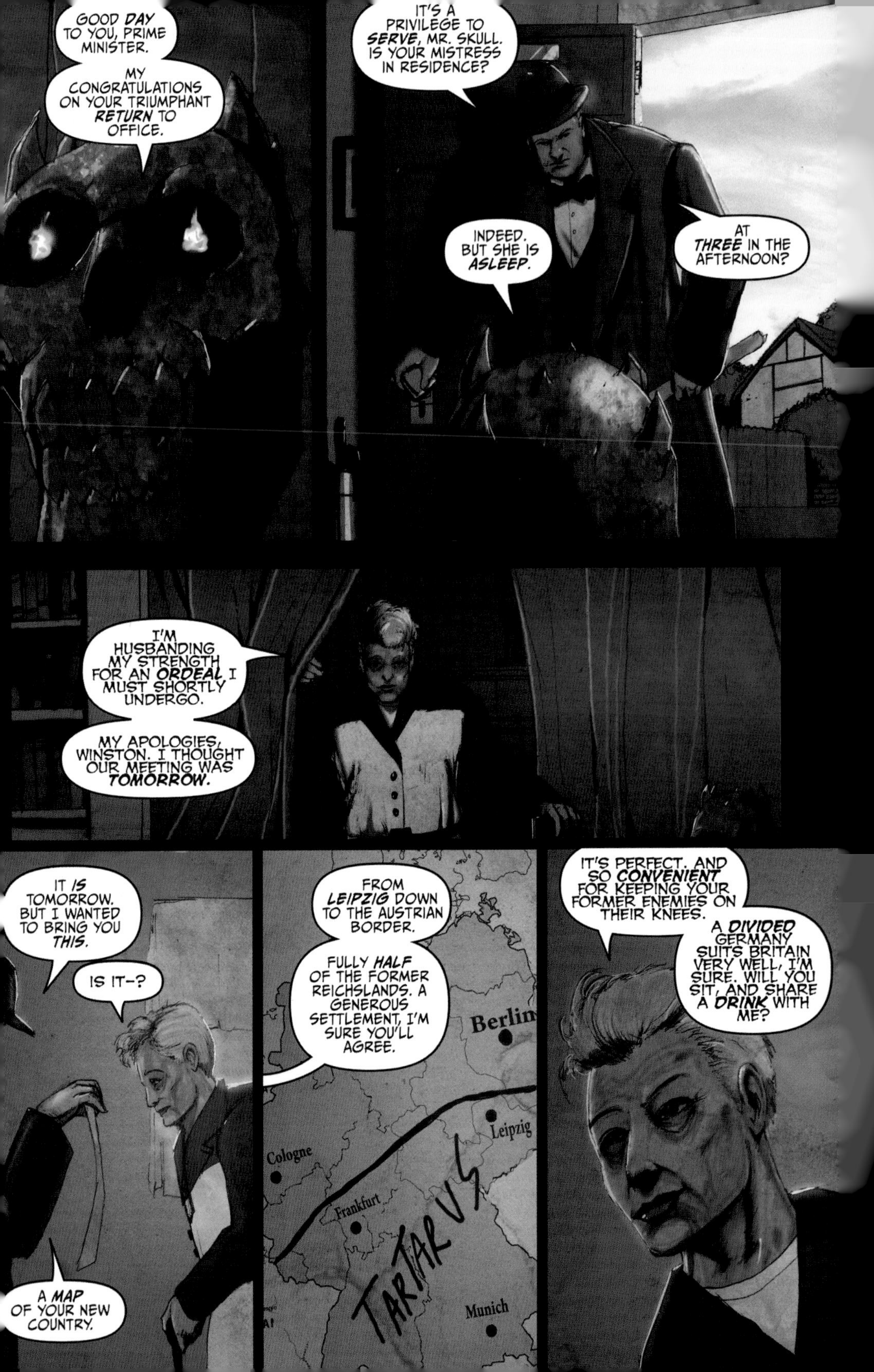
GOOD DAY TO YOU, PRIME MINISTER.
MY CONGRATULATIONS ON YOUR TRIUMPHANT RETURN TO OFFICE.
IT'S A PRIVILEGE TO SERVE, MR. SKULL. IS YOUR MISTRESS IN RESIDENCE?
INDEED. BUT SHE IS ASLEEP.
AT THREE IN THE AFTERNOON?
I'M HUSBANDING MY STRENGTH FOR AN ORDEAL I MUST SHORTLY UNDERGO.
MY APOLOGIES, WINSTON. I THOUGHT OUR MEETING WAS TOMORROW.
IT IS TOMORROW. BUT I WANTED TO BRING YOU THIS.
IS IT-?
A MAP OF YOUR NEW COUNTRY.
FROM LEIPZIG DOWN TO THE AUSTRIAN BORDER.
FULLY HALF OF THE FORMER REICHSLANDS. A GENEROUS SETTLEMENT, I'M SURE YOU'LL AGREE.
Berlin
Leipzig
Cologne
Frankfurt
TARTARUS
Munich
IT'S PERFECT. AND SO CONVENIENT FOR KEEPING YOUR FORMER ENEMIES ON THEIR KNEES.
A DIVIDED GERMANY SUITS BRITAIN VERY WELL, I'M SURE. WILL YOU SIT, AND SHARE A DRINK WITH ME?

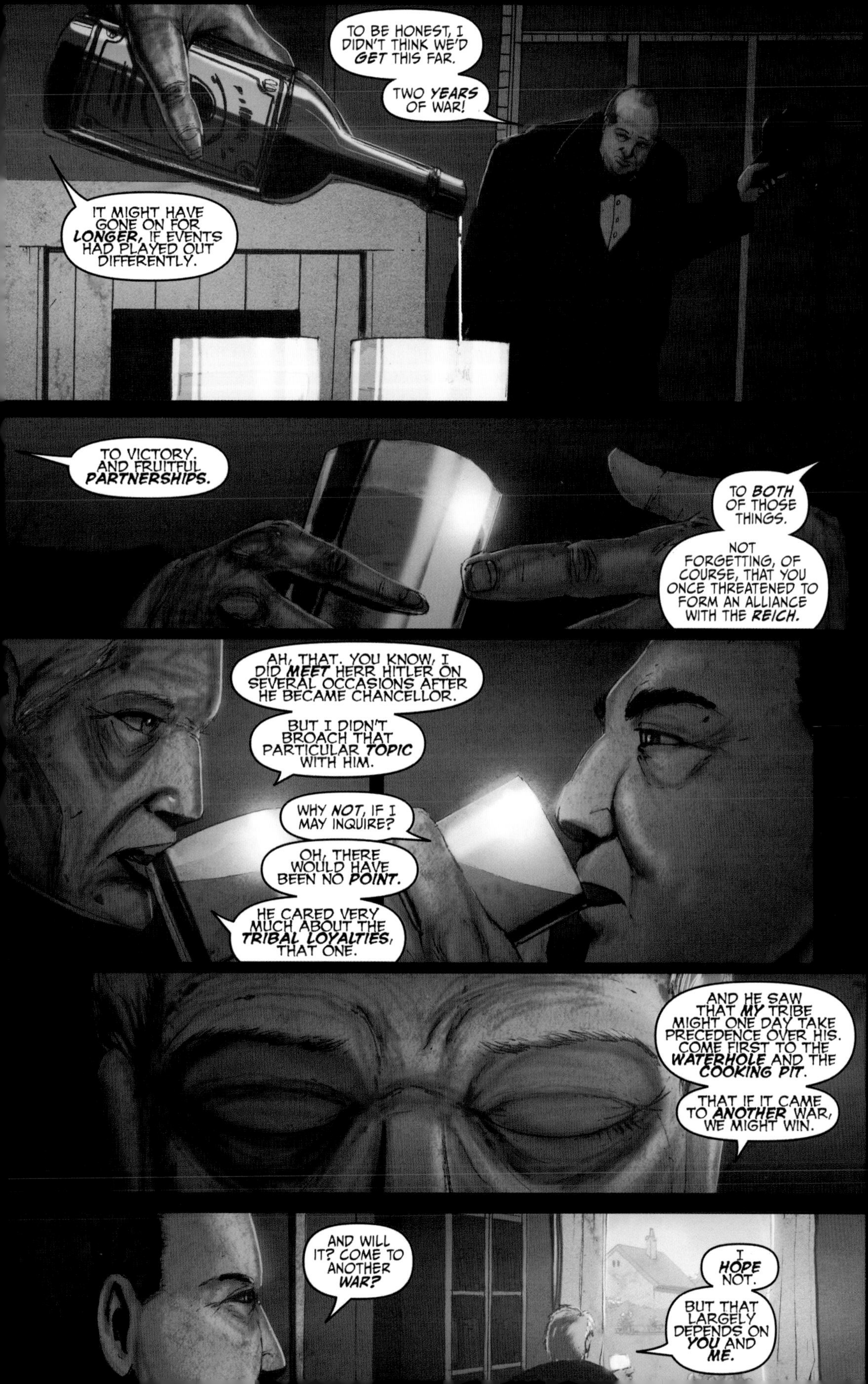
TO BE HONEST, I DIDN'T THINK WE'D GET THIS FAR.
TWO YEARS OF WAR!
IT MIGHT HAVE GONE ON FOR LONGER, IF EVENTS HAD PLAYED OUT DIFFERENTLY.
TO VICTORY. AND FRUITFUL PARTNERSHIPS.
TO BOTH OF THOSE THINGS.
NOT FORGETTING, OF COURSE, THAT YOU ONCE THREATENED TO FORM AN ALLIANCE WITH THE REICH.
AH, THAT. YOU KNOW, I DID MEET HERR HITLER ON SEVERAL OCCASIONS AFTER HE BECAME CHANCELLOR.
BUT I DIDN'T BROACH THAT PARTICULAR TOPIC WITH HIM.
WHY NOT, IF I MAY INQUIRE?
OH, THERE WOULD HAVE BEEN NO POINT.
HE CARED VERY MUCH ABOUT THE TRIBAL LOYALTIES, THAT ONE.
AND HE SAW THAT MY TRIBE MIGHT ONE DAY TAKE PRECEDENCE OVER HIS. COME FIRST TO THE WATERHOLE AND THE COOKING PIT.
THAT IF IT CAME TO ANOTHER WAR, WE MIGHT WIN.
AND WILL IT? COME TO ANOTHER WAR?
I HOPE NOT.
BUT THAT LARGELY DEPENDS ON YOU AND ME.

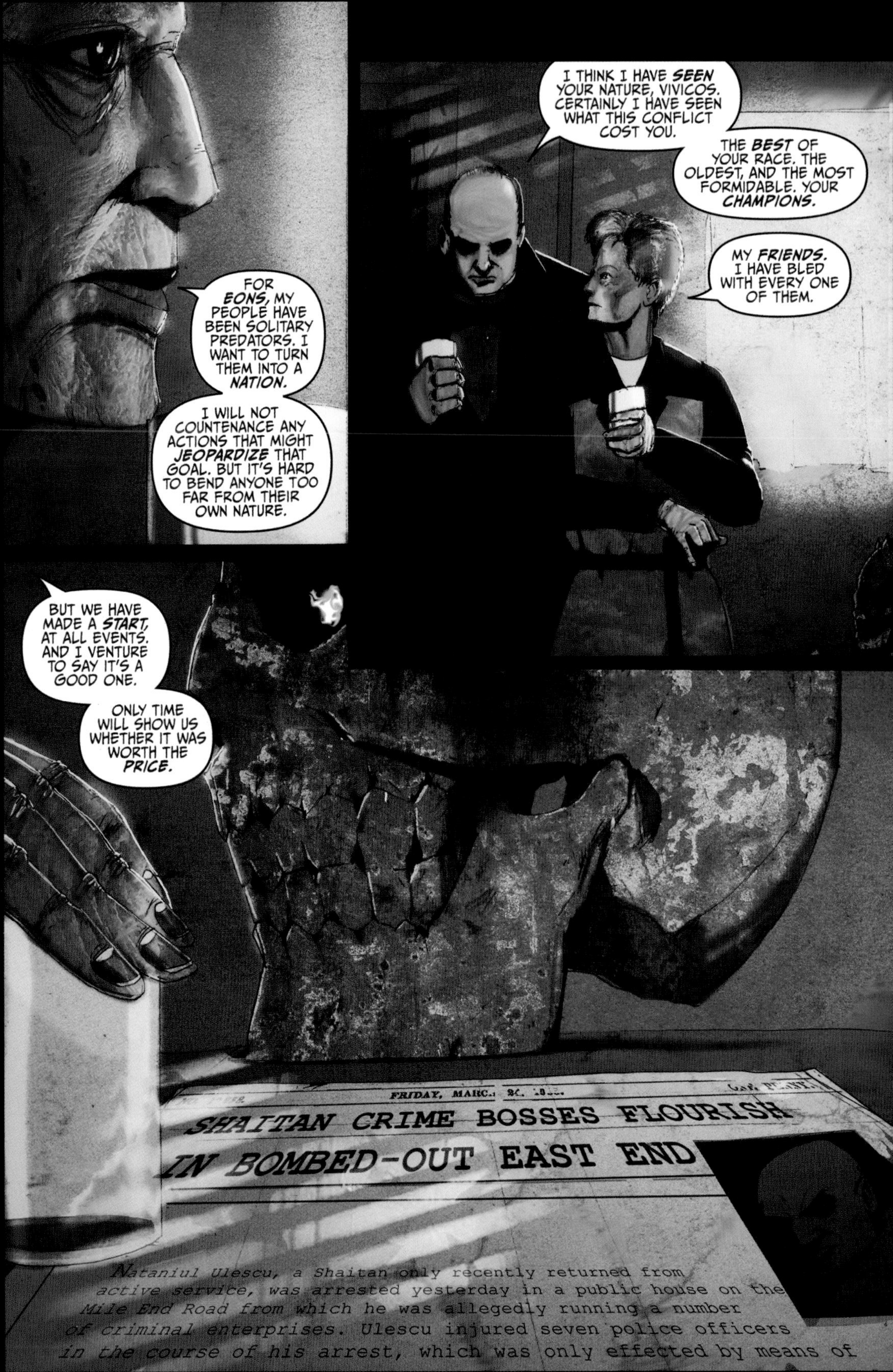
FOR EONS, MY PEOPLE HAVE BEEN SOLITARY PREDATORS. I WANT TO TURN THEM INTO A NATION.
I WILL NOT COUNTENANCE ANY ACTIONS THAT MIGHT JEOPARDIZE THAT GOAL. BUT IT'S HARD TO BEND ANYONE TOO FAR FROM THEIR OWN NATURE.
I THINK I HAVE SEEN YOUR NATURE, VIVICOS. CERTAINLY I HAVE SEEN WHAT THIS CONFLICT COST YOU.
THE BEST OF YOUR RACE. THE OLDEST, AND THE MOST FORMIDABLE. YOUR CHAMPIONS.
MY FRIENDS. I HAVE BLED WITH EVERY ONE OF THEM.
BUT WE HAVE MADE A START, AT ALL EVENTS. AND I VENTURE TO SAY IT'S A GOOD ONE.
ONLY TIME WILL SHOW US WHETHER IT WAS WORTH THE PRICE.
SHAITAN CRIME BOSSES FLOURISH IN BOMBED-OUT EAST END
Nataniul Ulescu, a Shaitan only recently returned from active service, was arrested yesterday in a public house on the Mile End Road from which he was allegedly running a number of criminal enterprises. Ulescu injured seven police officers in the course of his arrest, which was only effected by means of

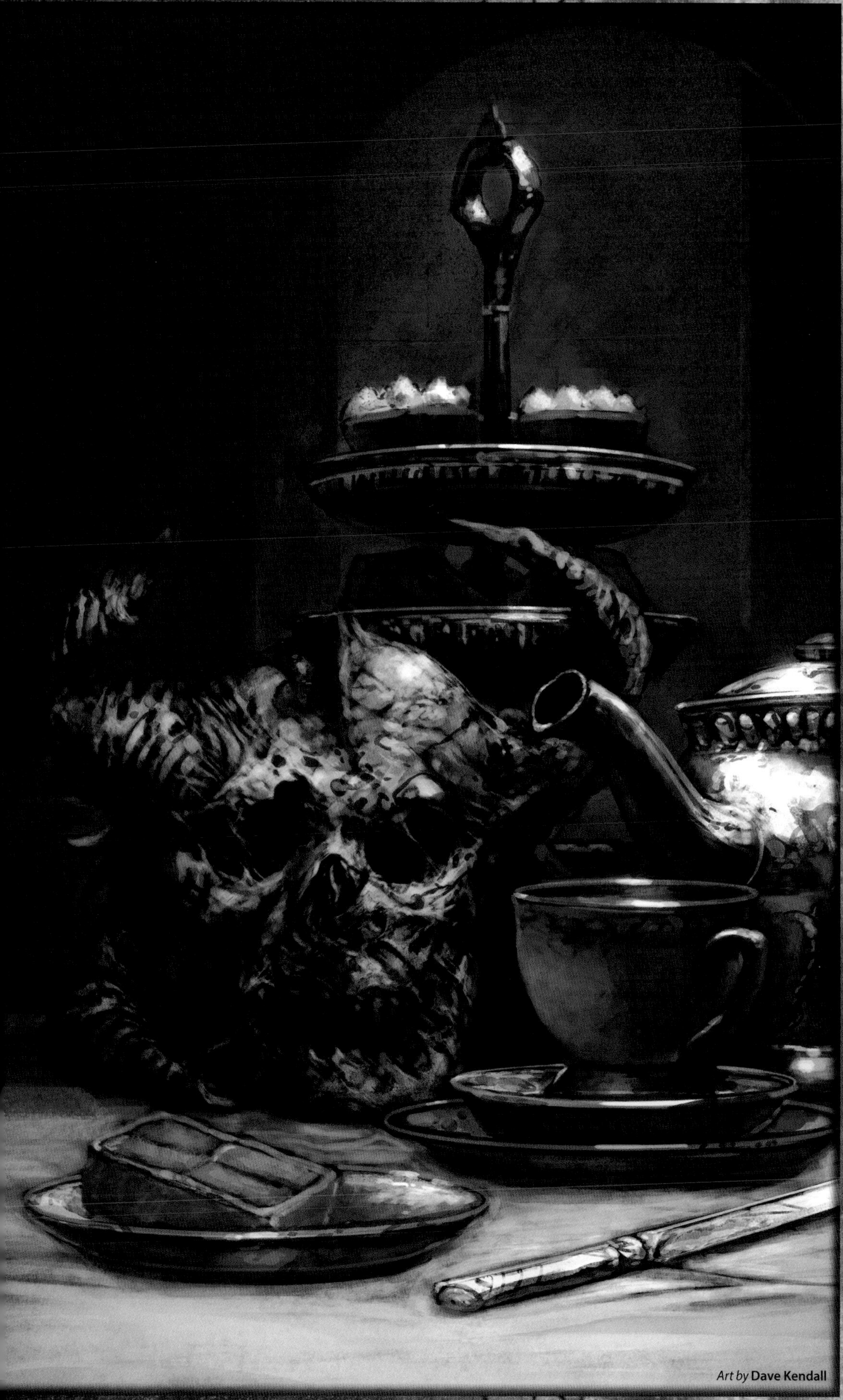

Art by **Dave Kendall**

CHAPTER 4

WHAT HATH NIGHT TO DO WITH SLEEP?

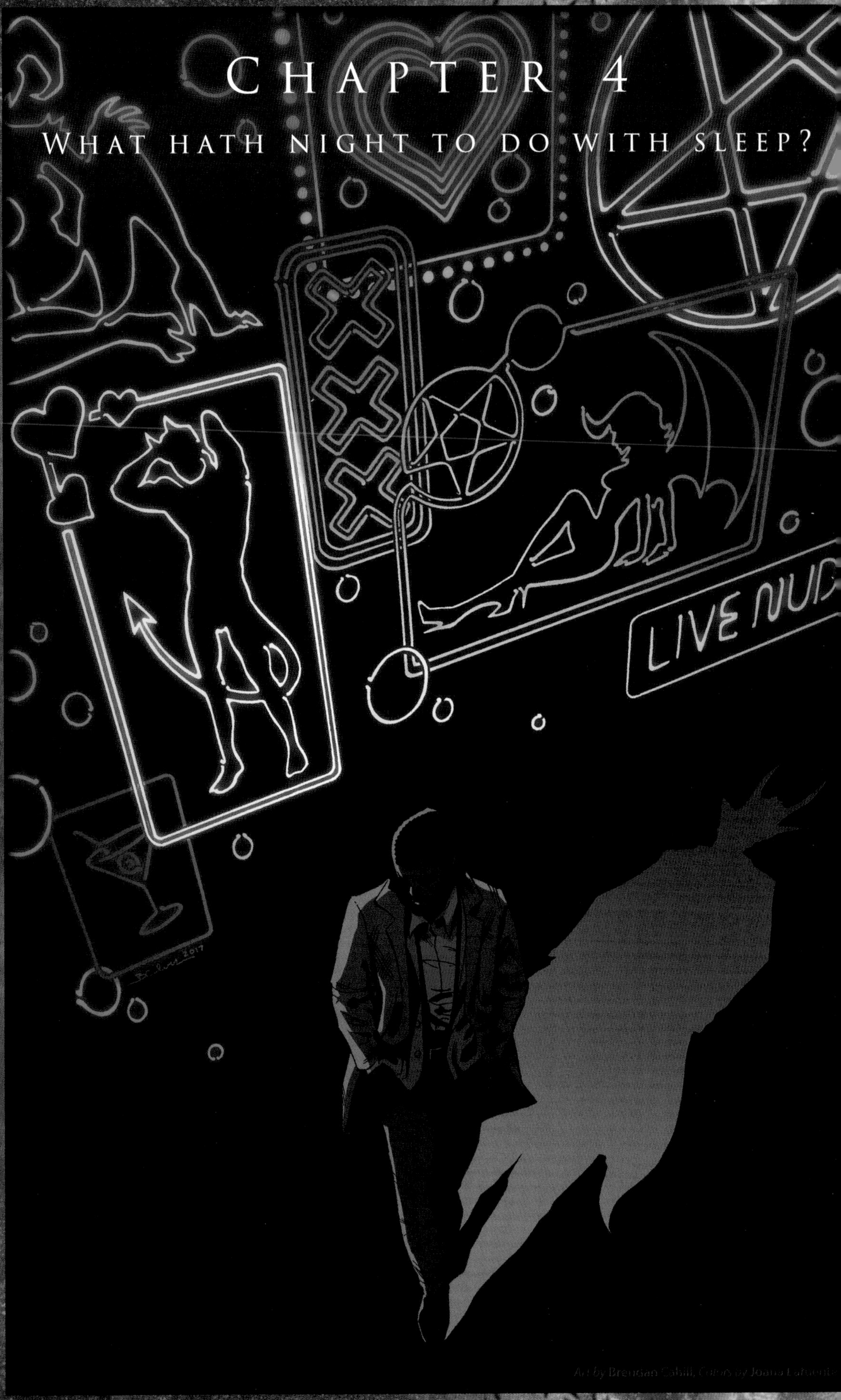
LIVE NUD

Art by Brendan Cahill, Colors by Joana Lafuente

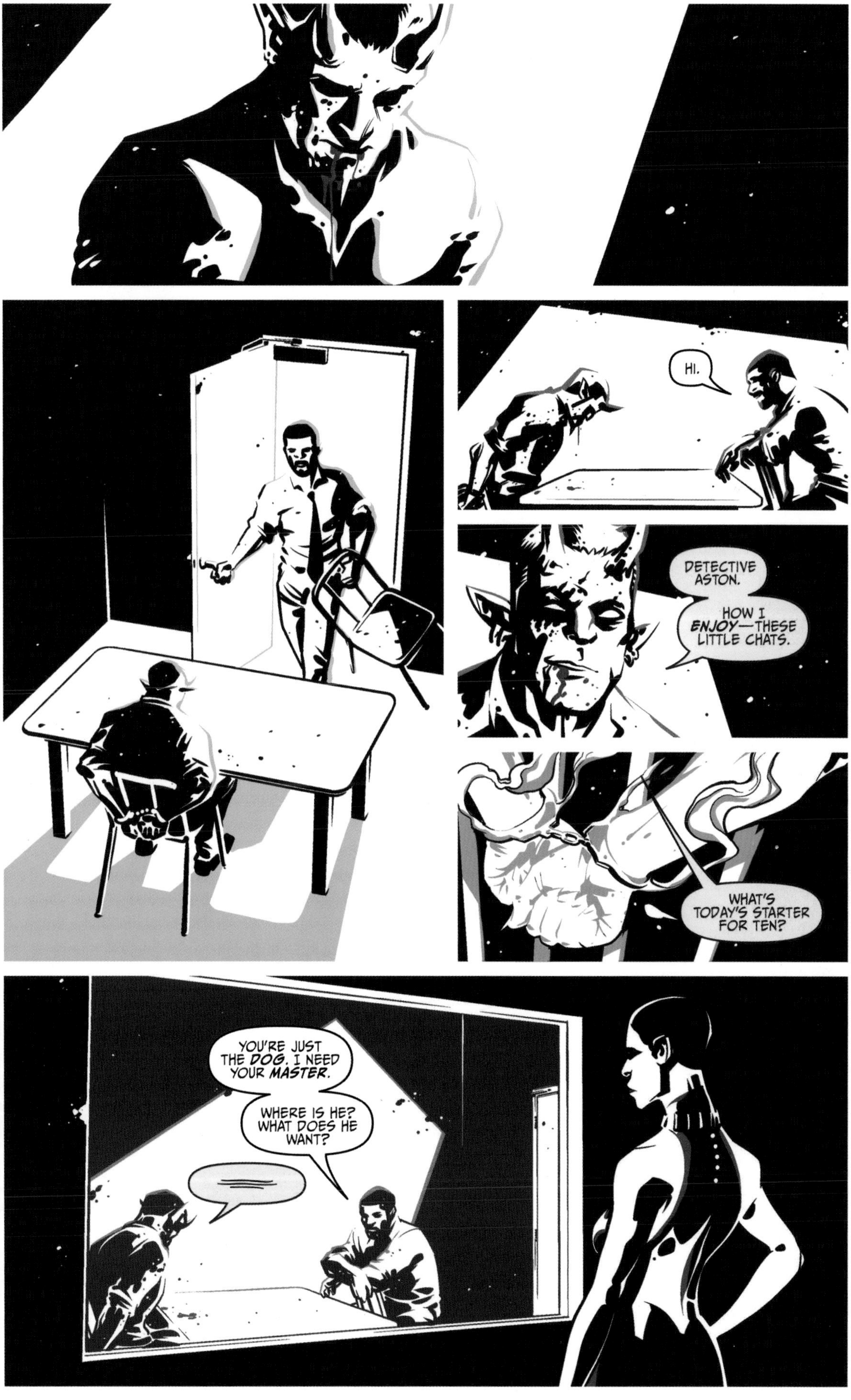
HI.
DETECTIVE ASTON.
HOW I ENJOY—THESE LITTLE CHATS.
WHAT'S TODAY'S STARTER FOR TEN?
YOU'RE JUST THE DOG. I NEED YOUR MASTER.
WHERE IS HE? WHAT DOES HE WANT?

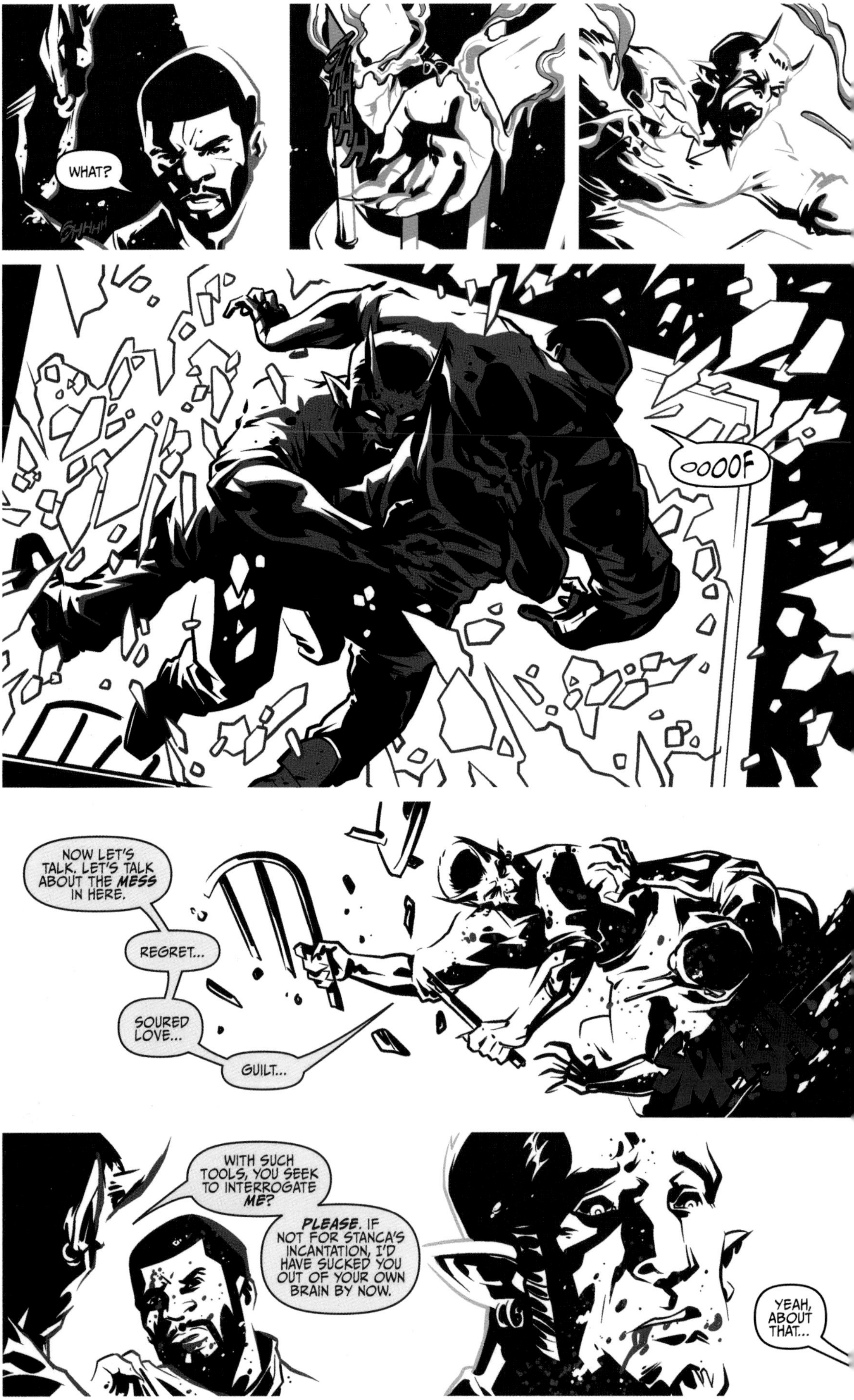
WHAT?
OOOOF
NOW LET'S TALK. LET'S TALK ABOUT THE *MESS* IN HERE.
REGRET...
SOURED LOVE...
GUILT...
WITH SUCH TOOLS, YOU SEEK TO INTERROGATE *ME*?
PLEASE. IF NOT FOR STANCA'S INCANTATION, I'D HAVE SUCKED YOU OUT OF YOUR OWN BRAIN BY NOW.
YEAH, ABOUT THAT...

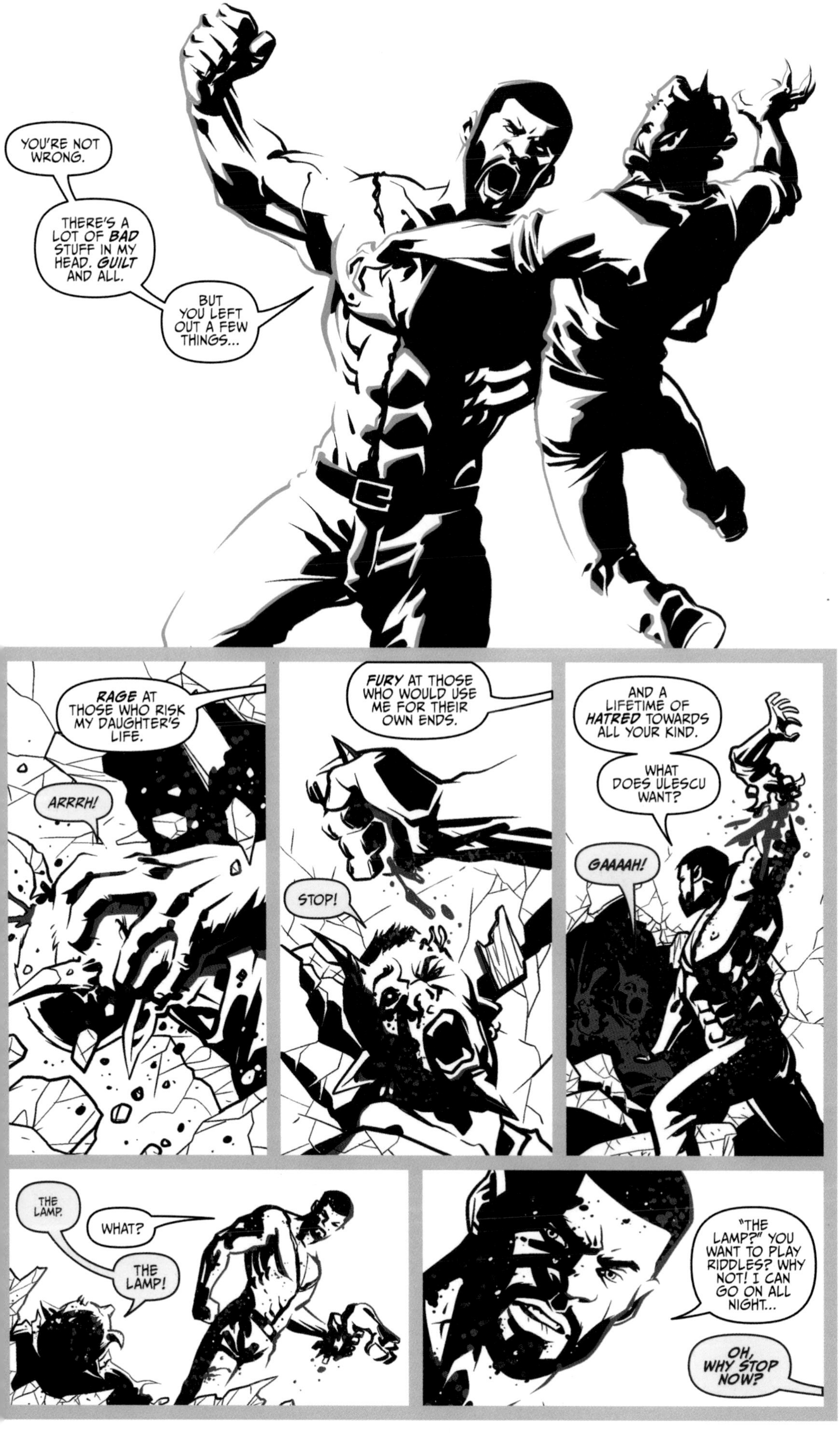

YOU'RE NOT WRONG.
THERE'S A LOT OF BAD STUFF IN MY HEAD. GUILT AND ALL.
BUT YOU LEFT OUT A FEW THINGS...
RAGE AT THOSE WHO RISK MY DAUGHTER'S LIFE.
ARRRH!
FURY AT THOSE WHO WOULD USE ME FOR THEIR OWN ENDS.
STOP!
AND A LIFETIME OF HATRED TOWARDS ALL YOUR KIND.
WHAT DOES ULESCU WANT?
GAAAAH!
THE LAMP.
WHAT?
THE LAMP!
"THE LAMP?" YOU WANT TO PLAY RIDDLES? WHY NOT! I CAN GO ON ALL NIGHT...
OH, WHY STOP NOW?

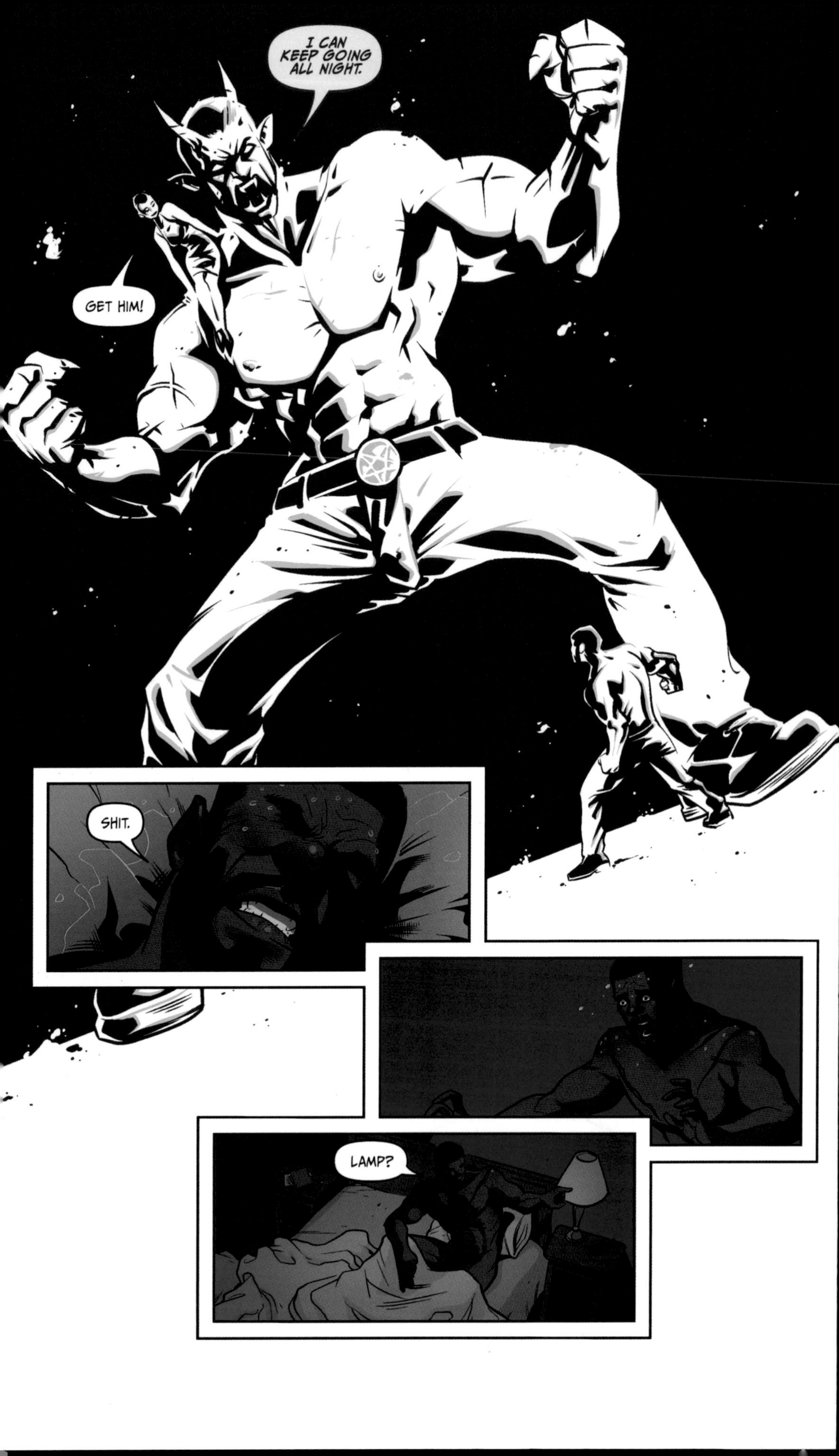
I CAN KEEP GOING ALL NIGHT.
GET HIM!
SHIT.
LAMP?

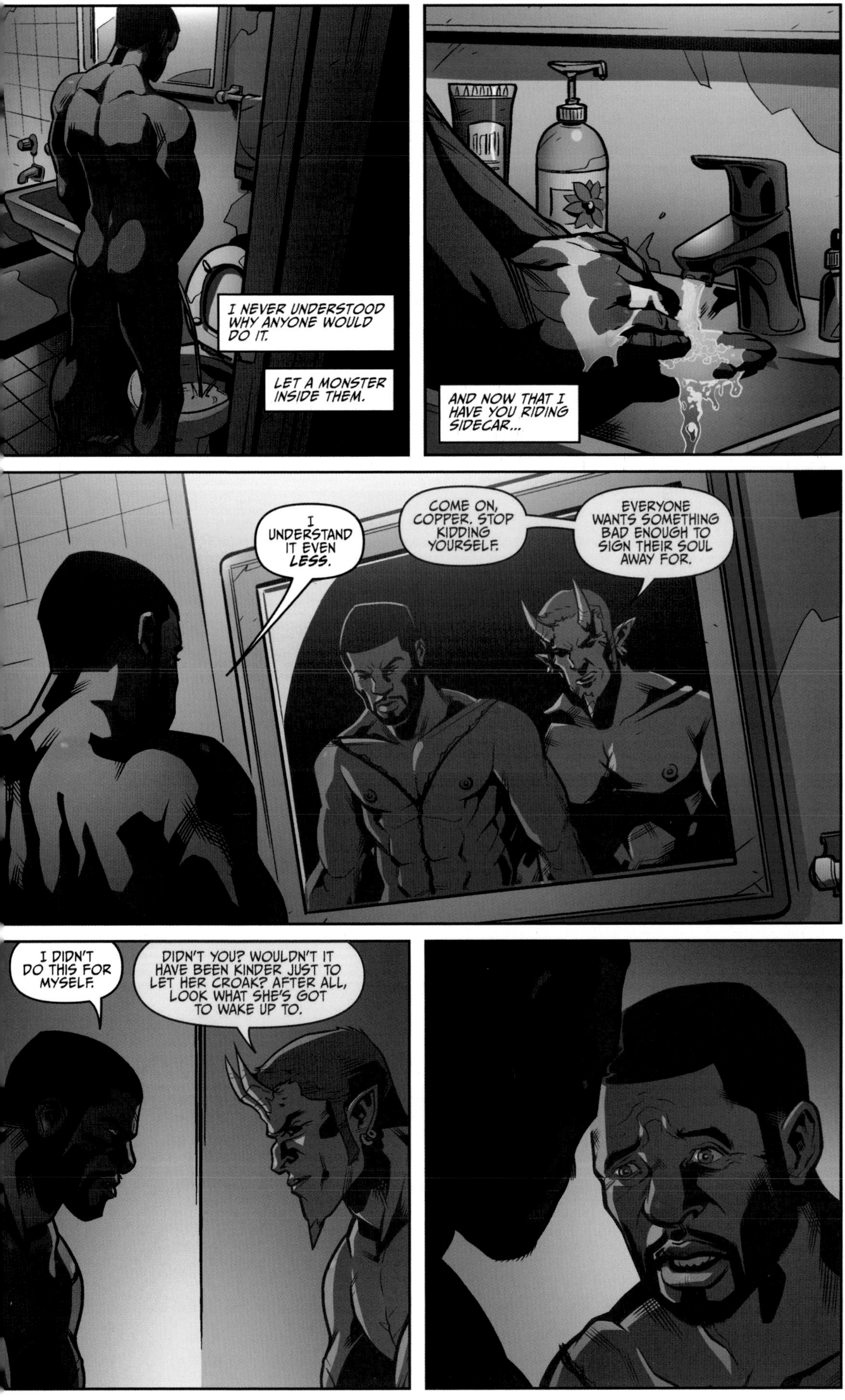
I NEVER UNDERSTOOD WHY ANYONE WOULD DO IT.
LET A MONSTER INSIDE THEM.
AND NOW THAT I HAVE YOU RIDING SIDECAR...
I UNDERSTAND IT EVEN LESS.
COME ON, COPPER. STOP KIDDING YOURSELF.
EVERYONE WANTS SOMETHING BAD ENOUGH TO SIGN THEIR SOUL AWAY FOR.
I DIDN'T DO THIS FOR MYSELF.
DIDN'T YOU? WOULDN'T IT HAVE BEEN KINDER JUST TO LET HER CROAK? AFTER ALL, LOOK WHAT SHE'S GOT TO WAKE UP TO.

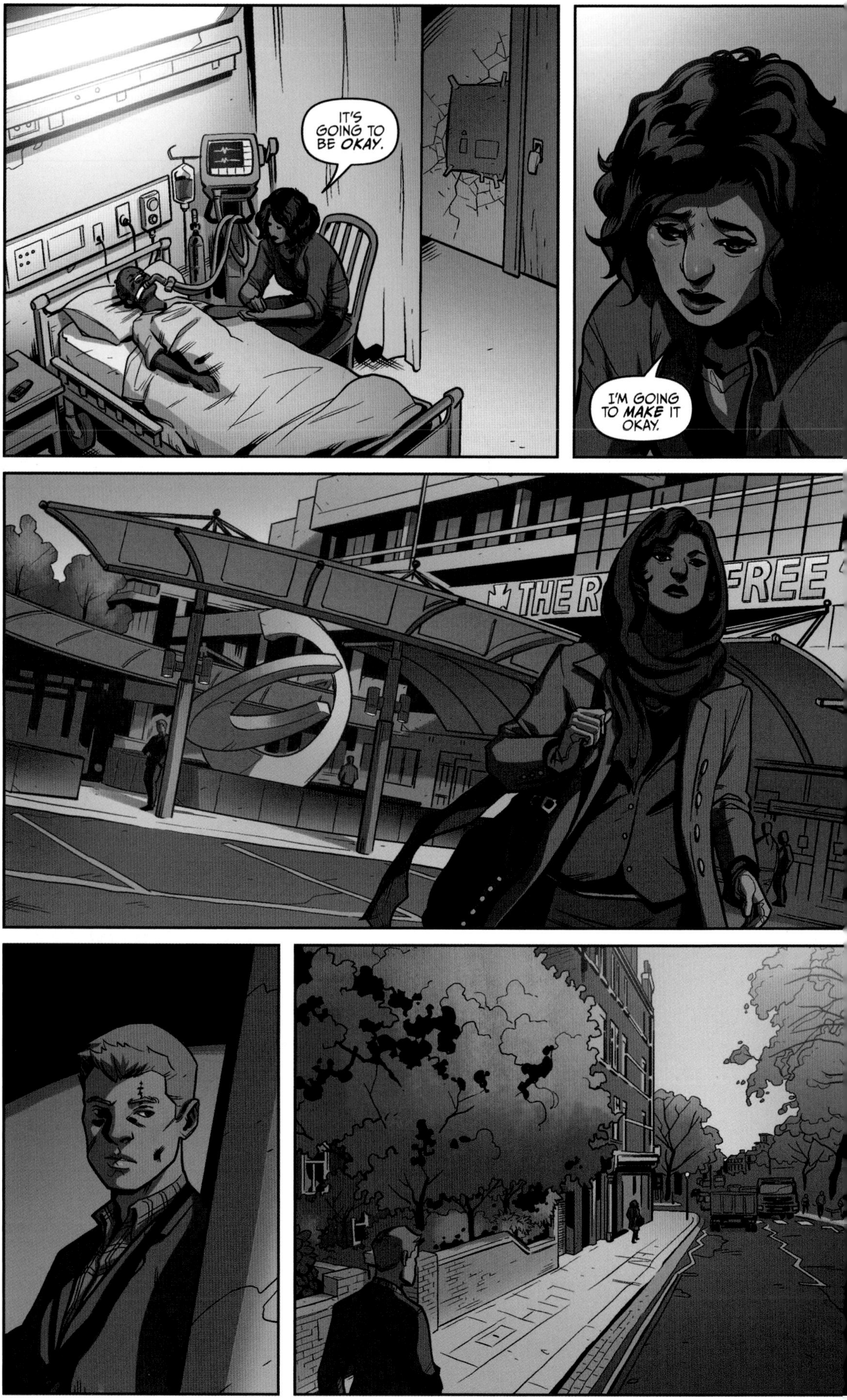
IT'S GOING TO BE OKAY.
I'M GOING TO MAKE IT OKAY.
THE R FREE

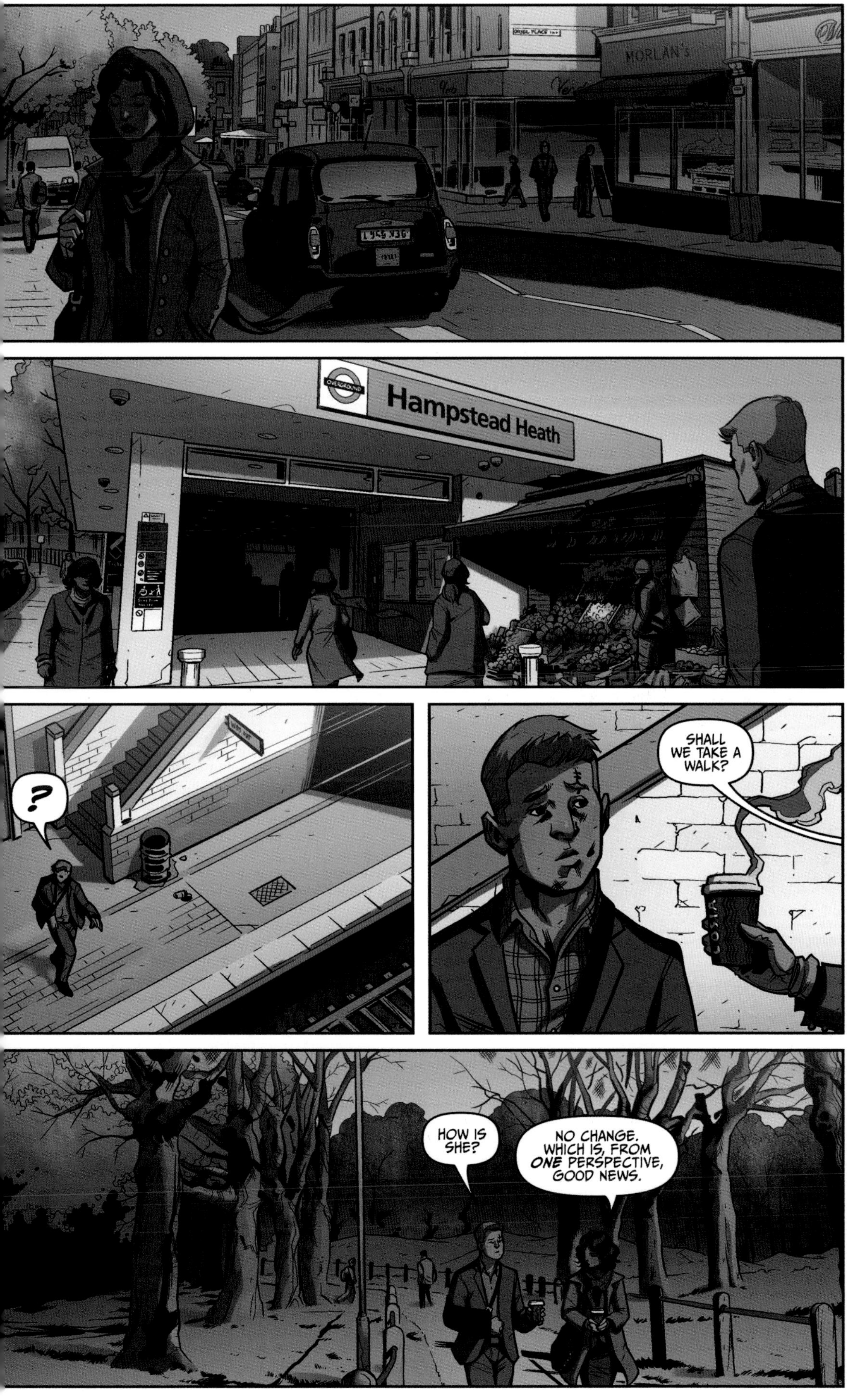
MORLAN's
Hampstead Heath
OVERGROUND
?
SHALL WE TAKE A WALK?
HOW IS SHE?
NO CHANGE. WHICH IS, FROM *ONE* PERSPECTIVE, GOOD NEWS.

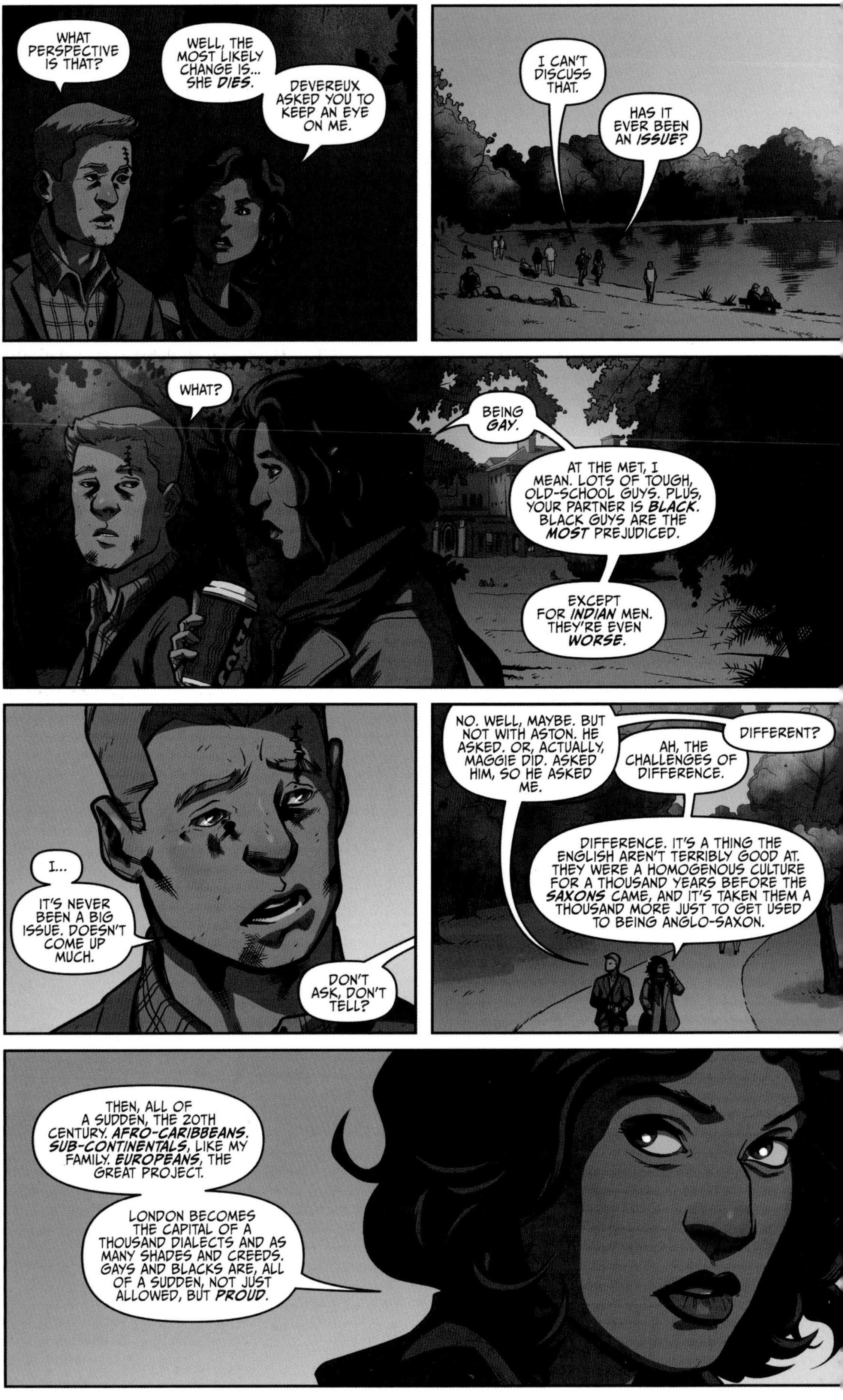
WHAT PERSPECTIVE IS THAT?
WELL, THE MOST LIKELY CHANGE IS... SHE *DIES*.
DEVEREUX ASKED YOU TO KEEP AN EYE ON ME.
I CAN'T DISCUSS THAT.
HAS IT EVER BEEN AN *ISSUE?*
WHAT?
BEING *GAY*.
AT THE MET, I MEAN. LOTS OF TOUGH, OLD-SCHOOL GUYS. PLUS, YOUR PARTNER IS *BLACK*. BLACK GUYS ARE THE *MOST* PREJUDICED.
EXCEPT FOR *INDIAN* MEN. THEY'RE EVEN *WORSE*.
I...
IT'S NEVER BEEN A BIG ISSUE. DOESN'T COME UP MUCH.
DON'T ASK, DON'T TELL?
NO. WELL, MAYBE. BUT NOT WITH ASTON. HE ASKED. OR, ACTUALLY, MAGGIE DID. ASKED HIM, SO HE ASKED ME.
DIFFERENT?
AH, THE CHALLENGES OF DIFFERENCE.
DIFFERENCE. IT'S A THING THE ENGLISH AREN'T TERRIBLY GOOD AT. THEY WERE A HOMOGENOUS CULTURE FOR A THOUSAND YEARS BEFORE THE *SAXONS* CAME, AND IT'S TAKEN THEM A THOUSAND MORE JUST TO GET USED TO BEING ANGLO-SAXON.
THEN, ALL OF A SUDDEN, THE 20TH CENTURY. *AFRO-CARIBBEANS*. *SUB-CONTINENTALS*, LIKE MY FAMILY. *EUROPEANS*, THE GREAT PROJECT.
LONDON BECOMES THE CAPITAL OF A THOUSAND DIALECTS AND AS MANY SHADES AND CREEDS. GAYS AND BLACKS ARE, ALL OF A SUDDEN, NOT JUST ALLOWED, BUT *PROUD*.

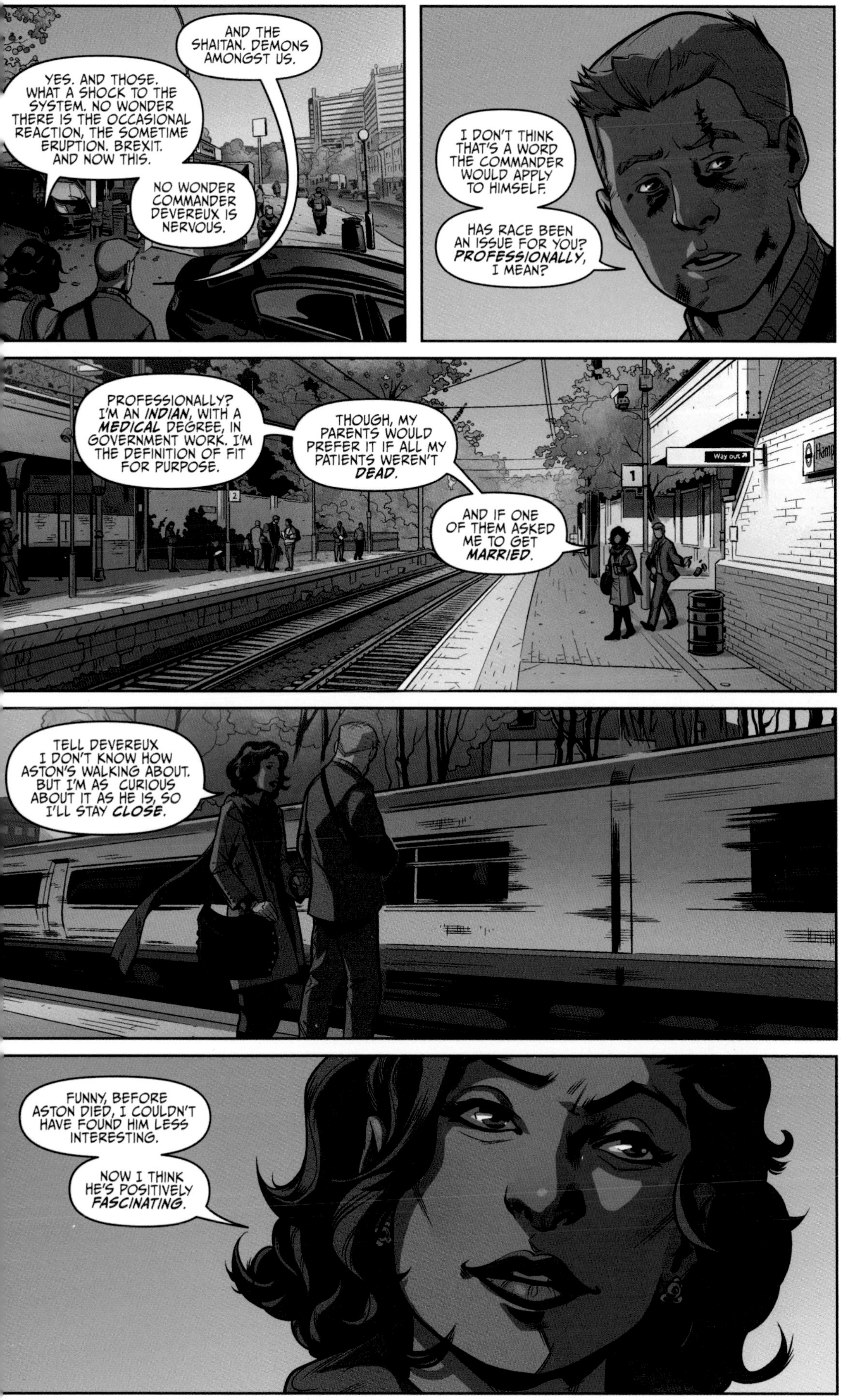
YES. AND THOSE. WHAT A SHOCK TO THE SYSTEM. NO WONDER THERE IS THE OCCASIONAL REACTION, THE SOMETIME ERUPTION. BREXIT. AND NOW THIS.
AND THE SHAITAN. DEMONS AMONGST US.
NO WONDER COMMANDER DEVEREUX IS NERVOUS.
I DON'T THINK THAT'S A WORD THE COMMANDER WOULD APPLY TO HIMSELF.
HAS RACE BEEN AN ISSUE FOR YOU? PROFESSIONALLY, I MEAN?
PROFESSIONALLY? I'M AN INDIAN, WITH A MEDICAL DEGREE, IN GOVERNMENT WORK. I'M THE DEFINITION OF FIT FOR PURPOSE.
THOUGH, MY PARENTS WOULD PREFER IT IF ALL MY PATIENTS WEREN'T DEAD.
AND IF ONE OF THEM ASKED ME TO GET MARRIED.
2
1
Way out
TELL DEVEREUX I DON'T KNOW HOW ASTON'S WALKING ABOUT. BUT I'M AS CURIOUS ABOUT IT AS HE IS, SO I'LL STAY CLOSE.
FUNNY, BEFORE ASTON DIED, I COULDN'T HAVE FOUND HIM LESS INTERESTING.
NOW I THINK HE'S POSITIVELY FASCINATING.

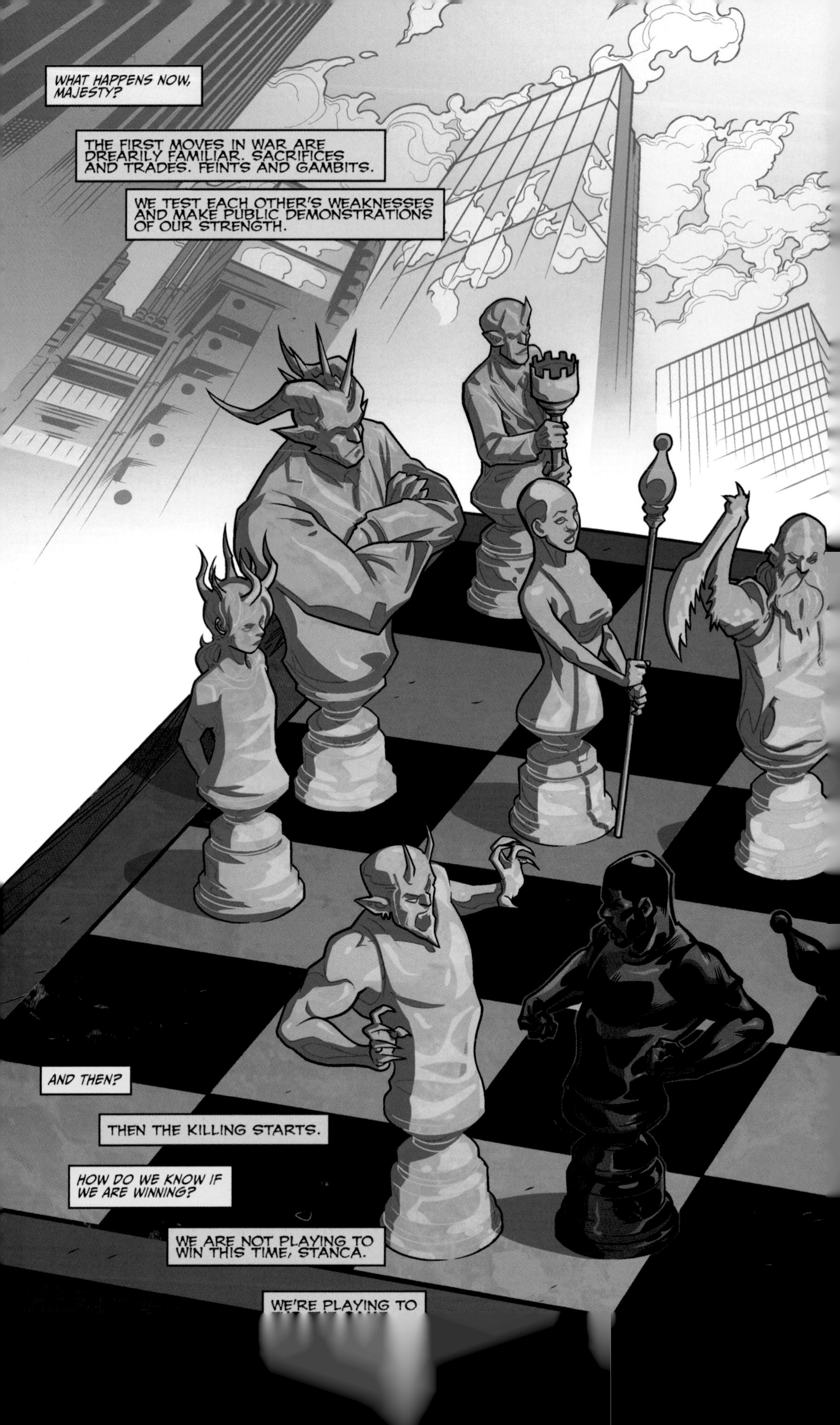
WHAT HAPPENS NOW, MAJESTY?
THE FIRST MOVES IN WAR ARE DREARILY FAMILIAR. SACRIFICES AND TRADES. FEINTS AND GAMBITS.
WE TEST EACH OTHER'S WEAKNESSES AND MAKE PUBLIC DEMONSTRATIONS OF OUR STRENGTH.
AND THEN?
THEN THE KILLING STARTS.
HOW DO WE KNOW IF WE ARE WINNING?
WE ARE NOT PLAYING TO WIN THIS TIME, STANCA.
WE'RE PLAYING TO

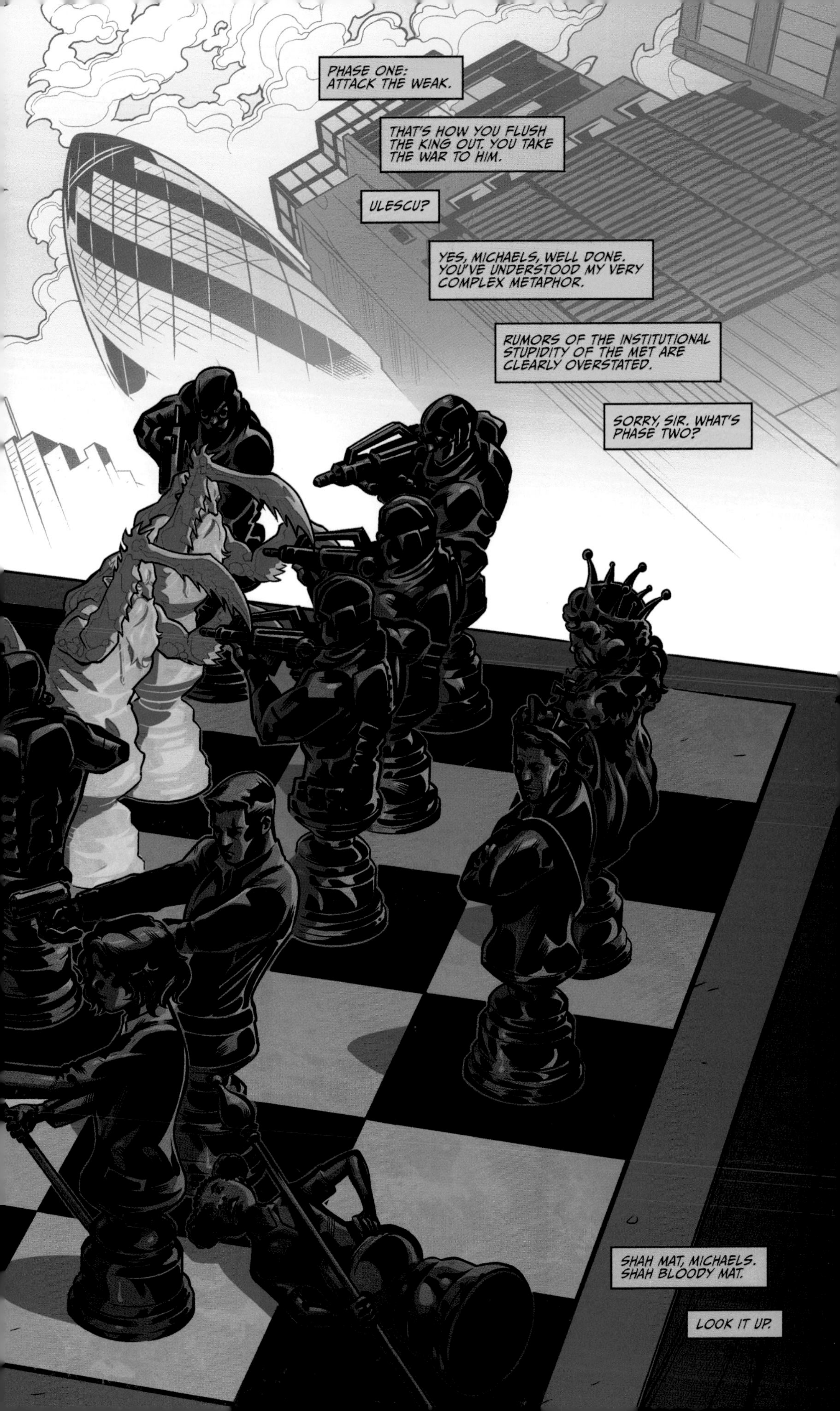
PHASE ONE: ATTACK THE WEAK.
THAT'S HOW YOU FLUSH THE KING OUT. YOU TAKE THE WAR TO HIM.
ULESCU?
YES, MICHAELS, WELL DONE. YOU'VE UNDERSTOOD MY VERY COMPLEX METAPHOR.
RUMORS OF THE INSTITUTIONAL STUPIDITY OF THE MET ARE CLEARLY OVERSTATED.
SORRY, SIR. WHAT'S PHASE TWO?
SHAH MAT, MICHAELS. SHAH BLOODY MAT.
LOOK IT UP.

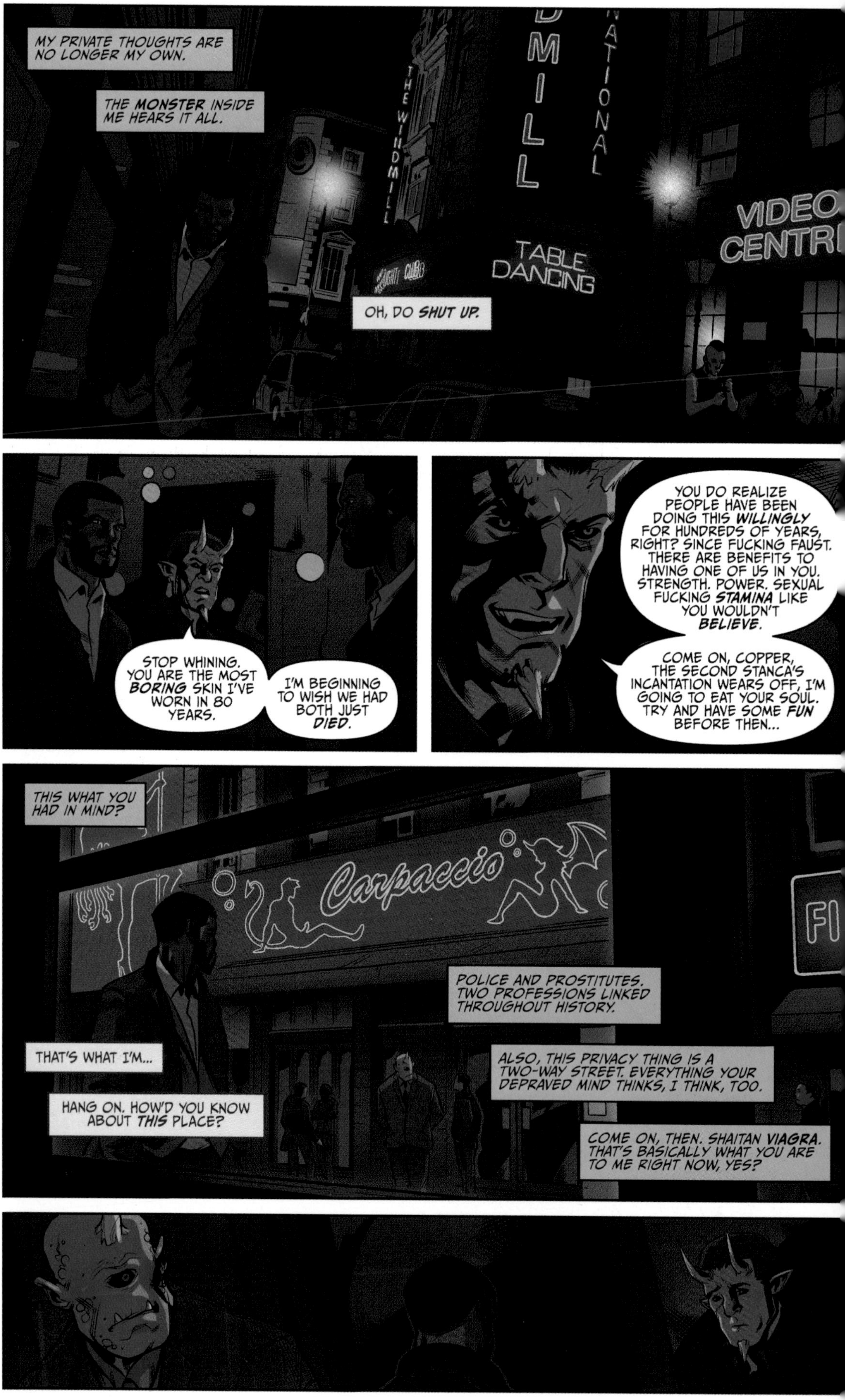

MY PRIVATE THOUGHTS ARE NO LONGER MY OWN.
THE MONSTER INSIDE ME HEARS IT ALL.
THE WINDMILL
INTERNATIONAL
TABLE DANCING
VIDEO CENTRE
OH, DO SHUT UP.
STOP WHINING. YOU ARE THE MOST BORING SKIN I'VE WORN IN 80 YEARS.
I'M BEGINNING TO WISH WE HAD BOTH JUST DIED.
YOU DO REALIZE PEOPLE HAVE BEEN DOING THIS WILLINGLY FOR HUNDREDS OF YEARS, RIGHT? SINCE FUCKING FAUST. THERE ARE BENEFITS TO HAVING ONE OF US IN YOU. STRENGTH. POWER. SEXUAL FUCKING STAMINA LIKE YOU WOULDN'T BELIEVE.
COME ON, COPPER, THE SECOND STANCA'S INCANTATION WEARS OFF, I'M GOING TO EAT YOUR SOUL. TRY AND HAVE SOME FUN BEFORE THEN...
THIS WHAT YOU HAD IN MIND?
Carpaccio
POLICE AND PROSTITUTES. TWO PROFESSIONS LINKED THROUGHOUT HISTORY.
THAT'S WHAT I'M...
HANG ON. HOW'D YOU KNOW ABOUT THIS PLACE?
ALSO, THIS PRIVACY THING IS A TWO-WAY STREET. EVERYTHING YOUR DEPRAVED MIND THINKS, I THINK, TOO.
COME ON, THEN. SHAITAN VIAGRA. THAT'S BASICALLY WHAT YOU ARE TO ME RIGHT NOW, YES?

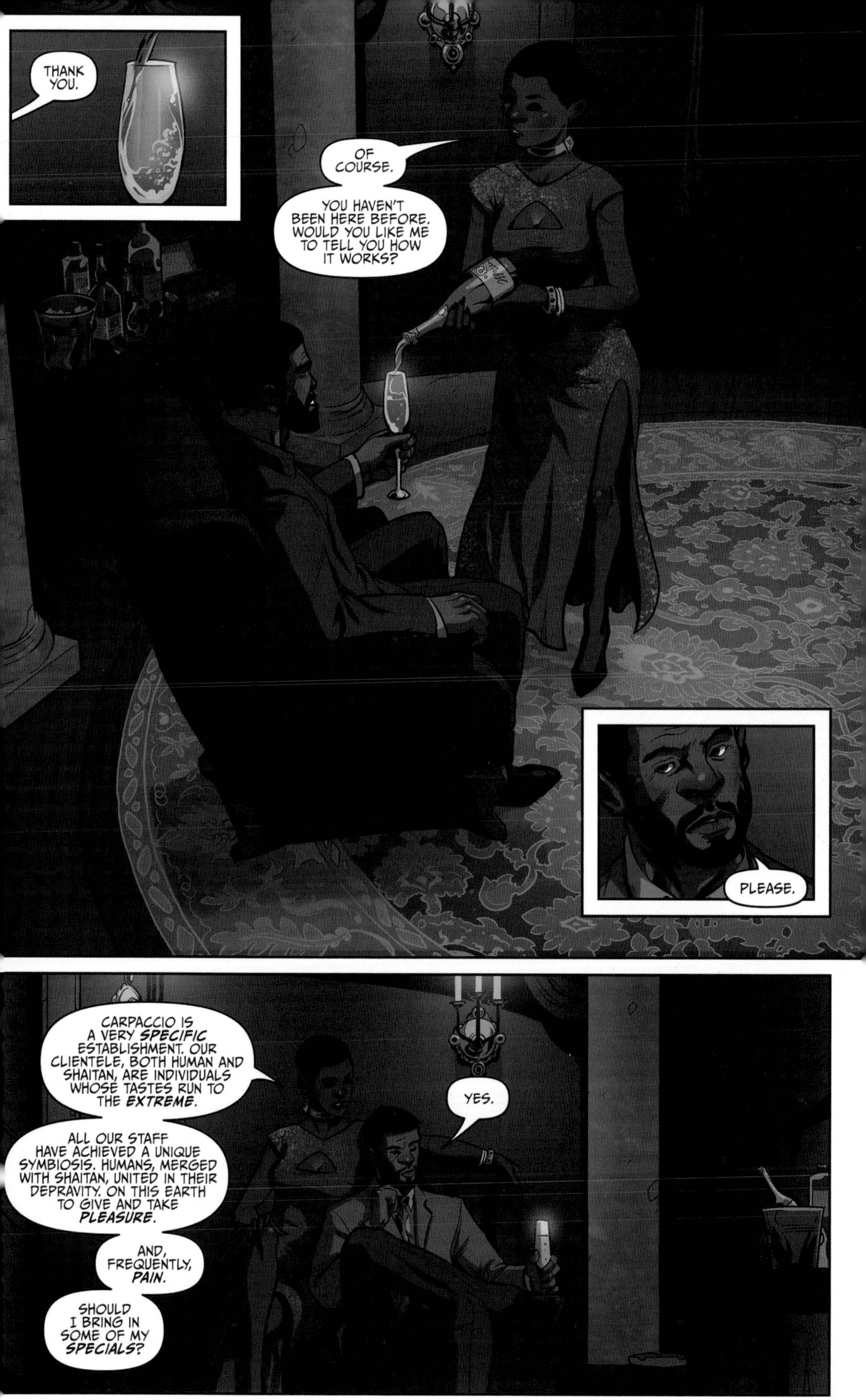
THANK YOU.
OF COURSE.
YOU HAVEN'T BEEN HERE BEFORE. WOULD YOU LIKE ME TO TELL YOU HOW IT WORKS?
PLEASE.
CARPACCIO IS A VERY SPECIFIC ESTABLISHMENT. OUR CLIENTELE, BOTH HUMAN AND SHAITAN, ARE INDIVIDUALS WHOSE TASTES RUN TO THE EXTREME.
YES.
ALL OUR STAFF HAVE ACHIEVED A UNIQUE SYMBIOSIS. HUMANS, MERGED WITH SHAITAN, UNITED IN THEIR DEPRAVITY. ON THIS EARTH TO GIVE AND TAKE PLEASURE.
AND, FREQUENTLY, PAIN.
SHOULD I BRING IN SOME OF MY SPECIALS?

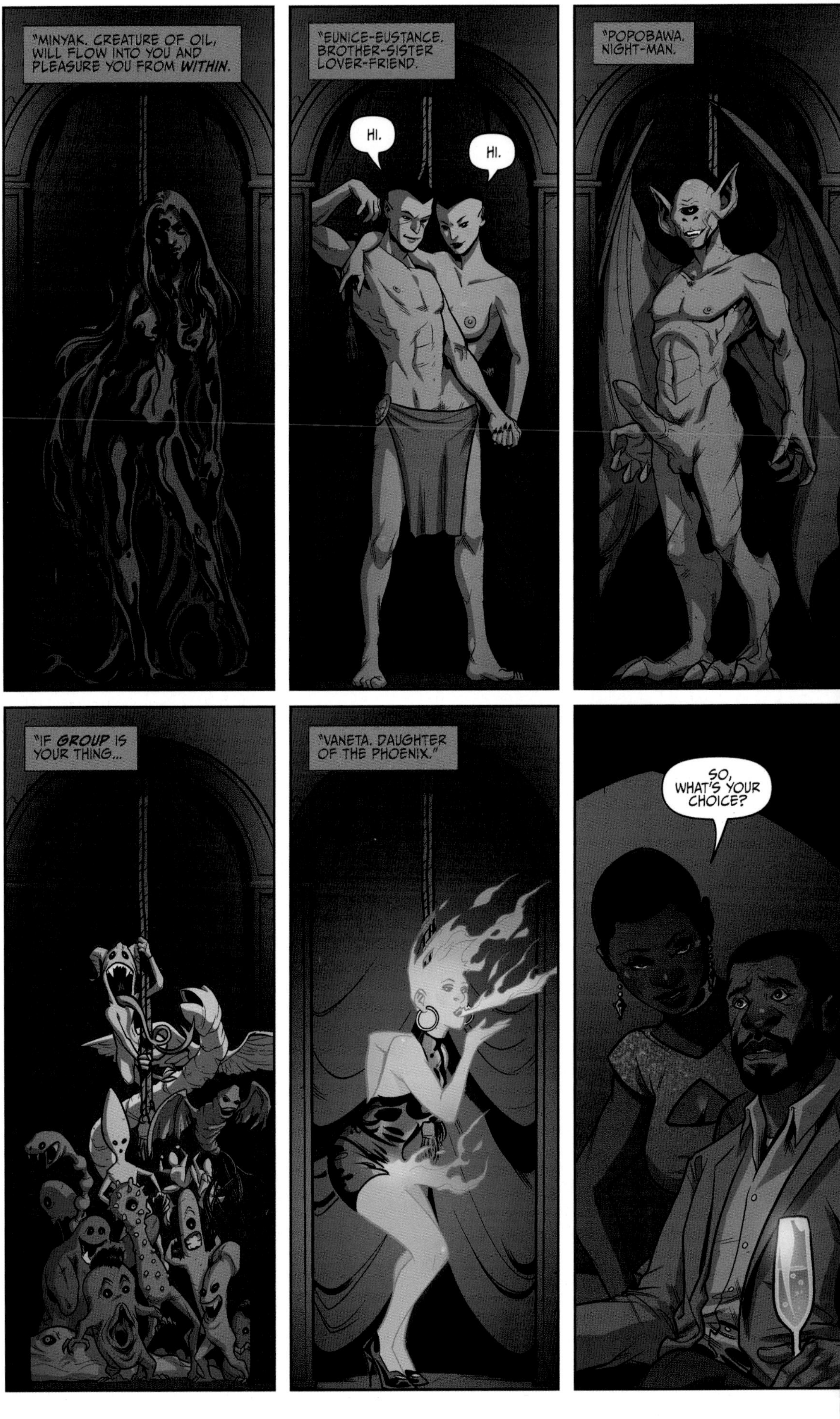
"MINYAK. CREATURE OF OIL, WILL FLOW INTO YOU AND PLEASURE YOU FROM WITHIN.
"EUNICE-EUSTANCE. BROTHER-SISTER LOVER-FRIEND.
HI.
HI.
"POPOBAWA. NIGHT-MAN.
"IF GROUP IS YOUR THING...
"VANETA. DAUGHTER OF THE PHOENIX."
SO, WHAT'S YOUR CHOICE?

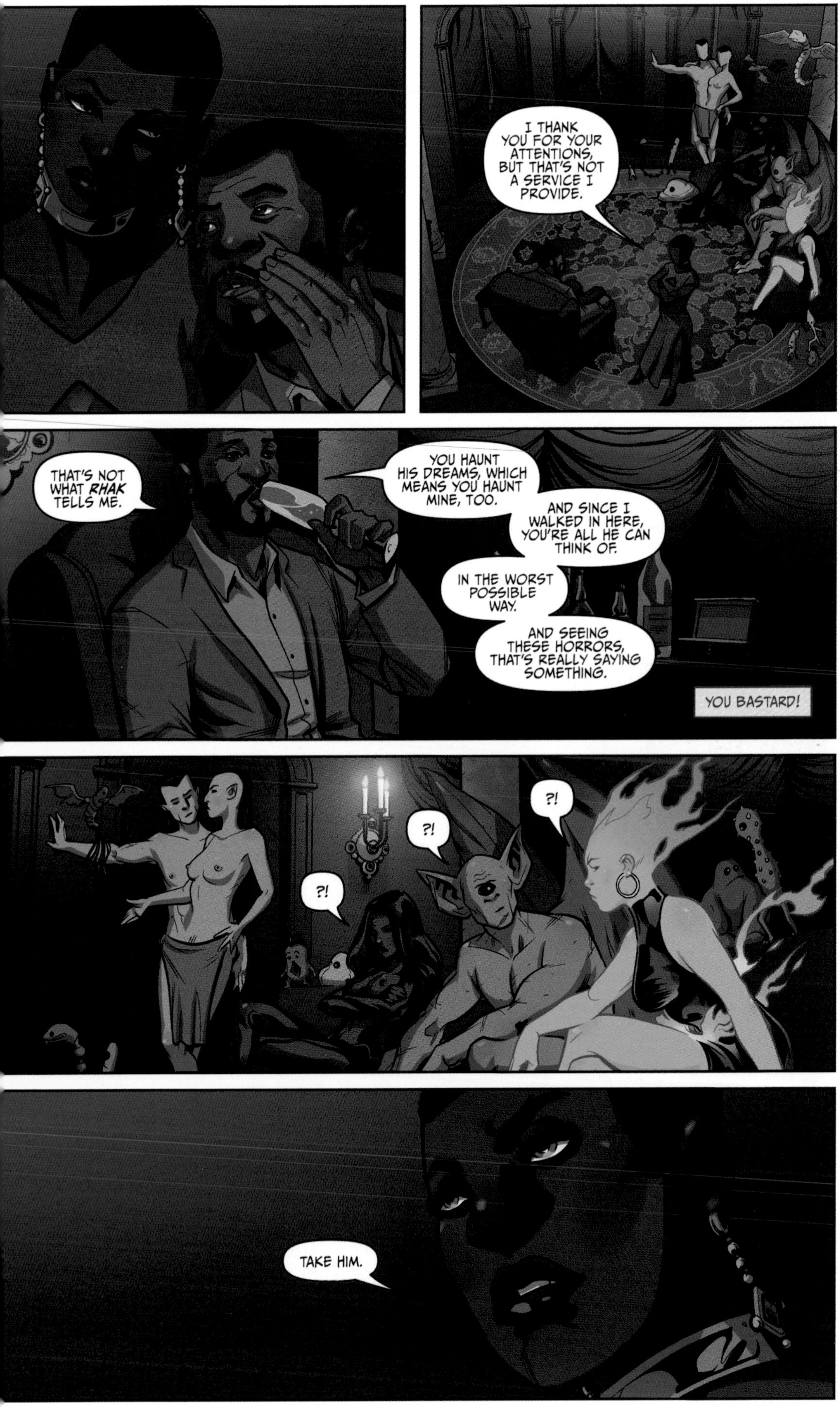
I THANK YOU FOR YOUR ATTENTIONS, BUT THAT'S NOT A SERVICE I PROVIDE.
THAT'S NOT WHAT *RHAK* TELLS ME.
YOU HAUNT HIS DREAMS, WHICH MEANS YOU HAUNT MINE, TOO.
AND SINCE I WALKED IN HERE, YOU'RE ALL HE CAN THINK OF.
IN THE WORST POSSIBLE WAY.
AND SEEING THESE HORRORS, THAT'S REALLY SAYING SOMETHING.
YOU BASTARD!
?!
?!
?!
TAKE HIM.

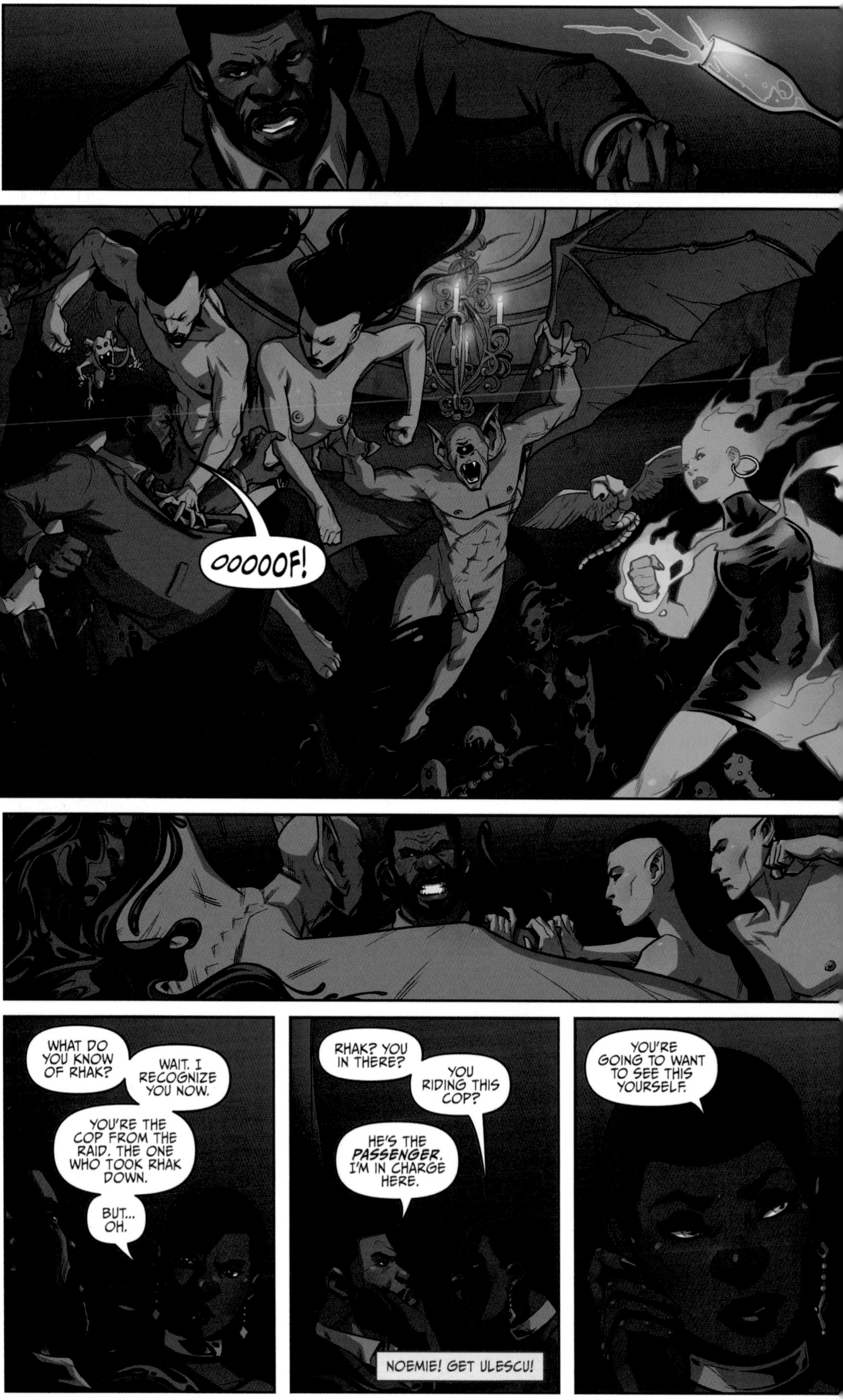
OOOOOF!
WHAT DO YOU KNOW OF RHAK?
WAIT. I RECOGNIZE YOU NOW.
YOU'RE THE COP FROM THE RAID. THE ONE WHO TOOK RHAK DOWN.
BUT... OH.
RHAK? YOU IN THERE?
YOU RIDING THIS COP?
HE'S THE *PASSENGER*. I'M IN CHARGE HERE.
NOEMIE! GET ULESCU!
YOU'RE GOING TO WANT TO SEE THIS YOURSELF.

NATHAN *ULESCU.*

FORMALLY KNOWN AS NATHAN *BLADE.*

I'M ARRESTING YOU UNDER THE SHAITAN CONTROL ACT OF 2003 ON *THREE* COUNTS OF TERRORISM, *SEVEN* COUNTS OF MURDER, *ONE* COUNT OF ATTEMPTED MURDER...

ON SOME LEVEL, I SHOULD *THANK YOU.* YOU'VE KEPT RHAK ALIVE.

HE IS *DEAR* TO ME. *MILLENNIA* OF ASSOCIATION WILL DO THAT.

HOWEVER, YOU'VE ALSO, BY SOME MEANS UNCLEAR TO ME, BECOME HIS *PRISON.*

THAT ISN'T *ACCEPTABLE.*

THE SYMBIOSIS BETWEEN SHAITAN AND HUMAN IS... *DELICATE.*

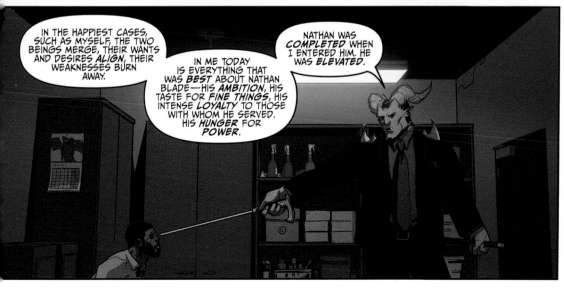

IN THE HAPPIEST CASES, SUCH AS MYSELF, THE TWO BEINGS MERGE, THEIR WANTS AND DESIRES *ALIGN,* THEIR WEAKNESSES BURN AWAY.

IN ME TODAY IS EVERYTHING THAT WAS *BEST* ABOUT NATHAN BLADE—HIS *AMBITION,* HIS TASTE FOR *FINE THINGS,* HIS INTENSE *LOYALTY* TO THOSE WITH WHOM HE SERVED. HIS *HUNGER* FOR *POWER.*

NATHAN WAS *COMPLETED* WHEN I ENTERED HIM. HE WAS *ELEVATED.*

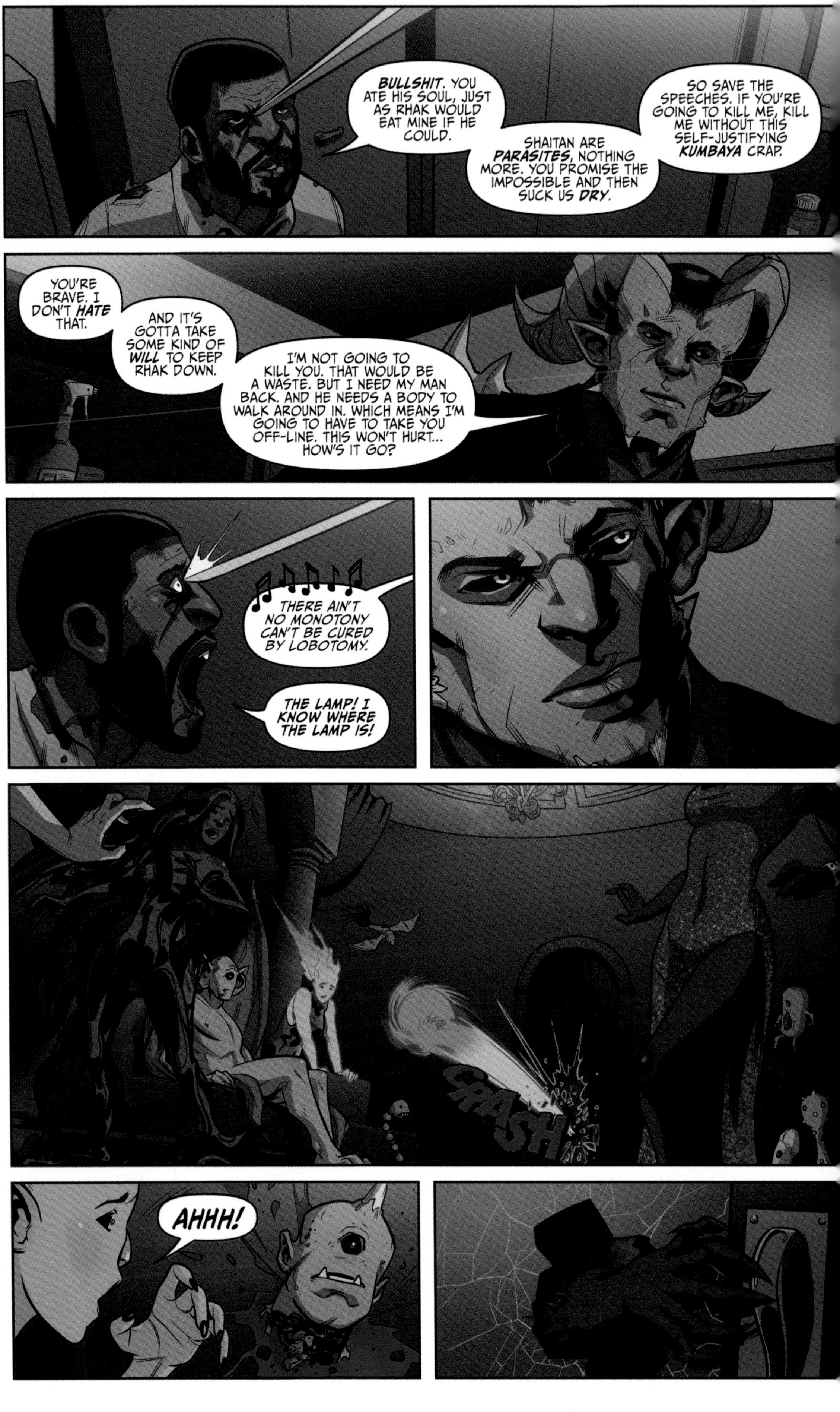

BULLSHIT. YOU ATE HIS SOUL, JUST AS RHAK WOULD EAT MINE IF HE COULD.
SHAITAN ARE **PARASITES**, NOTHING MORE. YOU PROMISE THE IMPOSSIBLE AND THEN SUCK US **DRY**.
SO SAVE THE SPEECHES. IF YOU'RE GOING TO KILL ME, KILL ME WITHOUT THIS SELF-JUSTIFYING **KUMBAYA** CRAP.
YOU'RE BRAVE. I DON'T **HATE** THAT.
AND IT'S GOTTA TAKE SOME KIND OF **WILL** TO KEEP RHAK DOWN.
I'M NOT GOING TO KILL YOU. THAT WOULD BE A WASTE. BUT I NEED MY MAN BACK. AND HE NEEDS A BODY TO WALK AROUND IN. WHICH MEANS I'M GOING TO HAVE TO TAKE YOU OFF-LINE. THIS WON'T HURT... HOW'S IT GO?
THERE AIN'T NO MONOTONY CAN'T BE CURED BY LOBOTOMY.
THE LAMP! I KNOW WHERE THE LAMP IS!
CRASH
AHHH!

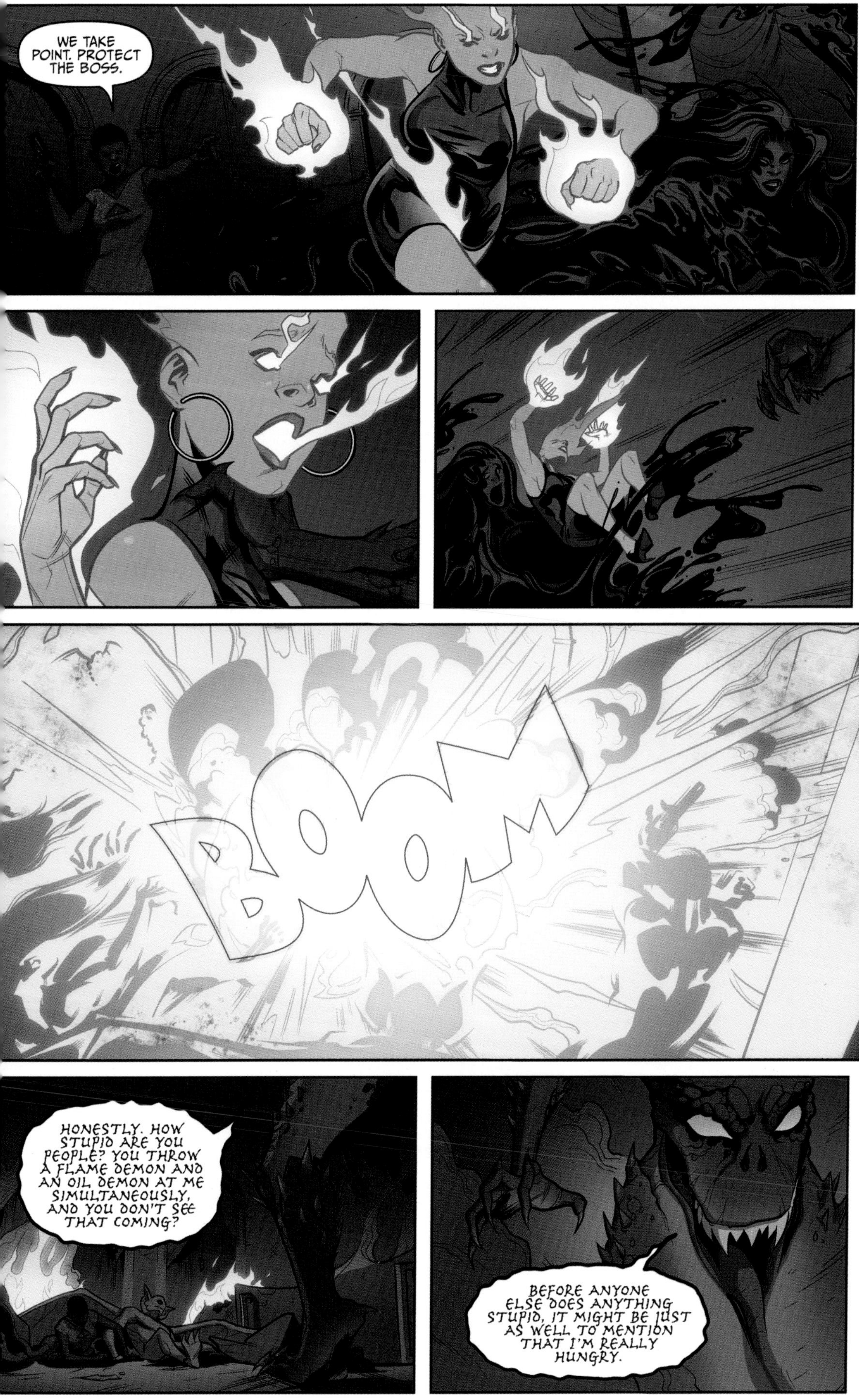
WE TAKE POINT. PROTECT THE BOSS.
BOOM
HONESTLY. HOW STUPID ARE YOU PEOPLE? YOU THROW A FLAME DEMON AND AN OIL DEMON AT ME SIMULTANEOUSLY, AND YOU DON'T SEE THAT COMING?
BEFORE ANYONE ELSE DOES ANYTHING STUPID, IT MIGHT BE JUST AS WELL TO MENTION THAT I'M REALLY HUNGRY.

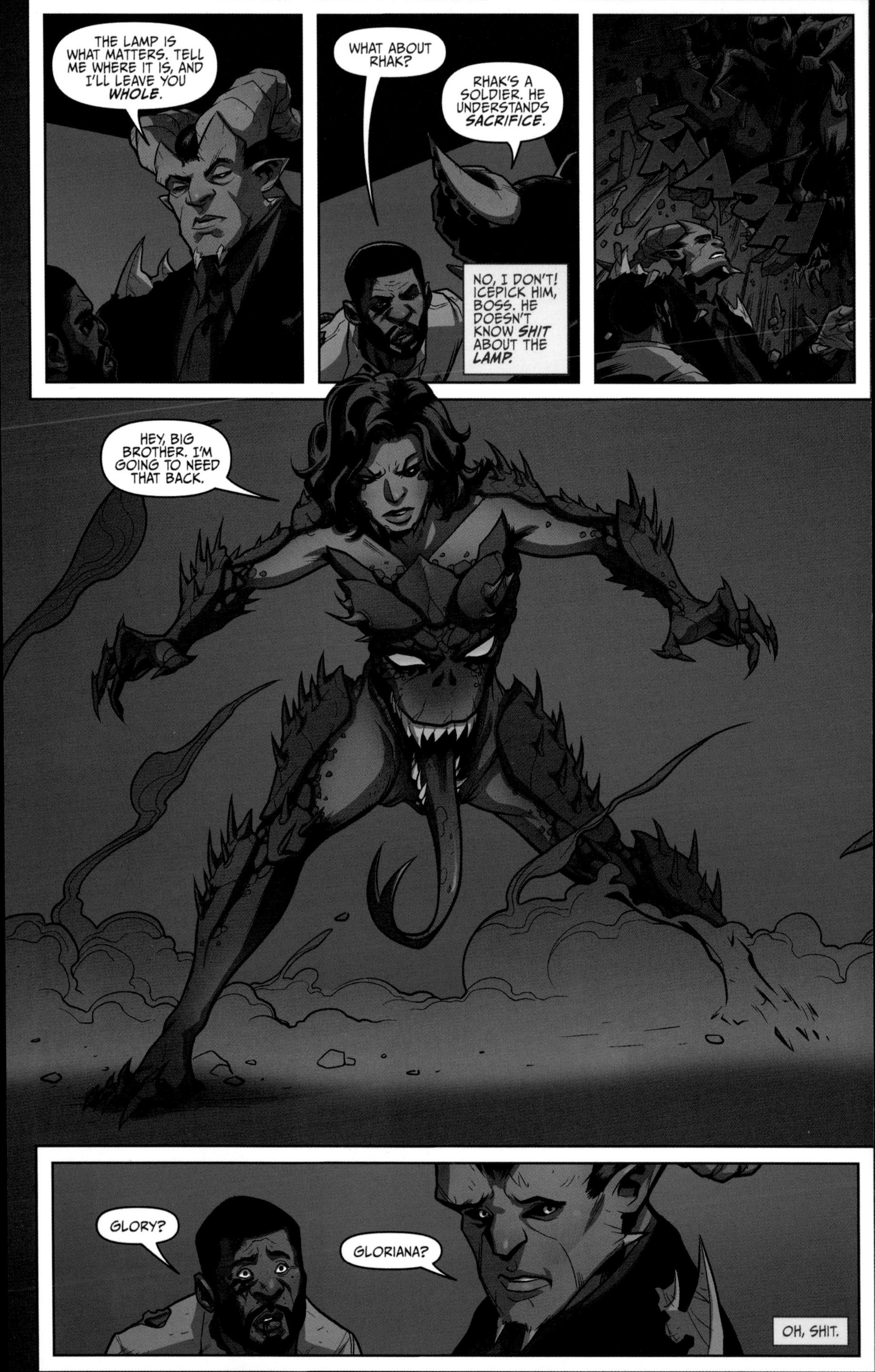
THE LAMP IS WHAT MATTERS. TELL ME WHERE IT IS, AND I'LL LEAVE YOU WHOLE.
WHAT ABOUT RHAK?
RHAK'S A SOLDIER. HE UNDERSTANDS SACRIFICE.
NO, I DON'T! ICEPICK HIM, BOSS. HE DOESN'T KNOW SHIT ABOUT THE LAMP.
SMASH
HEY, BIG BROTHER. I'M GOING TO NEED THAT BACK.
GLORY?
GLORIANA?
OH, SHIT.

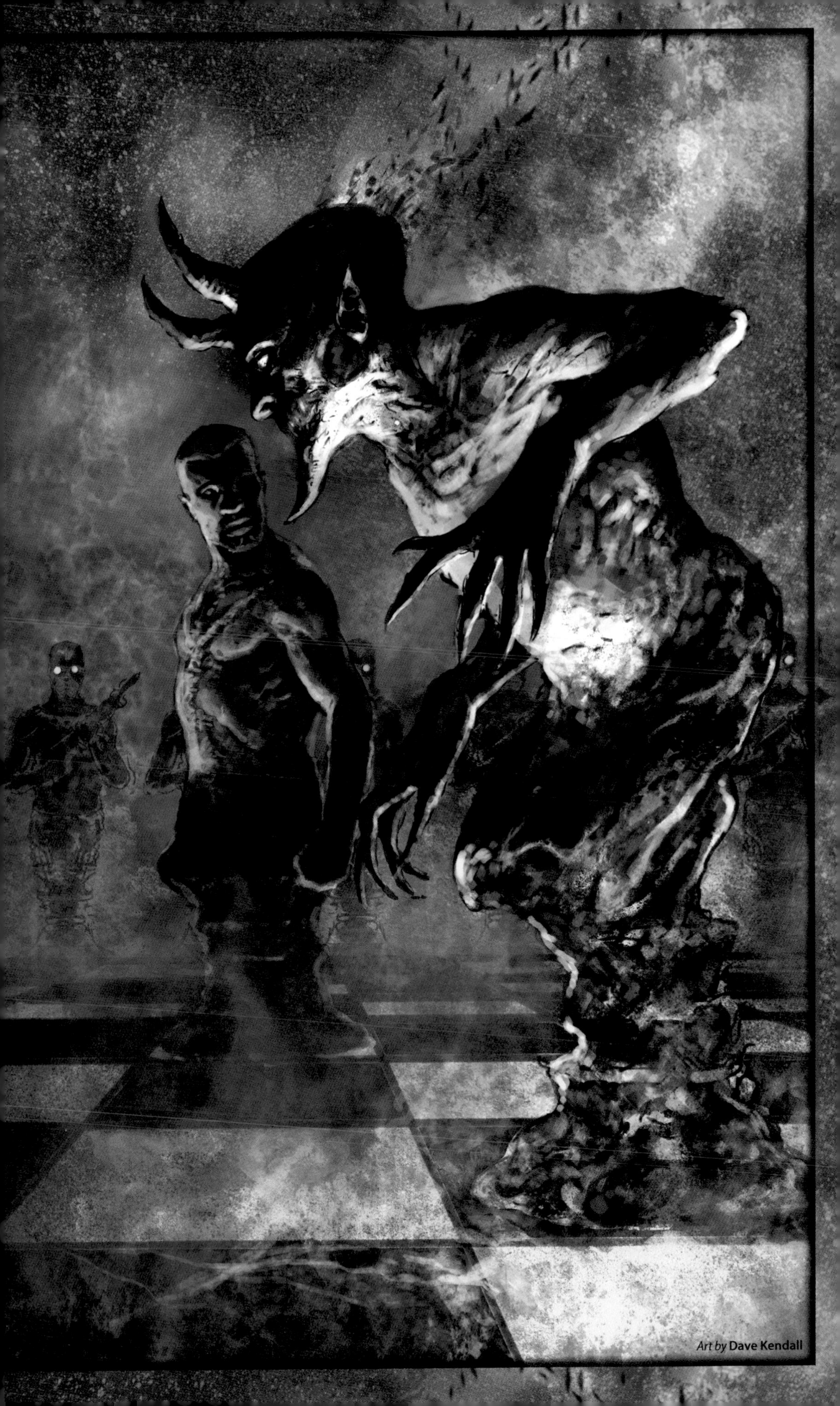
Art by Dave Kendall

Chapter 5
The Bastard Truth

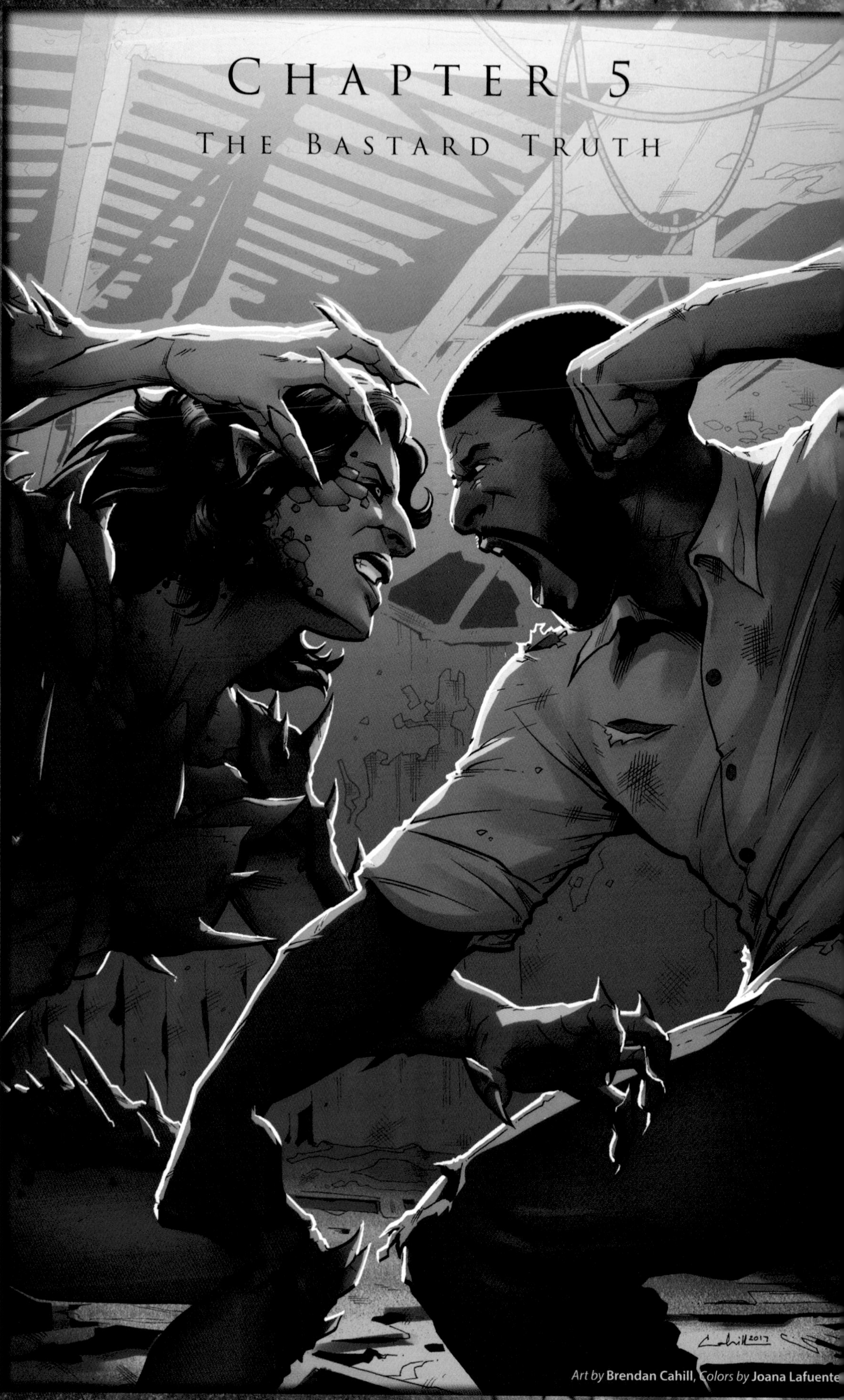

Art by **Brendan Cahill**, *Colors by* **Joana Lafuente**

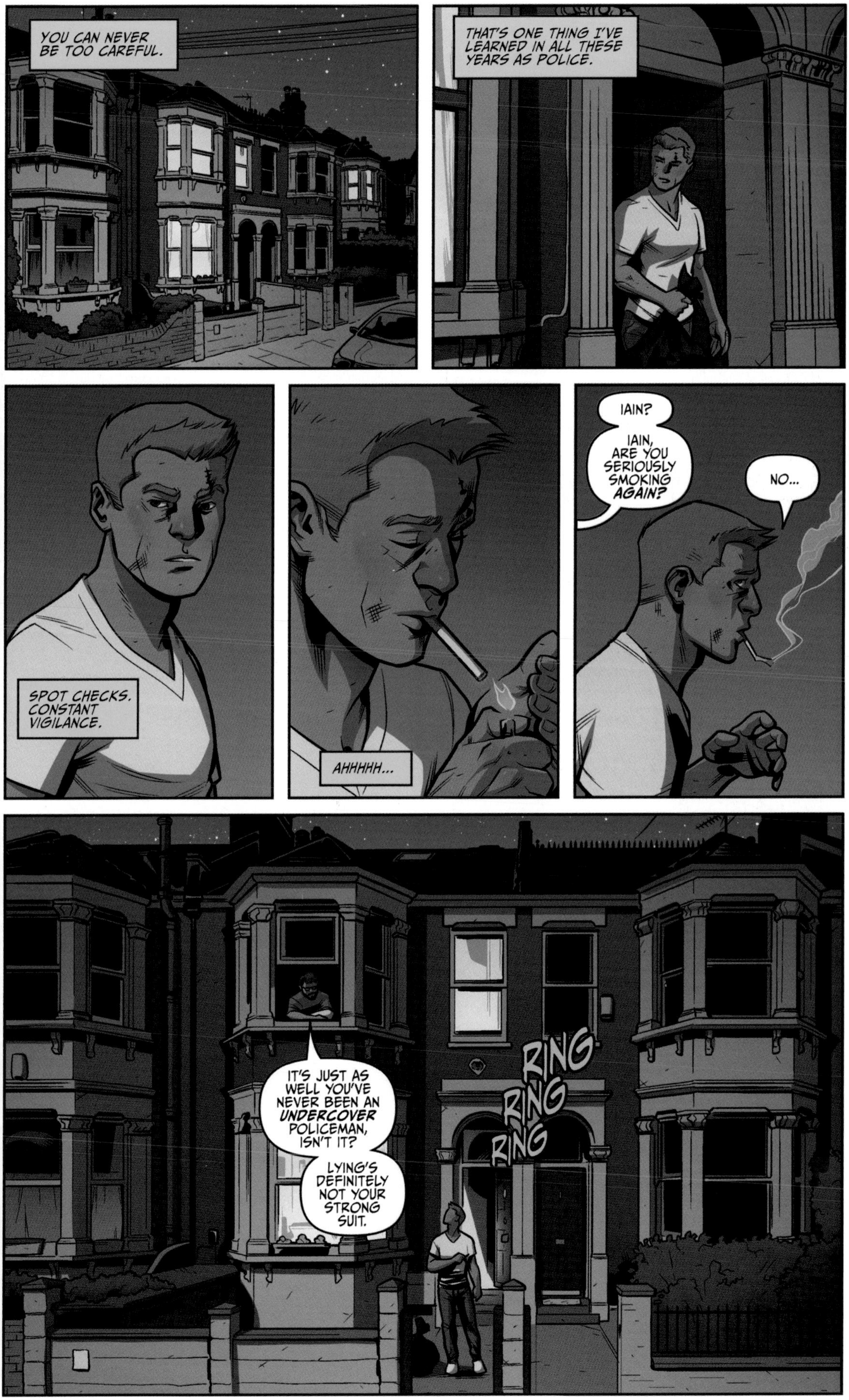
YOU CAN NEVER BE TOO CAREFUL.
THAT'S ONE THING I'VE LEARNED IN ALL THESE YEARS AS POLICE.
SPOT CHECKS. CONSTANT VIGILANCE.
AHHHHH...
IAIN?
IAIN, ARE YOU SERIOUSLY SMOKING AGAIN?
NO...
IT'S JUST AS WELL YOU'VE NEVER BEEN AN UNDERCOVER POLICEMAN, ISN'T IT?
LYING'S DEFINITELY NOT YOUR STRONG SUIT.
RING RING RING

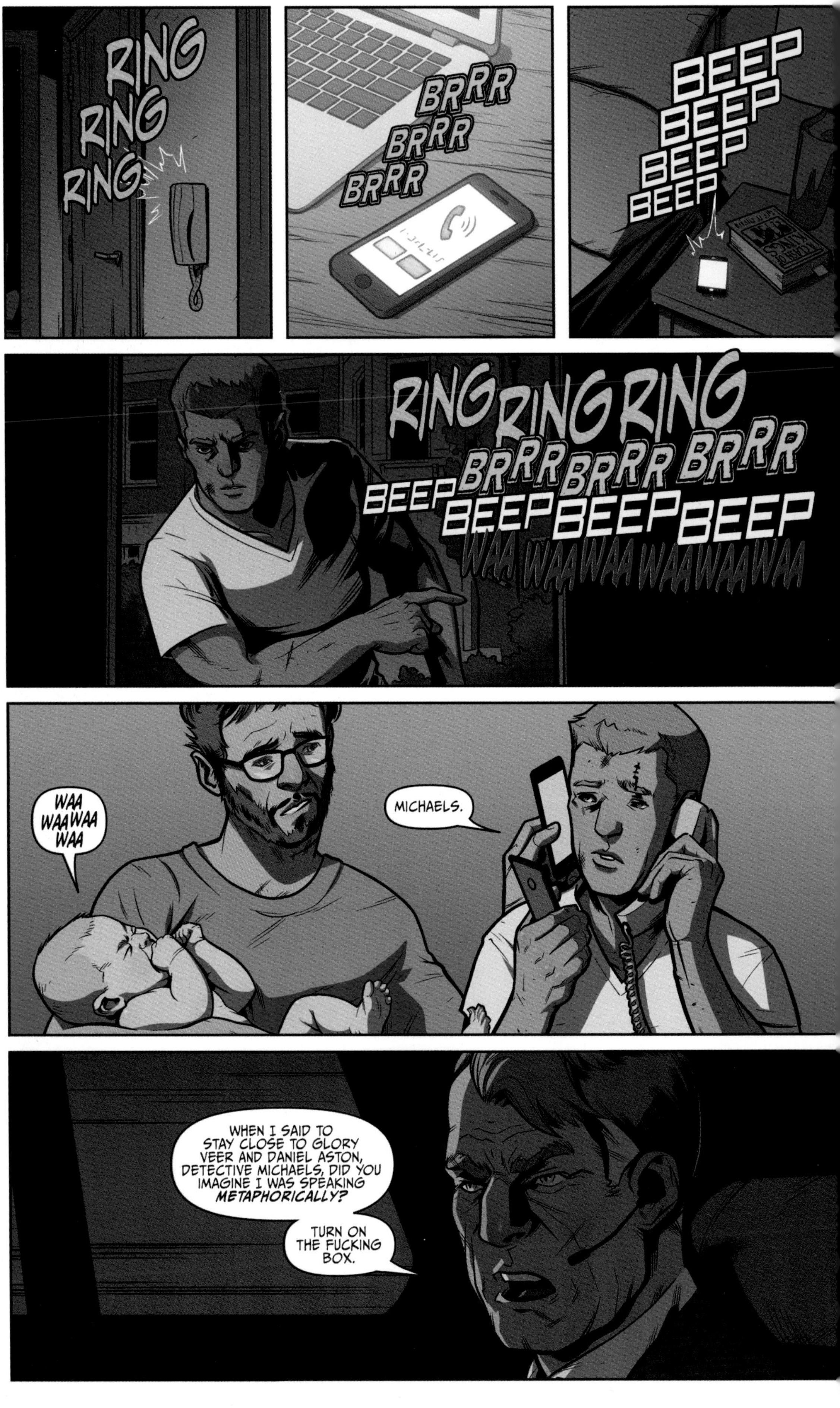
RING
RING
RING
BRRR
BRRR
BRRR
BEEP
BEEP
BEEP
BEEP
RING RING RING
BRRR BRRR BRRR
BEEP BEEP BEEP BEEP
WAA WAA WAA WAA WAA WAA
WAA WAA WAA WAA
MICHAELS.
WHEN I SAID TO STAY CLOSE TO GLORY VEER AND DANIEL ASTON, DETECTIVE MICHAELS, DID YOU IMAGINE I WAS SPEAKING *METAPHORICALLY?*
TURN ON THE FUCKING BOX.

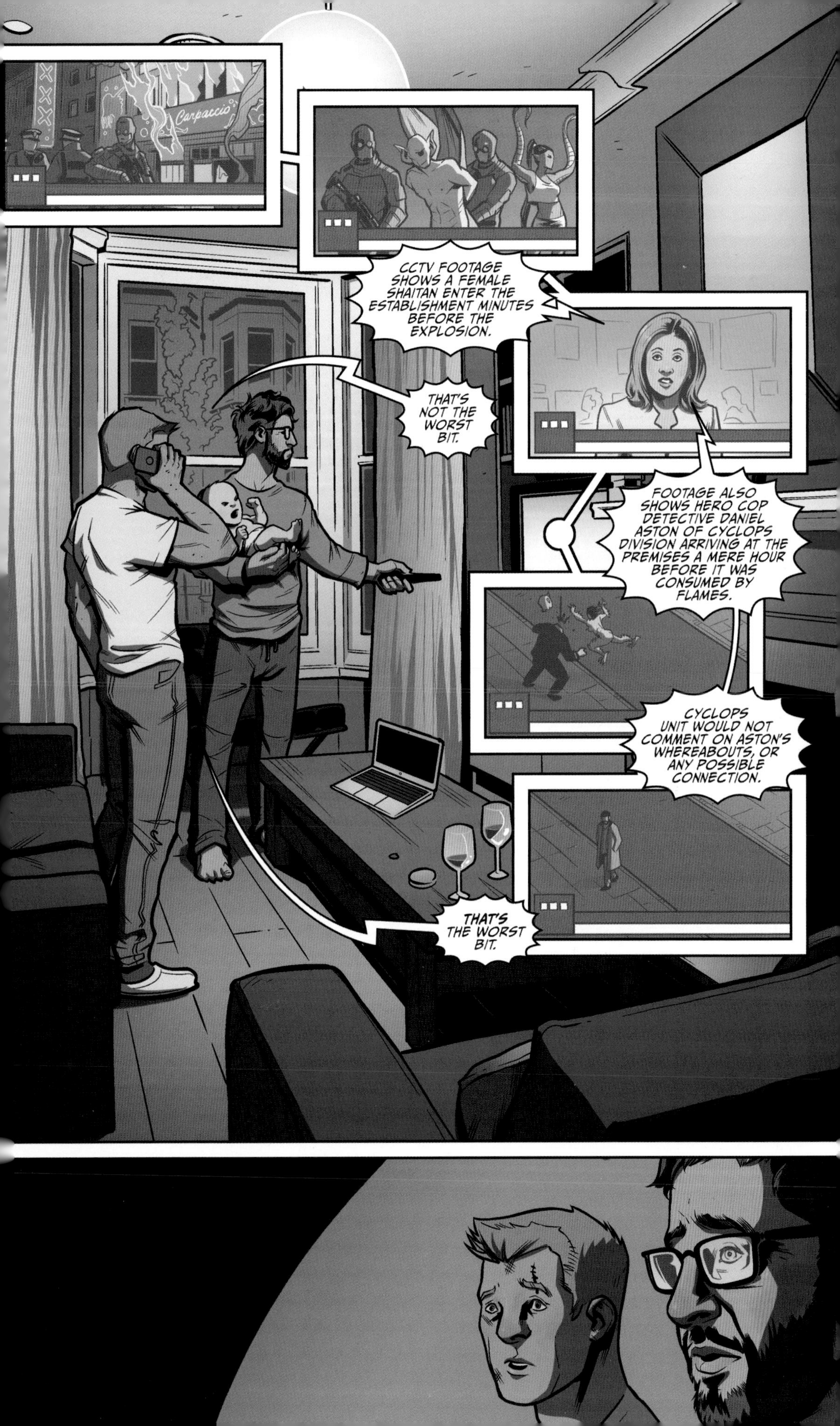

Carpaccio
CCTV FOOTAGE SHOWS A FEMALE SHAITAN ENTER THE ESTABLISHMENT MINUTES BEFORE THE EXPLOSION.
THAT'S NOT THE WORST BIT.
FOOTAGE ALSO SHOWS HERO COP DETECTIVE DANIEL ASTON OF CYCLOPS DIVISION ARRIVING AT THE PREMISES A MERE HOUR BEFORE IT WAS CONSUMED BY FLAMES.
CYCLOPS UNIT WOULD NOT COMMENT ON ASTON'S WHEREABOUTS, OR ANY POSSIBLE CONNECTION.
THAT'S THE WORST BIT.

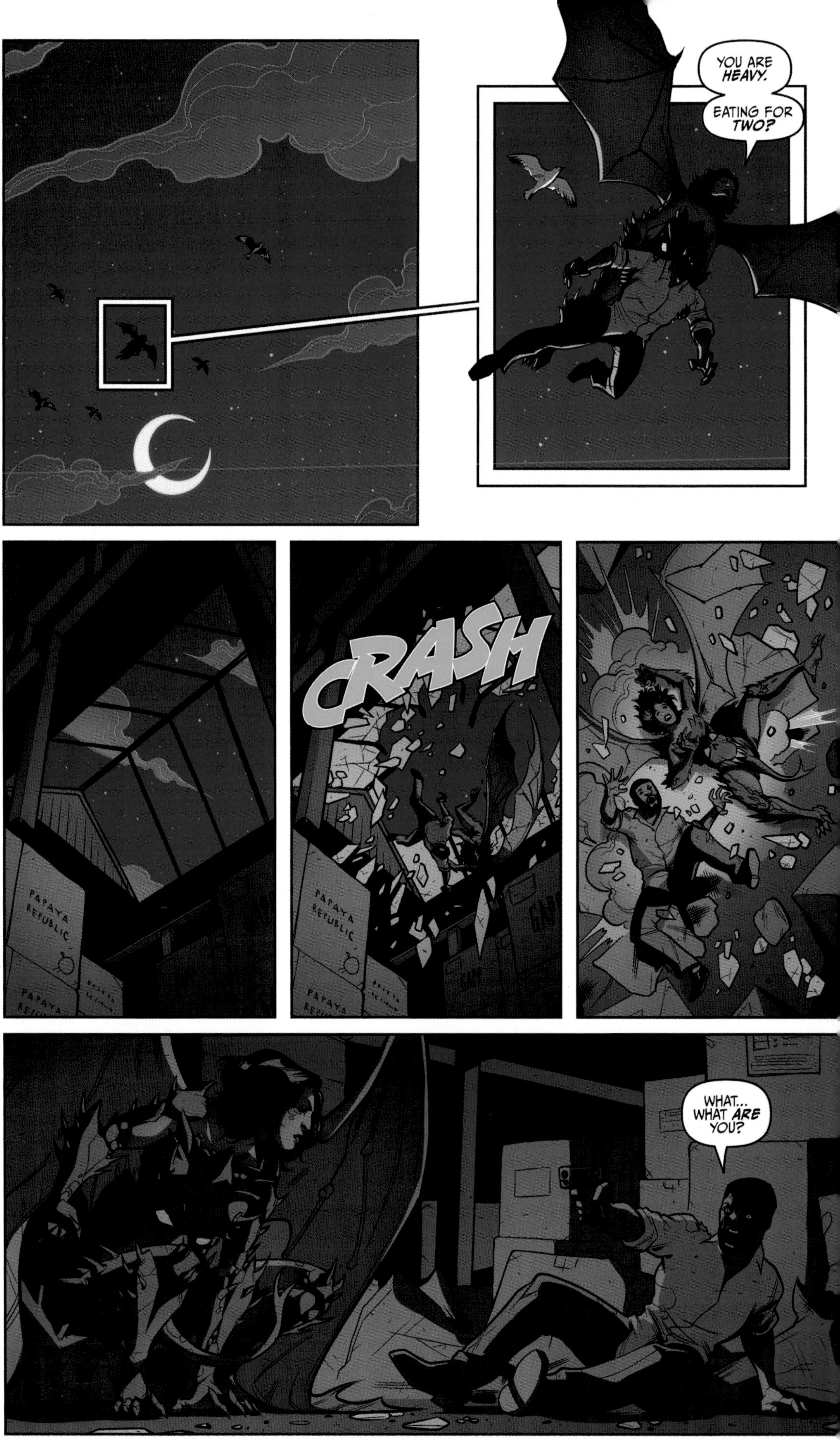
YOU ARE HEAVY.
EATING FOR TWO?
CRASH
PAPAYA REPUBLIC
WHAT... WHAT ARE YOU?

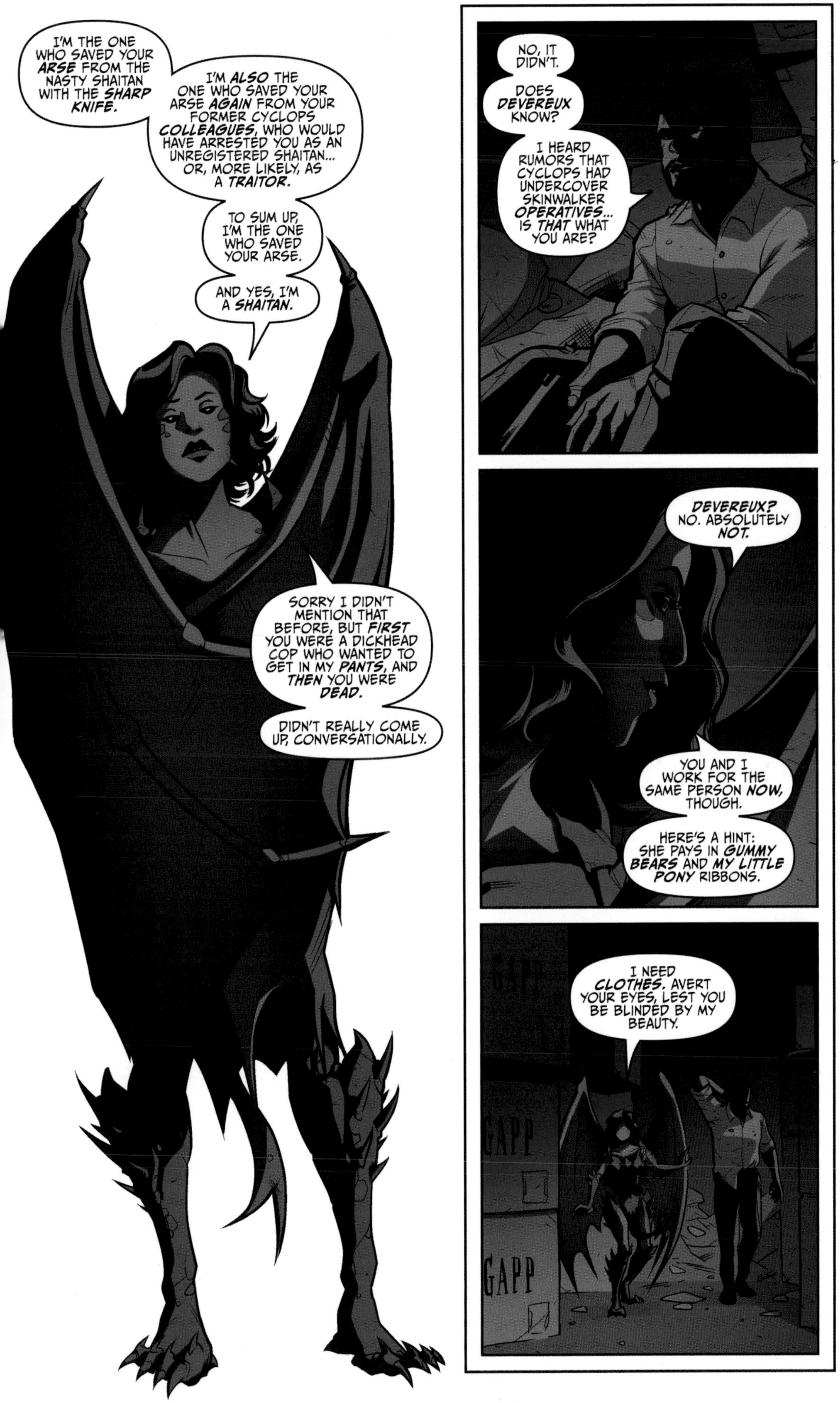

I'M THE ONE WHO SAVED YOUR ARSE FROM THE NASTY SHAITAN WITH THE SHARP KNIFE.
I'M ALSO THE ONE WHO SAVED YOUR ARSE AGAIN FROM YOUR FORMER CYCLOPS COLLEAGUES, WHO WOULD HAVE ARRESTED YOU AS AN UNREGISTERED SHAITAN... OR, MORE LIKELY, AS A TRAITOR.
TO SUM UP, I'M THE ONE WHO SAVED YOUR ARSE.
AND YES, I'M A SHAITAN.
SORRY I DIDN'T MENTION THAT BEFORE, BUT FIRST YOU WERE A DICKHEAD COP WHO WANTED TO GET IN MY PANTS, AND THEN YOU WERE DEAD.
DIDN'T REALLY COME UP, CONVERSATIONALLY.
NO, IT DIDN'T.
DOES DEVEREUX KNOW?
I HEARD RUMORS THAT CYCLOPS HAD UNDERCOVER SKINWALKER OPERATIVES... IS THAT WHAT YOU ARE?
DEVEREUX? NO. ABSOLUTELY NOT.
YOU AND I WORK FOR THE SAME PERSON NOW, THOUGH.
HERE'S A HINT: SHE PAYS IN GUMMY BEARS AND MY LITTLE PONY RIBBONS.
GAPP
I NEED CLOTHES. AVERT YOUR EYES, LEST YOU BE BLINDED BY MY BEAUTY.
GAPP
GAPP

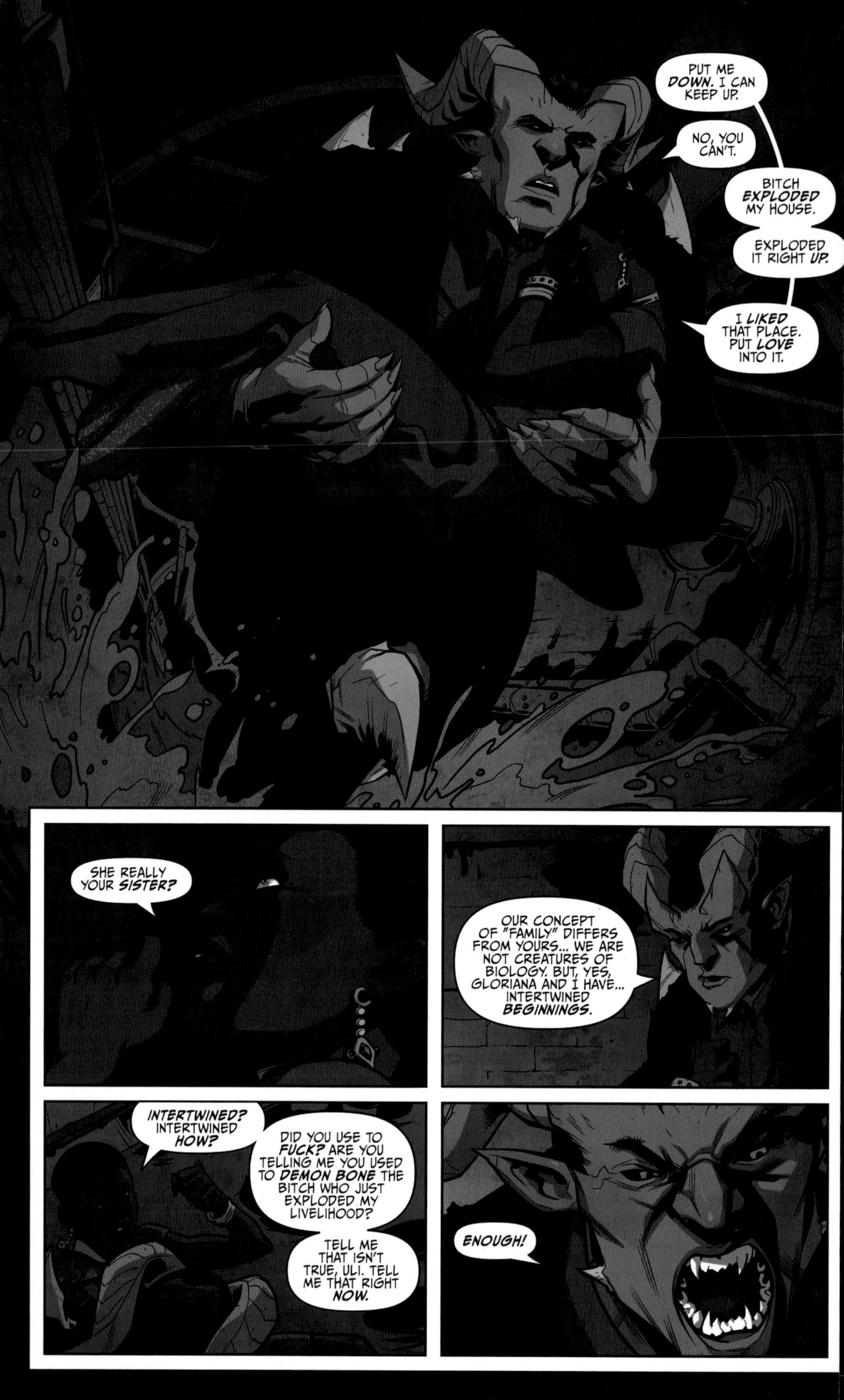
PUT ME DOWN. I CAN KEEP UP.
NO, YOU CAN'T.
BITCH EXPLODED MY HOUSE.
EXPLODED IT RIGHT UP.
I LIKED THAT PLACE. PUT LOVE INTO IT.
SHE REALLY YOUR SISTER?
OUR CONCEPT OF "FAMILY" DIFFERS FROM YOURS... WE ARE NOT CREATURES OF BIOLOGY. BUT, YES, GLORIANA AND I HAVE... INTERTWINED BEGINNINGS.
INTERTWINED? INTERTWINED HOW?
DID YOU USE TO FUCK? ARE YOU TELLING ME YOU USED TO DEMON BONE THE BITCH WHO JUST EXPLODED MY LIVELIHOOD?
TELL ME THAT ISN'T TRUE, ULI. TELL ME THAT RIGHT NOW.
ENOUGH!

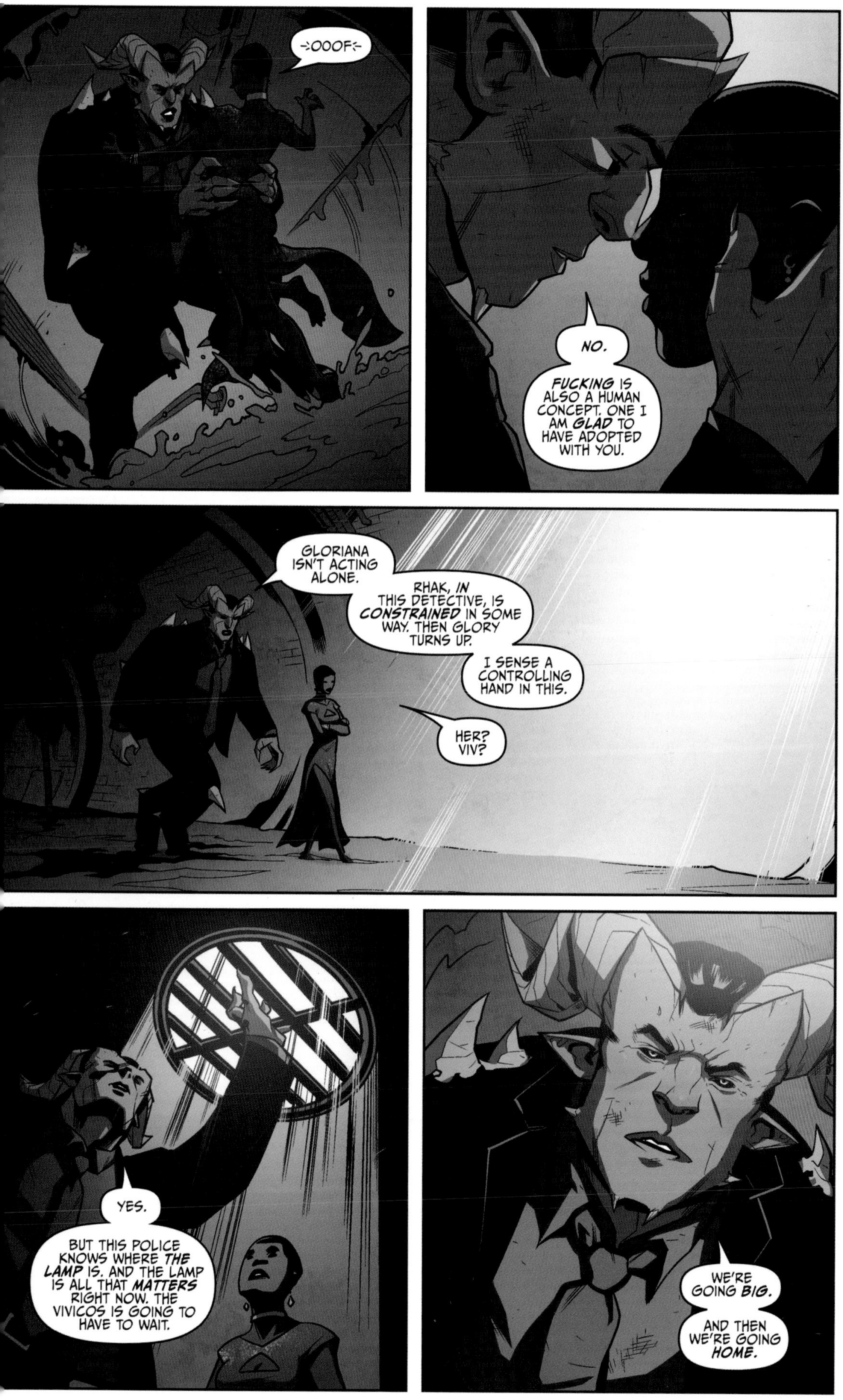

-OOOF-
NO.
FUCKING IS ALSO A HUMAN CONCEPT. ONE I AM GLAD TO HAVE ADOPTED WITH YOU.
GLORIANA ISN'T ACTING ALONE.
RHAK, IN THIS DETECTIVE, IS CONSTRAINED IN SOME WAY. THEN GLORY TURNS UP.
I SENSE A CONTROLLING HAND IN THIS.
HER? VIV?
YES.
BUT THIS POLICE KNOWS WHERE THE LAMP IS. AND THE LAMP IS ALL THAT MATTERS RIGHT NOW. THE VIVICOS IS GOING TO HAVE TO WAIT.
WE'RE GOING BIG.
AND THEN WE'RE GOING HOME.

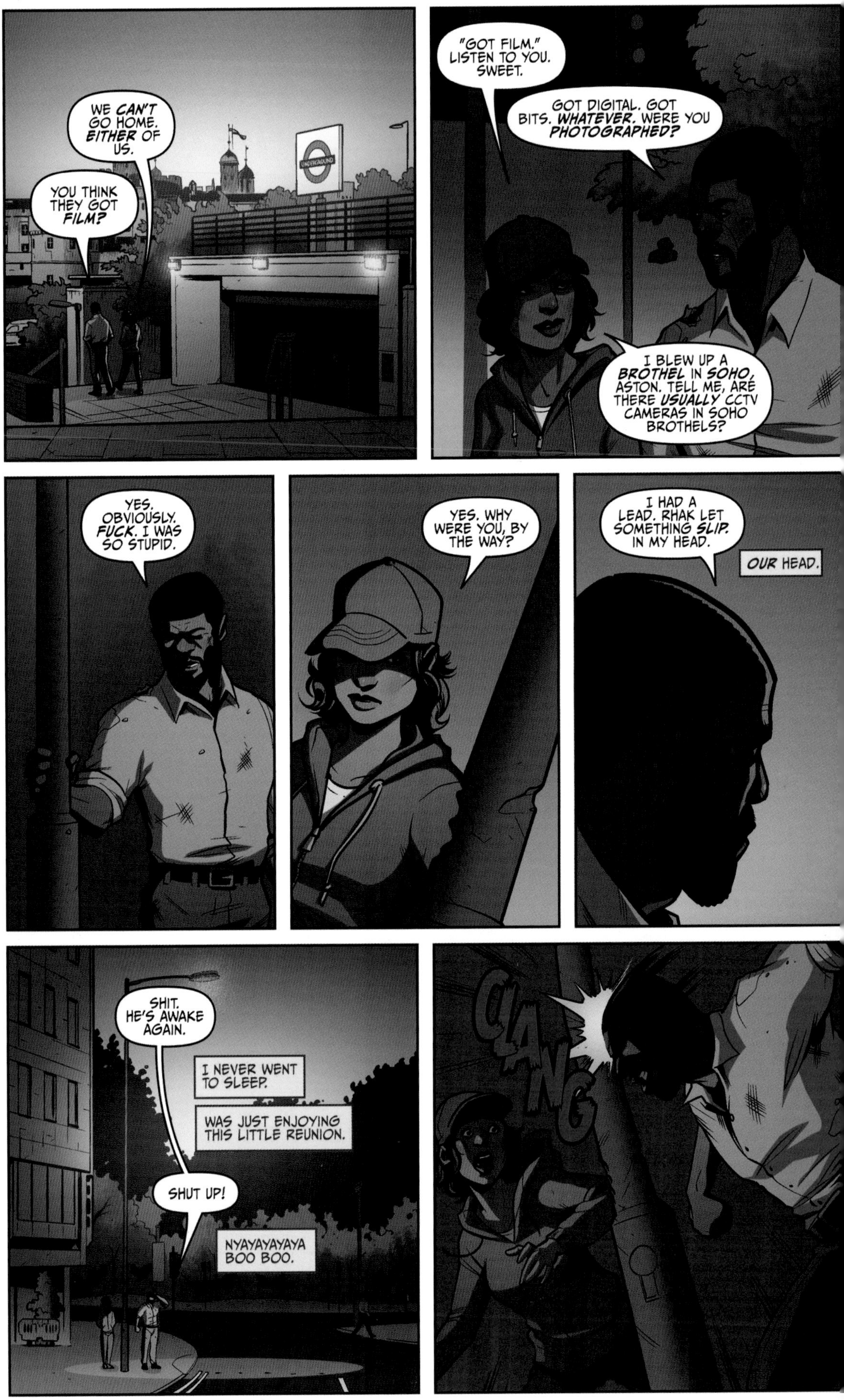
WE CAN'T GO HOME. EITHER OF US.
YOU THINK THEY GOT FILM?
"GOT FILM." LISTEN TO YOU. SWEET.
GOT DIGITAL. GOT BITS. WHATEVER. WERE YOU PHOTOGRAPHED?
I BLEW UP A BROTHEL IN SOHO, ASTON. TELL ME, ARE THERE USUALLY CCTV CAMERAS IN SOHO BROTHELS?
YES. OBVIOUSLY. FUCK. I WAS SO STUPID.
YES. WHY WERE YOU, BY THE WAY?
I HAD A LEAD. RHAK LET SOMETHING SLIP. IN MY HEAD.
OUR HEAD.
SHIT. HE'S AWAKE AGAIN.
I NEVER WENT TO SLEEP.
WAS JUST ENJOYING THIS LITTLE REUNION.
SHUT UP!
NYAYAYAYAYA BOO BOO.
CLANG

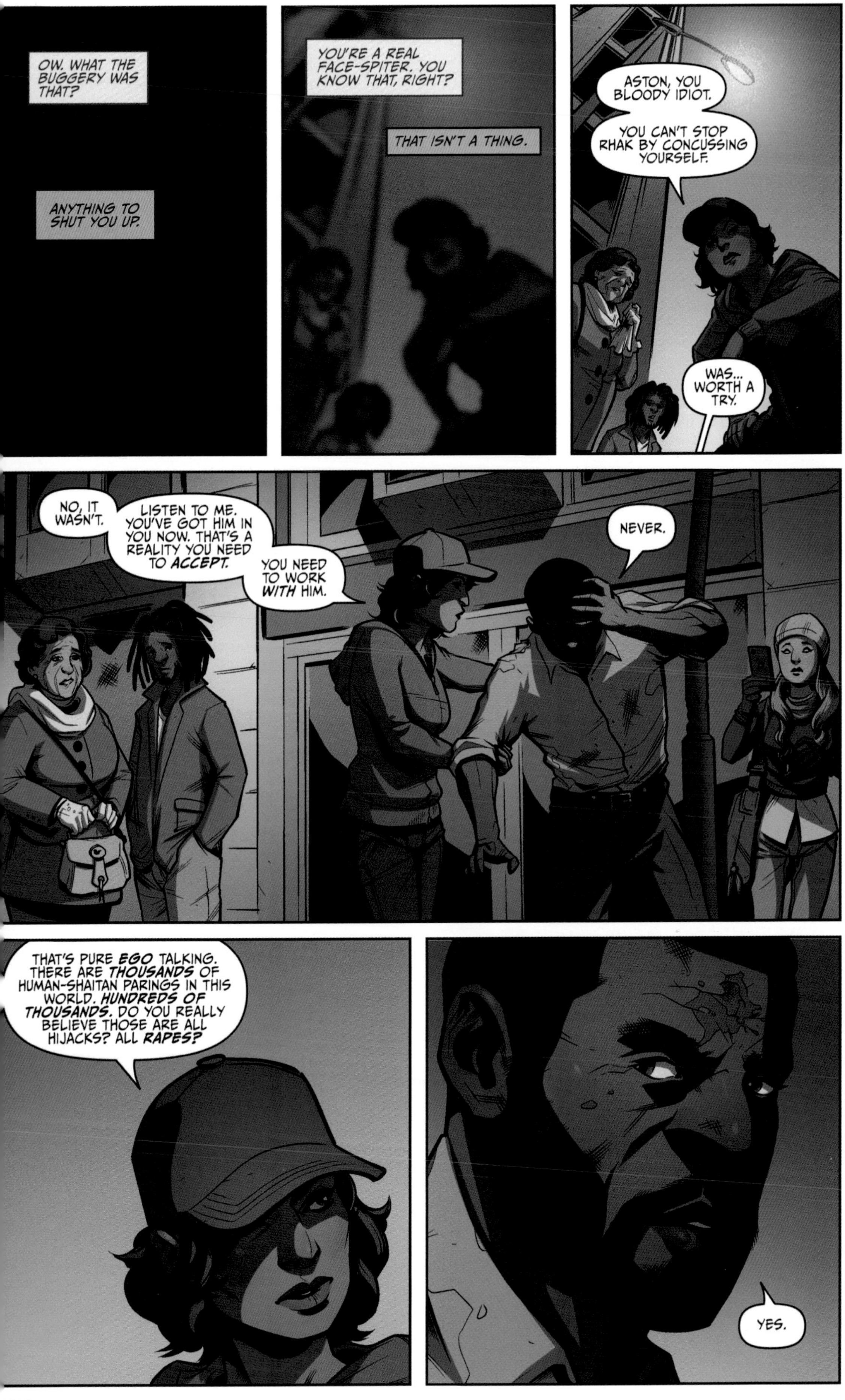
OW. WHAT THE BUGGERY WAS THAT?
ANYTHING TO SHUT YOU UP.
YOU'RE A REAL FACE-SPITER. YOU KNOW THAT, RIGHT?
THAT ISN'T A THING.
ASTON, YOU BLOODY IDIOT.
YOU CAN'T STOP RHAK BY CONCUSSING YOURSELF.
WAS... WORTH A TRY.
NO, IT WASN'T.
LISTEN TO ME. YOU'VE GOT HIM IN YOU NOW. THAT'S A REALITY YOU NEED TO ACCEPT.
YOU NEED TO WORK WITH HIM.
NEVER.
THAT'S PURE EGO TALKING. THERE ARE THOUSANDS OF HUMAN-SHAITAN PARINGS IN THIS WORLD. HUNDREDS OF THOUSANDS. DO YOU REALLY BELIEVE THOSE ARE ALL HIJACKS? ALL RAPES?
YES.

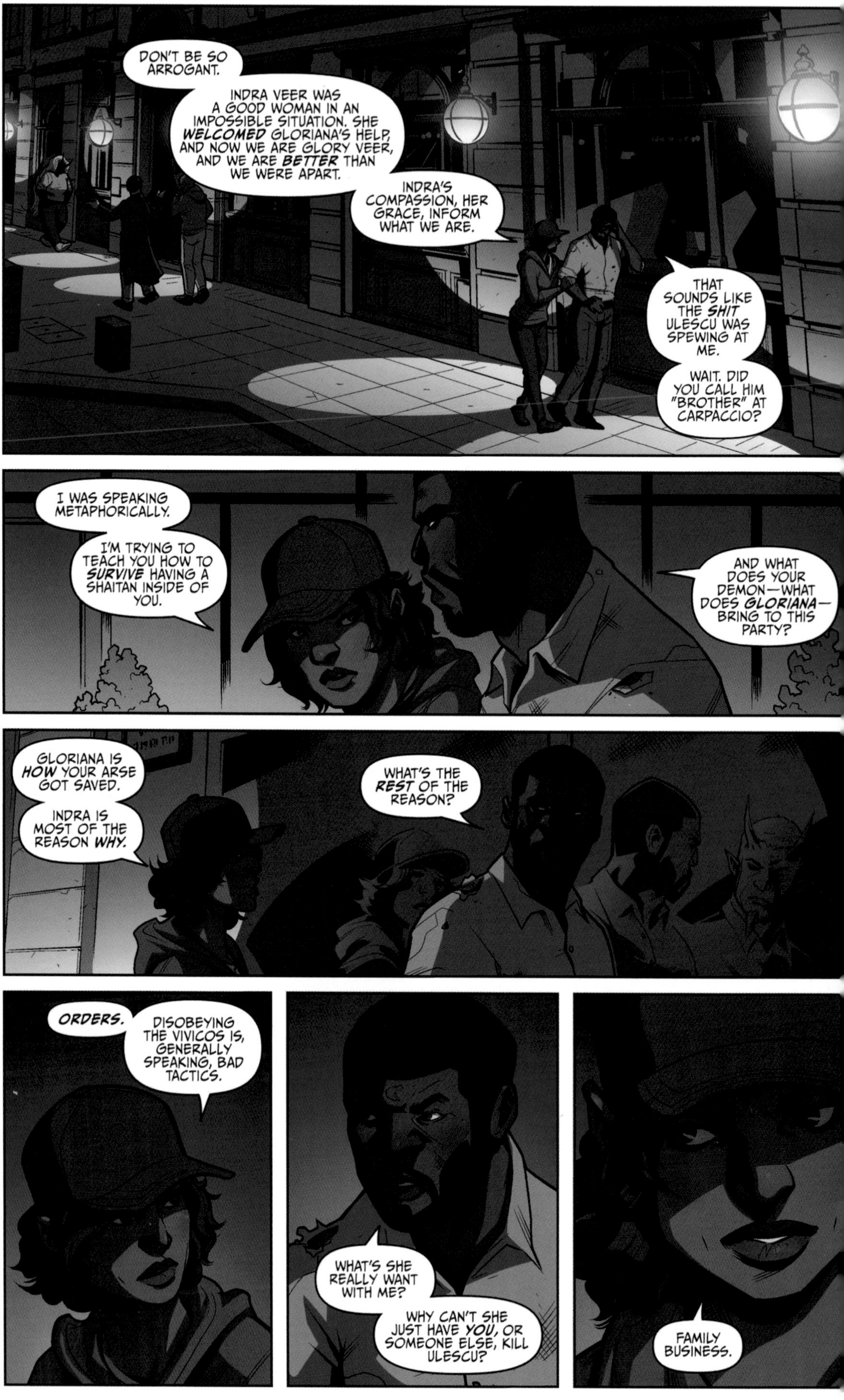
DON'T BE SO ARROGANT.
INDRA VEER WAS A GOOD WOMAN IN AN IMPOSSIBLE SITUATION. SHE WELCOMED GLORIANA'S HELP, AND NOW WE ARE GLORY VEER, AND WE ARE BETTER THAN WE WERE APART.
INDRA'S COMPASSION, HER GRACE, INFORM WHAT WE ARE.
THAT SOUNDS LIKE THE SHIT ULESCU WAS SPEWING AT ME.
WAIT. DID YOU CALL HIM "BROTHER" AT CARPACCIO?
I WAS SPEAKING METAPHORICALLY.
I'M TRYING TO TEACH YOU HOW TO SURVIVE HAVING A SHAITAN INSIDE OF YOU.
AND WHAT DOES YOUR DEMON—WHAT DOES GLORIANA—BRING TO THIS PARTY?
GLORIANA IS HOW YOUR ARSE GOT SAVED.
INDRA IS MOST OF THE REASON WHY.
WHAT'S THE REST OF THE REASON?
ORDERS.
DISOBEYING THE VIVICOS IS, GENERALLY SPEAKING, BAD TACTICS.
WHAT'S SHE REALLY WANT WITH ME?
WHY CAN'T SHE JUST HAVE YOU, OR SOMEONE ELSE, KILL ULESCU?
FAMILY BUSINESS.

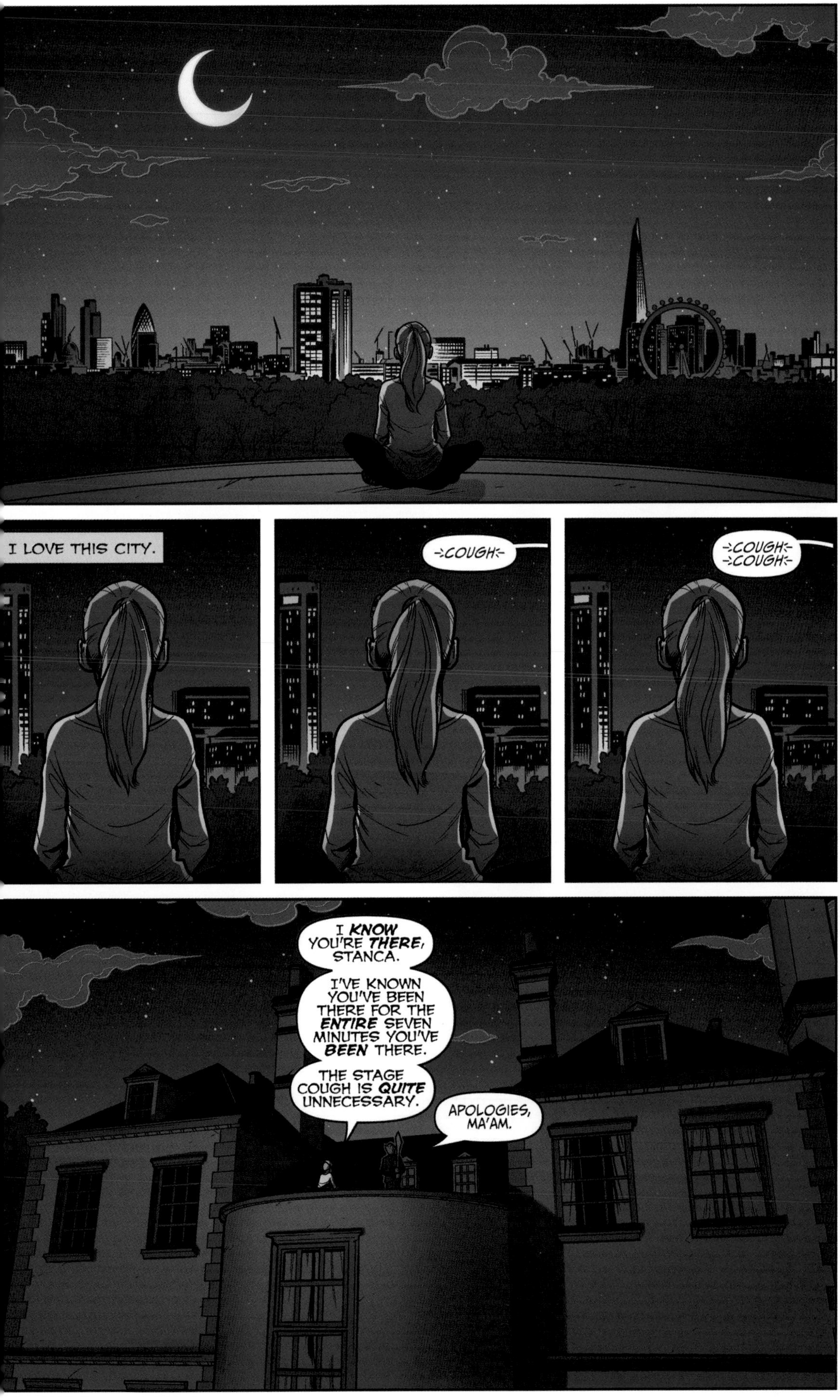
I LOVE THIS CITY.
-COUGH-
-COUGH- -COUGH-
I KNOW YOU'RE THERE, STANCA.
I'VE KNOWN YOU'VE BEEN THERE FOR THE ENTIRE SEVEN MINUTES YOU'VE BEEN THERE.
THE STAGE COUGH IS QUITE UNNECESSARY.
APOLOGIES, MA'AM.

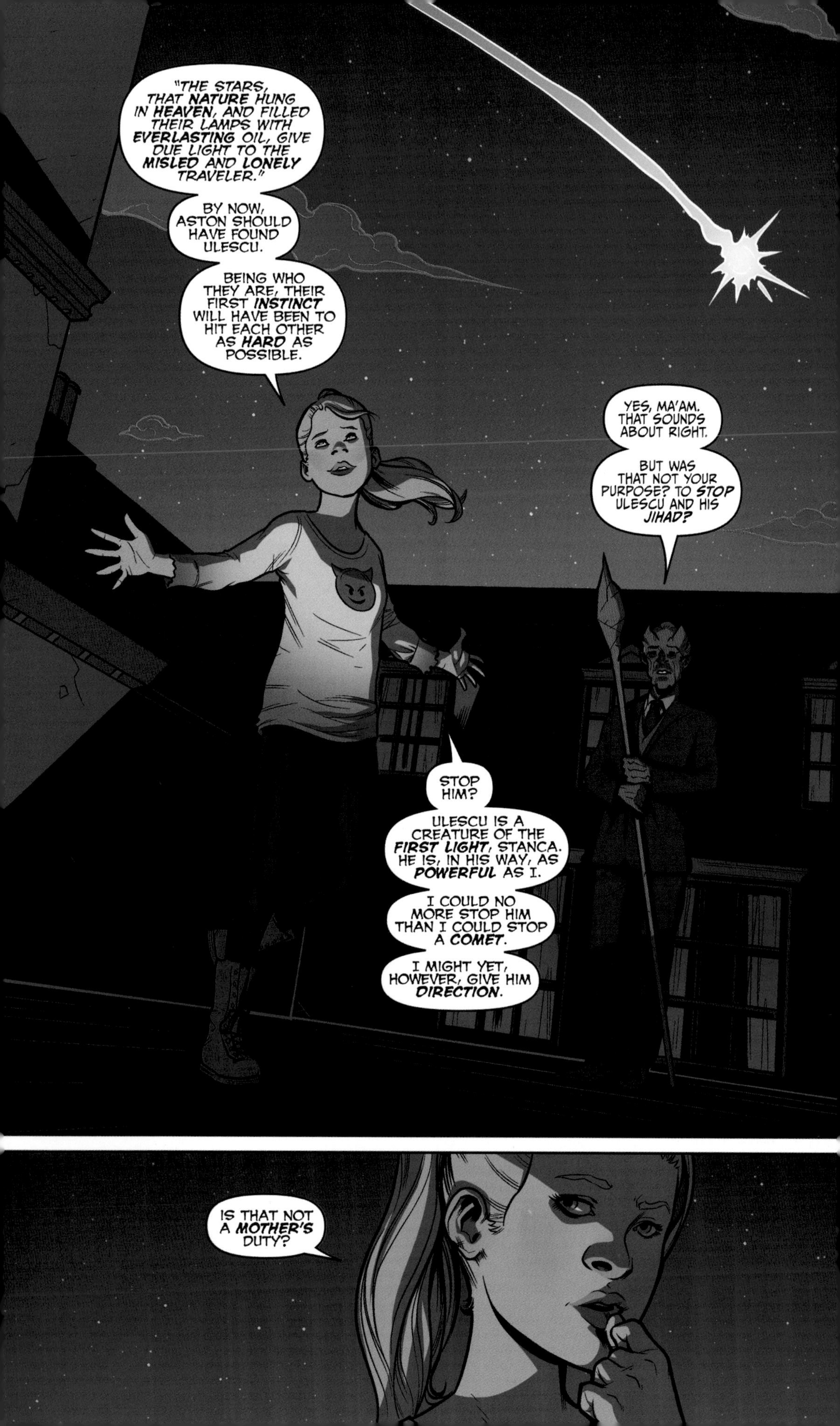
"THE STARS, THAT NATURE HUNG IN HEAVEN, AND FILLED THEIR LAMPS WITH EVERLASTING OIL, GIVE DUE LIGHT TO THE MISLED AND LONELY TRAVELER."
BY NOW, ASTON SHOULD HAVE FOUND ULESCU.
BEING WHO THEY ARE, THEIR FIRST INSTINCT WILL HAVE BEEN TO HIT EACH OTHER AS HARD AS POSSIBLE.
YES, MA'AM. THAT SOUNDS ABOUT RIGHT.
BUT WAS THAT NOT YOUR PURPOSE? TO STOP ULESCU AND HIS JIHAD?
STOP HIM?
ULESCU IS A CREATURE OF THE FIRST LIGHT, STANCA. HE IS, IN HIS WAY, AS POWERFUL AS I.
I COULD NO MORE STOP HIM THAN I COULD STOP A COMET.
I MIGHT YET, HOWEVER, GIVE HIM DIRECTION.
IS THAT NOT A MOTHER'S DUTY?

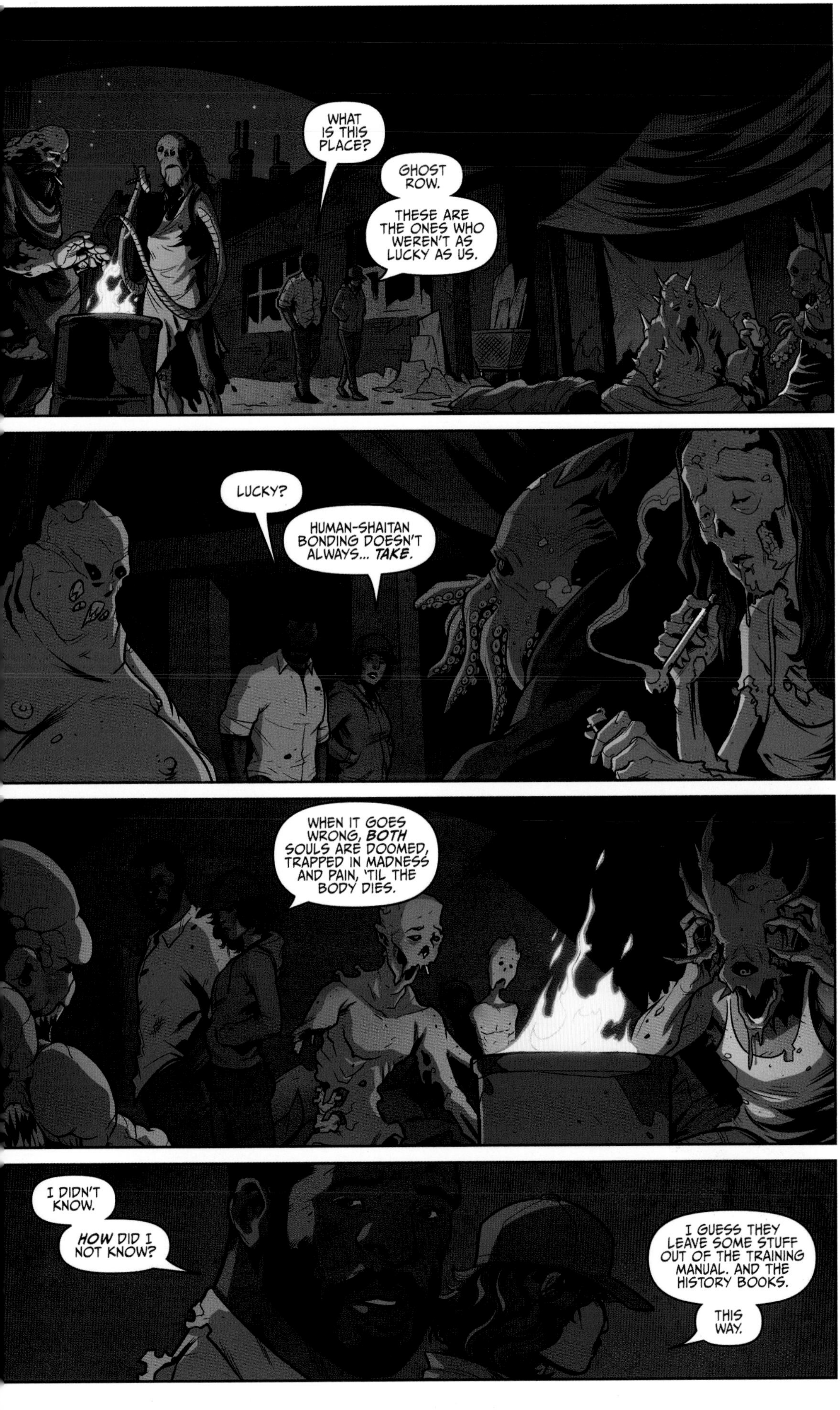

WHAT IS THIS PLACE?
GHOST ROW.
THESE ARE THE ONES WHO WEREN'T AS LUCKY AS US.
LUCKY?
HUMAN-SHAITAN BONDING DOESN'T ALWAYS... *TAKE.*
WHEN IT GOES WRONG, *BOTH* SOULS ARE DOOMED, TRAPPED IN MADNESS AND PAIN, 'TIL THE BODY DIES.
I DIDN'T KNOW.
HOW DID I NOT KNOW?
I GUESS THEY LEAVE SOME STUFF OUT OF THE TRAINING MANUAL. AND THE HISTORY BOOKS.
THIS WAY.

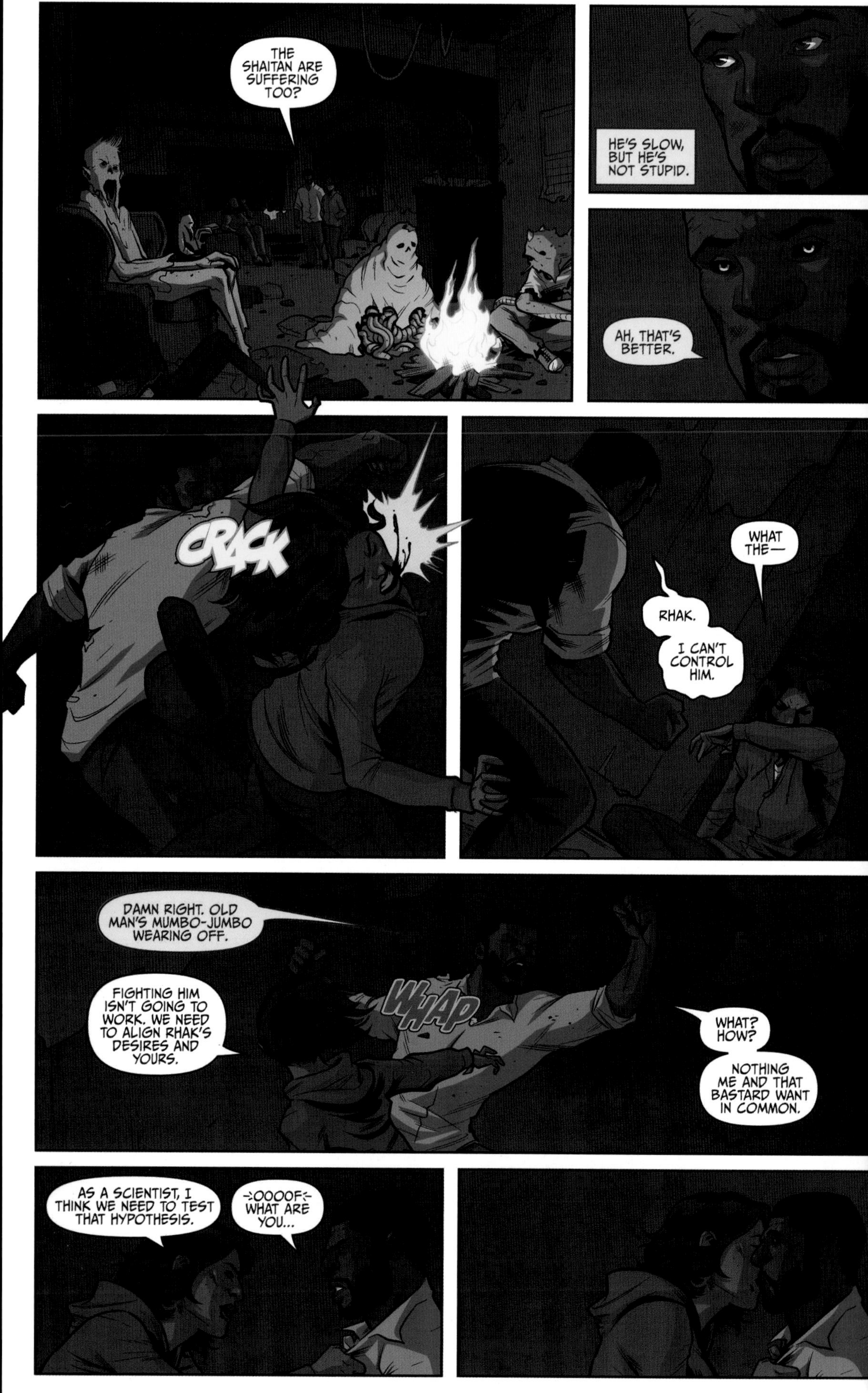
THE SHAITAN ARE SUFFERING TOO?
HE'S SLOW, BUT HE'S NOT STUPID.
AH, THAT'S BETTER.
CRACK
WHAT THE—
RHAK.
I CAN'T CONTROL HIM.
DAMN RIGHT. OLD MAN'S MUMBO-JUMBO WEARING OFF.
FIGHTING HIM ISN'T GOING TO WORK. WE NEED TO ALIGN RHAK'S DESIRES AND YOURS.
WHAP
WHAT? HOW?
NOTHING ME AND THAT BASTARD WANT IN COMMON.
AS A SCIENTIST, I THINK WE NEED TO TEST THAT HYPOTHESIS.
-OOOOF- WHAT ARE YOU...

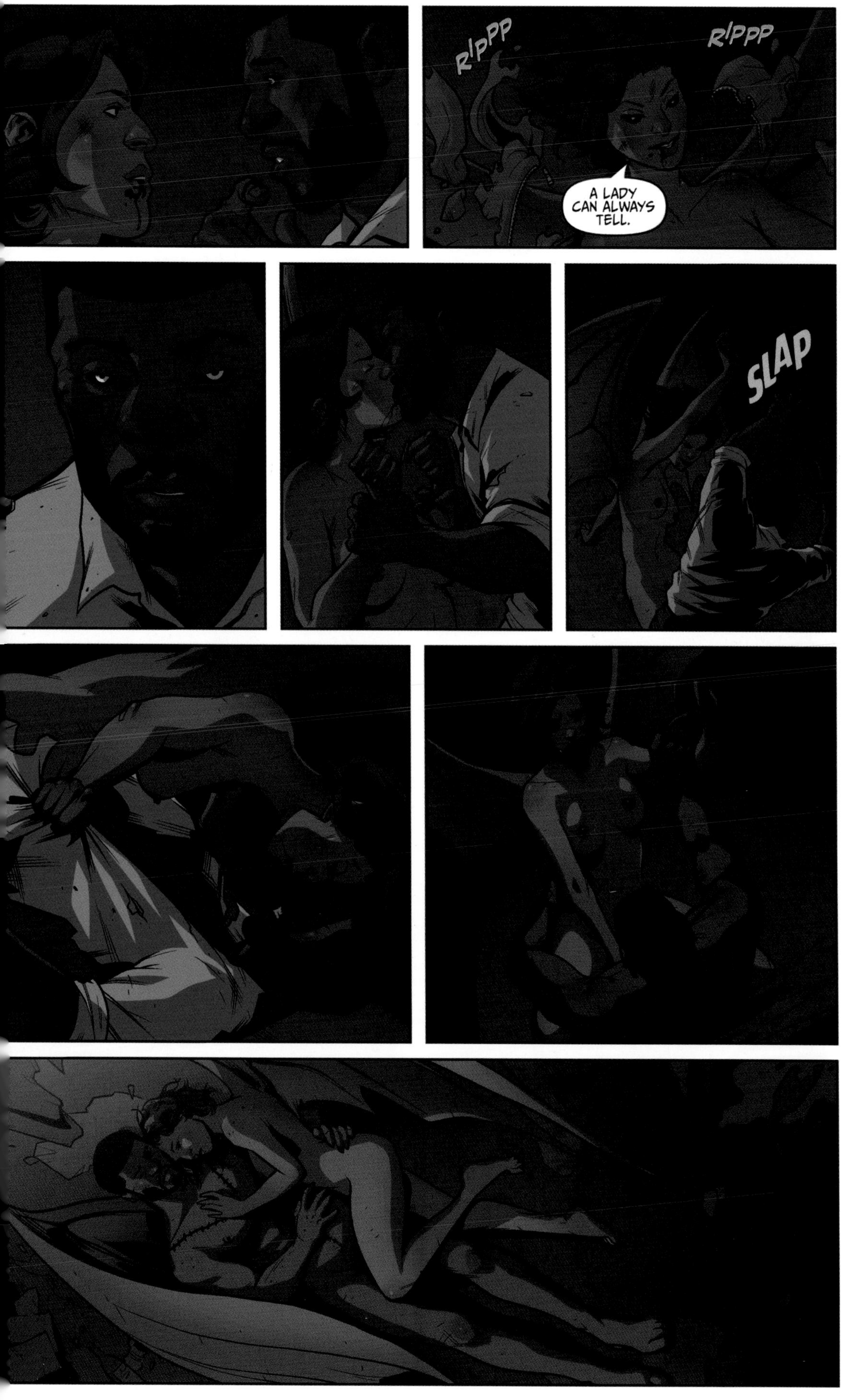
RIPPP
RIPPP
A LADY CAN ALWAYS TELL.
SLAP

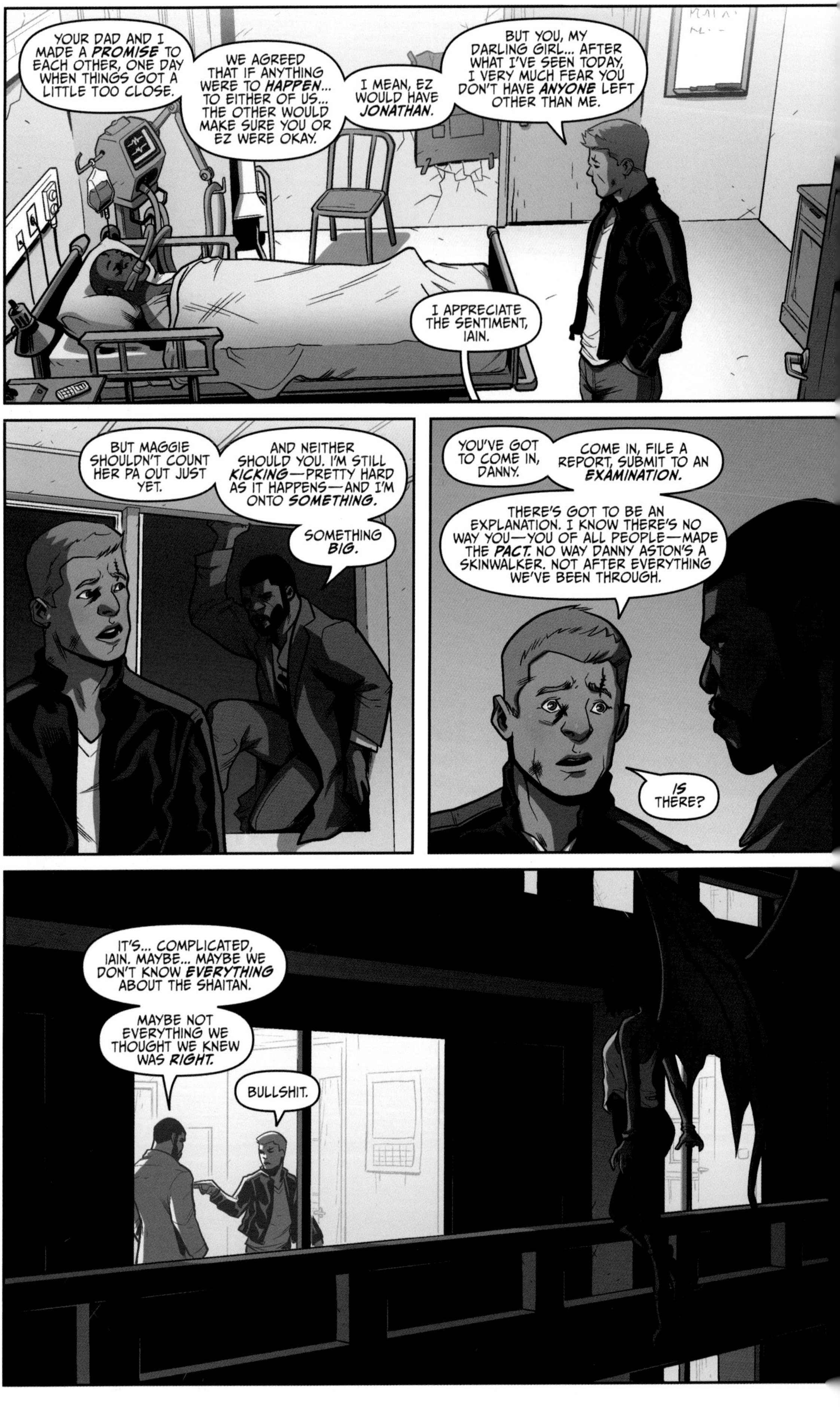

YOUR DAD AND I MADE A PROMISE TO EACH OTHER, ONE DAY WHEN THINGS GOT A LITTLE TOO CLOSE.
WE AGREED THAT IF ANYTHING WERE TO HAPPEN... TO EITHER OF US... THE OTHER WOULD MAKE SURE YOU OR EZ WERE OKAY.
I MEAN, EZ WOULD HAVE JONATHAN.
BUT YOU, MY DARLING GIRL... AFTER WHAT I'VE SEEN TODAY, I VERY MUCH FEAR YOU DON'T HAVE ANYONE LEFT OTHER THAN ME.
I APPRECIATE THE SENTIMENT, IAIN.
BUT MAGGIE SHOULDN'T COUNT HER PA OUT JUST YET.
AND NEITHER SHOULD YOU. I'M STILL KICKING—PRETTY HARD AS IT HAPPENS—AND I'M ONTO SOMETHING.
SOMETHING BIG.
YOU'VE GOT TO COME IN, DANNY.
COME IN, FILE A REPORT, SUBMIT TO AN EXAMINATION.
THERE'S GOT TO BE AN EXPLANATION. I KNOW THERE'S NO WAY YOU—YOU OF ALL PEOPLE—MADE THE PACT. NO WAY DANNY ASTON'S A SKINWALKER. NOT AFTER EVERYTHING WE'VE BEEN THROUGH.
IS THERE?
IT'S... COMPLICATED, IAIN. MAYBE... MAYBE WE DON'T KNOW EVERYTHING ABOUT THE SHAITAN.
MAYBE NOT EVERYTHING WE THOUGHT WE KNEW WAS RIGHT.
BULLSHIT.

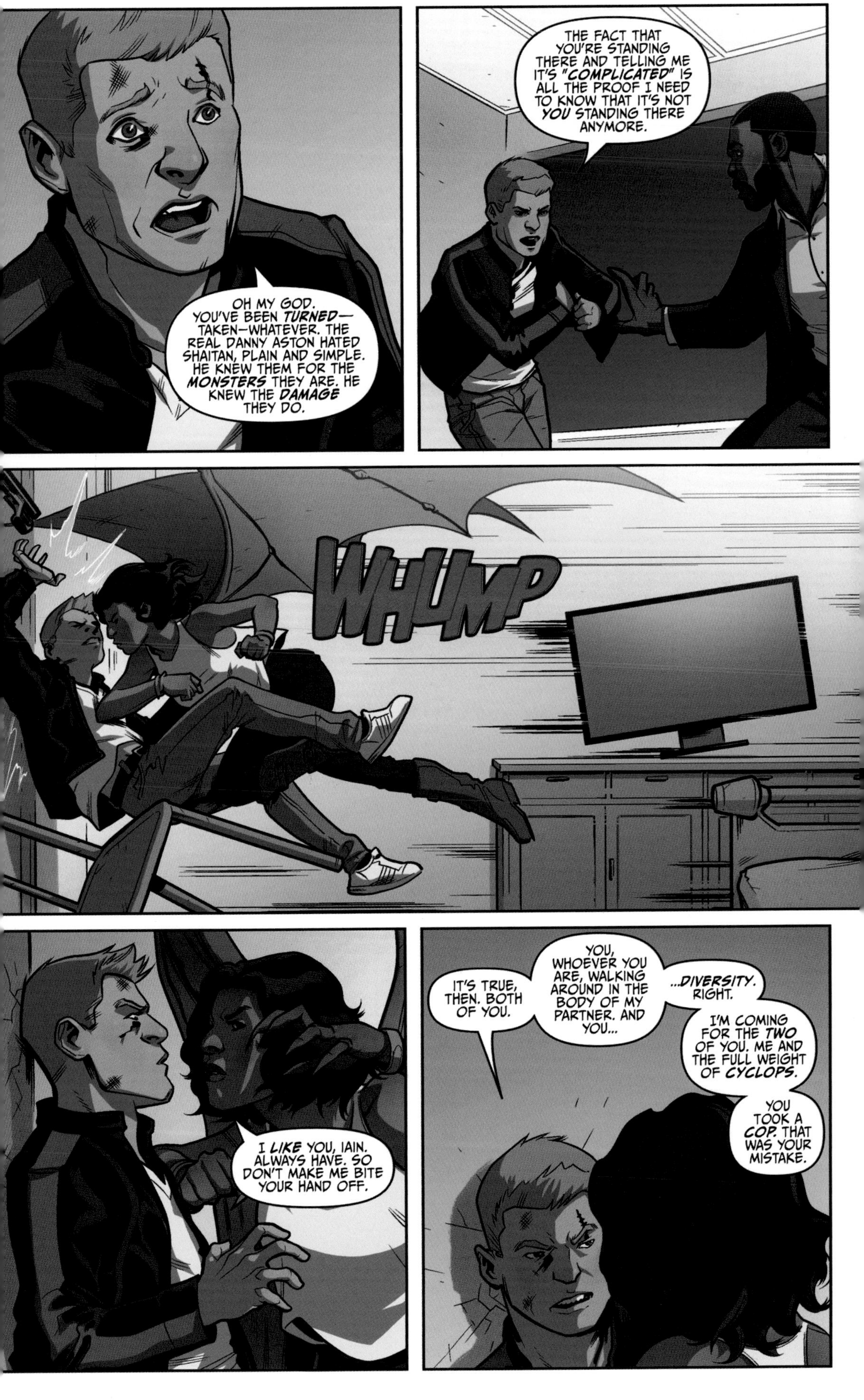
OH MY GOD. YOU'VE BEEN TURNED—TAKEN—WHATEVER. THE REAL DANNY ASTON HATED SHAITAN, PLAIN AND SIMPLE. HE KNEW THEM FOR THE MONSTERS THEY ARE. HE KNEW THE DAMAGE THEY DO.
THE FACT THAT YOU'RE STANDING THERE AND TELLING ME IT'S "COMPLICATED" IS ALL THE PROOF I NEED TO KNOW THAT IT'S NOT YOU STANDING THERE ANYMORE.
WHUMP
I LIKE YOU, IAIN. ALWAYS HAVE. SO DON'T MAKE ME BITE YOUR HAND OFF.
IT'S TRUE, THEN. BOTH OF YOU.
YOU, WHOEVER YOU ARE, WALKING AROUND IN THE BODY OF MY PARTNER. AND YOU...
...DIVERSITY. RIGHT.
I'M COMING FOR THE TWO OF YOU. ME AND THE FULL WEIGHT OF CYCLOPS.
YOU TOOK A COP. THAT WAS YOUR MISTAKE.

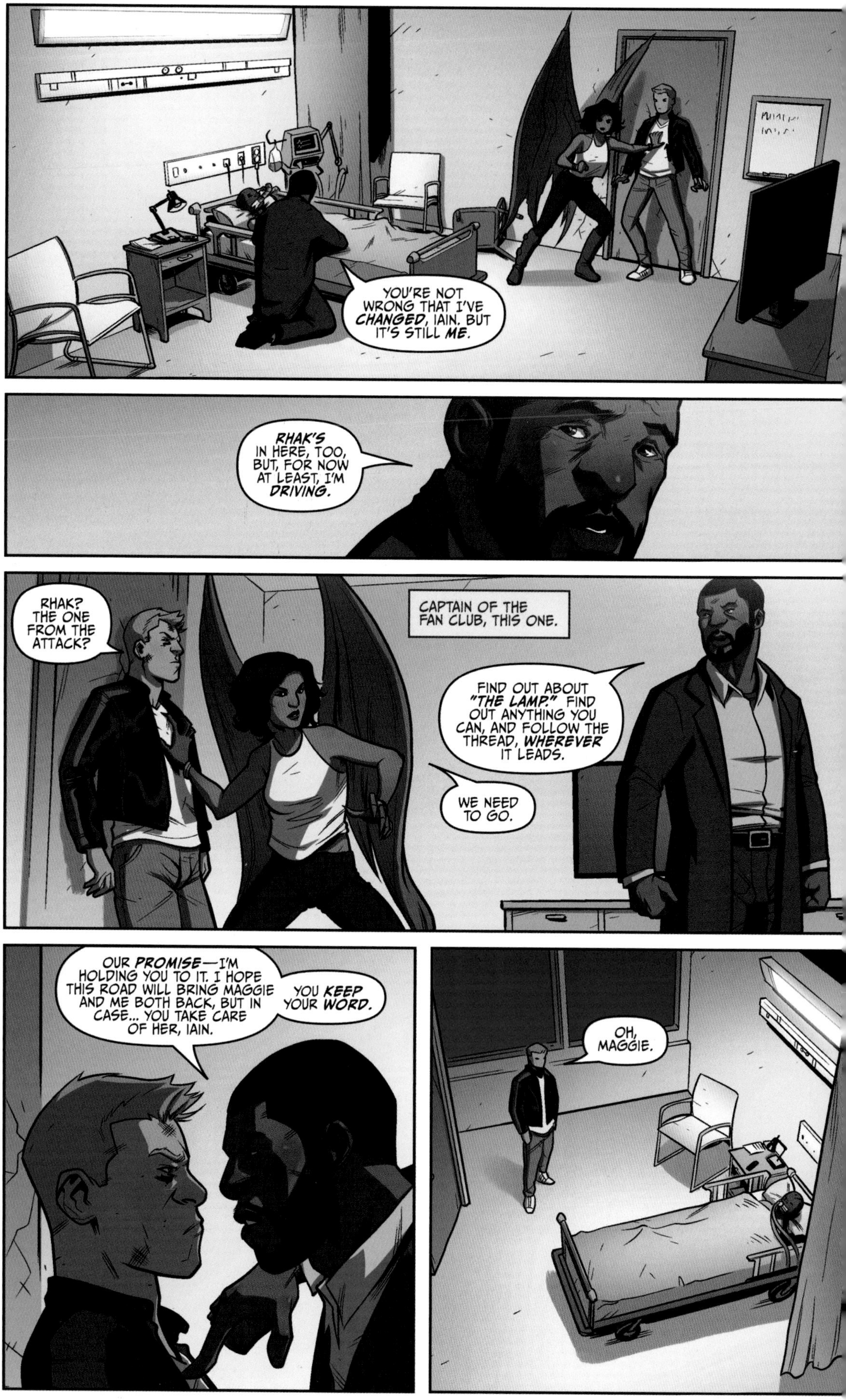
YOU'RE NOT WRONG THAT I'VE CHANGED, IAIN. BUT IT'S STILL ME.
RHAK'S IN HERE, TOO, BUT, FOR NOW AT LEAST, I'M DRIVING.
RHAK? THE ONE FROM THE ATTACK?
CAPTAIN OF THE FAN CLUB, THIS ONE.
FIND OUT ABOUT "THE LAMP." FIND OUT ANYTHING YOU CAN, AND FOLLOW THE THREAD, WHEREVER IT LEADS.
WE NEED TO GO.
OUR PROMISE—I'M HOLDING YOU TO IT. I HOPE THIS ROAD WILL BRING MAGGIE AND ME BOTH BACK, BUT IN CASE... YOU TAKE CARE OF HER, IAIN.
YOU KEEP YOUR WORD.
OH, MAGGIE.

-:WHIMPER:-
-:WHIMPER:-

CLACK

WHO'S THERE? WHAT DO YOU WANT?

WHAT IS THIS PLACE?

CAN I GO HOME?

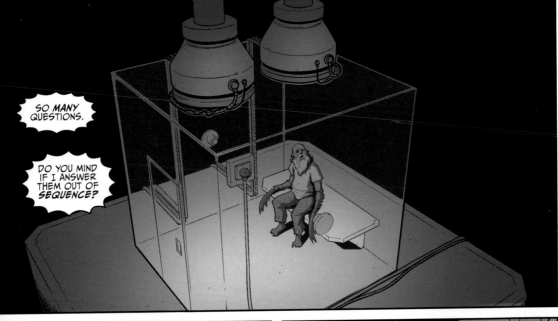

SO MANY QUESTIONS.

DO YOU MIND IF I ANSWER THEM OUT OF SEQUENCE?

SECOND, WHAT I WANT IS TO RESTORE THE BALANCE OF THE WORLD. THAT'S ALL.

A BALANCE YOU CREATURES BROKE WHEN YOU CRAWLED OUT OF HELL.

THIRD, THIS PLACE IS A PLACE OF SCIENCE.

BECAUSE SCIENCE... SCIENCE IS A CANDLE IN THE DARK.

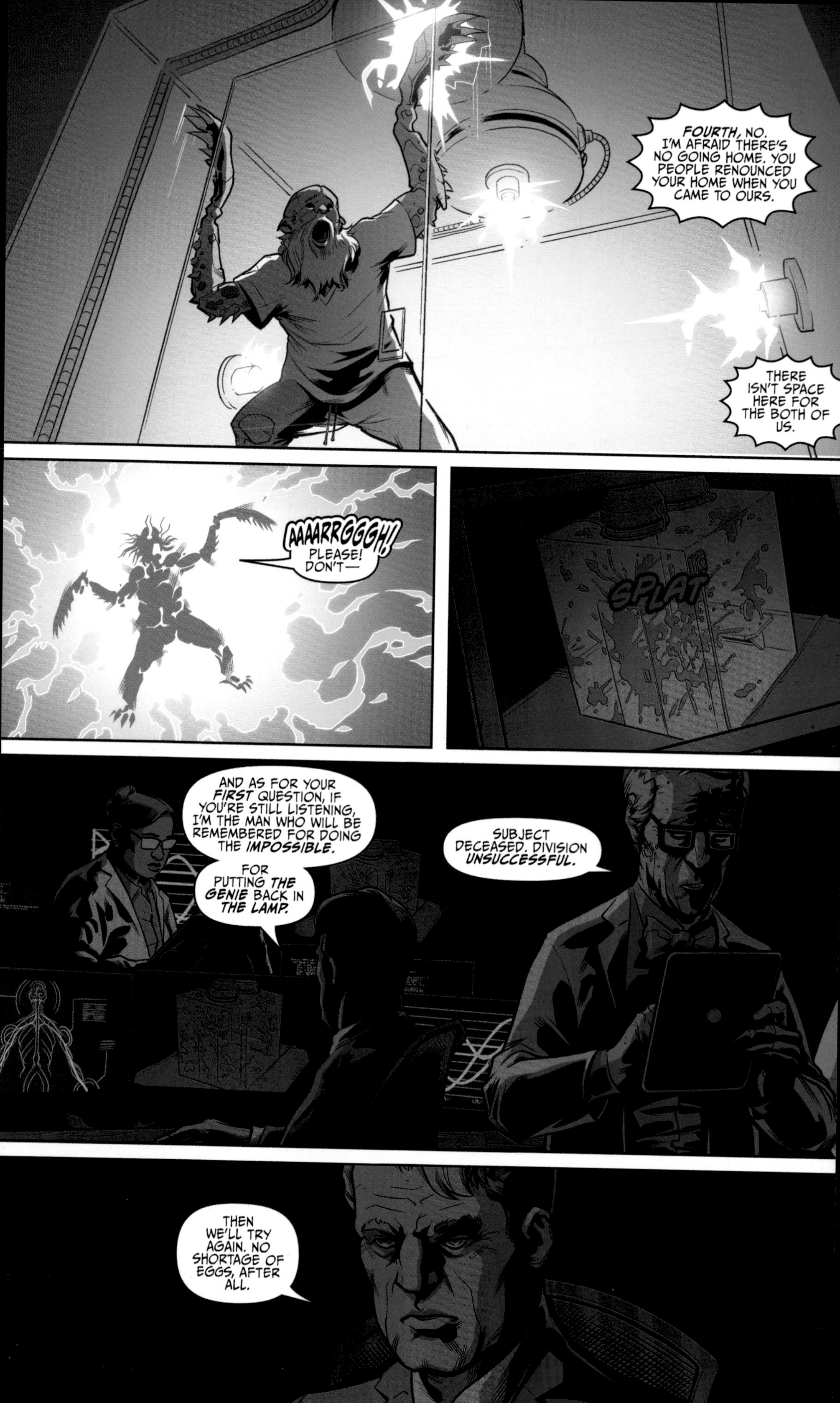

FOURTH, NO. I'M AFRAID THERE'S NO GOING HOME. YOU PEOPLE RENOUNCED YOUR HOME WHEN YOU CAME TO OURS.
THERE ISN'T SPACE HERE FOR THE BOTH OF US.
AAAARRGGGH! PLEASE! DON'T—
SPLAT
AND AS FOR YOUR FIRST QUESTION, IF YOU'RE STILL LISTENING, I'M THE MAN WHO WILL BE REMEMBERED FOR DOING THE IMPOSSIBLE.
FOR PUTTING THE GENIE BACK IN THE LAMP.
SUBJECT DECEASED. DIVISION UNSUCCESSFUL.
THEN WE'LL TRY AGAIN. NO SHORTAGE OF EGGS, AFTER ALL.

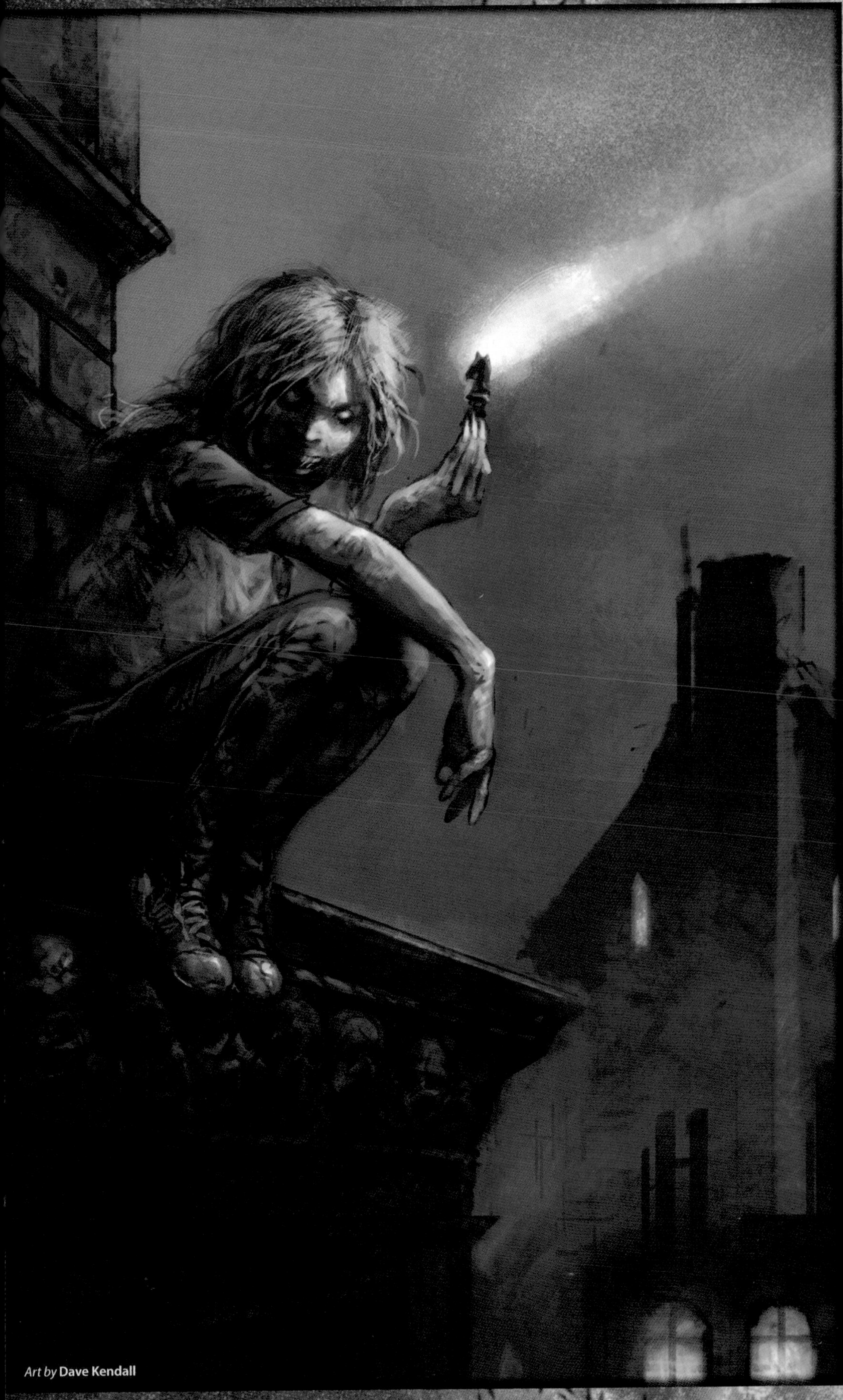

Art by **Dave Kendall**

CHAPTER 6

501

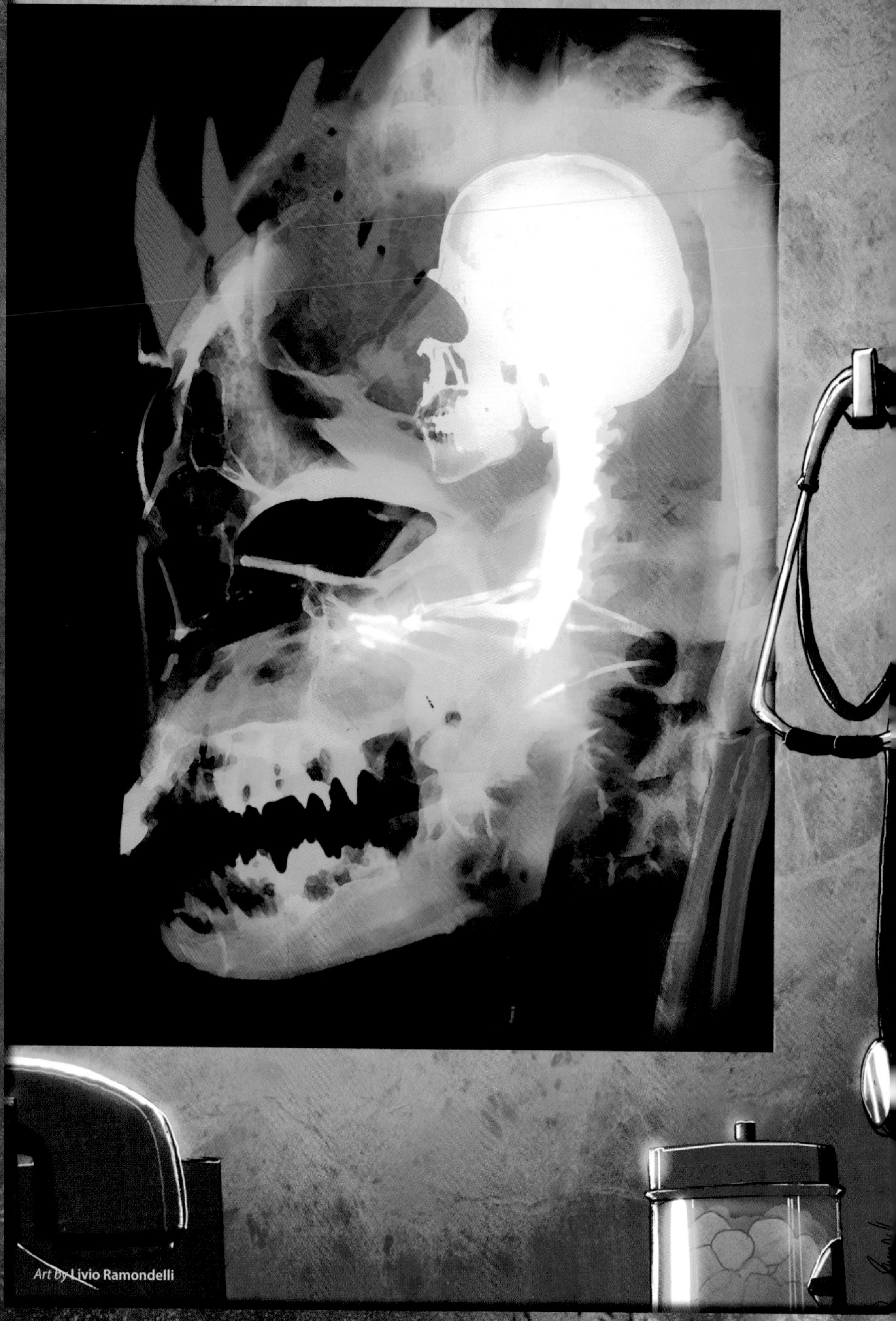

Art by Livio Ramondelli

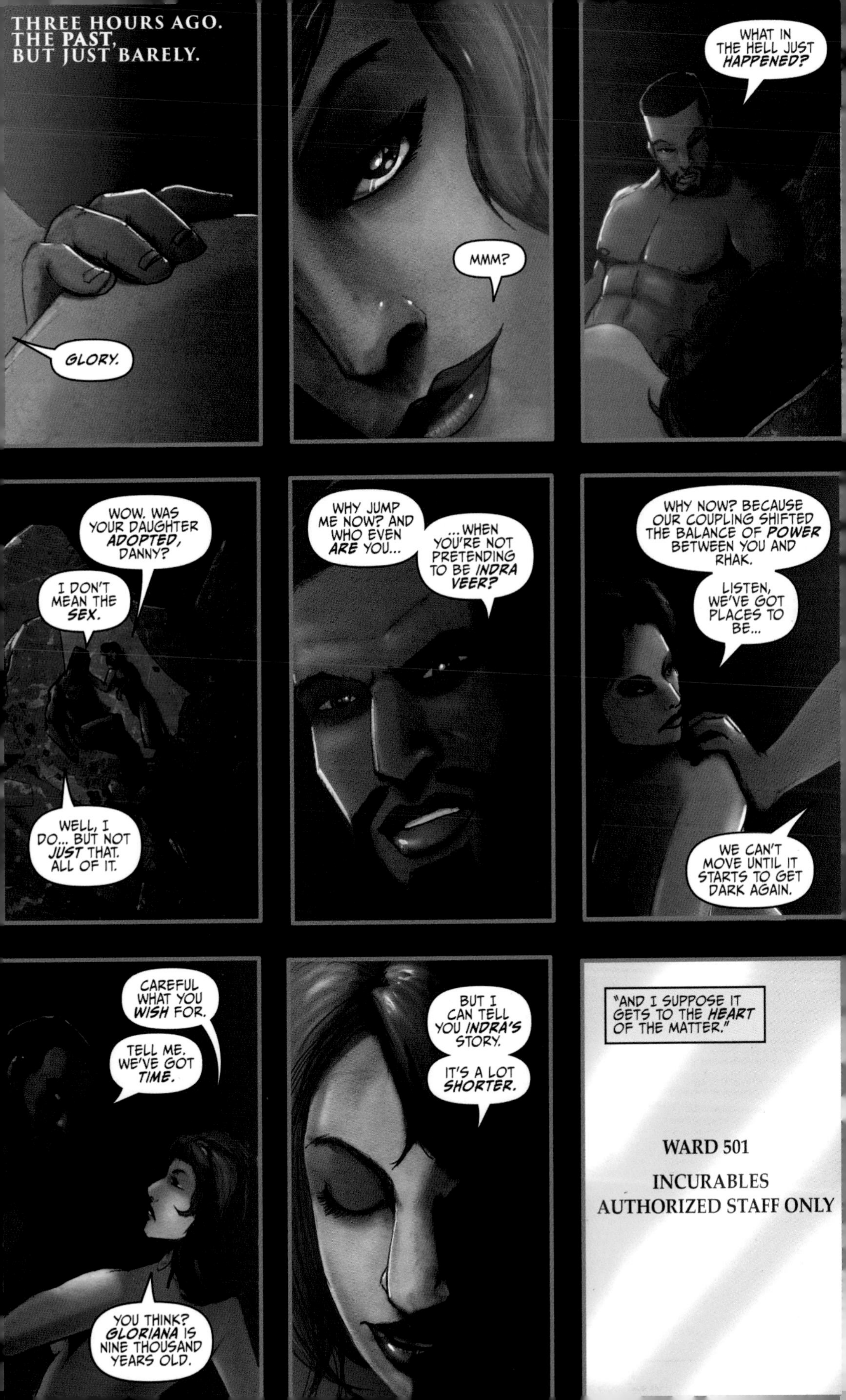
THREE HOURS AGO. THE PAST, BUT JUST BARELY.
GLORY.
MMM?
WHAT IN THE HELL JUST HAPPENED?
WOW. WAS YOUR DAUGHTER ADOPTED, DANNY?
I DON'T MEAN THE SEX.
WELL, I DO... BUT NOT JUST THAT. ALL OF IT.
WHY JUMP ME NOW? AND WHO EVEN ARE YOU...
...WHEN YOU'RE NOT PRETENDING TO BE INDRA VEER?
WHY NOW? BECAUSE OUR COUPLING SHIFTED THE BALANCE OF POWER BETWEEN YOU AND RHAK.
LISTEN, WE'VE GOT PLACES TO BE...
WE CAN'T MOVE UNTIL IT STARTS TO GET DARK AGAIN.
CAREFUL WHAT YOU WISH FOR.
TELL ME. WE'VE GOT TIME.
YOU THINK? GLORIANA IS NINE THOUSAND YEARS OLD.
BUT I CAN TELL YOU INDRA'S STORY.
IT'S A LOT SHORTER.
"AND I SUPPOSE IT GETS TO THE HEART OF THE MATTER."
WARD 501
INCURABLES
AUTHORIZED STAFF ONLY

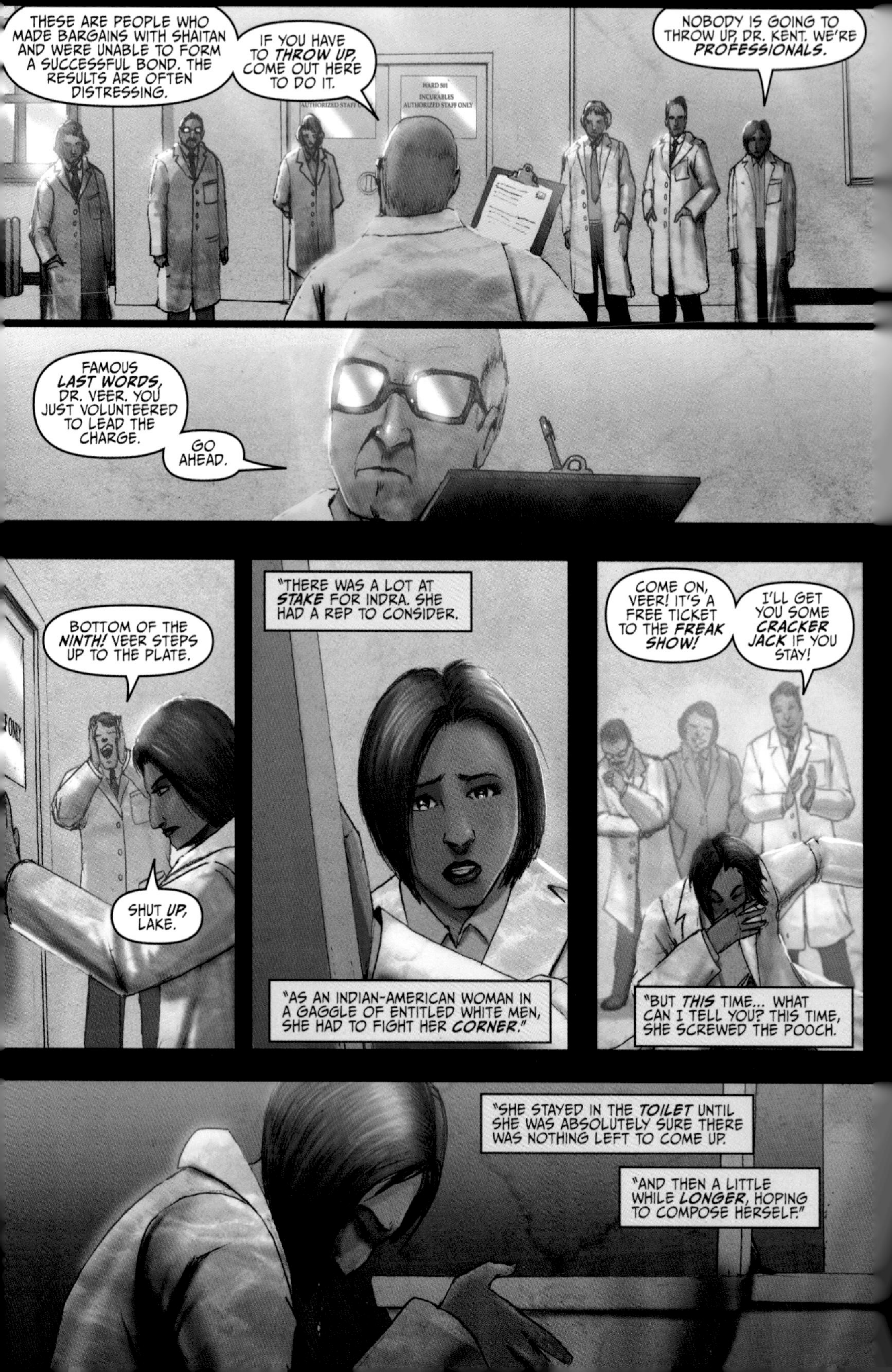
THESE ARE PEOPLE WHO MADE BARGAINS WITH SHAITAN AND WERE UNABLE TO FORM A SUCCESSFUL BOND. THE RESULTS ARE OFTEN DISTRESSING.
IF YOU HAVE TO THROW UP, COME OUT HERE TO DO IT.
WARD 501
INCURABLES
AUTHORIZED STAFF ONLY
NOBODY IS GOING TO THROW UP, DR. KENT. WE'RE PROFESSIONALS.
FAMOUS LAST WORDS, DR. VEER. YOU JUST VOLUNTEERED TO LEAD THE CHARGE.
GO AHEAD.
BOTTOM OF THE NINTH! VEER STEPS UP TO THE PLATE.
SHUT UP, LAKE.
"THERE WAS A LOT AT STAKE FOR INDRA. SHE HAD A REP TO CONSIDER.
"AS AN INDIAN-AMERICAN WOMAN IN A GAGGLE OF ENTITLED WHITE MEN, SHE HAD TO FIGHT HER CORNER."
COME ON, VEER! IT'S A FREE TICKET TO THE FREAK SHOW!
I'LL GET YOU SOME CRACKER JACK IF YOU STAY!
"BUT THIS TIME... WHAT CAN I TELL YOU? THIS TIME, SHE SCREWED THE POOCH.
"SHE STAYED IN THE TOILET UNTIL SHE WAS ABSOLUTELY SURE THERE WAS NOTHING LEFT TO COME UP.
"AND THEN A LITTLE WHILE LONGER, HOPING TO COMPOSE HERSELF."

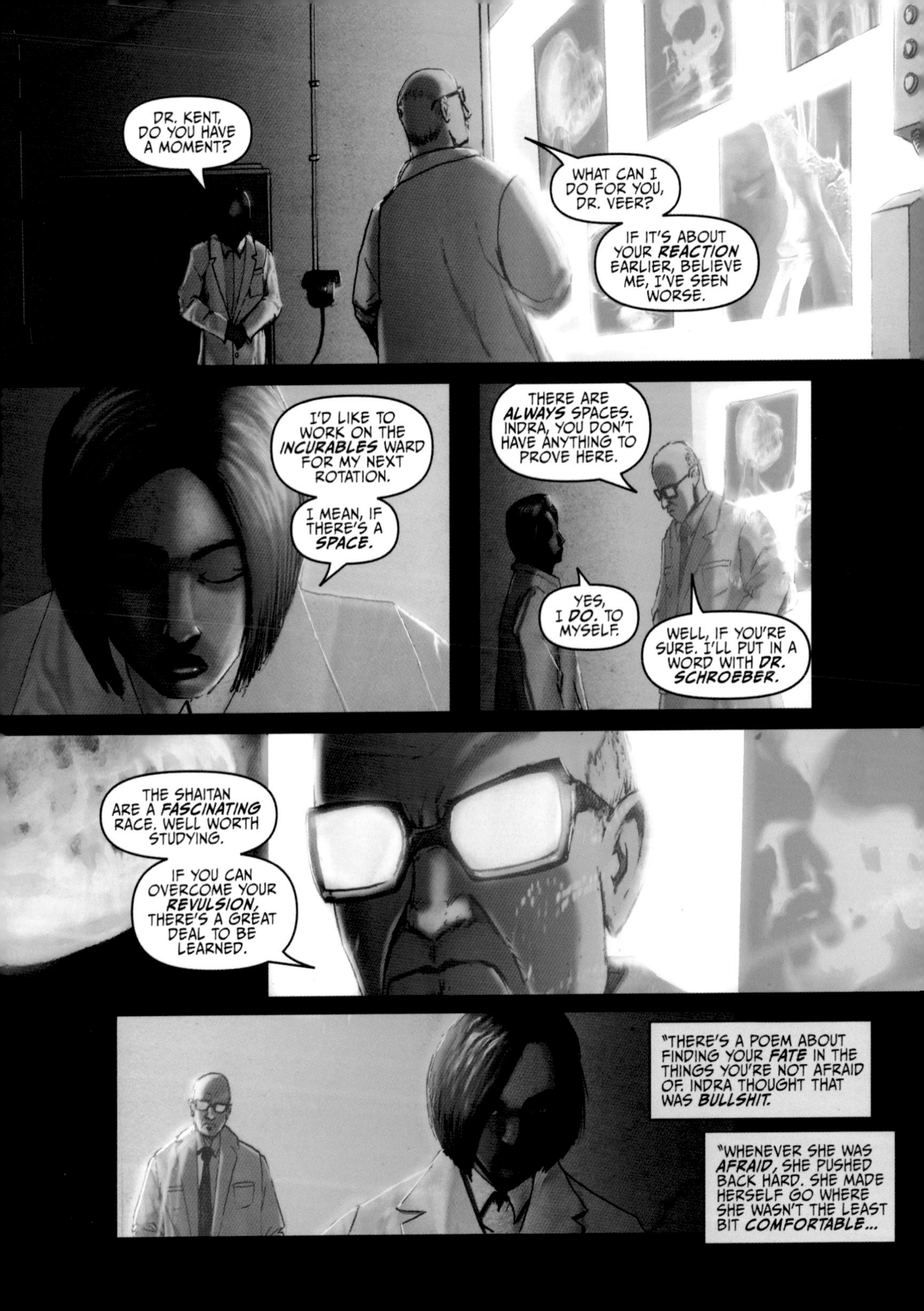
DR. KENT, DO YOU HAVE A MOMENT?
WHAT CAN I DO FOR YOU, DR. VEER?
IF IT'S ABOUT YOUR REACTION EARLIER, BELIEVE ME, I'VE SEEN WORSE.
I'D LIKE TO WORK ON THE INCURABLES WARD FOR MY NEXT ROTATION.
I MEAN, IF THERE'S A SPACE.
THERE ARE ALWAYS SPACES. INDRA, YOU DON'T HAVE ANYTHING TO PROVE HERE.
YES, I DO. TO MYSELF.
WELL, IF YOU'RE SURE. I'LL PUT IN A WORD WITH DR. SCHROEBER.
THE SHAITAN ARE A FASCINATING RACE. WELL WORTH STUDYING.
IF YOU CAN OVERCOME YOUR REVULSION, THERE'S A GREAT DEAL TO BE LEARNED.
"THERE'S A POEM ABOUT FINDING YOUR FATE IN THE THINGS YOU'RE NOT AFRAID OF. INDRA THOUGHT THAT WAS BULLSHIT.
"WHENEVER SHE WAS AFRAID, SHE PUSHED BACK HARD. SHE MADE HERSELF GO WHERE SHE WASN'T THE LEAST BIT COMFORTABLE...

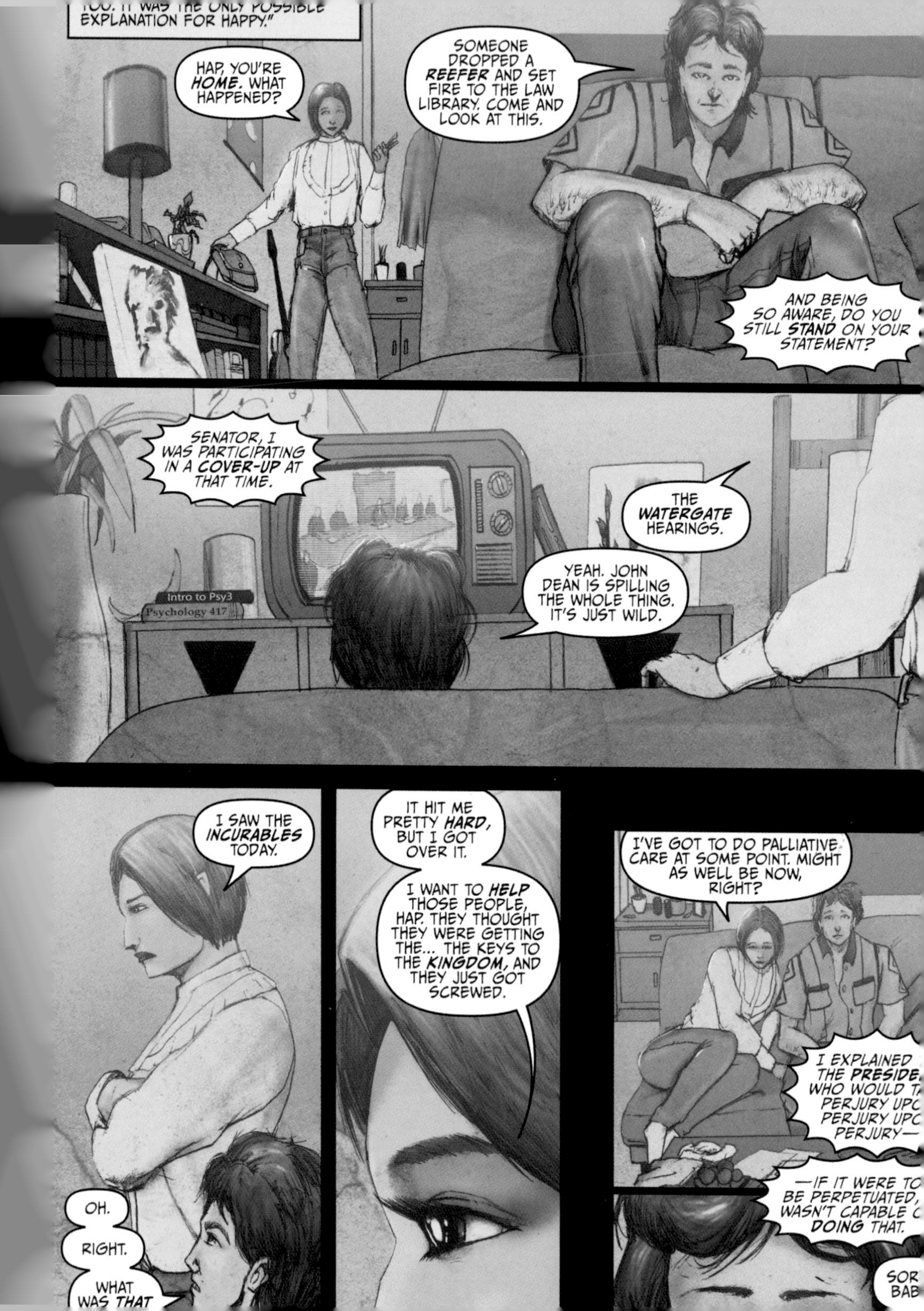

EXPLANATION FOR HAPPY."
HAP, YOU'RE HOME. WHAT HAPPENED?
SOMEONE DROPPED A REEFER AND SET FIRE TO THE LAW LIBRARY. COME AND LOOK AT THIS.
AND BEING SO AWARE, DO YOU STILL STAND ON YOUR STATEMENT?
SENATOR, I WAS PARTICIPATING IN A COVER-UP AT THAT TIME.
THE WATERGATE HEARINGS.
YEAH. JOHN DEAN IS SPILLING THE WHOLE THING. IT'S JUST WILD.
Intro to Psy3
Psychology 417
I SAW THE INCURABLES TODAY.
OH.
RIGHT.
WHAT WAS THAT
IT HIT ME PRETTY HARD, BUT I GOT OVER IT.
I WANT TO HELP THOSE PEOPLE, HAP. THEY THOUGHT THEY WERE GETTING THE... THE KEYS TO THE KINGDOM, AND THEY JUST GOT SCREWED.
I'VE GOT TO DO PALLIATIVE CARE AT SOME POINT. MIGHT AS WELL BE NOW, RIGHT?
I EXPLAINED THE PRESIDE WHO WOULD T PERJURY UPC PERJURY UPC PERJURY—
—IF IT WERE TO BE PERPETUATED, WASN'T CAPABLE C DOING THAT.
SOR BAB

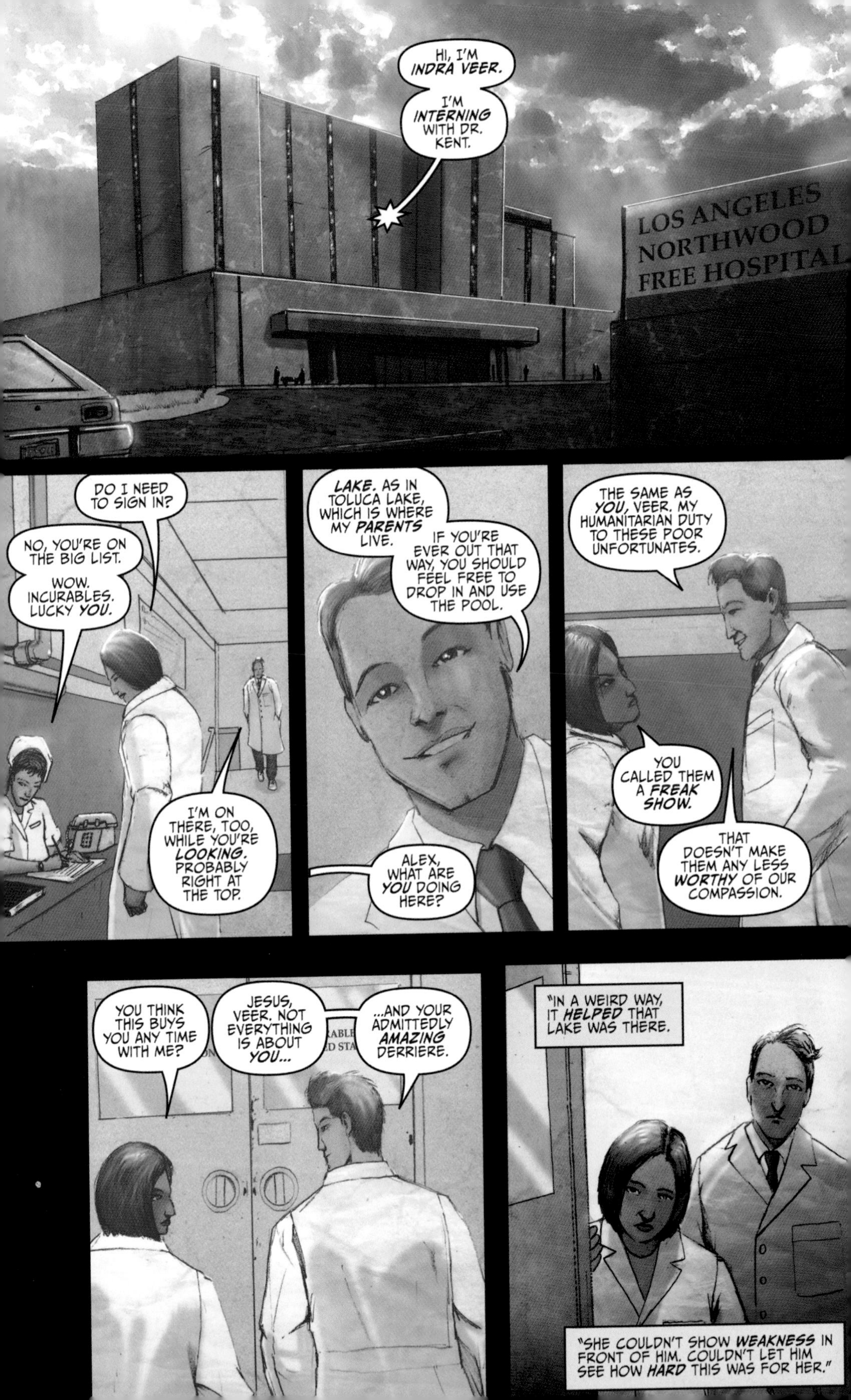
HI, I'M INDRA VEER.
I'M INTERNING WITH DR. KENT.
LOS ANGELES NORTHWOOD FREE HOSPITAL
DO I NEED TO SIGN IN?
NO, YOU'RE ON THE BIG LIST.
WOW. INCURABLES. LUCKY YOU.
I'M ON THERE, TOO, WHILE YOU'RE LOOKING. PROBABLY RIGHT AT THE TOP.
ALEX, WHAT ARE YOU DOING HERE?
LAKE. AS IN TOLUCA LAKE, WHICH IS WHERE MY PARENTS LIVE.
IF YOU'RE EVER OUT THAT WAY, YOU SHOULD FEEL FREE TO DROP IN AND USE THE POOL.
THE SAME AS YOU, VEER. MY HUMANITARIAN DUTY TO THESE POOR UNFORTUNATES.
YOU CALLED THEM A FREAK SHOW.
THAT DOESN'T MAKE THEM ANY LESS WORTHY OF OUR COMPASSION.
YOU THINK THIS BUYS YOU ANY TIME WITH ME?
JESUS, VEER. NOT EVERYTHING IS ABOUT YOU...
...AND YOUR ADMITTEDLY AMAZING DERRIERE.
"IN A WEIRD WAY, IT HELPED THAT LAKE WAS THERE.
"SHE COULDN'T SHOW WEAKNESS IN FRONT OF HIM. COULDN'T LET HIM SEE HOW HARD THIS WAS FOR HER."

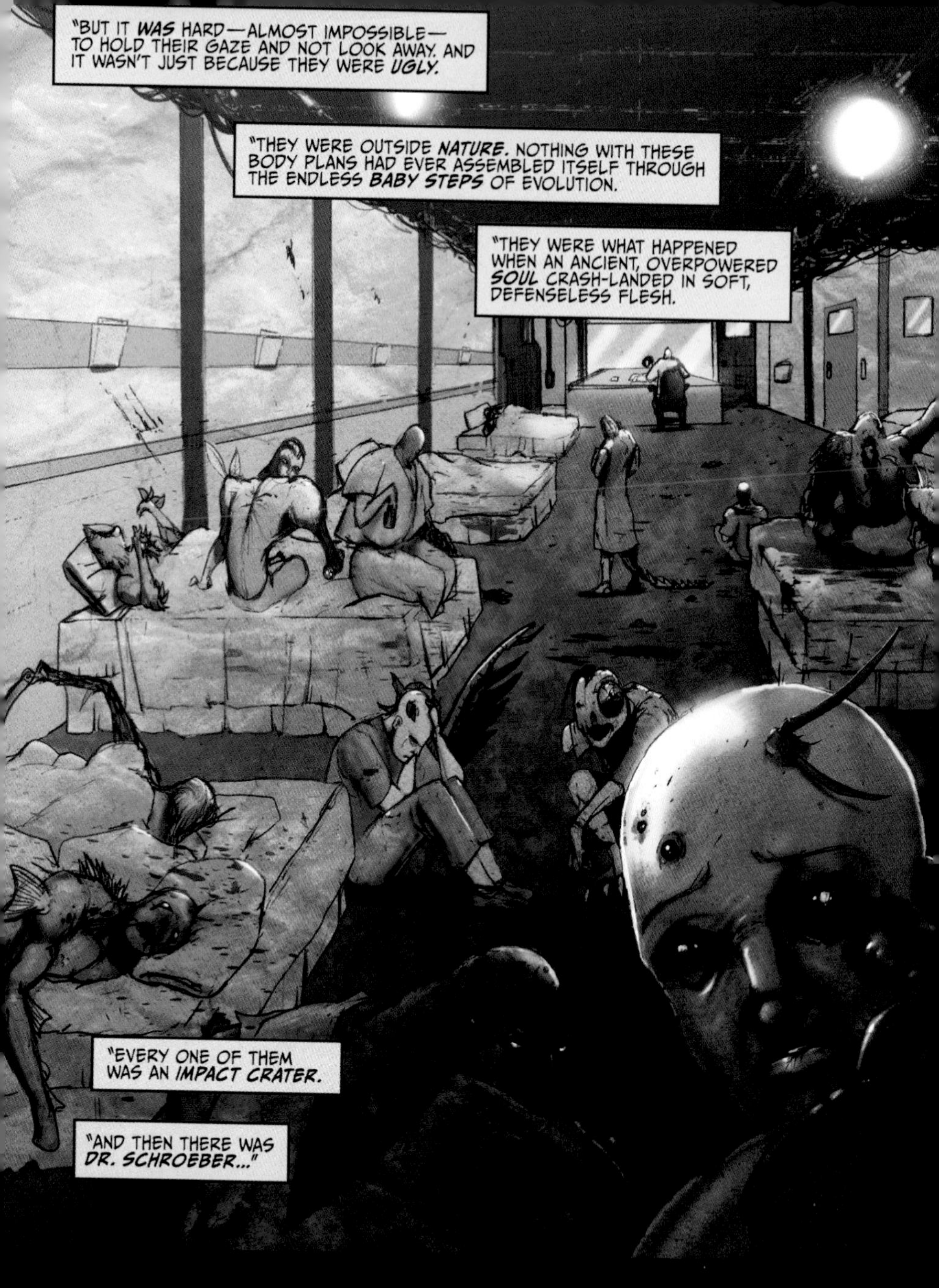
"BUT IT WAS HARD—ALMOST IMPOSSIBLE—TO HOLD THEIR GAZE AND NOT LOOK AWAY. AND IT WASN'T JUST BECAUSE THEY WERE UGLY.
"THEY WERE OUTSIDE NATURE. NOTHING WITH THESE BODY PLANS HAD EVER ASSEMBLED ITSELF THROUGH THE ENDLESS BABY STEPS OF EVOLUTION.
"THEY WERE WHAT HAPPENED WHEN AN ANCIENT, OVERPOWERED SOUL CRASH-LANDED IN SOFT, DEFENSELESS FLESH.
"EVERY ONE OF THEM WAS AN IMPACT CRATER.
"AND THEN THERE WAS DR. SCHROEBER..."

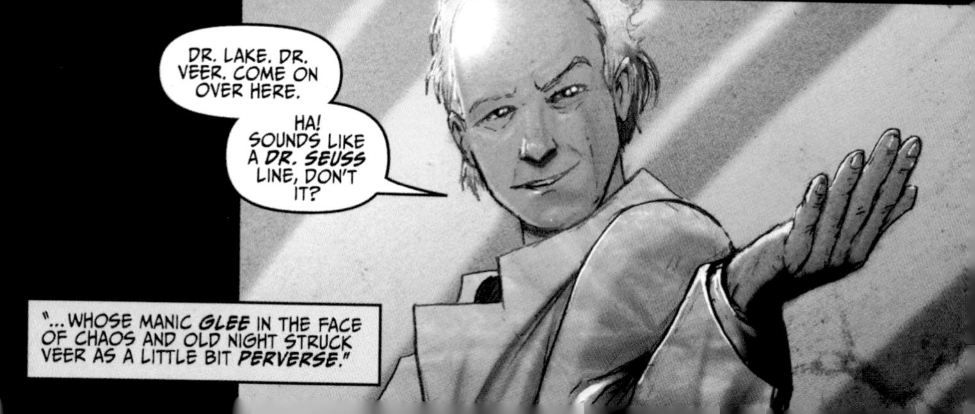
DR. LAKE. DR. VEER. COME ON OVER HERE.
HA! SOUNDS LIKE A DR. SEUSS LINE, DON'T IT?
"...WHOSE MANIC GLEE IN THE FACE OF CHAOS AND OLD NIGHT STRUCK VEER AS A LITTLE BIT PERVERSE."

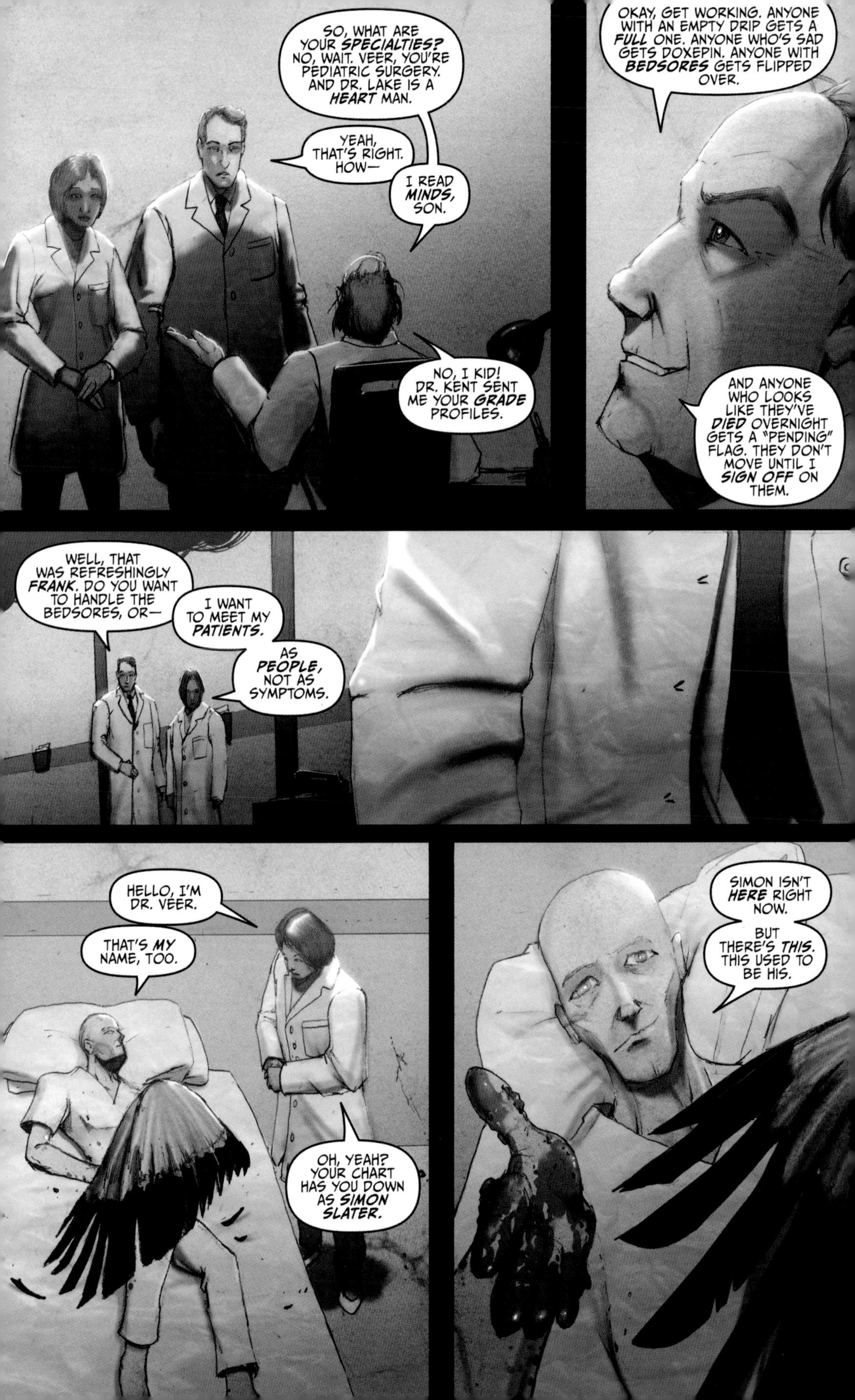
SO, WHAT ARE YOUR SPECIALTIES? NO, WAIT. VEER, YOU'RE PEDIATRIC SURGERY. AND DR. LAKE IS A HEART MAN.
YEAH, THAT'S RIGHT. HOW—
I READ MINDS, SON.
NO, I KID! DR. KENT SENT ME YOUR GRADE PROFILES.
OKAY, GET WORKING. ANYONE WITH AN EMPTY DRIP GETS A FULL ONE. ANYONE WHO'S SAD GETS DOXEPIN. ANYONE WITH BEDSORES GETS FLIPPED OVER.
AND ANYONE WHO LOOKS LIKE THEY'VE DIED OVERNIGHT GETS A "PENDING" FLAG. THEY DON'T MOVE UNTIL I SIGN OFF ON THEM.
WELL, THAT WAS REFRESHINGLY FRANK. DO YOU WANT TO HANDLE THE BEDSORES, OR—
I WANT TO MEET MY PATIENTS.
AS PEOPLE, NOT AS SYMPTOMS.
HELLO, I'M DR. VEER.
THAT'S MY NAME, TOO.
OH, YEAH? YOUR CHART HAS YOU DOWN AS SIMON SLATER.
SIMON ISN'T HERE RIGHT NOW.
BUT THERE'S THIS. THIS USED TO BE HIS.

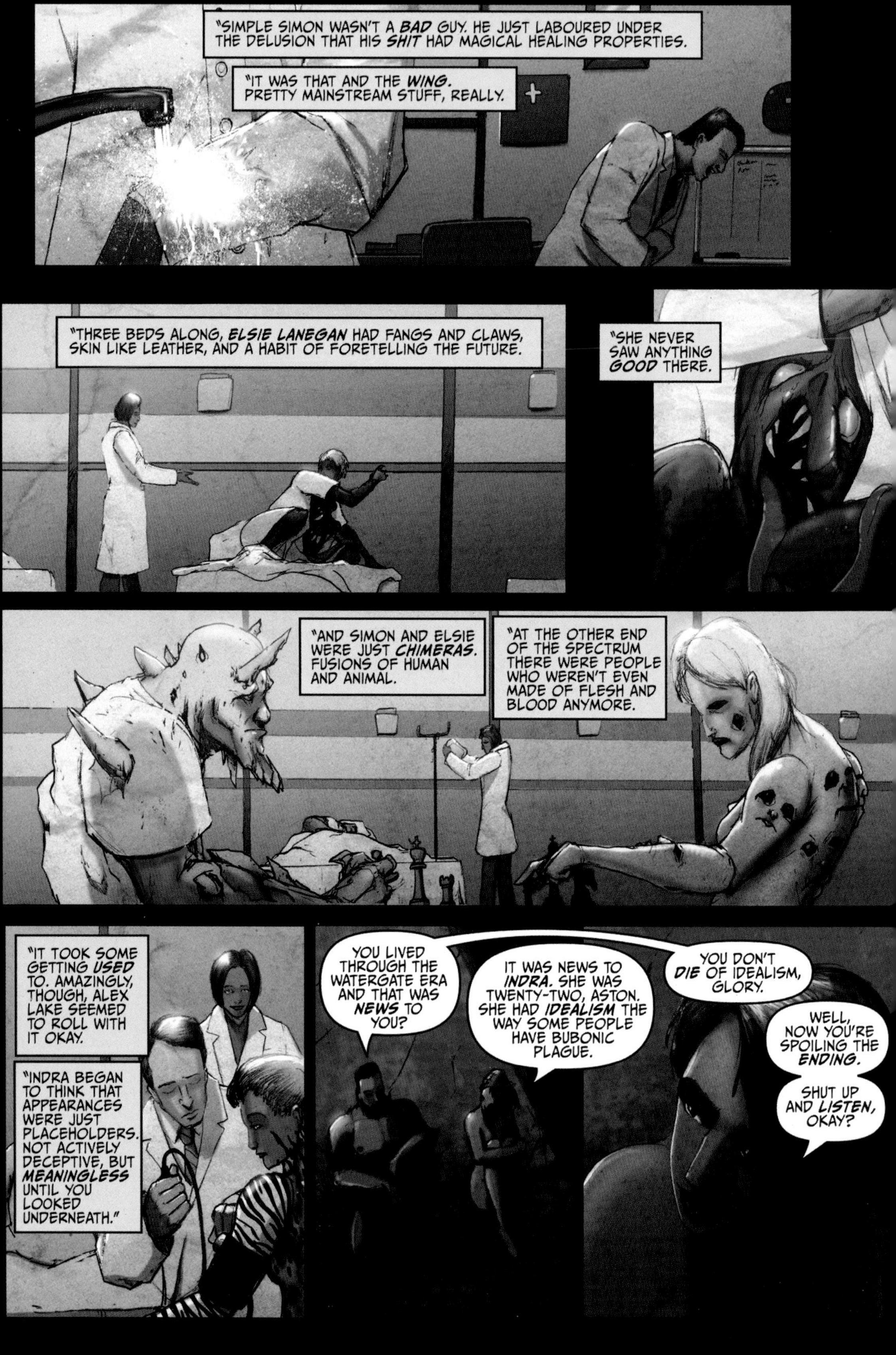
"SIMPLE SIMON WASN'T A *BAD* GUY. HE JUST LABOURED UNDER THE DELUSION THAT HIS *SHIT* HAD MAGICAL HEALING PROPERTIES.
"IT WAS THAT AND THE *WING.* PRETTY MAINSTREAM STUFF, REALLY.
"THREE BEDS ALONG, *ELSIE LANEGAN* HAD FANGS AND CLAWS, SKIN LIKE LEATHER, AND A HABIT OF FORETELLING THE FUTURE.
"SHE NEVER SAW ANYTHING *GOOD* THERE.
"AND SIMON AND ELSIE WERE JUST *CHIMERAS.* FUSIONS OF HUMAN AND ANIMAL.
"AT THE OTHER END OF THE SPECTRUM THERE WERE PEOPLE WHO WEREN'T EVEN MADE OF FLESH AND BLOOD ANYMORE.
"IT TOOK SOME GETTING *USED* TO. AMAZINGLY, THOUGH, ALEX LAKE SEEMED TO ROLL WITH IT OKAY.
"INDRA BEGAN TO THINK THAT APPEARANCES WERE JUST PLACEHOLDERS. NOT ACTIVELY DECEPTIVE, BUT *MEANINGLESS* UNTIL YOU LOOKED UNDERNEATH."
YOU LIVED THROUGH THE WATERGATE ERA AND THAT WAS *NEWS* TO YOU?
IT WAS NEWS TO *INDRA.* SHE WAS TWENTY-TWO, ASTON. SHE HAD *IDEALISM* THE WAY SOME PEOPLE HAVE BUBONIC PLAGUE.
YOU DON'T *DIE* OF IDEALISM, GLORY.
WELL, NOW YOU'RE SPOILING THE *ENDING.*
SHUT UP AND *LISTEN,* OKAY?

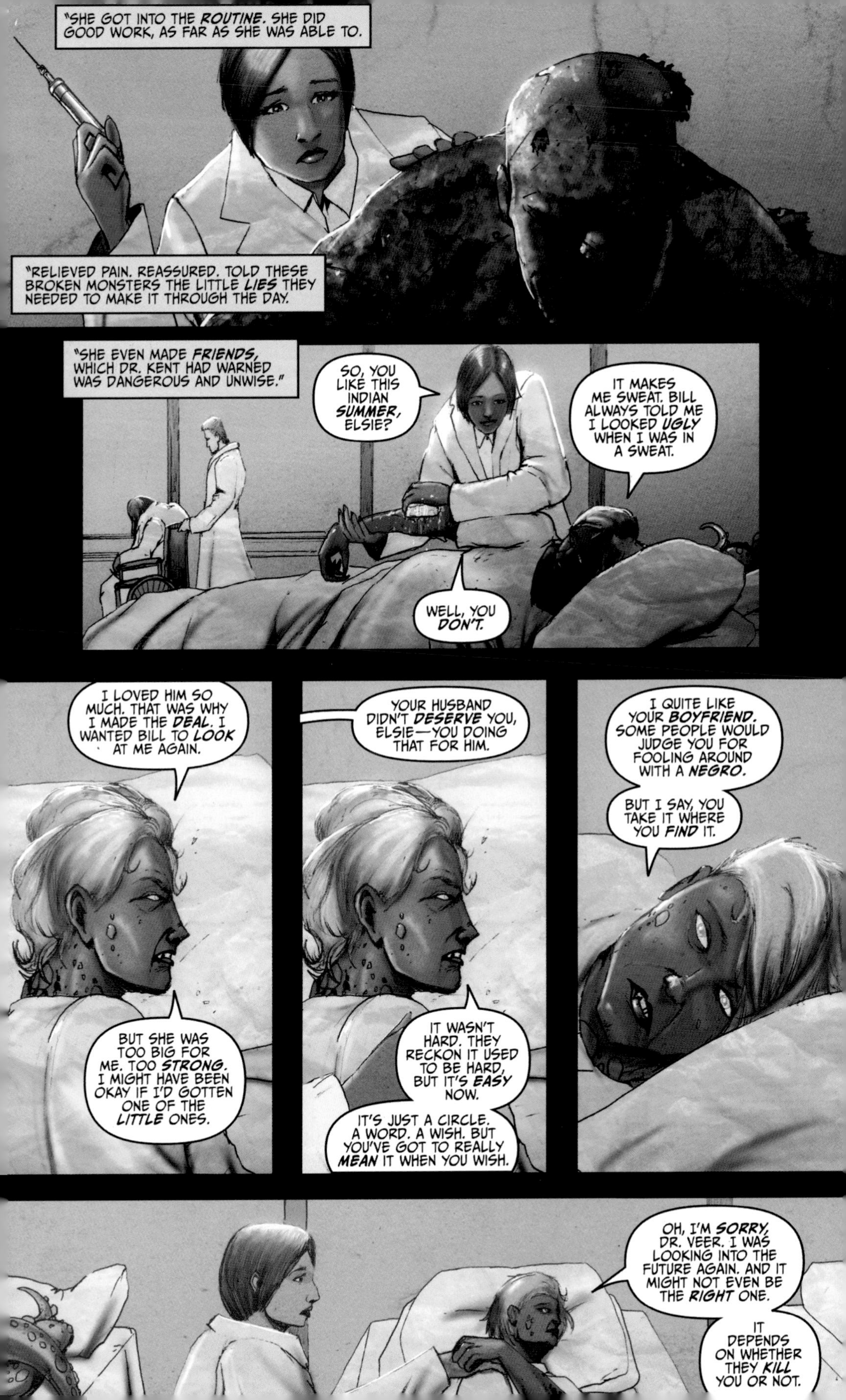
"SHE GOT INTO THE ROUTINE. SHE DID GOOD WORK, AS FAR AS SHE WAS ABLE TO.
"RELIEVED PAIN. REASSURED. TOLD THESE BROKEN MONSTERS THE LITTLE LIES THEY NEEDED TO MAKE IT THROUGH THE DAY.
"SHE EVEN MADE FRIENDS, WHICH DR. KENT HAD WARNED WAS DANGEROUS AND UNWISE."
SO, YOU LIKE THIS INDIAN SUMMER, ELSIE?
IT MAKES ME SWEAT. BILL ALWAYS TOLD ME I LOOKED UGLY WHEN I WAS IN A SWEAT.
WELL, YOU DON'T.
I LOVED HIM SO MUCH. THAT WAS WHY I MADE THE DEAL. I WANTED BILL TO LOOK AT ME AGAIN.
BUT SHE WAS TOO BIG FOR ME. TOO STRONG. I MIGHT HAVE BEEN OKAY IF I'D GOTTEN ONE OF THE LITTLE ONES.
YOUR HUSBAND DIDN'T DESERVE YOU, ELSIE—YOU DOING THAT FOR HIM.
IT WASN'T HARD. THEY RECKON IT USED TO BE HARD, BUT IT'S EASY NOW.
IT'S JUST A CIRCLE. A WORD. A WISH. BUT YOU'VE GOT TO REALLY MEAN IT WHEN YOU WISH.
I QUITE LIKE YOUR BOYFRIEND. SOME PEOPLE WOULD JUDGE YOU FOR FOOLING AROUND WITH A NEGRO.
BUT I SAY, YOU TAKE IT WHERE YOU FIND IT.
OH, I'M SORRY, DR. VEER. I WAS LOOKING INTO THE FUTURE AGAIN. AND IT MIGHT NOT EVEN BE THE RIGHT ONE.
IT DEPENDS ON WHETHER THEY KILL YOU OR NOT.

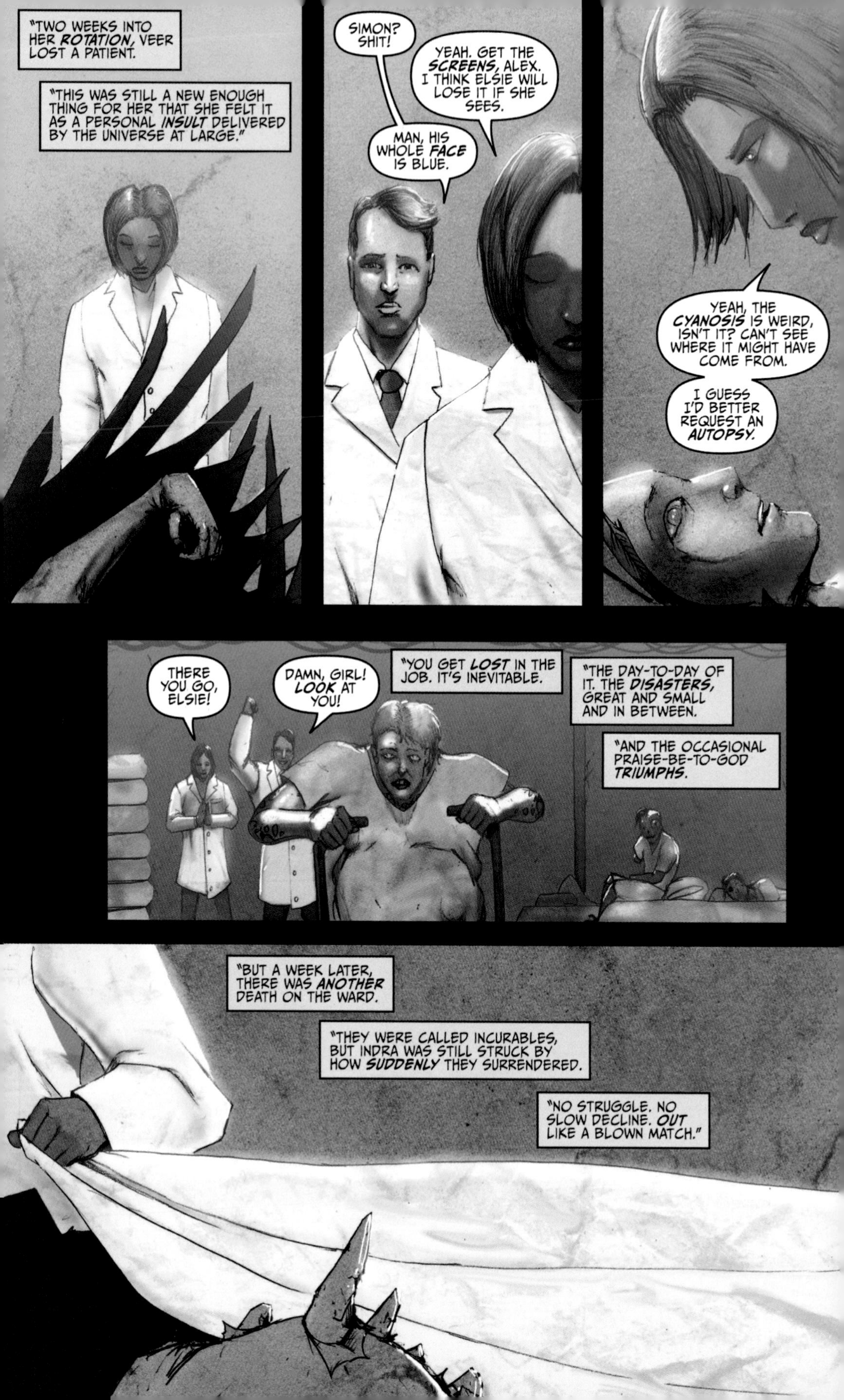
"TWO WEEKS INTO HER ROTATION, VEER LOST A PATIENT.
"THIS WAS STILL A NEW ENOUGH THING FOR HER THAT SHE FELT IT AS A PERSONAL INSULT DELIVERED BY THE UNIVERSE AT LARGE."
SIMON? SHIT!
MAN, HIS WHOLE FACE IS BLUE.
YEAH. GET THE SCREENS, ALEX. I THINK ELSIE WILL LOSE IT IF SHE SEES.
YEAH, THE CYANOSIS IS WEIRD, ISN'T IT? CAN'T SEE WHERE IT MIGHT HAVE COME FROM.
I GUESS I'D BETTER REQUEST AN AUTOPSY.
THERE YOU GO, ELSIE!
DAMN, GIRL! LOOK AT YOU!
"YOU GET LOST IN THE JOB. IT'S INEVITABLE.
"THE DAY-TO-DAY OF IT. THE DISASTERS, GREAT AND SMALL AND IN BETWEEN.
"AND THE OCCASIONAL PRAISE-BE-TO-GOD TRIUMPHS.
"BUT A WEEK LATER, THERE WAS ANOTHER DEATH ON THE WARD.
"THEY WERE CALLED INCURABLES, BUT INDRA WAS STILL STRUCK BY HOW SUDDENLY THEY SURRENDERED.
"NO STRUGGLE. NO SLOW DECLINE. OUT LIKE A BLOWN MATCH."

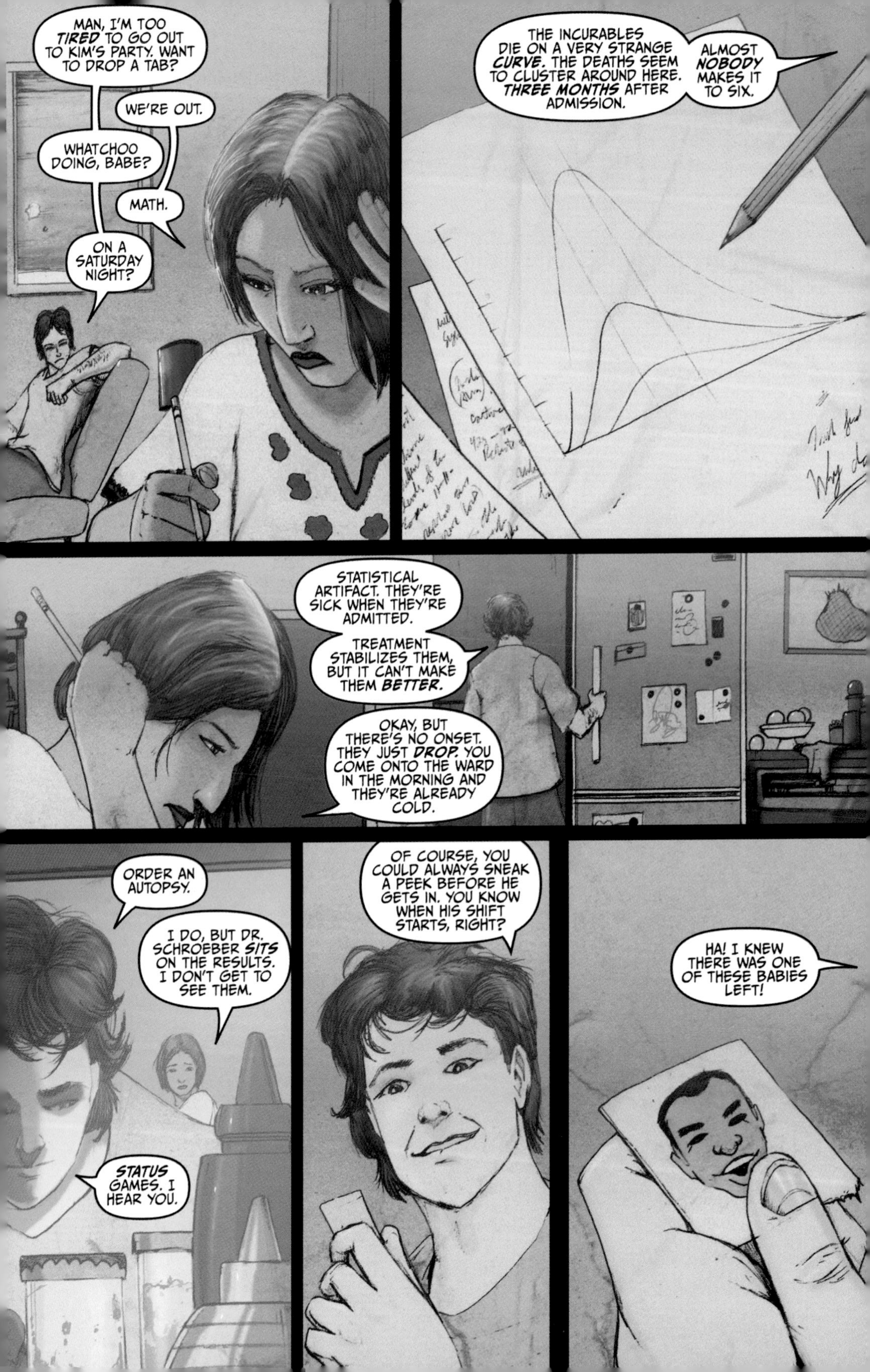
MAN, I'M TOO TIRED TO GO OUT TO KIM'S PARTY. WANT TO DROP A TAB?
WE'RE OUT.
WHATCHOO DOING, BABE?
MATH.
ON A SATURDAY NIGHT?
THE INCURABLES DIE ON A VERY STRANGE CURVE. THE DEATHS SEEM TO CLUSTER AROUND HERE. THREE MONTHS AFTER ADMISSION.
ALMOST NOBODY MAKES IT TO SIX.
STATISTICAL ARTIFACT. THEY'RE SICK WHEN THEY'RE ADMITTED.
TREATMENT STABILIZES THEM, BUT IT CAN'T MAKE THEM BETTER.
OKAY, BUT THERE'S NO ONSET. THEY JUST DROP. YOU COME ONTO THE WARD IN THE MORNING AND THEY'RE ALREADY COLD.
ORDER AN AUTOPSY.
I DO, BUT DR. SCHROEBER SITS ON THE RESULTS. I DON'T GET TO SEE THEM.
STATUS GAMES. I HEAR YOU.
OF COURSE, YOU COULD ALWAYS SNEAK A PEEK BEFORE HE GETS IN. YOU KNOW WHEN HIS SHIFT STARTS, RIGHT?
HA! I KNEW THERE WAS ONE OF THESE BABIES LEFT!

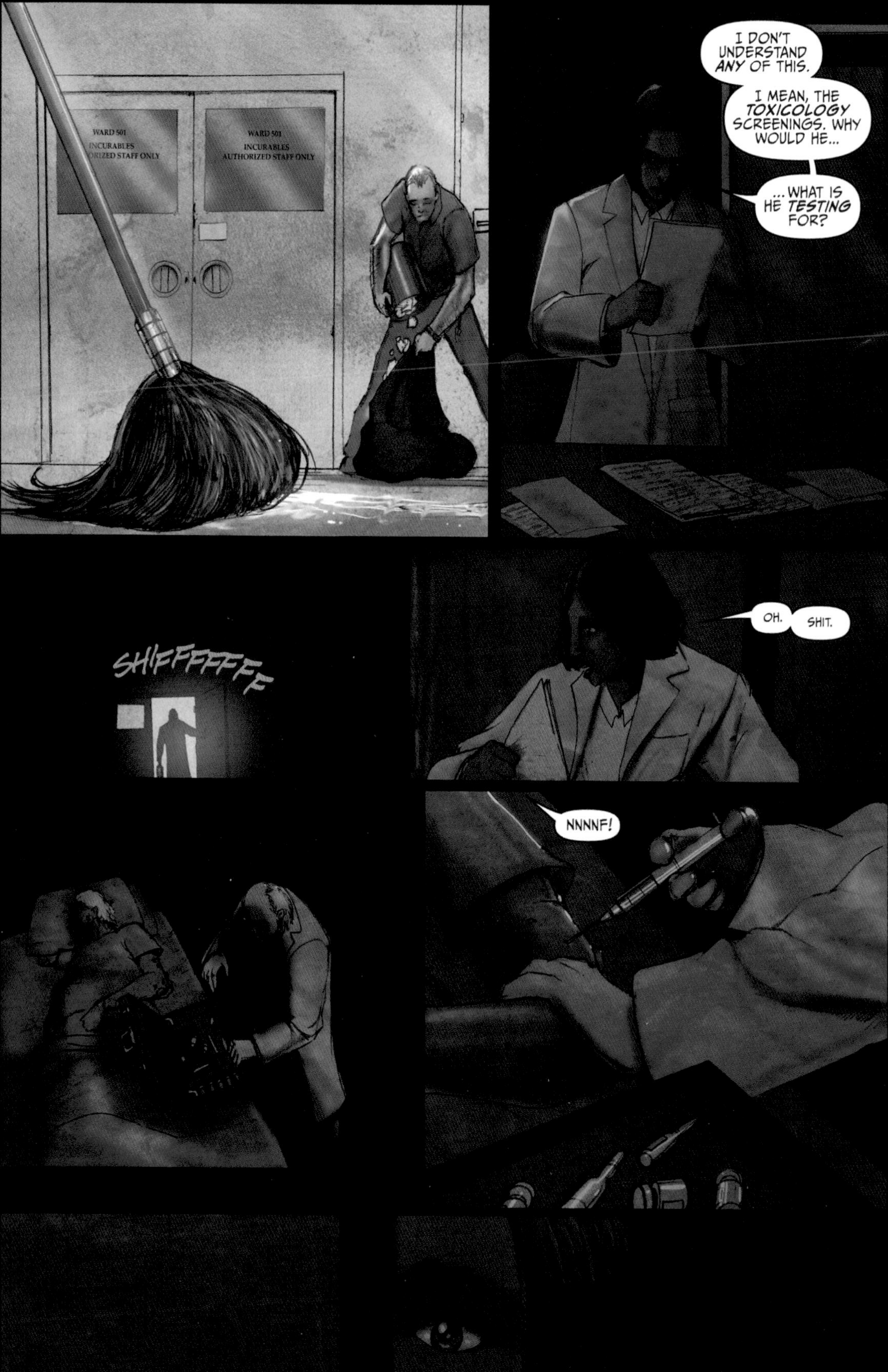
WARD 501
INCURABLES
AUTHORIZED STAFF ONLY
WARD 501
INCURABLES
AUTHORIZED STAFF ONLY
I DON'T UNDERSTAND *ANY* OF THIS.
I MEAN, THE *TOXICOLOGY* SCREENINGS. WHY WOULD HE...
...WHAT IS HE *TESTING* FOR?
SHIFFFFFFF
OH.
SHIT.
NNNNF!

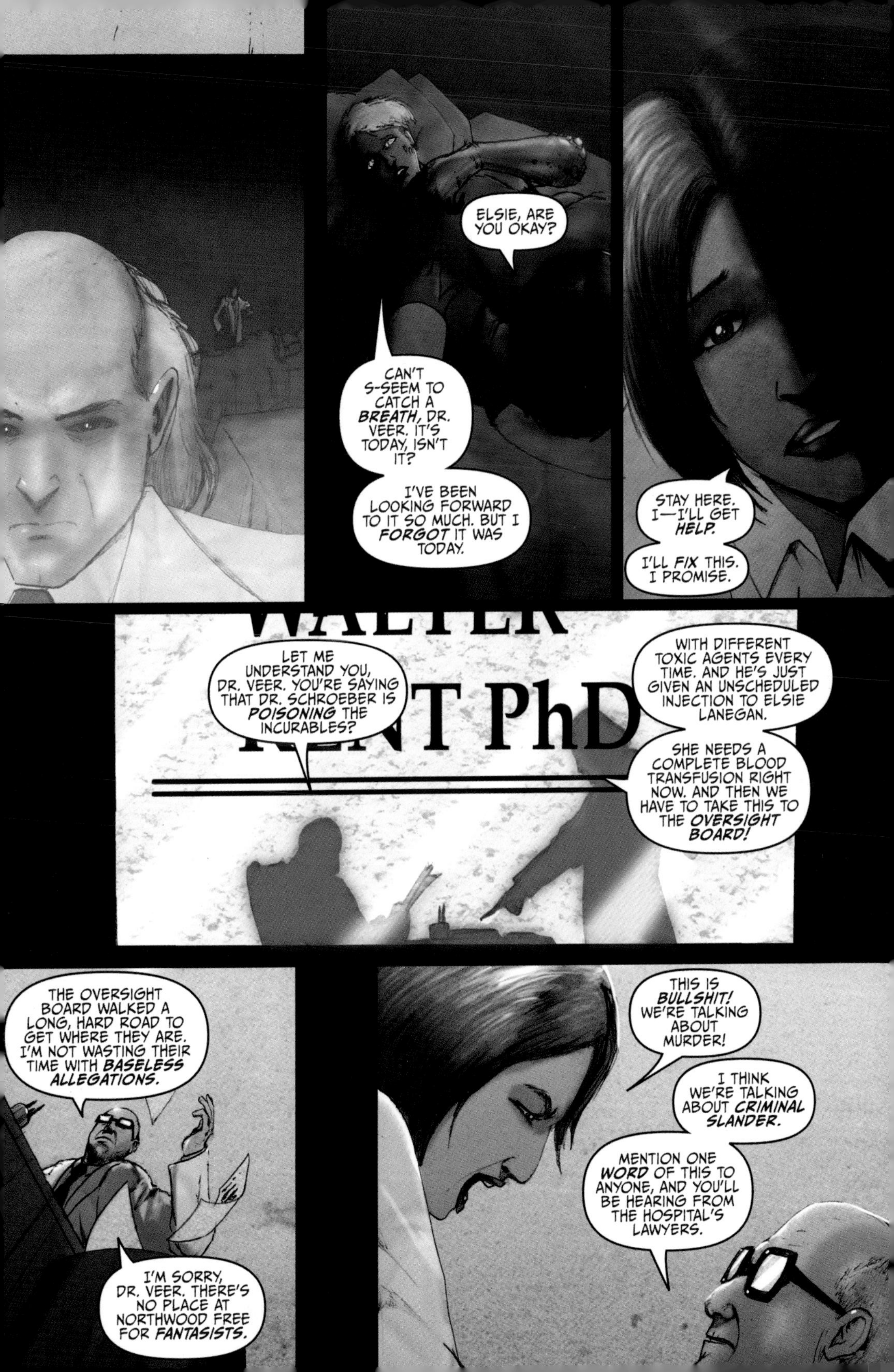
ELSIE, ARE YOU OKAY?
CAN'T S-SEEM TO CATCH A BREATH, DR. VEER. IT'S TODAY, ISN'T IT?
I'VE BEEN LOOKING FORWARD TO IT SO MUCH. BUT I FORGOT IT WAS TODAY.
STAY HERE. I—I'LL GET HELP.
I'LL FIX THIS. I PROMISE.
KENT PhD
LET ME UNDERSTAND YOU, DR. VEER. YOU'RE SAYING THAT DR. SCHROEBER IS POISONING THE INCURABLES?
WITH DIFFERENT TOXIC AGENTS EVERY TIME. AND HE'S JUST GIVEN AN UNSCHEDULED INJECTION TO ELSIE LANEGAN.
SHE NEEDS A COMPLETE BLOOD TRANSFUSION RIGHT NOW. AND THEN WE HAVE TO TAKE THIS TO THE OVERSIGHT BOARD!
THE OVERSIGHT BOARD WALKED A LONG, HARD ROAD TO GET WHERE THEY ARE. I'M NOT WASTING THEIR TIME WITH BASELESS ALLEGATIONS.
I'M SORRY, DR. VEER. THERE'S NO PLACE AT NORTHWOOD FREE FOR FANTASISTS.
THIS IS BULLSHIT! WE'RE TALKING ABOUT MURDER!
I THINK WE'RE TALKING ABOUT CRIMINAL SLANDER.
MENTION ONE WORD OF THIS TO ANYONE, AND YOU'LL BE HEARING FROM THE HOSPITAL'S LAWYERS.

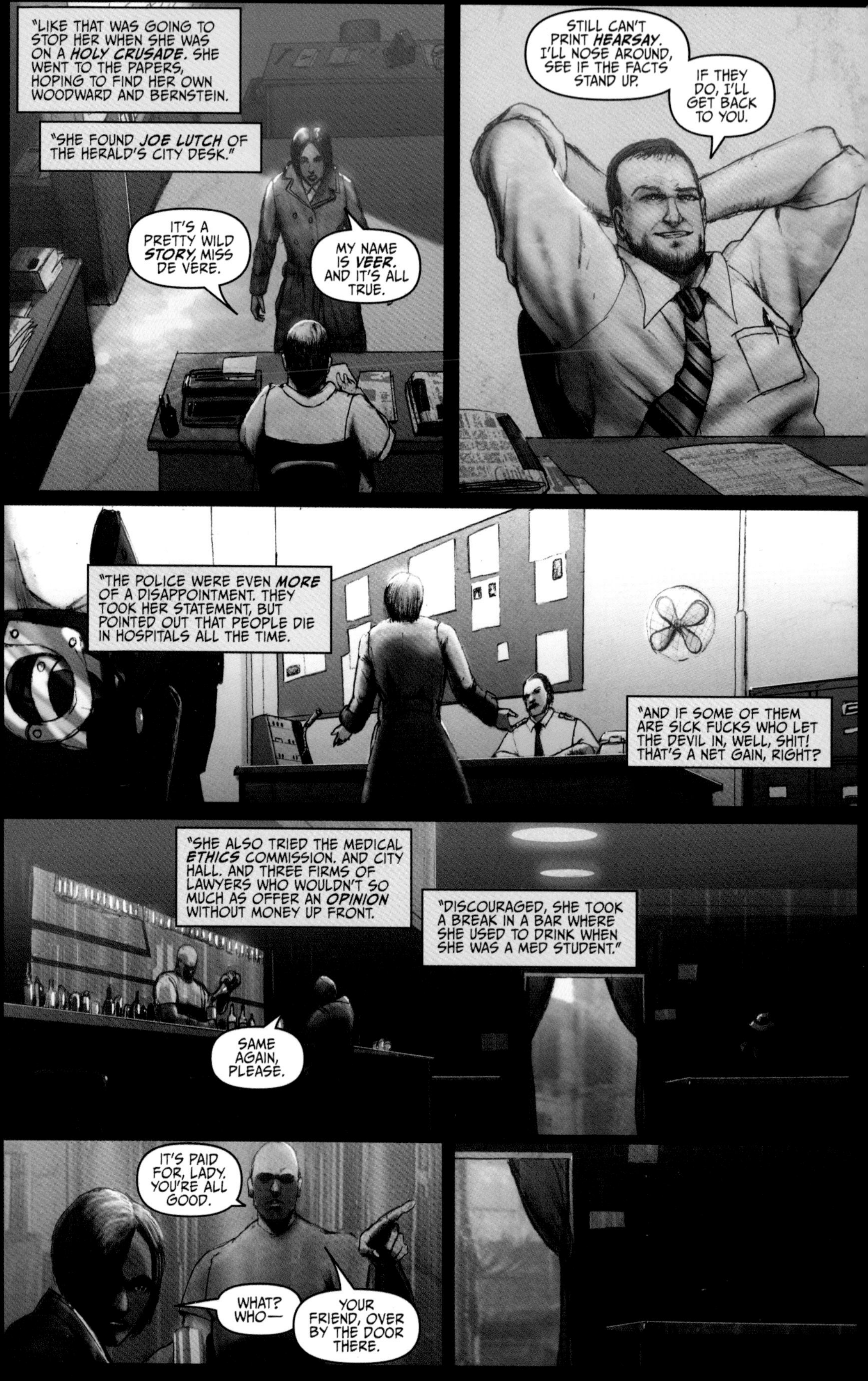
"LIKE THAT WAS GOING TO STOP HER WHEN SHE WAS ON A HOLY CRUSADE. SHE WENT TO THE PAPERS, HOPING TO FIND HER OWN WOODWARD AND BERNSTEIN.
"SHE FOUND JOE LUTCH OF THE HERALD'S CITY DESK."
IT'S A PRETTY WILD STORY, MISS DE VÈRE.
MY NAME IS VEER. AND IT'S ALL TRUE.
STILL CAN'T PRINT HEARSAY. I'LL NOSE AROUND, SEE IF THE FACTS STAND UP.
IF THEY DO, I'LL GET BACK TO YOU.
"THE POLICE WERE EVEN MORE OF A DISAPPOINTMENT. THEY TOOK HER STATEMENT, BUT POINTED OUT THAT PEOPLE DIE IN HOSPITALS ALL THE TIME.
"AND IF SOME OF THEM ARE SICK FUCKS WHO LET THE DEVIL IN, WELL, SHIT! THAT'S A NET GAIN, RIGHT?
"SHE ALSO TRIED THE MEDICAL ETHICS COMMISSION. AND CITY HALL. AND THREE FIRMS OF LAWYERS WHO WOULDN'T SO MUCH AS OFFER AN OPINION WITHOUT MONEY UP FRONT.
"DISCOURAGED, SHE TOOK A BREAK IN A BAR WHERE SHE USED TO DRINK WHEN SHE WAS A MED STUDENT."
SAME AGAIN, PLEASE.
IT'S PAID FOR, LADY. YOU'RE ALL GOOD.
WHAT? WHO—
YOUR FRIEND, OVER BY THE DOOR THERE.

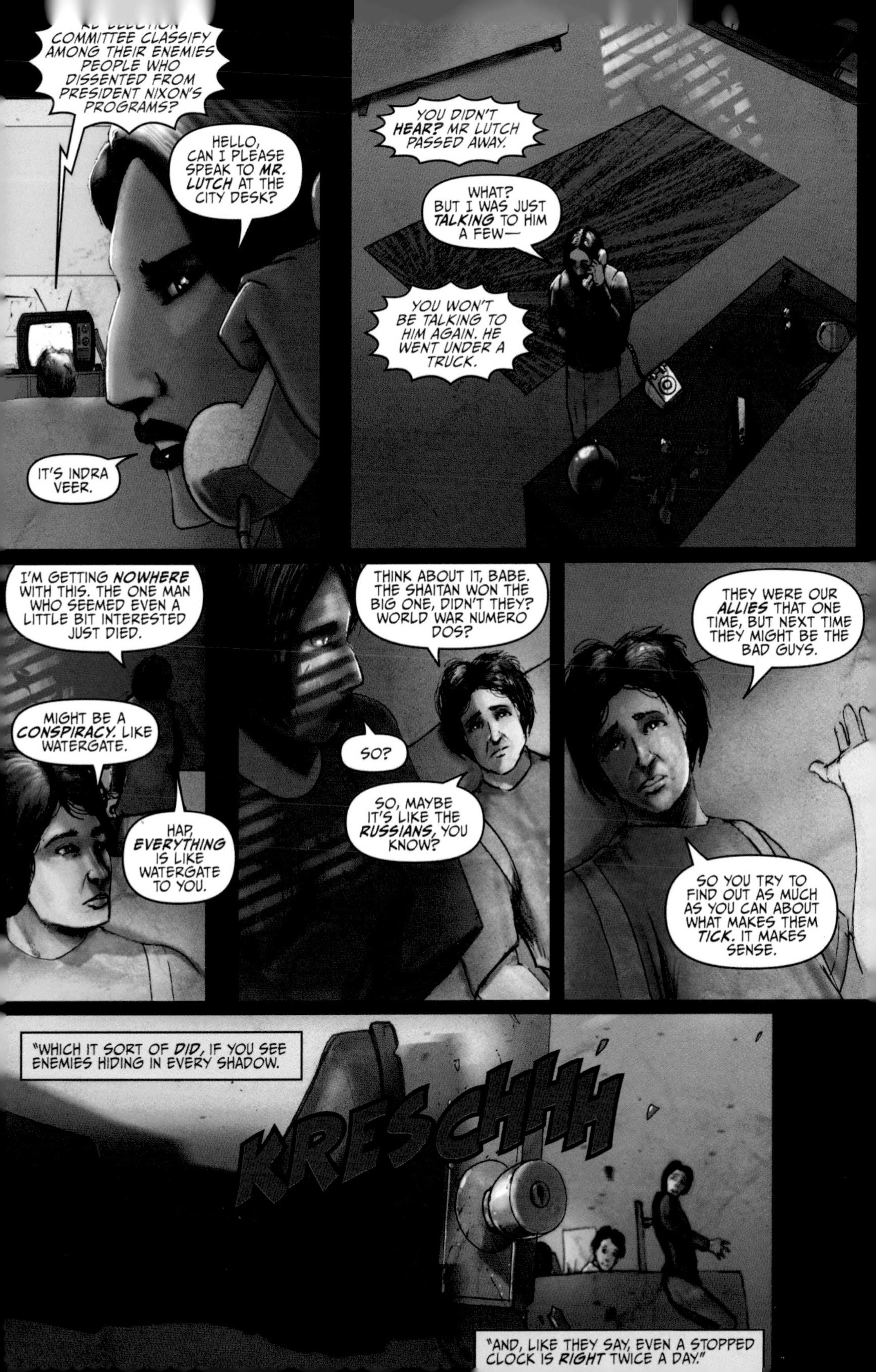
COMMITTEE CLASSIFY AMONG THEIR ENEMIES PEOPLE WHO DISSENTED FROM PRESIDENT NIXON'S PROGRAMS?
HELLO, CAN I PLEASE SPEAK TO MR. LUTCH AT THE CITY DESK?
IT'S INDRA VEER.
YOU DIDN'T HEAR? MR LUTCH PASSED AWAY.
WHAT? BUT I WAS JUST TALKING TO HIM A FEW—
YOU WON'T BE TALKING TO HIM AGAIN. HE WENT UNDER A TRUCK.
I'M GETTING NOWHERE WITH THIS. THE ONE MAN WHO SEEMED EVEN A LITTLE BIT INTERESTED JUST DIED.
MIGHT BE A CONSPIRACY. LIKE WATERGATE.
HAP, EVERYTHING IS LIKE WATERGATE TO YOU.
THINK ABOUT IT, BABE. THE SHAITAN WON THE BIG ONE, DIDN'T THEY? WORLD WAR NUMERO DOS?
SO?
SO, MAYBE IT'S LIKE THE RUSSIANS, YOU KNOW?
THEY WERE OUR ALLIES THAT ONE TIME, BUT NEXT TIME THEY MIGHT BE THE BAD GUYS.
SO YOU TRY TO FIND OUT AS MUCH AS YOU CAN ABOUT WHAT MAKES THEM TICK. IT MAKES SENSE.
"WHICH IT SORT OF DID, IF YOU SEE ENEMIES HIDING IN EVERY SHADOW.
KRESCHHH
"AND, LIKE THEY SAY, EVEN A STOPPED CLOCK IS RIGHT TWICE A DAY."

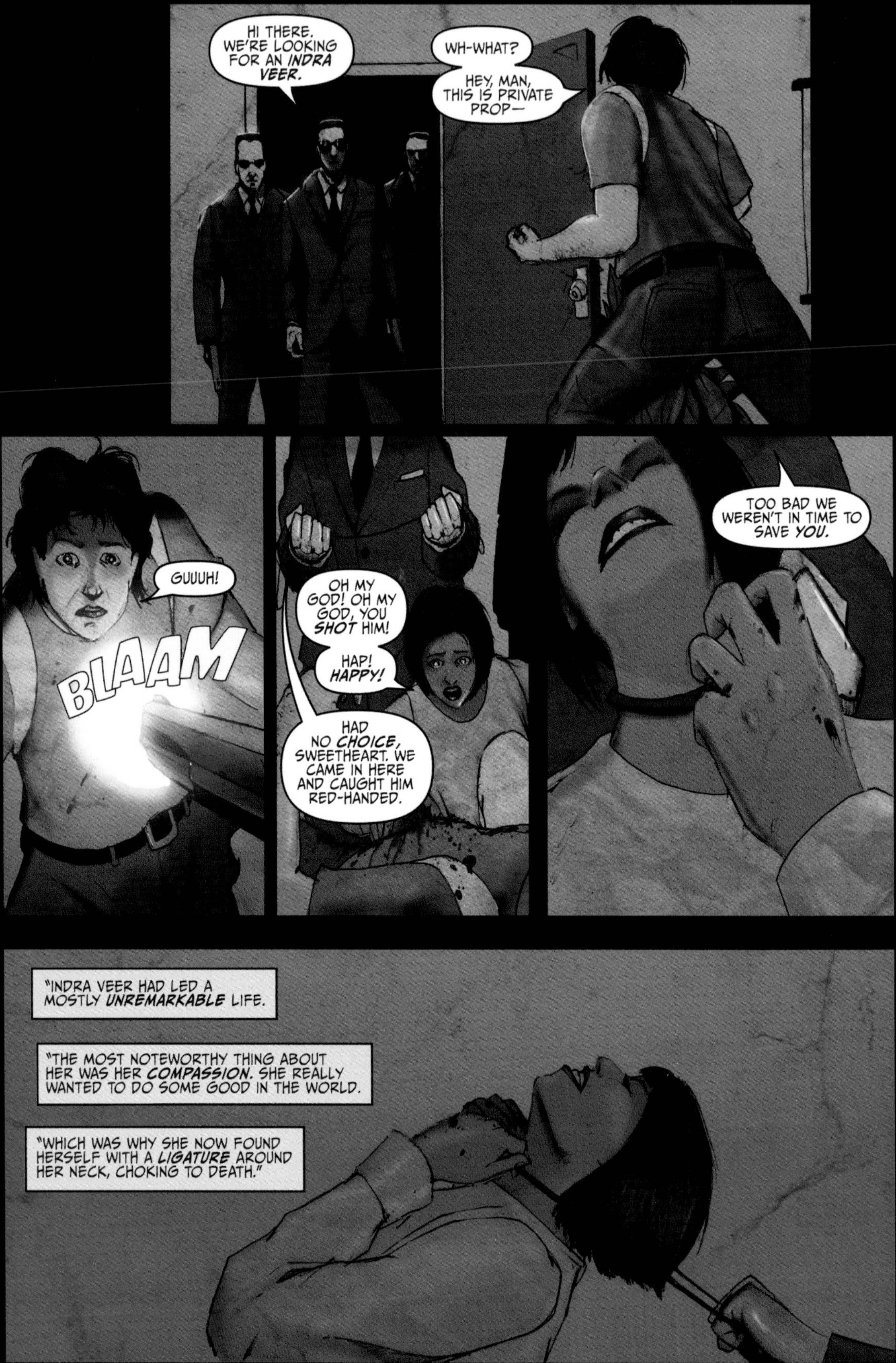
HI THERE. WE'RE LOOKING FOR AN *INDRA VEER.*
WH-WHAT?
HEY, MAN, THIS IS PRIVATE PROP—
GUUUH!
BLAAM
OH MY GOD! OH MY GOD, YOU *SHOT* HIM!
HAP! *HAPPY!*
HAD NO *CHOICE*, SWEETHEART. WE CAME IN HERE AND CAUGHT HIM RED-HANDED.
TOO BAD WE WEREN'T IN TIME TO SAVE *YOU.*
"INDRA VEER HAD LED A MOSTLY *UNREMARKABLE* LIFE.
"THE MOST NOTEWORTHY THING ABOUT HER WAS HER *COMPASSION.* SHE REALLY WANTED TO DO SOME GOOD IN THE WORLD.
"WHICH WAS WHY SHE NOW FOUND HERSELF WITH A *LIGATURE* AROUND HER NECK, CHOKING TO DEATH."

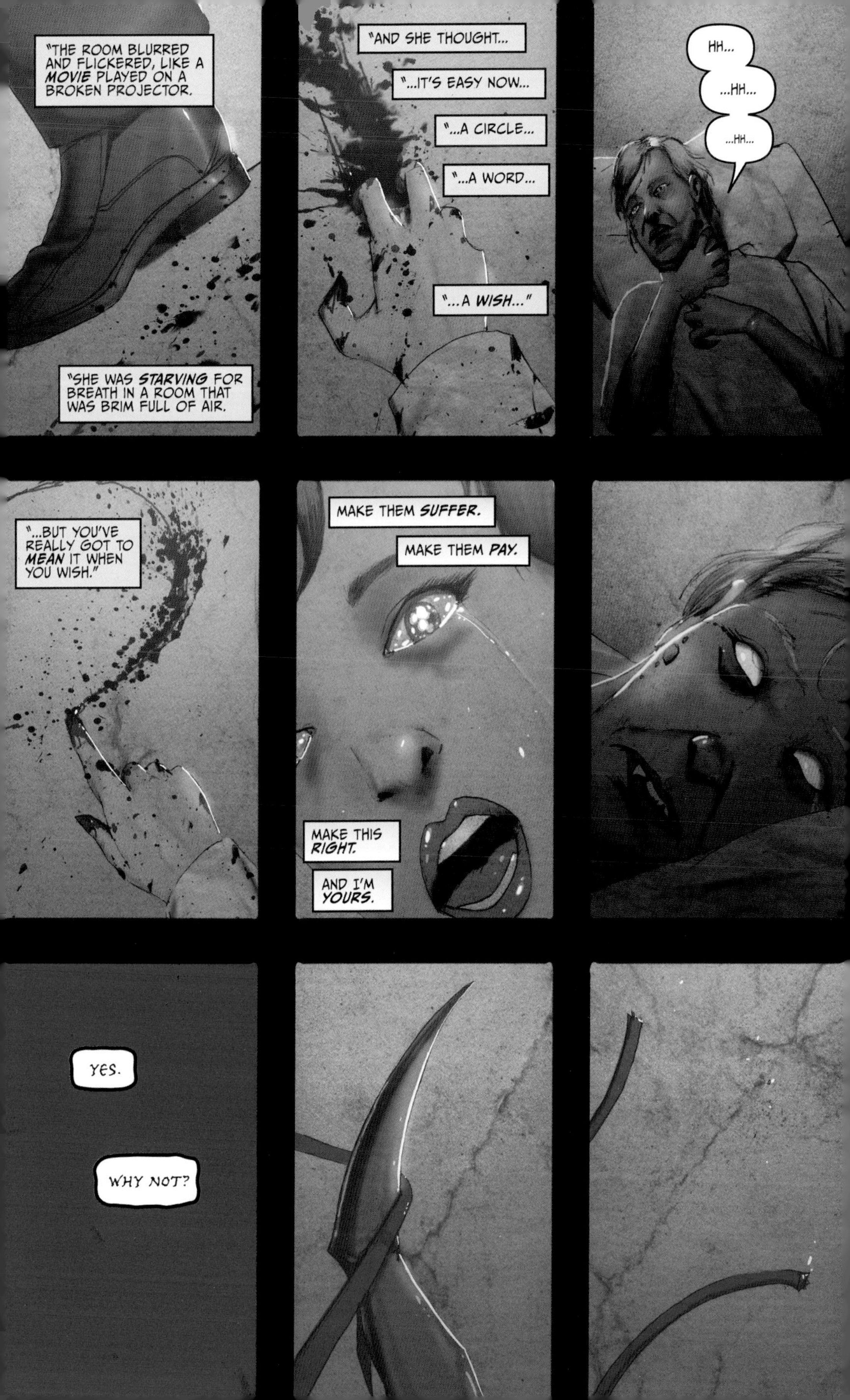
"THE ROOM BLURRED AND FLICKERED, LIKE A MOVIE PLAYED ON A BROKEN PROJECTOR.
"SHE WAS STARVING FOR BREATH IN A ROOM THAT WAS BRIM FULL OF AIR.
"AND SHE THOUGHT...
"...IT'S EASY NOW...
"...A CIRCLE...
"...A WORD...
"...A WISH..."
HH...
...HH...
...HH...
"...BUT YOU'VE REALLY GOT TO MEAN IT WHEN YOU WISH."
MAKE THEM SUFFER.
MAKE THEM PAY.
MAKE THIS RIGHT.
AND I'M YOURS.
YES.
WHY NOT?

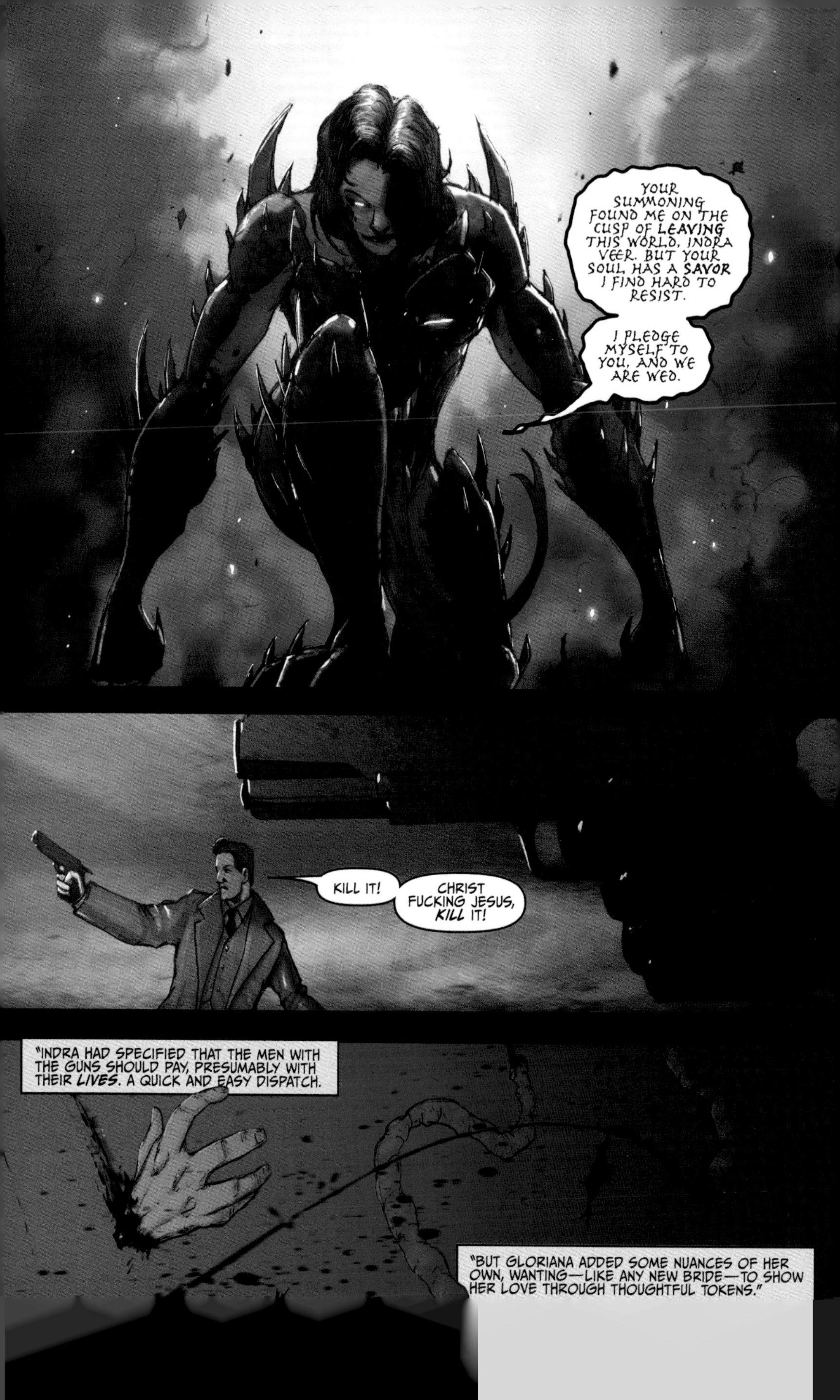
YOUR SUMMONING FOUND ME ON THE CUSP OF **LEAVING** THIS WORLD, INDRA VEER. BUT YOUR SOUL HAS A **SAVOR** I FIND HARD TO RESIST.
I PLEDGE MYSELF TO YOU, AND WE ARE WED.
KILL IT!
CHRIST FUCKING JESUS, ***KILL*** IT!
"INDRA HAD SPECIFIED THAT THE MEN WITH THE GUNS SHOULD PAY, PRESUMABLY WITH THEIR ***LIVES***. A QUICK AND EASY DISPATCH.
"BUT GLORIANA ADDED SOME NUANCES OF HER OWN, WANTING—LIKE ANY NEW BRIDE—TO SHOW HER LOVE THROUGH THOUGHTFUL TOKENS."

"WHAT *ELSE* IS THERE TO TELL?"

"DR. KENT'S FAMOUS LAST WORDS WERE SNATCHED FROM HIS LIPS BY THE SPEED OF HIS FALL."

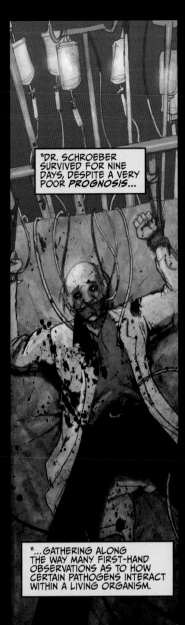

"DR. SCHROEBER SURVIVED FOR NINE DAYS, DESPITE A VERY POOR *PROGNOSIS*..."

"...GATHERING ALONG THE WAY MANY FIRST-HAND OBSERVATIONS AS TO HOW CERTAIN PATHOGENS INTERACT WITHIN A LIVING ORGANISM."

"AS FOR THE *OVERSIGHT BOARD*..."

"...THEY WALKED—AS KENT MIGHT HAVE SAID— A LONG, HARD ROAD."

"WITH ONLY *TEARS* AT THE END OF IT."

SO THAT WAS...

THEIR *WEDDING* DAY. GLORIANA AND VEER'S. AND MY CONCEPTION. THE DAY THEY CHOSE EACH OTHER AND SOMETHING CAME INTO BEING THAT WAS EVENTUALLY *ME*.

I DIDN'T REALIZE IT HAPPENED SO *LONG* AGO.

DANNY, THE *MILLENNIA* I LIVED IN NO FLESH AT ALL WERE LONG. HUMAN LIFE IS A *HEARTBEAT*.

LET'S FILL IT WITH SOMETHING THAT *MATTERS*.

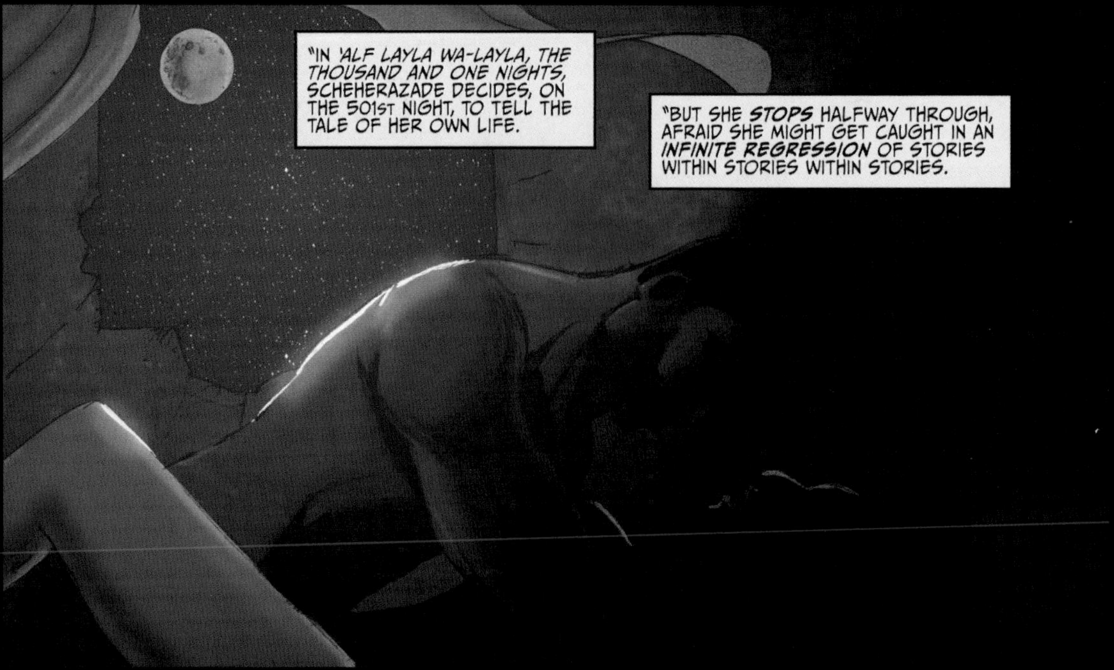
"IN 'ALF LAYLA WA-LAYLA, THE THOUSAND AND ONE NIGHTS, SCHEHERAZADE DECIDES, ON THE 501st NIGHT, TO TELL THE TALE OF HER OWN LIFE.
"BUT SHE STOPS HALFWAY THROUGH, AFRAID SHE MIGHT GET CAUGHT IN AN INFINITE REGRESSION OF STORIES WITHIN STORIES WITHIN STORIES.

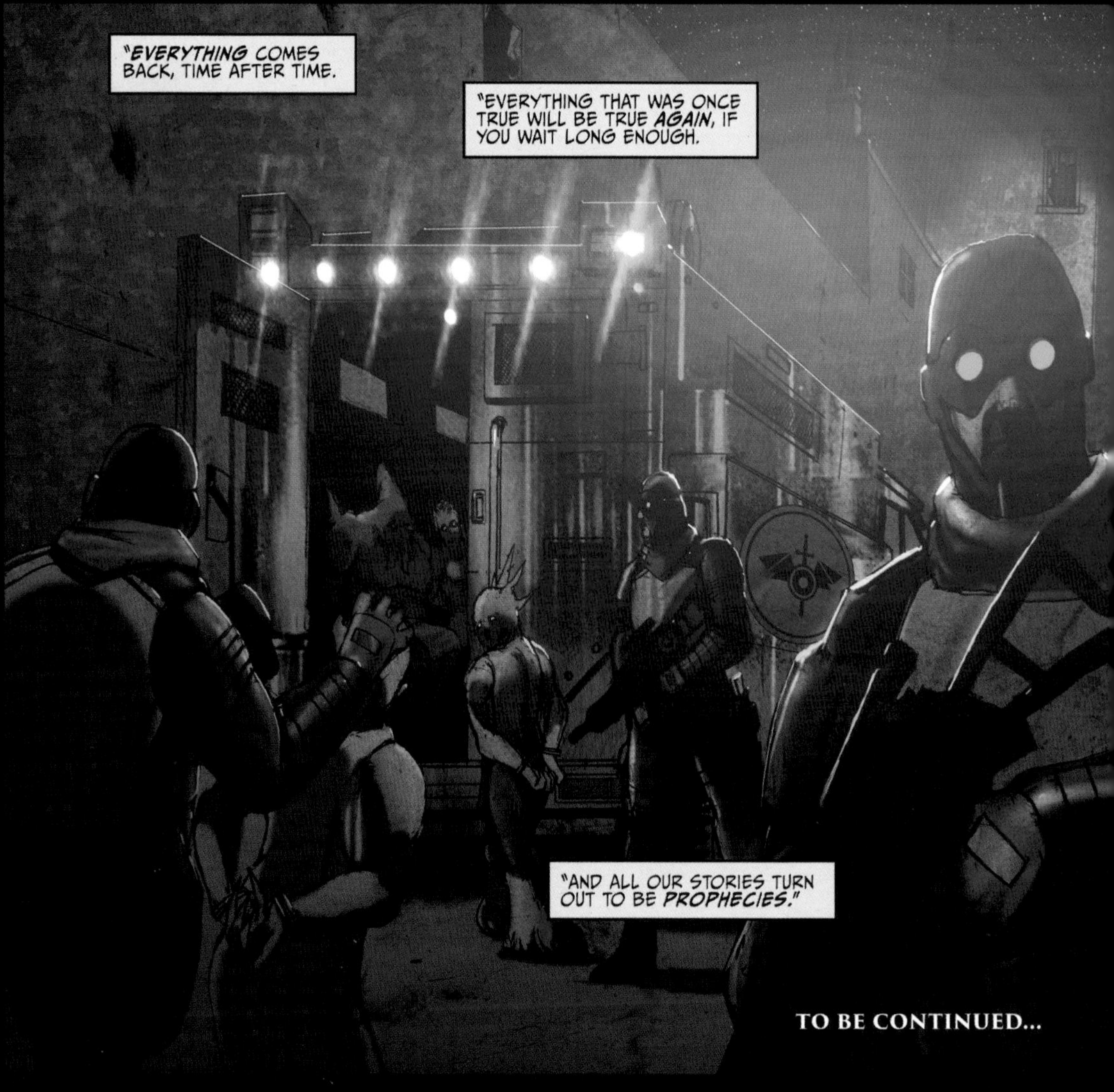
"EVERYTHING COMES BACK, TIME AFTER TIME.
"EVERYTHING THAT WAS ONCE TRUE WILL BE TRUE AGAIN, IF YOU WAIT LONG ENOUGH.
"AND ALL OUR STORIES TURN OUT TO BE PROPHECIES."
TO BE CONTINUED...

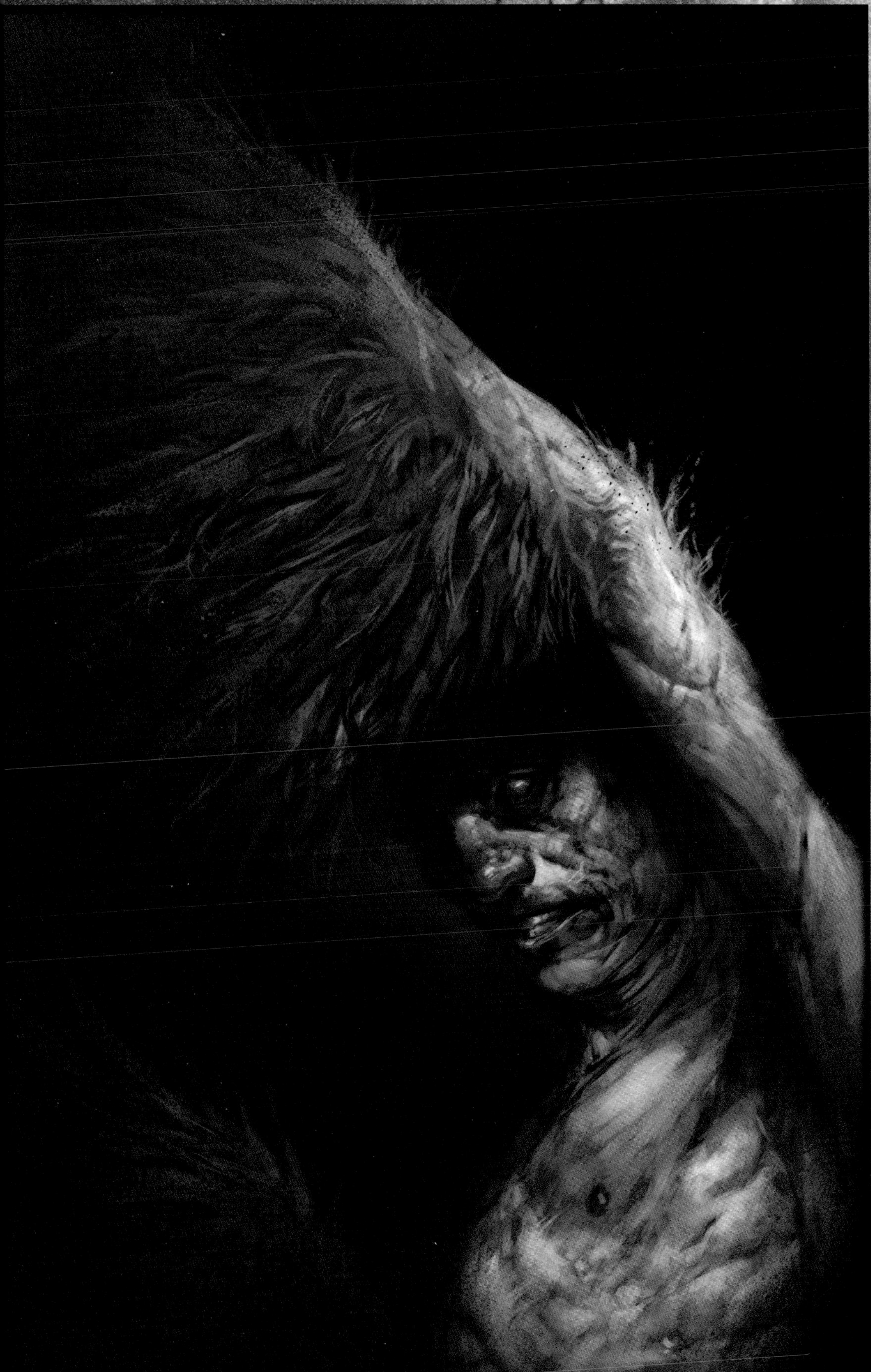

Art by **Dave Kendall**

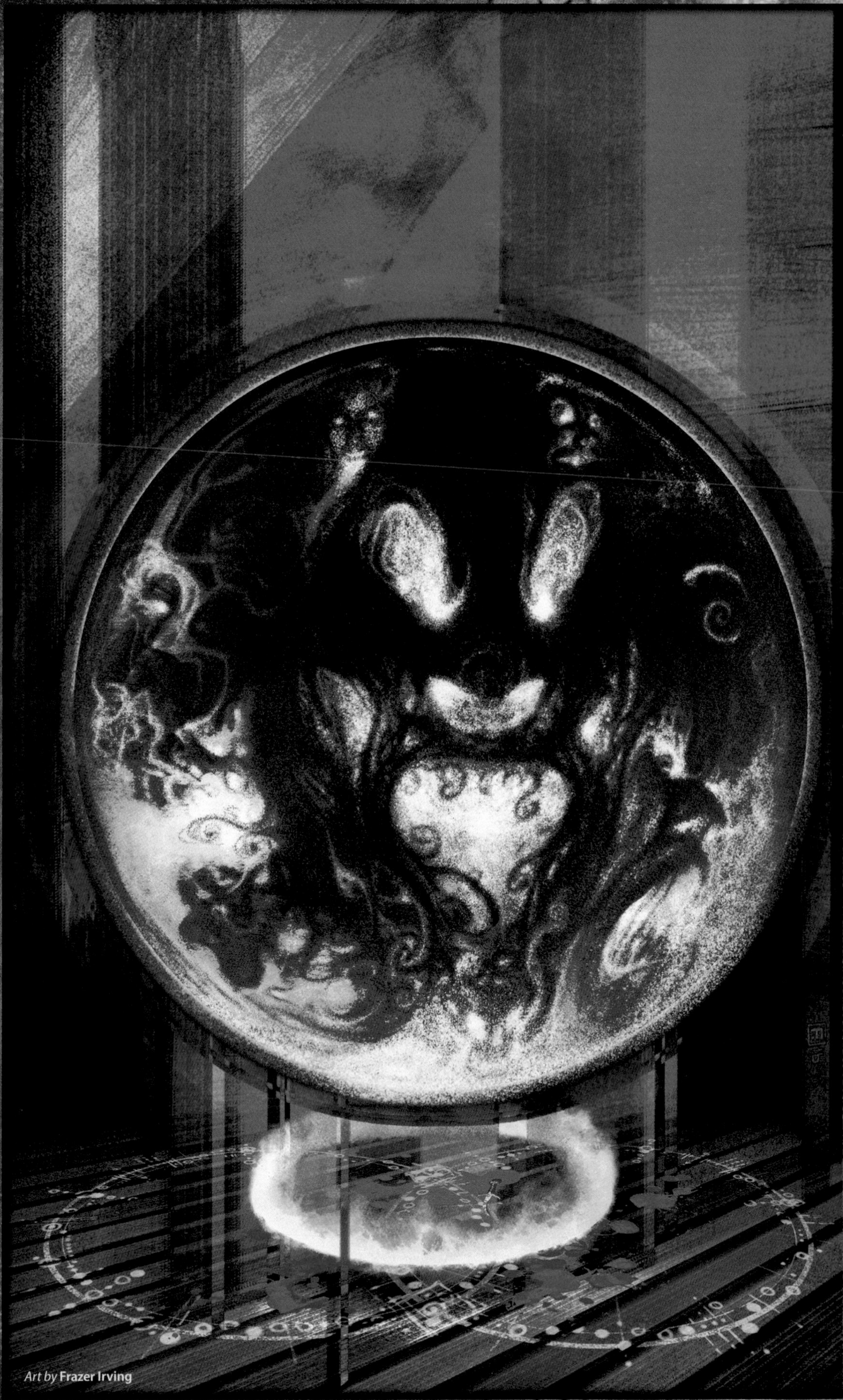

Art by **Frazer Irving**

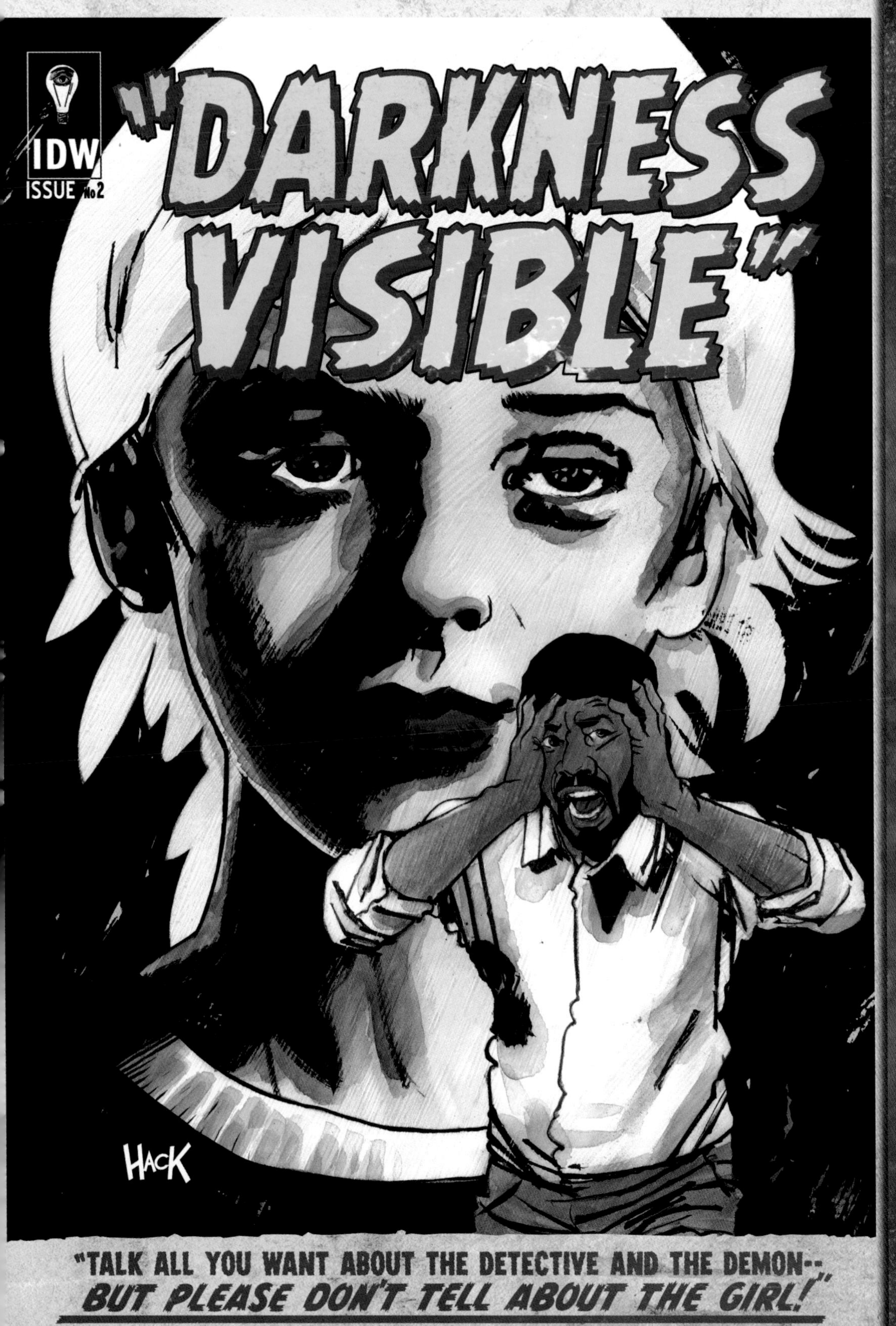
IDW
ISSUE No 2
"DARKNESS VISIBLE"
HACK
"TALK ALL YOU WANT ABOUT THE DETECTIVE AND THE DEMON--
BUT PLEASE DON'T TELL ABOUT THE GIRL!"
MIKE CAREY ARVIND ETHAN DAVID BRENDAN CAHILL JOANA LAFUENTE

Art by **Robert Hack**

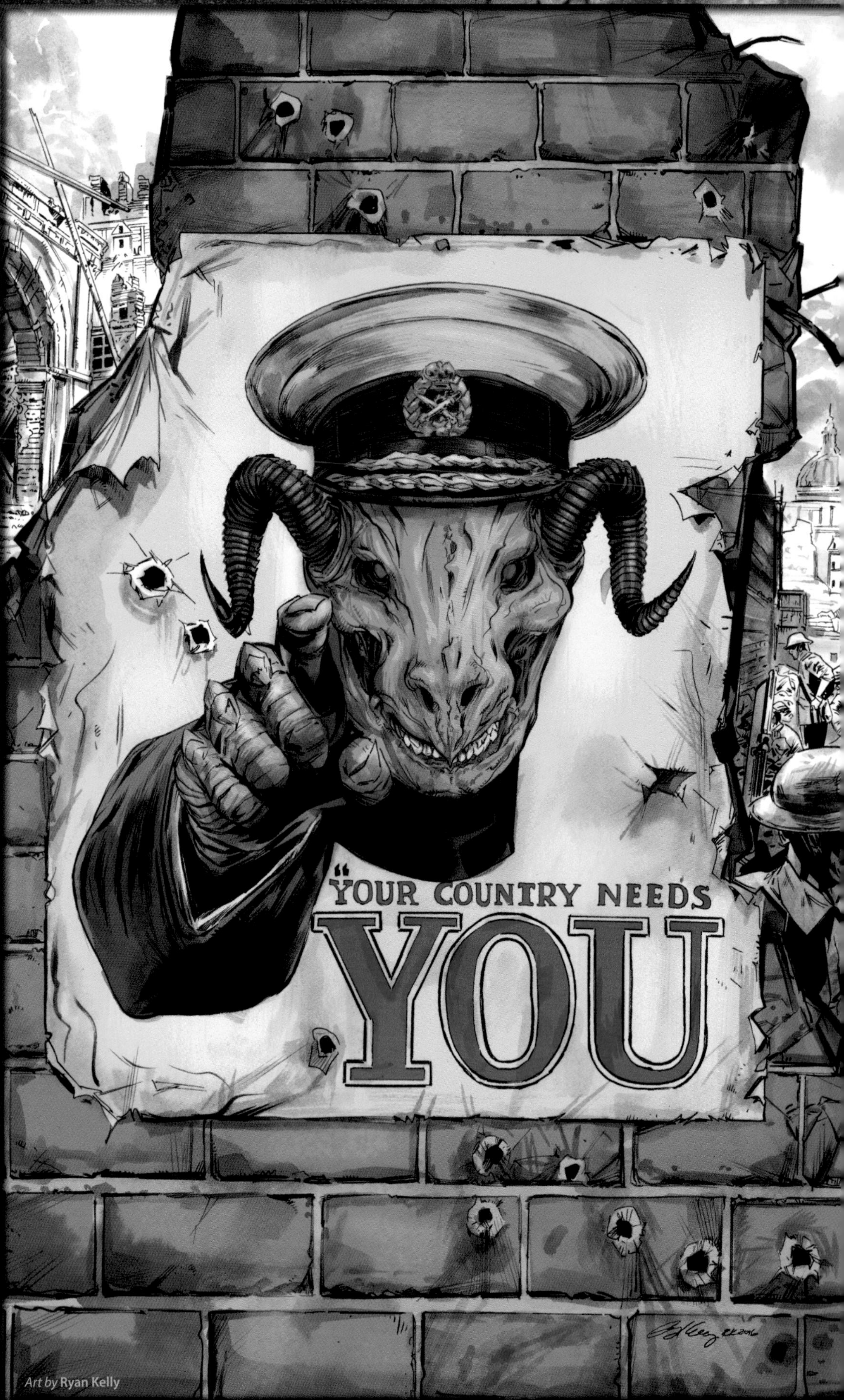
"YOUR COUNTRY NEEDS
YOU

Art by Ryan Kelly

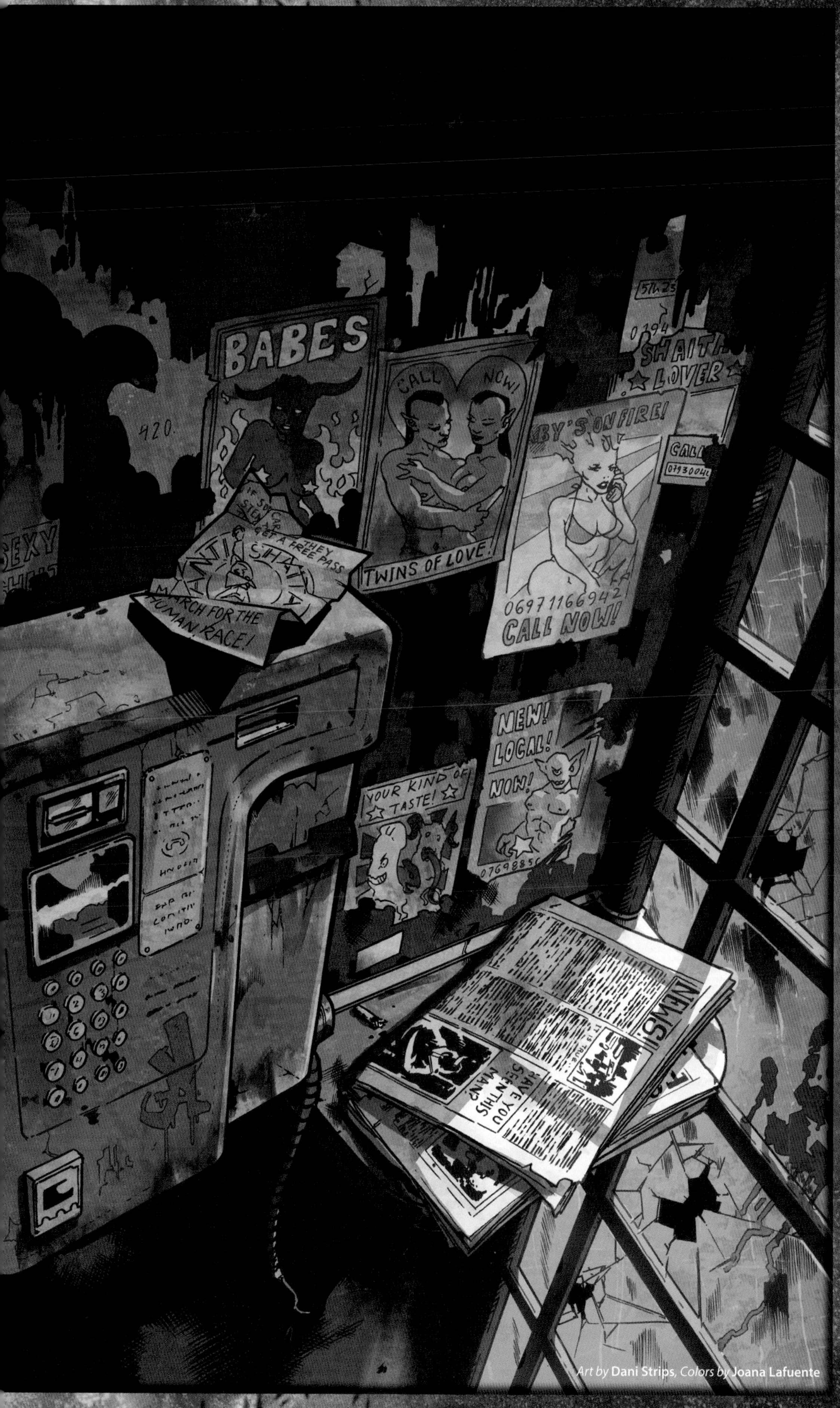

BABES
420.
CALL NOW!
TWINS OF LOVE
SHAITH LOVER
06971166942
CALL NOW!
THEY GET A FREE PASS
ANTI SHAITH
MARCH FOR THE HUMAN RACE!
YOUR KIND OF TASTE!
NEW! LOCAL! NOW!
NEWS
HAVE YOU SEEN THIS MAN?
IT IS TRUE.

Art by **Dani Strips**, *Colors by* **Joana Lafuente**

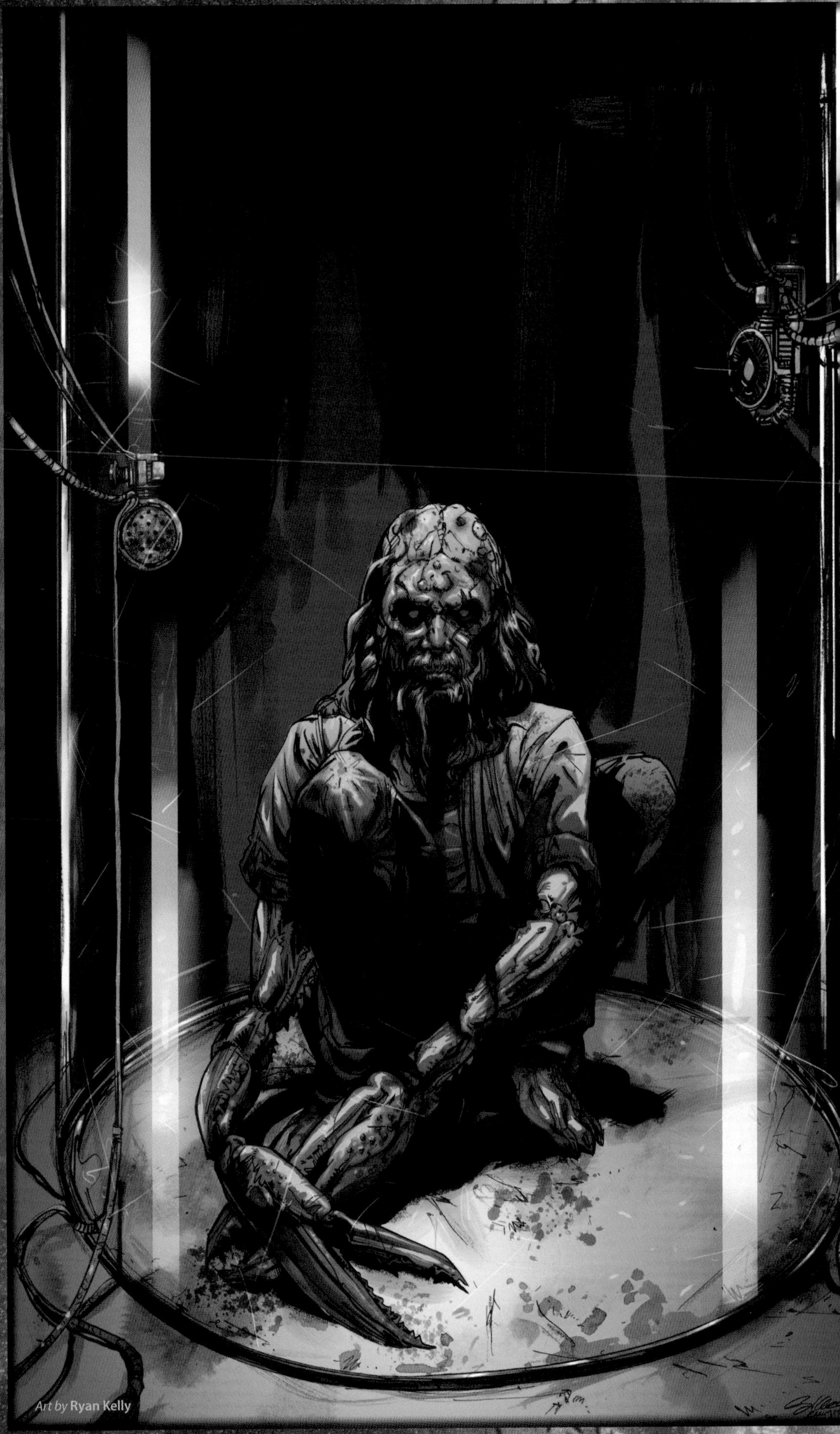
Art by **Ryan Kelly**

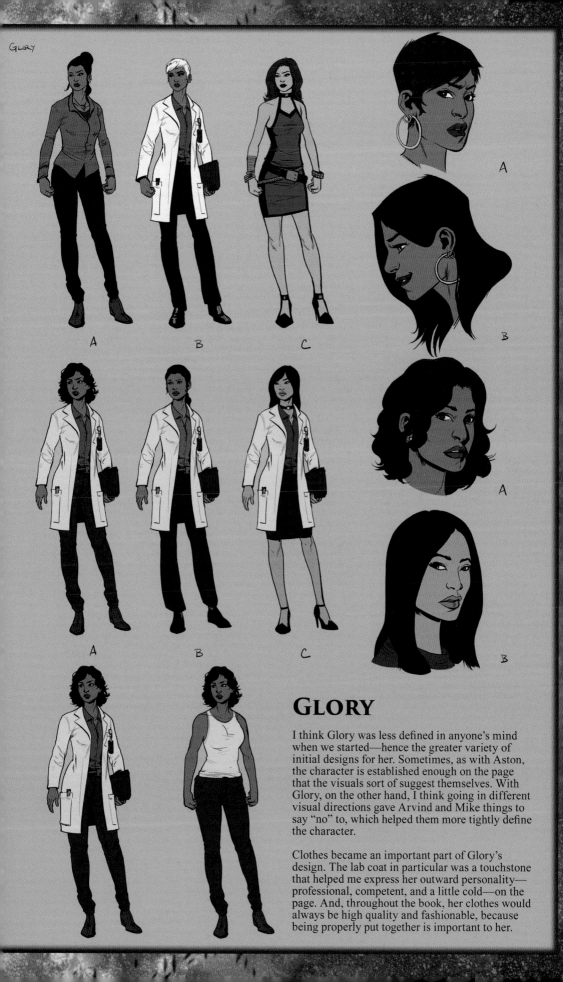

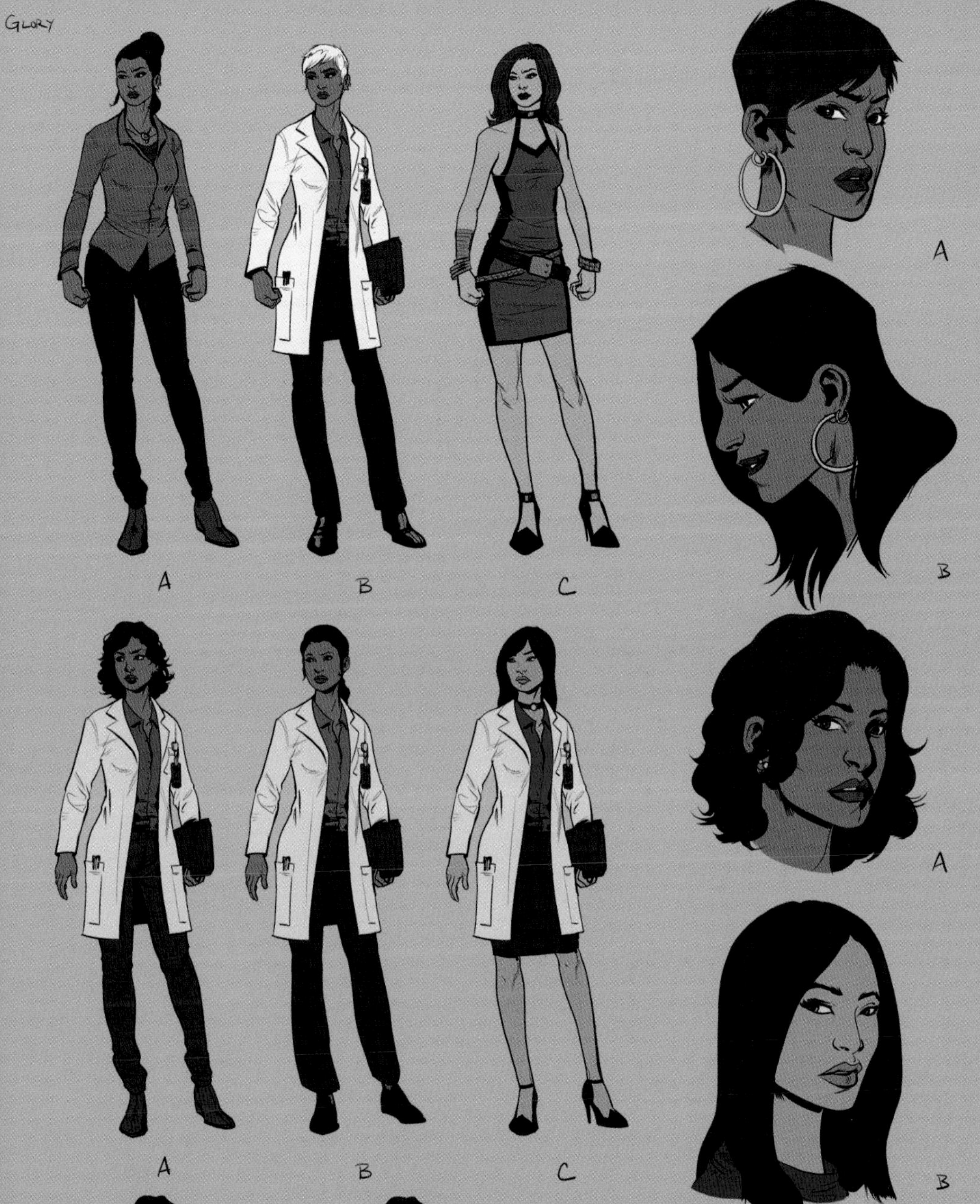
GLORY
A
A
B
C
B
A
B
C
A
B

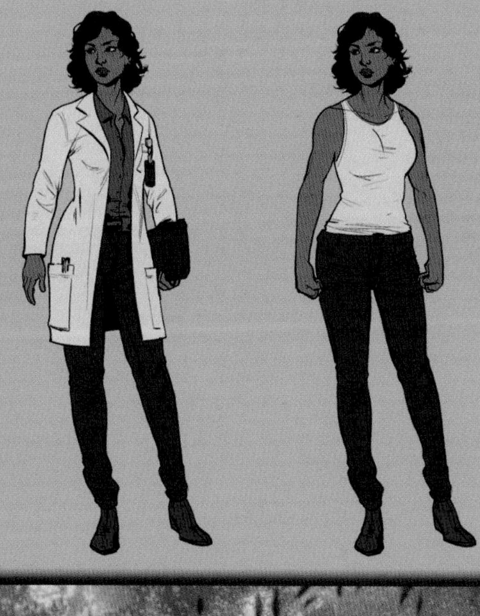

GLORY

I think Glory was less defined in anyone's mind when we started—hence the greater variety of initial designs for her. Sometimes, as with Aston, the character is established enough on the page that the visuals sort of suggest themselves. With Glory, on the other hand, I think going in different visual directions gave Arvind and Mike things to say "no" to, which helped them more tightly define the character.

Clothes became an important part of Glory's design. The lab coat in particular was a touchstone that helped me express her outward personality—professional, competent, and a little cold—on the page. And, throughout the book, her clothes would always be high quality and fashionable, because being properly put together is important to her.

ASTON

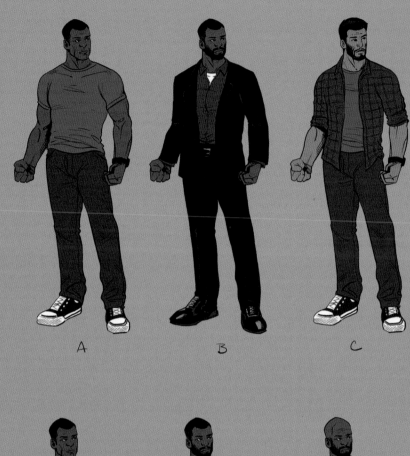

A   B   C

A   B   C

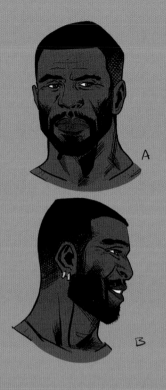

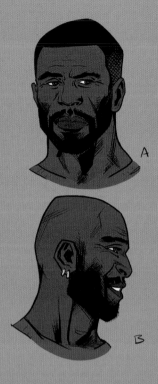

ASTON

Aston was always intended to be big and physically powerful, imposing due to his authority as a cop, and his deep anger issues. A war with a demon was going to play out inside him, and we wanted his body to look like an appropriate battleground.

You can see that we tried a couple of different looks for him, but settled on our general direction pretty quickly, at which point it was just down to things like hairstyle, beard, and jewelry.

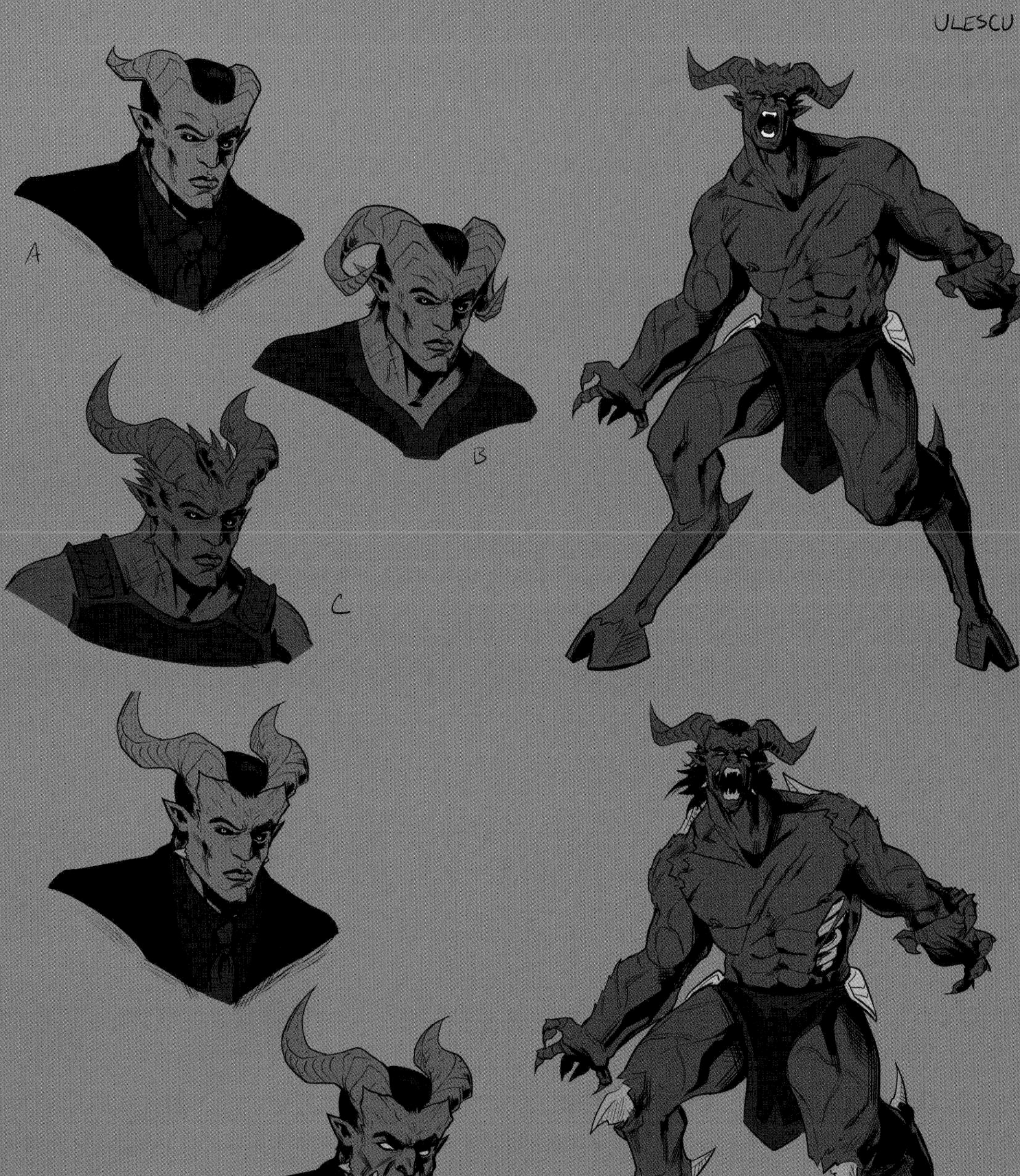
ULESCU
A
B
C

ULESCU

We knew going in that Ulescu was going to be our most "demony" demon—we wanted to go full-on horns, spikes, and hooves with him, and make him bigger and more physically imposing than any of the other characters.

We tried a few different horn styles, and a few different clothing styles, from modern to more medieval-looking tunics and armor. We all liked the "demon in a suit" thing, and that helped Arvind and Mike build out the Shaitan a little more as a culture—they figured that many Shaitan would tend to stick with clothes from the time they first came to our world and took a host. So, Ulescu dresses like the Kray twins because he's a '50s East End gangster at heart, and always will be.

We also decided early on that as Ulescu's emotional intensity increased, his body would distort further. You'll see in the book that as the story goes on, he has more spikes and horns, and his skin starts splitting open to reveal bone beneath, and those changes are actually manifestations of his inner turmoil, not continuity mistakes. (Though I'm sure there are some of those, too!)

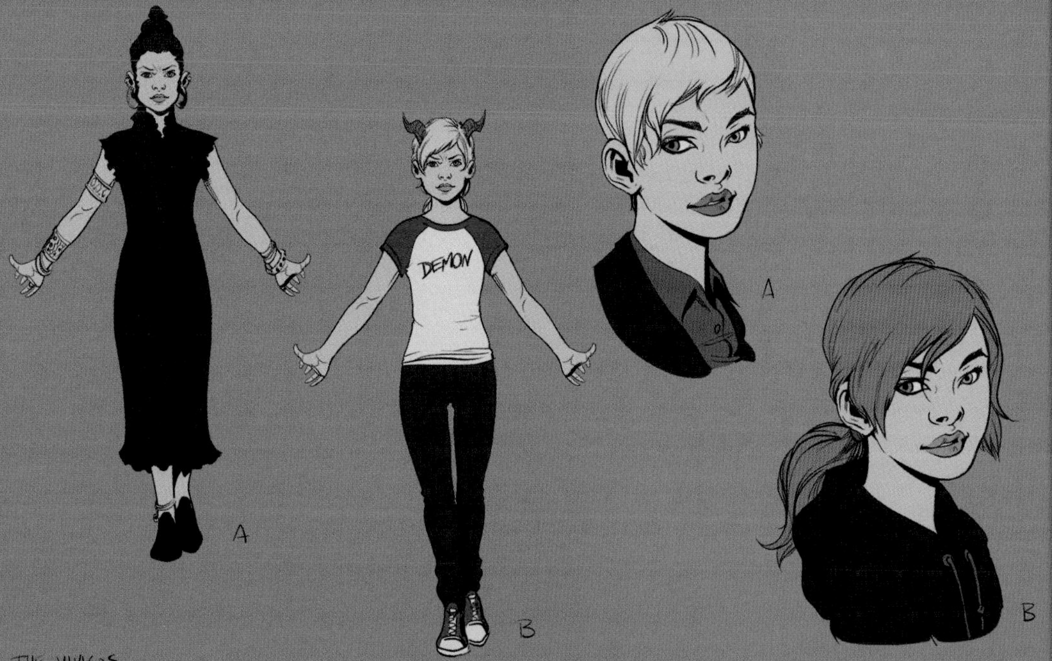
DEMON
A
B
A
B

THE VIVICOS

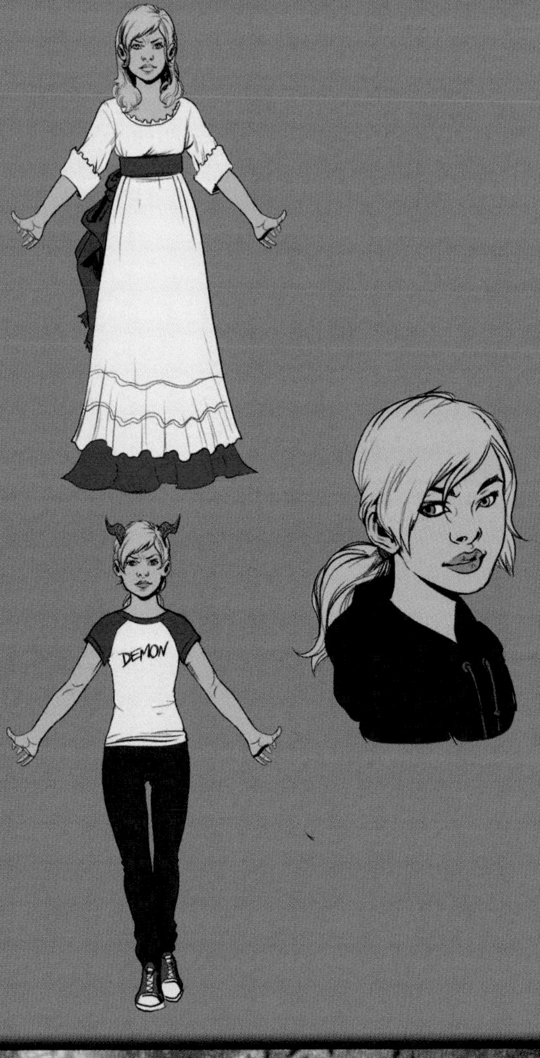
DEMON

THE VIVICOS

Viv was always intended to appear as a child, but there was a lot to figure out about how that would play out. She's very old and very powerful, and part of her character is that she can control her host body's form much better than other Shaitan. So, she doesn't have horns or a tail or anything unless she wants to. To fuck with you.

We put her in some older, more ceremonial, and/or more formal clothes to see how that looked, and decided that, at least for her introduction, she really should just look like a kid, wearing kid clothes, nondescript. Except for her mismatched eyes, which was something I hit on early in the process. I wanted her theme colors to be purple and gold—to evoke royalty—and liked the idea of making her eyes purple and gold as well. A little thing that makes her just a little bit off.

I always liked the "DEMON" shirt, and we've toyed with putting it in the actual book, but have resisted so far. (Though I did give her the "Smiling Face With Horns Emoji" shirt in issue #5!)

Other Characters

The other characters we wanted to take a stab at before we began work on the book itself were Maggie, Rhak, and Stanca.

Maggie's look came together easily, and survived pretty much intact as we went into production.

We kept Rhak's basic look, but wanted to make him more of a big, dumb bruiser, so in the book, he's physically bigger, a bit uglier, and has less styled hair. Basically, we took a couple layers of polish off of him.

With Stanca, I had an initial impression that he was kind of a garrulous back-slapper, but that wasn't where the character ended up. In the book, he's older-looking, thinner, and more dignified, in keeping with his position as the seneschal to the most powerful demon on Earth.

RHAK

MAGGIE

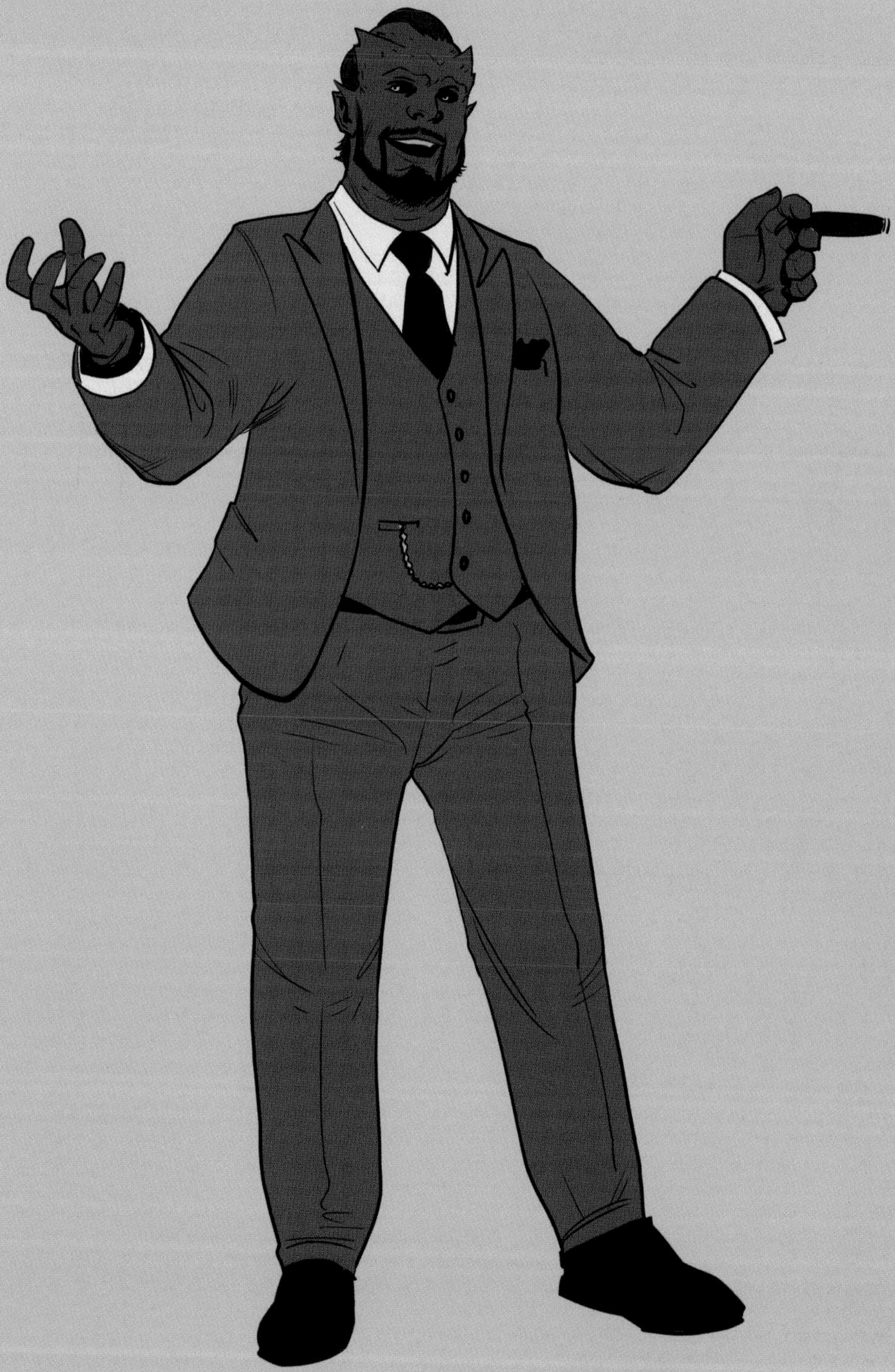

Stanca

Cyclops

Cyclops is the law enforcement agency that deals with supernatural/superpowered threats, so right from the beginning, they had to be more militaristic than a standard police force. My first designs leaned into this a bit too much, and they came off looking like Nazis. While there is something of a fascistic element in Cyclops we wanted to play with, we didn't want it to be so heavy-handed, so we dialed it down.

Early on, I did a design for a heavy suit of powered armor they'd use to deal with the really powerful Shaitan, but we decided ultimately that it took us too far away from our focus. The book is about injecting demons into the real world, and so the world around the demons should feel as "real" as we could get it, and sci-fi mech stuff didn't quite fit.

I also developed a number of potential logos for Cyclops, to give them a "brand." I really like the one we ended up with, which you see throughout the book.

CYCLOPS

CYCLOPS

CYCLOPS

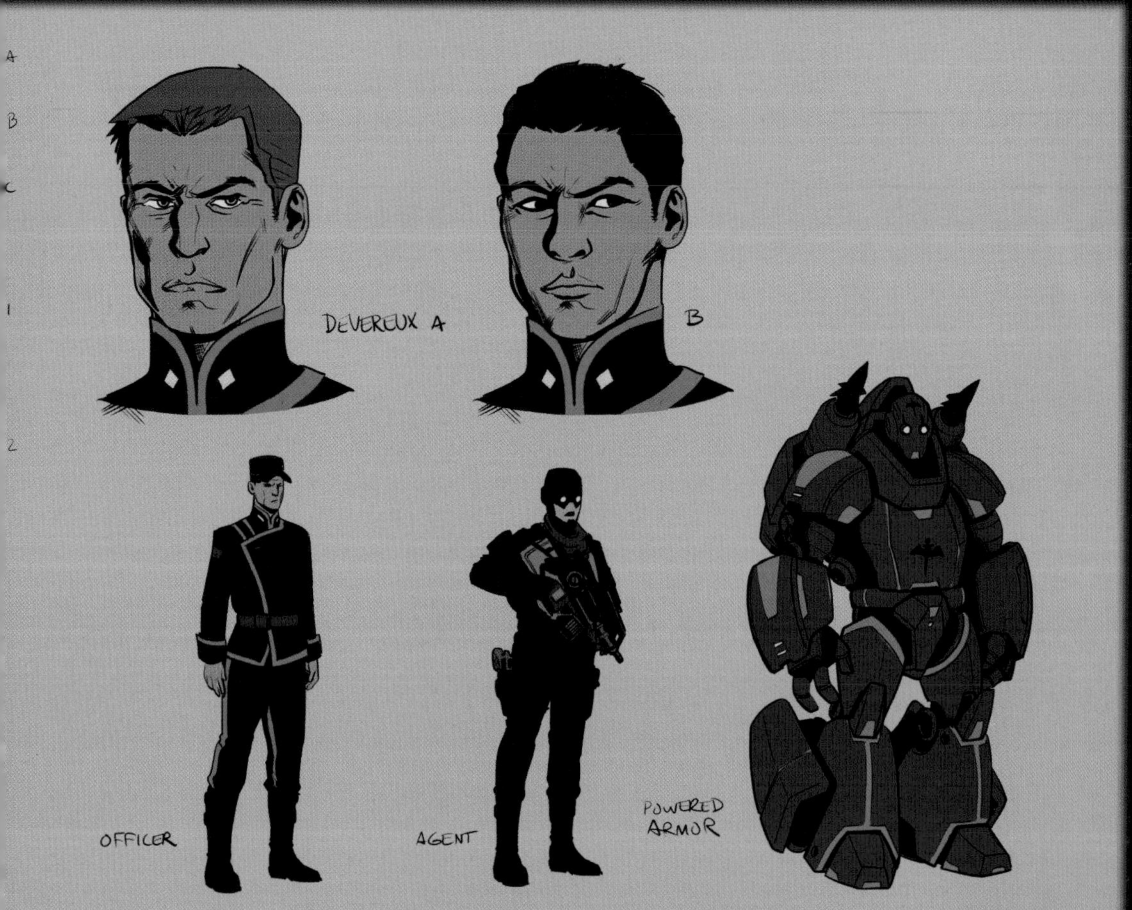
DEVEREUX A
B
OFFICER
AGENT
POWERED ARMOR

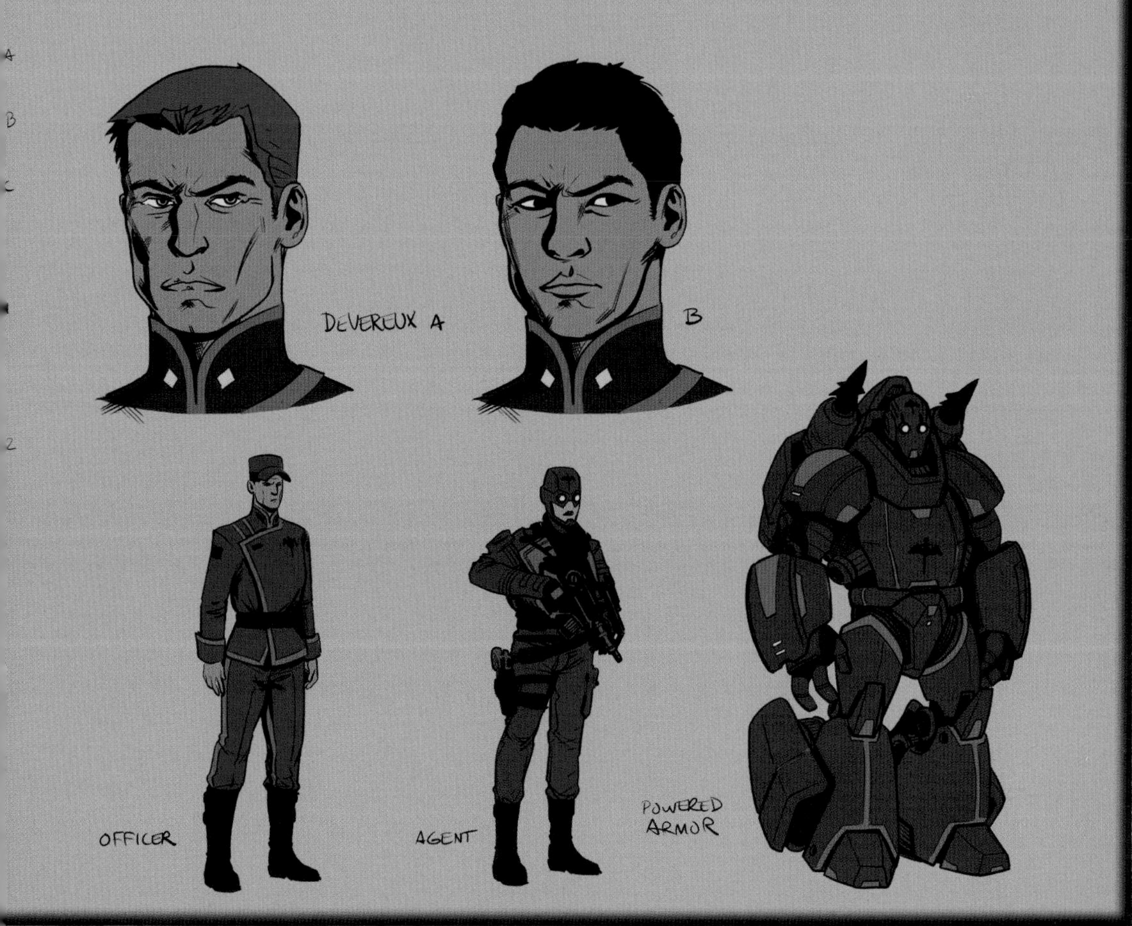
DEVEREUX A
B
OFFICER
AGENT
POWERED ARMOR

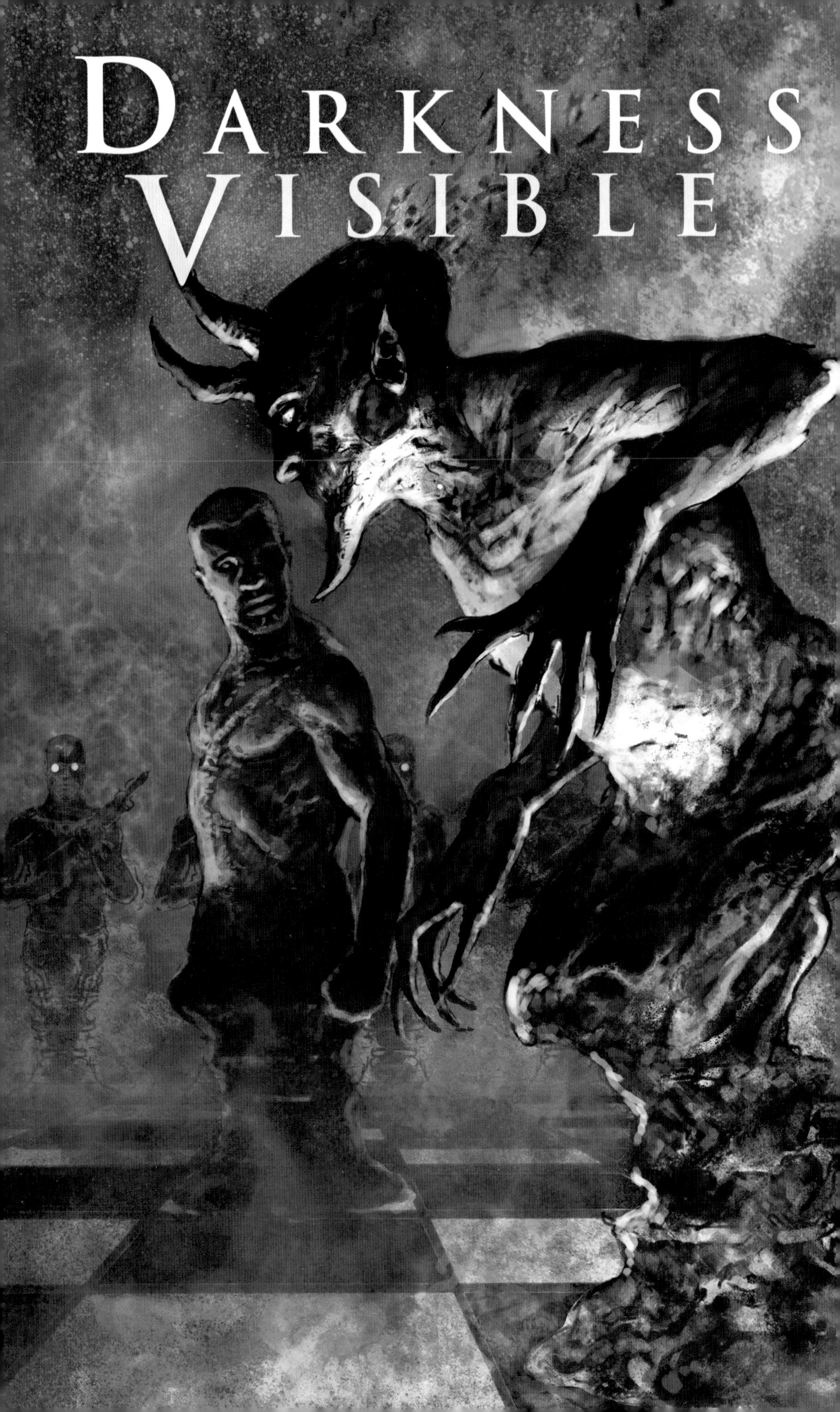
DARKNESS
VISIBLE